EDUCATING ALL THE CHILDREN

Strategies for Primary Schooling in the South

Educating All
the Children

Strategies for Primary Schooling
in the South

CHRISTOPHER COLCLOUGH

with

Keith Lewin

CLARENDON PRESS · OXFORD

1993

Oxford University Press, Walton Street, Oxford OX2 6DP

Oxford New York Toronto
Delhi Bombay Calcutta Madras Karachi
Kuala Lumpur Singapore Hong Kong Tokyo
Nairobi Dar es Salaam Cape Town
Melbourne Auckland Madrid
and associated companies in
Berlin Ibadan

Oxford is a trade mark of Oxford University Press

Published in the United States
by Oxford University Press Inc., New York

British Library Cataloguing in Publication Data
Data available

Library of Congress Cataloging in Publication Data
Colclough, Christopher.
Educating all the children / Christopher Colclough with
Keith Lewin.
p.   cm.
Includes bibliographical references (p.   ) and index.
ISBN 0-19-828746-1 (pbk.)
1. Education, Elementary—Developing countries—Statistics.
2. Education and state—Developing countries—Statistics.
3. Educational equalization—Developing countries—Statistics.
I. Lewin, Keith.   II. Title.
LC2608.C65   1993   372.9172'4'021—dc20   92-32445
ISBN 0-19-828747-X

Typeset by Best-set Typesetter Ltd., Hong Kong

Printed in Great Britain
on acid-free paper by
Biddles Ltd.

Preface

This book, which is about primary schooling in developing countries, had its origins in a co-authored paper with the same title, which was prepared for the World Conference on Education for All, held in Jomtien, Thailand, in March 1990. Discussions with delegates and panelists at that conference led to a broadening of the scope of the work.

The project was directed by Christopher Colclough. Keith Lewin wrote the case-studies of China and Sri-Lanka, and Sections 3 and 4 of Chapter 4. He wrote most of Chapter 5, although the methods and assumptions which are described in that chapter were jointly determined. He also contributed to the Technical Appendix. Christopher Colclough wrote the other parts of the book.

Assistance was received from Robin Horn, Terri Demsky, and Carolyn Winter in the initial production of case-study material. Able research assistance was also provided, at different stages of the project, by Thierry Sanders, Harry Patrinos, Jerker Edstrom, and Ana Marr. Many others gave comments and constructive suggestions at seminars held at the World Bank in Washington, UNICEF in New York, UNESCO in Paris, the Overseas Development Administration in London, the Swedish International Development Authority in Stockholm, and at the Universities of Oxford, Reading, and Sussex.

Particular thanks are due to Richard Jolly, Aklilu Habte and staff from the Education Cluster in UNICEF, and to Tony Davison, Stephen McCarthy, Peter Williams, and Adrian Wood, each of whom commented extensively and helpfully on the entire draft. Useful comments were also received on particular chapters from Peter Fallon, Angela Little, and Adriaan Verspoor. None of the above, however, bears any responsibility for the ways in which their comments have been used. Thanks are also due to staff from UNESCO who made available the software for the model utilized in Chapters 5 and 6, and to both UNICEF and the ODA, for the financial support which allowed the research to proceed.

C.C.

K.L.

Brighton
June 1992

Contents

List of Figures

List of Tables

Summary of the Argument
and Main Findings

Access to good-quality primary schooling is of central importance to national development. Nevertheless, it is still far from being universally available. In fact, only about three-quarters of eligible children attend primary schools in developing countries. Furthermore, many schools offer an education of very poor quality. In 1990 those who were out of school comprised about 130 million girls and boys; they were mainly illiterate, and had either never attended school, or had left before completing the primary cycle. This book asks why such high levels of underenrolment persist, how the trend could be reversed, and what resources and policy changes would be required, nationally and internationally, in order that all the world's children should receive schooling of an acceptable quality.

The Importance of Good-Quality Primary Schooling

Primary schooling has been formally accepted as a human right for almost fifty years, but the case for its provision on more strictly economic criteria is more recent. There is now a substantial body of evidence that primary schooling is productive in an economic sense, and that it affects people's behaviour in ways which support a wide range of development goals. This evidence, which is reviewed in Chapter 1, is of several kinds. First, studies of the costs and benefits of schooling, using formal sector earnings as a measure of benefits, consistently indicate that average rates of return to education are high in comparison with returns to expenditures in other sectors, and that they are highest for primary schooling. These results hold for both social and private rates of return. Second, primary schooling appears to improve productivity not only in the formal sector, but also in the rural and urban informal sectors. Third, reductions in fertility, improvements to family health and nutrition, and reductions in infant and child mortality are each statistically associated with primary-school attendance, particularly for women. Although there are interpretative difficulties which are pointed to in the text, these, and other non-market effects and externalities, considerably strengthen the case for the developmental importance of primary schooling.

The quality of schools in developing countries affects the cognitive achievements of their pupils to a greater extent than in richer countries. The critical variables appear to be the qualifications, experience, and educational levels of teachers, and the availability of good textbooks. Although, eventually, there appear to be diminishing returns to further expenditures on school quality, most low- and middle-income countries are still at an earlier stage, where there are increasing returns to such expenditures.

Why does Underenrolment Persist?

Given the apparently strong social benefits which accrue from primary schooling, why, then, have developing countries been so tardy in ensuring its universal provision? After all, their announced intention, as indicated by the declarations of a series of regional conferences organized during the early 1960s by Unesco, was to achieve universal primary education (UPE) by 1980, at the latest. In the event, there were many reasons for failure. School systems did expand rapidly. But in most countries, population growth continued at much higher rates than had been imagined in the 1960s, thereby making the quantitative task more difficult than had been forecast. Educational costs also rose more sharply, owing to the links between salaries and teacher qualifications, and to the budgetary burden imposed by the rapid expansion of higher education. After 1980, the pace of enrolment growth slumped, as recession hit educational expenditures by the State. This was particularly so in Africa, where real educational spending, per head of population, fell by two-thirds during 1980–7, and where, in consequence, both gross and net primary-enrolment ratios fell below their 1980 levels.

Equally, the targets were badly specified: many of the 130 million out-of-school children live in countries where UPE, defined as 'the circumstance of having a primary gross enrolment ratio (GER) of 100 or more', has already been achieved.[1] Colombia and Lesotho represent extremes, where primary GERs are around 115, yet where only about 70 per cent of children in the official school-age group actually attend school. There are many other countries with school systems which are only slightly more efficient, and where a 20-point difference between gross and net enrolment ratios—the result (mainly) of high rates of repetition—remains common. Schooling for all (SFA) is a better target. This we define as 'the circumstance of having a school system in which all eligible children are enrolled in schools of at least minimally acceptable quality'.

---

[1] The gross enrolment ratio is defined as the number of children who are enrolled in primary school expressed as a proportion of the number of children in the age-group who are eligible to attend.

On these definitions, UPE becomes a necessary, but not a sufficient condition for the achievement of SFA. The latter is more difficult, and more expensive to achieve, than the former. But only when SFA is attained can one truly say that primary schooling has been universalized.

The fact that one-quarter of children remain out of primary school is not only the result of action, or inaction, by governments. It is also caused by the demand for schooling amongst some private households remaining low. This, at first sight, seems puzzling, given the high private returns to primary schooling mentioned above, together with the additional 'external' benefits, some of which—such as better health and nutrition—are privately captured.

The most important cause of low demand is poverty. Even where returns are high, the direct and indirect costs of school attendance are often too great for poor families to afford. During the 1980s, household incomes in many parts of the world fell—often in countries where the costs of attending school rose, as governments introduced or raised school fees and other charges. The result has often been a fall in demand for primary schooling—particularly so in Africa—and declining enrolments.

In addition, the non-monetary benefits of schooling are often not known by families, and even if they were, assessment of their value, for comparison with private costs, would hardly be an easy task. Furthermore, not all population groups within countries face similar private benefits from schooling: minority castes or tribes, isolated populations or those in poor regions, and women, often have reason to expect lower monetary returns to schooling than the average. Finally, there are a range of powerful economic and customary reasons for parents favouring the education of sons over that of daughters in many countries. This helps to explain why almost two-thirds of the children who are not enrolled in primary schools are girls.

Clearly, there is no single answer to the question as to why underenrolment persists. The reasons differ between countries, and are strongly influenced by differences in domestic history, culture, and politics, as well as in economic and educational policies. It is, however, possible to identify a range of factors which appear to have influenced enrolment outcomes, whilst recognizing that the weight given to each varies from country to country.

The cross-country statistical analysis presented in Chapter 2 identifies a number of important characteristics which are systematically associated with underenrolment at primary level around the world. It is demonstrated there that countries with low GERs tend to have low per capita incomes. On the supply side, this is partly because the poorer countries have high rates of population growth, and thus face a proportionately greater task in achieving SFA than do richer countries. Nevertheless in about half of the low GER cases, the public commitment to achieving

SFA appears to be low: in Nigeria, Uganda, Pakistan, Bangladesh, Nepal, Bolivia, and some other countries, the necessary amount of public spending needed for GERs of 100 would be less than the equivalent of 2 per cent of GNP. Elsewhere, and particularly in West and Central Africa, the task is more difficult: there, high levels of educational costs would require public expenditures equivalent to between 3 and 7 per cent of GNP, even for UPE to be attained. In those countries, cost-reduction strategies will be needed if UPE and SFA are to be achieved.

We also document the strong relationship between low primary enrolments and an underenrolment of girls. This indicates that the demand for girls' schooling is lower in poorer countries, reflecting lower net benefits—as perceived by their parents—in such circumstances. Nevertheless, tradition and culture are also important determinants of demand. We demonstrate, for example, that the proportion of Muslims in the population is significantly associated with low GERs, even after allowing for differences in per capita incomes, and that the main manifestation of this is the lower proportion of female primary enrolments in such communities. Thus, customary and cultural influences help to determine the level of female enrolments, in addition to economic ones, and these, in turn, are a further cause of low GERs.

Policy Responses

Although low primary enrolments are more usually found amongst the poorer countries, exceptions are frequent. Equally, although low public spending may indicate a weak 'commitment' to primary schooling, high expenditures (relative to GNP) do not seem to be a necessary condition for SFA to be achieved. The reality is more complex. It is the interaction between these and a range of other variables, including the public and private costs of schooling, and the ideologies which inform both state and private behaviour, which determine SFA outcomes. An important question thus concerns the extent to which changes in public policy can affect these variables in ways which are supportive of SFA.

Six countries are selected for particular study. In four of them UPE (but not SFA) has already been attained, two being low income (China and Sri Lanka) and two being from the middle-income group (Zimbabwe and Colombia). In the remaining countries—Ghana (low income) and Senegal (middle income)—UPE remains some way off. However, in all six countries important educational reforms have recently been introduced, with the intention of achieving universal access to higher-quality primary schooling.

China's record is important: although it remains amongst the 20 or so poorest countries, and has one-fifth of the world's population, China has achieved UPE with a lower proportion of GNP being spent on education than most other countries. This is partly because of its successful policies for slowing population growth, which latter has, for some years, been running at only about half that in other low-income States. Thus, the task of maintaining UPE, and of achieving SFA, is more manageable than in many other countries, since in China the size of the school-age cohort is small relative to the population, and is shrinking. In addition, however, teachers' salaries are much lower than elsewhere. In China, they are about equal to per capita income, whereas in other countries they are (again, relative to per capita income) typically between four and six times as large. Reforms to the salary structure have introduced substantial performance-related elements, whilst keeping total costs low. Funding the primary school system has been diversified, to include central and local governments, income taxes from state employees, factories which help to run schools, and private voluntary contributions. The quality of schooling is low, but improving at modest cost.

Zimbabwe's experience, in managing to double primary enrolments in the early 1980s, is remarkable. After only two years of independence the primary GER had risen from 60 to around 100. Within a very short period of time, the system was transformed from one in which resources for education were profoundly maldistributed, and heavily orientated towards the white community, to one where there is open access to education for all, where primary schooling is compulsory, and where all who so wish may proceed to secondary school after completing Standard 7. The main reforms which facilitated these achievements were the introduction of double-session teaching in urban and some rural schools, the extensive use of untrained teachers, increases in class-size, rationalization of the curriculum, and a devolution of financial responsibility to communities—for the construction of schools, and to contribute to school expenses. Our assessment of the Zimbabwe case is, ultimately, critical, since it has resulted in a highly differentiated quality of schooling which, because of the devolved means of financing, is strongly related to the household incomes and general prosperity of the communities served by particular schools. Nevertheless, there are many positive aspects to the experience, which pose a sharp challenge to those who believe that administrative and fiscal constraints must inevitably frustrate rapid moves towards SFA in the developing world.

The theme of cost-recovery has also been important in Sri Lanka, with similar consequences for equity as in the Zimbabwe case. Those schools with the greatest need for improvement are usually those with the least capacity to raise additional resources from the communities they serve. Financing mechanisms are needed which provide positive discrimination in favour of the most deprived schools and areas. Our discussion of a project supporting Tamil schools, where both achievement levels and enrolments were much lower than the national average, provides an illustration of how this can be done, and of how donor assistance can be important in helping to promote it.

Ghana and Senegal are examples of African countries which have been exceptionally hard hit by recession. Both have faced a chronic lack of public resources, and their governments have introduced educational and fiscal reforms in the face of low, and declining, primary enrolments. In Ghana, where the primary GER fell from 80 to around 70 by the mid-1980s, efficiency savings were obtained by reducing the length of the pre-university school cycle, by cuts in administrative staff in schools, and by introducing double shifts at primary level. Some costs, as in the other cases discussed, were passed from the State to parents and communities. As a result primary enrolments increased by one-fifth over the first two years of the reforms, for little additional budgetary cost.

Senegal is one of those West African countries where the major constraint on educational expansion has been the high level of recurrent costs: teachers' salaries were, on average, twelve times as high as per capita incomes in the early 1980s—more than twice the average for the rest of Sub-Saharan Africa at that time. Senegal's reforms sought to reduce unit costs in a number of different ways: the proportion of low-cost assistant teachers employed was increased by one-fifth; large numbers of educational administrators (equivalent to about 10 per cent of the teaching force) were redeployed as teachers (as in Ghana) at no net additional costs; double-shift teaching was widely introduced in urban schools, and multigrade methods (whereby each teacher is responsible for more than one class) were introduced in rural schools. These and other measures led to a sharp increase in primary enrolments with, according to recent evaluations of progress, no noticeable decline in school quality.

Finally, Colombia's radical approach to improve the relevance and efficiency of rural primary schooling appears to have been highly effective. 'Escuela Nueva' has evolved over a period of about twenty years, and incorporates a number of the reforms discussed in the cases of other countries: assistant teachers, multigrade teaching, and strong links with local communities are important elements. In addition, the curriculum is flexible, allowing for student absence during periods of peak agricultural activity. Costs are lower, drop-outs from school appear much reduced (as with BRAC in Bangladesh, discussed in Chapter 4), and the quality of schooling, judged by student performance, appears better than in more conventional schools.

The case-studies show that in some countries which are poor, and where initial enrolment levels are very low, UPE—and, perhaps, SFA—can be attained over comparatively short periods of time if a determined and imaginative approach to policy change is adopted. The methods used in these six countries do not, however, exhaust the possibilities confronting reformist States. Accordingly, Chapter 4 synthesizes the lessons from the case-studies, and integrates these with additional evidence from the wider research literature.

There is a potential trade-off between the achievement of budgetary savings and the maintenance of school quality. This is confronted, in our analysis, when assessing the extent to which particular reform measures can improve the efficiency of, or enhance resources available for, primary schooling. We identify sets of policies which hold promise of increasing the capacity to expand enrolments, whilst at the same time giving greatest benefit (or doing least harm) to the quality of schooling. Examples are provided under four headings, which correspond to the main objectives of the relevant categories of policy change. These objectives are, respectively, to reduce the unit costs of schooling by affecting teacher-costs per student; to reduce the total costs per school-leaver via changes to the organization and length of the school cycle; to redistribute expenditures towards primary schooling from other items, both within education and from other sectors; and, finally, to raise additional financial resources for education in general, and for primary schooling in particular, through taxation, various forms of cost-recovery, or other fiscal measures.

Enrolment and Cost Implications of Achieving SFA

The enrolment and cost implications of achieving UPE and SFA have been simulated for all low- and middle-income countries separately. National data for enrolments, population growth, and a wide variety of parameters which determine educational costs have been utilized. An enrolment-transition model has been developed for these analyses, which permits investigation of the cost implications of the expansion of school systems under present, or changed, policies.

Based upon the research results and case-studies reviewed earlier, a number of efficiency reforms are selected which appear to offer the most cost-effective means of financing further school expansion. These include a group of reforms to save costs, via increasing the extent of double-shift teaching, increasing the size of classes in cases where there is scope for this, and increasing the proportion of teacher-helpers and assistants. A second group of reforms shifts more of the costs of education to households, by encouraging some increase in private schooling, and by passing on more of the costs of tertiary education to users. In addition, a number of quality-enhancing reforms are introduced, in order to simulate the difference between the mere expansion of existing primary systems to UPE levels, and the substantial qualitative improvement necessary, in most countries, for SFA to be achieved. These include a substantial reduction in present rates of repetition and drop-out, the allocation of a minimum amount of resources per child for learning materials, and increased real expenditures on teachers' salaries. This set of measures is sensitive to the initial circumstances in each country, and it identifies a minimum set of conditions necessary to satisfy the qualitative criteria of SFA.

The results show that if every country were to achieve UPE by the year 2000, an additional 114 million primary school places would by then be required, in comparison with 1990. The achievement of SFA would require about 156 million additional places by the end of the century— about 30 per cent more than 1990 levels—rising to about 212 million additional places by the year 2005. Although in aggregate these needs are modest, requiring no more than 2 or 3 per cent growth in enrolments per year, their incidence is very unequally distributed. In many countries with low GERs and high rates of population growth, very rapid enrolment growth would be required to meet these targets. The scale of the problem will be worst in the countries of Sub-Saharan Africa (SSA) and in Pakistan and Bangladesh. In SSA, primary enrolments would have to double to reach SFA by the century's end. Although this region contained only 11 per cent of all primary enrolments in developing countries in 1990, it accounts for more than 40 per cent of all the additional school places required for SFA. Further, in eight countries in the region, as in Pakistan, enrolments would have to triple if SFA were to be reached within a decade.

The total additional recurrent costs of achieving UPE by the end of the century would, in the absence of policy reforms, amount to some $146 billion, in 1986 prices, over the years 1990–2005. These costs are additional to 1990 expenditures (running at about $100 billion), cumulated over the whole fifteen-year period, and they include the minimum cost of enrolment increases at secondary level which the move to UPE is likely to bring. Capital costs are excluded from these estimates: our work shows that these would be small compared to the recurrent-cost burden. SFA could also be achieved within this cost ceiling, provided all countries introduced the full package of cost-saving and cost-shifting reforms which we have simulated. Thus, the efficiency savings which we propose are capable of financing the improvements to school quality which separate UPE from SFA.

Given a willingness to implement the policy reforms, a majority of developing countries would be able to meet these costs of SFA, provided that real spending on education increased at least as fast as their populations, over the period 1990–2005. This, of course, is a demanding requirement, particularly for the poorer countries of Africa. And even so, forty countries would still incur combined deficits (in the sense of unfinanced expenditures on education) of around $44 billion over the period unless education spending increased more rapidly than this. Nevertheless, reallocation of recurrent resources from defence, or other sectors, to education provides additional means of financing SFA. Our analyses suggest that the combined deficit could be further reduced to around $20 billion, in thirty-five countries, if the proportion of the recurrent budget allocated by each country to education in the late 1980s were increased by 2 percentage points, and kept constant over 1990–2005.

Implications for Aid Policy

It is obviously not possible to forecast the precise magnitude of aid transfers required to finance SFA throughout the developing world. Aid requirements will depend upon what developing countries actually do themselves in order to increase expenditures on education, and to reform both their systems of schooling and the methods whereby they are financed. However, our analysis suggests that the $20 billion (in 1986 prices) mentioned above represents a minimum estimate for foreign resources required. Aid would need to be greater than that to the extent that countries were unable to introduce all the efficiency reforms, that the rates of economic growth were lower than expected, or that the required budgetary reallocations towards education, and away from defence or other sectors, were not achieved. Even if these (and other) conditions were satisfied, additional aid would still be needed to help countries other than the thirty-five deficit cases to introduce the reforms necessary for them to achieve SFA.

For these, and other reasons, our work suggests that the likely additional aid requirement over 1990–2005 would amount to around $30 billion. Most of this would need to be recurrent support, directed towards the countries which had not achieved UPE by 1990. About half of it would be needed for Africa. Target flows of an additional $2 billion (1986 prices) per year are thus implied, which, in terms of 1990 prices amounts to some $2.5 billion, annually, over fifteen years.

Additional resources of this magnitude would increase annual aid to education by about 50 per cent, in real terms, above recent levels. That is a very substantial increase, but it would no more than compensate for the downward trend in such aid which has occurred since the mid-1970s. Furthermore, pledges made during 1990/1 were significant, and up to half the additional resources needed for education were allocated by the World Bank. However, we demonstrate that some change in the composition of Bank lending, towards a greater utilization of IDA financing, would be needed if these funds were genuinely to support SFA. If that happened, and provided that the value of Bank programmes were sustained in real terms at 1991 levels, other donors would need to increase the value of their support to education by about 25 per cent beyond 1990 levels in order to reach the $2.5 billion which is annually required. In aggregate, it is not impossible that these monies will be found.

Danger Signals

Even if that is so, however, it will be the start, rather than the end of the task in hand. There are many reasons to fear that the achievement of SFA will be delayed, or that its costs will be higher than need be, owing to a range of factors which are analysed in the last chapter of the book. It will require a more efficient approach to programme management and policy implementation on the part of both aid agencies and national governments than has been typical in the past. As regards the northern part of the bargain, it will be necessary to review afresh the geographical disposition of educational aid: at present, for example, very few World Bank funds go to the educationally most disadvantaged countries identified in this book. It will also be necessary to shift away from capital aid towards recurrent support, to substitute southern for northern purchasing wherever possible, and to ensure that aid genuinely supports SFA policy, assisted by a policy dialogue leading to specific agreement on the timing and phasing of national policy reforms.

Equally, in developing countries themselves there are a range of constraints that are likely to hinder progress. The process of policy reform often involves offending the interests of some groups—including the parents of children who attend the best schools—in ways which not all governments will find easy. Planners and administrators would need to move rapidly, often devolving more of their authority to the local level. Teachers would be better paid, but would also have more responsibilities than in the pre-reform period, which may not always be easy for them to accept. There are also technical and economic reasons which might prevent the reform process from delivering quite as much as expected in the circumstances of some countries.

Finally, supply-side and demand-side policies must go hand in hand. The policies to improve both the quality and the availability of primary schooling will, of course, have effects upon demand. Reductions in the average walking-distance to school sharply reduce the private costs (and, for girls, the dangers) of attendance. Automatic promotion reduces the time it takes to graduate from school. Qualitative improvements make schools more enjoyable, and their effects more productive. Each of these changes will help to stimulate demand.

Nevertheless, where demand for schooling is particularly low, more direct policy measures will also be needed in order to attain SFA. Critical, here, would be measures to mitigate the costs of school attendance. Community financing would need to be confined to the wealthier areas and schools, and all direct costs, such as fees or charges for books, materials, and other consumables, would need to be reduced and, where possible, removed. Measures to alleviate the costs for girls, or to give parents special incentives to enrol their daughters, will often be a priority, owing to higher opportunity costs, or cultural biases, which discourage female enrolments. The most important ingredient for successful policy design will be careful analysis of the factors which constrain enrolments in each case. Circumstances differ, and a range of policies will typically be needed, affecting both demand and supply, in order effectively and rapidly to increase the enrolment of both girls and boys.

Conclusion

At the World Conference on Education for All, held in Thailand in March 1990, delegates from 155 governments, and a similar number of non-governmental organizations and agencies, declared their commitment to the achievement of 'universal access to, and completion of, primary education by the year 2000'. There were echoes here of the Unesco regional conferences, thirty years earlier, which had espoused similar goals. If failure is not to be repeated, policy changes and additional resources, of the dimensions documented in this book, will need to be secured. Universal primary schooling, in all countries, is a viable goal for the turn of the century—not just in the sense of UPE, but the more demanding SFA, as we have here defined it. But if it is to be achieved resources would need to increase, and policies would need to change at a faster pace than happened over the first three years of the present decade.

1

The Problem Outlined

1. Introduction

In 1990, only about three-quarters of children of primary-school-age in developing countries were actually attending school. The remainder, amounting to about 130 million children, had either never attended school, or had dropped out before completing the primary cycle. Most of them were illiterate, and were likely to remain so. These stark facts represent a lost opportunity for developing countries of immense proportions. This book asks why such high levels of underenrolment persist, if and how they may be eliminated, and what the costs of so doing would comprise. In this first chapter, however, we begin by placing current educational problems in their historical context: naturally, they have not emerged overnight, and their character can properly be understood only by examining something of the dynamic which has delivered them. Secondly, we set out the reasons why the enrolment record summarized above represents such a tragic 'lost opportunity'—not just for the millions of individuals affected, but, more broadly, for the societies in which they live and for the generations which will succeed them.

2. Post-Independence Expansion of School Systems

2.1. Early promise fades

A convenient date to begin a consideration of the changing availability of schooling around the world is 1960. By then, independence had been achieved in a good number of the erstwhile colonized countries, and for the rest it was shortly to come. Thus the outset of that decade marks, for many countries, a watershed between the colonial educational inheritance —which was often meagre—and the results of nationally determined development policies, which typically placed fairly central importance upon the early expansion of schooling.

Also, it was during the early 1960s that Unesco convened a series of conferences on the development of education in each of the major regional blocks of developing countries. These were held between 1960 and 1966, for African, Asian, Latin American, and Arab countries separately.[1] Almost all countries in these regional groupings were represented at the conferences and were thus signatories to the resolutions passed. The latter were ambitious. They set a timetable for the expansion of each level of education which was energetic by any standards—but particularly so in comparison with the rather gradual approach to educational development which had typified earlier years. For example, in Africa, secondary enrolments were planned to increase sixfold, and tertiary enrolments by more than tenfold over the two decades to 1980. Given that less than 5 per cent of the relevant age-group attended secondary school in Africa in 1960, and that only about half of one per cent had any post-secondary education, these rates of expansion would, it was hoped, lead to a transformation of the educational attainments of Africans over a fairly short period of time. Nevertheless, the major effort—in terms of the absolute increase in enrolments—was to occur at primary level, such that all eligible children were to be enrolled in primary school by 1980. This pattern was reflected in the other regions. The conferences held in Karachi and Tripoli also called for universal and free primary education to be attained by 1980 in Asia and the Arab States, respectively, and that held in Santiago set a similar target for Latin America, to be achieved by the much earlier date of 1970.

It is important to recognize that the documents that emerged from these conferences were not plans in the usual sense of that term: since they were issued by a UN agency, they neither committed the governments to actions along the lines proposed, nor did they carry with them (or propose serious strategies for raising) the resources necessary to finance the expansion programmes which they described. They were, nevertheless, substantially more than exercises in hopeful anticipation. They set out the first substantive statistical overview of the state of education in the developing world; the regional targets were well researched (given the data constraints of the time), being based upon information supplied by planning and education ministries in each country, and they were costed in a competent fashion; their resolutions were adopted by delegates drawn from the highest levels of the national bureaucracies of the member States; finally, they reflected, and further helped to strengthen, the view that educational policy and expansion would be critical to development success, particularly in the new nation States of Africa and Asia. It would, therefore, require a rather cynical interpretation to argue that these meetings had no relevance to the design

---

[1] The dates and locations of these conferences were as follows: Karachi, 1960 for the Asian region; Addis Ababa, 1961 for the African region; Santiago, 1962 for Latin America; Tripoli, 1966 for the Arab States. See Unesco (1960, 1961*b*, 1962, 1966 respectively) for the final reports of these conferences and for the resolutions passed by each.

The Problem Outlined

TABLE 1.1. *School and college enrolment[a] by major developing-country region, 1960–1987 (millions)*

	Year(s)	First level	Second level	Third level	Total
Africa[b]	1960	19.5	1.7	0.2	21.4
	1975	40.2	7.8	0.8	48.8
	1980	59.2	13.7	1.4	74.3
	1987	68.3	20.7	2.1	91.0
Annual growth (%)					
	1960–75	5.0	10.5	10.6	5.7
	1975–80	8.0	11.9	11.3	8.7
	1980–7	2.1	6.0	5.7	2.9
Asia[c]	1960	89.7	26.6	2.7	119.0
	1975	160.1	60.5	9.8	230.4
	1980	184.5	77.0	12.7	274.3
	1987	216.8	114.4	18.9	347.3
Annual growth (%)					
	1960–75	3.9	5.6	9.0	4.5
	1975–80	2.9	4.9	5.4	3.5
	1980–7	2.3	5.4	5.8	3.4
Latin America and	1960	26.6	4.1	0.6	31.3
Caribbean	1975	56.3	12.6	3.6	72.5
	1980	64.8	17.6	4.9	87.3
	1987	71.8	22.8	6.9	101.4
Annual growth (%)					
	1960–75	5.1	7.8	13.1	5.8
	1975–80	2.9	6.9	6.0	3.8
	1980–7	1.5	3.7	5.0	2.2

[a] Not including pre-primary, special, and adult education.
[b] Excludes South Africa.
[c] Excludes China, since data are not available for 1960.
Sources: Calculated from data in Unesco (1977, 1989).

of national educational policies. Indeed, as is shown below, later developments were in some important respects consistent with these early educational aims, and the Unesco targets were frequently used as the touchstones against which subsequent national success, or failure, was gauged.

In the event, educational expansion over the decade or two following this round of conferences took place at historically unprecedented rates. The pattern of enrolment growth in developing countries since 1960 is summarized in Table 1.1. Schooling at all levels expanded rapidly, but the fastest rates of increase in enrolments generally occurred at tertiary level, whilst secondary schooling also increased more rapidly than that at primary level. This hierarchy was anticipated at the Unesco conferences, and partly reflected the much smaller bases from which secondary and tertiary expansion began. Even at primary level, however, enrolments doubled in Asia and Latin America over the two decades to 1980, whilst in Africa they more than tripled over the period. These increases in the capacity of school systems in developing countries comfortably exceeded those envisaged by the Unesco conferences of the early 1960s—at least at primary- and secondary-school levels. Perhaps, then, the optimism and target-setting of that time was vindicated by subsequent events.

A shadow falls across this record of progress, however, from 1980 onwards. It can be seen from Table 1.1 that rates of expansion were sharply reduced between 1980 and 1987. This was particularly so in Africa and Latin America, where the growth rates of secondary and tertiary enrolments were halved, and those of primary enrolments fell to between one-quarter and one-third of their earlier levels. What, then, accounts for this change in the rate of expansion of school systems in the developing world?

It might be thought that, at least at primary level, such a result was inescapable: if, as we reported above, the achieved rates of growth of primary enrolments were somewhat faster than those envisaged in the Unesco conferences, and if the latter had been premissed upon the attainment of universal enrolment by 1980, continued expansion at rates faster than that of the growth of population could not be expected to continue after 1980. Sadly, though the logic is impeccable, the conclusion is flawed, because the population of developing countries increased much faster than the planners in 1960 had predicted. Thus, although the rates of school expansion recommended by the Unesco conferences were achieved, they were nowhere near enough to provide primary schooling for all of the eligible age-group by 1970 in Latin America, nor by 1980 in the rest of the developing world. In the Africa case (excluding the five Arab nations of North Africa), for example, it had been thought that 33 million places would be sufficient to provide for universal primary enrolment by 1980. In fact, actual enrolments in the same year had risen to 44.8 million,[2] but about 56 million places would by then have been required if all the children within the eligible age-range for primary schooling were to have been enrolled. As in so many other areas of economic and social policy, rapid population growth has continually undermined the ability of countries to meet their educational targets: the location of the goalposts has shifted as the game has progressed.

---

[2] This statistic is calculated from Unesco (1989), and comprises all Sub-Saharan African primary enrolments in 1980 less those in Mozambique, Angola, Namibia, and South Africa. Those countries were not included in the Addis Ababa conference. The North African Arab States of Egypt, Morocco, Tunisia, Algeria, and Libya were invited to send observers, but they were more formally covered by the meeting in Tripoli 5 years later.

TABLE 1.2. *Gross enrolment ratios in the developing world*

	Primary			Secondary			Tertiary		
	1960	1980	1987	1960	1980	1987	1960	1980	1987
Africa[a]	42	80	76	5	23	31	0.7	3.5	4.3
Asia	85	97	104	21	38	42	2.6	5.6	7.3
Latin America	73	105	108	15	45	54	3.0	13.5	16.9

[a] Excludes South Africa.
Source: Unesco (1989, Table 2.10).

2.2. Differences between gross and net enrolments

The results of the interaction between population growth and the expansion of school places are summarized in Table 1.2. This table shows
changes in gross enrolment ratios (GER) for each level of schooling in
the southern continents over 1960–87. Before considering the implications of the table, a word of explanation is needed about how to interpret
this ratio. The GER is the most widely used indicator of schooling
availability. It is derived by expressing total enrolment at a given level of
education—irrespective of the age of the students—as a percentage of
the population which, according to national regulations, is of an age to
attend at that level.[3] Universal primary enrolment (UPE) is conventionally said to have been achieved when the primary GER reaches a value of
100.

By 1970, then, Latin American countries had succeeded in raising their
combined GERs only to 90, and it was not until the later years of that
decade that UPE, in the above sense, was achieved. Table 1.2 shows that
by 1980 it had been increased to a value of 105, and that Asia was not far
behind, with a GER of 97 in that year. Africa, on the other hand, still fell
well short of UPE, with total enrolments equal to only 80 per cent of the
number of children of primary-school-age. Further progress was made to
1987 in Asia and Latin America, but in Africa, as a result of the sharp
decline in enrolment growth to a level less than that of the increase in the
school-age population, the GER actually fell back some four points below
the level achieved in 1980.

---

[3] GERs calculated in the above way are thus adjusted for individual national school
systems and structures. They may also be calculated by standardizing the ratios, across all
countries, with respect to a given age-group used in the denominator and/or a given number
of years of schooling used in the numerator. Standardized ratios are not used in any of the
tables in this book.

Does this imply, then, that the remaining challenge of achieving UPE is confined to Africa—that all of the out-of-school children are to be found in that continent? This is not so, for two main reasons. First, although the regional values for the GER in Latin America and Asia are now in excess of 100, there remain a number of individual countries in these regions where GERs of 100 are far from being attained. The average value thus reflects the influence of other countries (such as, in Asia, China) where primary enrolments are far greater than the number of children who are formally eligible to attend.

Secondly, a moment's thought will reveal that the GER provides a rather narrow measure of progress towards universal enrolment. This is because it does not take account of the age-structure of those enrolled. The existence of significant numbers of over-age pupils need not imply that schools enrol children with scant regard for their ages, or for whether they happen to fall within the officially designated age-group (although many school principals do act thus, particularly where their salary levels are determined partly by the size of their schools). A more common cause is that in most developing countries repetition rates are high at both primary and secondary levels. Thus, a typical country with a primary repetition rate of 12 per cent, would be likely to have a similar rate of over-age enrolment, concentrated mainly in the highest grade. This would imply that, even if the GER stood at 100, around 12 per cent of children of primary age would still not be enrolled in school.

Thus, the GER measures the *capacity* of school systems, relative to the population eligible to attend. A GER value of 100 indicates that a country is, in principle, able to accommodate all of its school-age population, but it does not indicate the proportion actually enrolled. The achievement of a GER of 100 is therefore a necessary but not sufficient condition for enrolling all eligible children in school.[4]

The fallibility of the GER as a measure of progress towards universal *attendance* at school, as opposed to universal *capacity*, has emerged relatively recently.[5] The Unesco targets for UPE were defined in terms of capacity. The extent of over-age enrolment was, at that time, viewed to be a temporary problem, which would quickly disappear after the growth

[4] Although a country with a GER of 100 has, by definition, enough school places to accommodate all children in the eligible age-group, whether this could be achieved in practice is likely to depend upon rather more than changes in policies regarding repetition. It would e.g. require a particular pattern for the geographic distribution of schools relative to the location of populations. Furthermore the successful enrolment of all eligible children may require policies to stimulate the demand for schooling, irrespective of the supply of available places.

[5] Williams (1979) adds a further category—that of universal accessibility of primary schooling. In the absence of universal attendance, universal capacity does not necessarily deliver accessible school places for all primary-age children. Universal accessibility would thus become an important intermediate policy-goal prior to universal attendance being gained.

The Problem Outlined

TABLE 1.3. *Primary enrolments amongst*
6–11-year-olds as % of age-group 6–11

	1960	1980	1987
Africa[a]	32	60	59
Asia	52	71	80
Latin America and Caribbean	58	82	86
All developing	48	70	76
All developed	91	92	92

[a] Excludes South Africa.
Source: Unesco (1989, Table 2.11).

of school places had caught up with the size of the population eligible to attend. This seemed to have happened in the industrialized countries, where the differences between gross and net enrolment ratios appeared to be (and remain) small,[6] and it was also expected to follow as a natural consequence of educational expansion in the poorer countries of the world.

Thus, GERs quickly became the accepted statistical means of monitoring the progress of nations towards UPE. This convention was strengthened by the fact that net enrolment ratios are difficult to measure. It is much easier merely to count and report the number of children in school than it is to classify them, additionally, by age-group. This is particularly so where both parents and teachers have an incentive— such as is provided by regulations specifying the appropriate ages for attendance at school—not to reveal the true extent of over-age (or under-age) enrolments. Accordingly, age-adjusted enrolment ratios are available for fewer countries, and are generally less reliable, than are GERs. For these reasons, most studies which attempt to measure the progress of developing countries towards UPE continue to depend upon the attainment of a GER value of 100 as the main indicator of success.[7]

Notwithstanding the data problems involved, some estimates for the proportions of children aged 6–11 years who were actually enrolled in primary schools over the years 1960–87 are shown in Table 1.3. It is not surprising to find a much less satisfactory position than that suggested by Table 1.2. For developing countries, only three-quarters of children in this age-group were enrolled in school in 1987, compared with about 92

---

[6] For further discussion of this point, see Ch. 2, below.
[7] See e.g. Fredriksen (1981, 1983); and Berstecher and Carr-Hill (1990). For an exception, see Lee (1988), which reports an interesting attempt to use NERs in a cross-country analysis of prospects for UPE in Africa.

per cent in the industrialized world. If the latter were taken as a maximum feasible target,[8] developing countries as a group were 83 per cent enrolled in 1987. The ratio was slightly higher for Asia and Latin America, but substantially lower for Africa, where only two-thirds of 'attainable" primary enrolments had been achieved.

Both the practical and financial difficulties of moving towards 90 or 95 per cent net enrolments are likely to be considerably greater than those associated with earlier stages of expansion of the primary system. This is because those children who are last to be enrolled are likely to be different, in important respects, from the rest of their peers.[9] If they are urban dwellers, they are likely to be poorer than the children already at school, and more likely to be providing a source of income upon which their parents and families depend. Greater poverty is also a likely characteristic of those out of school in rural areas. In addition, they may be living in more scattered population groups which are too small to provide for a normally sized school. They may be migrants, nomads, or members of religious or linguistic minorities, who may find schooling dysfunctional to their traditional ways of life. In short, the continued underenrolment of some children may be as much caused by the demand for schooling as its supply. We return to a consideration of the problem of low demand later in this chapter. Meanwhile, it should be noted that, although the demand for primary schooling can be affected, and increased, by public policy, the marginal costs of so doing may, in some circumstances, be high.

Nevertheless, as the experiences of a large number of countries testify, the task of enrolling the final 10 or 20 per cent of children in school is by no means insurmountable. It seems clear, therefore, that the sharp decline in the rate of growth of primary enrolments in developing countries was not merely a product of the special problems mentioned above, still less of universal primary enrolment (in the sense of universal attendance) already having been generally achieved. After all, the reduced expansion of enrolments was not just confined to primary schooling: Table 1.1 has shown that secondary and tertiary systems—where enrolment ratios remain very small—were also severely affected. The main explanation for the decline is that it was a product of the much worsened economic circumstances that characterized the 1980s in most parts of the developing world.

[8] A target value for the net enrolment ratio of 100 would be too ambitious: not all primary systems start at age 6, e.g. in all the Scandinavian countries the entry age is 7; in most countries a small proportion of parents will exercise their right to educate their children at home; finally, illness and disability further reduce the level of attainable enrolments.

[9] A useful check-list of policy alternatives to tackle the problem of enrolling the 'last 10 per cent' is given in Williams (1983).

TABLE 1.4. *Public expenditure on education by major world region, 1980 and 1987*

	Public expenditure on education as % GNP		Public expenditure[a] on education per inhabitant ($)	
	1980	1987	1980	1987
Africa excluding Arab States[b]	4.7	4.8	32	15
Asia excluding Arab States	4.6	4.4	37	58
Arab States	4.4	6.6	112	134
Latin America and Caribbean	3.8	4.1	88	78
All developed countries	6.0	5.9	469	704

[a] These are current prices. A constant price series is not available.
[b] Equivalent to Sub-Saharan Africa, excluding Somalia, Sudan, and South Africa.
Source: Unesco (1989, Table 2.12).

2.3. The impact of recession and adjustment

On this theme, Table 1.4 indicates that—perhaps contrary to expectations—developing countries maintained and, if anything, slightly increased public expenditures on education, expressed as a proportion of their national incomes, during the 1980s. But the table also shows some startling changes in the dollar value of these expenditures, expressed in per capita terms. It can be seen that public expenditures on education per inhabitant in African countries (excluding the Arab States) fell by more than one-half between 1980 and 1987. In Latin America, over the same period, they fell by 11 per cent. By contrast, expenditures in Arab countries increased by one-fifth, and in the rest of Asia and in industrialized countries by more than one-half. The latter is roughly what would have been necessary in order to maintain the real value of per capita expenditures over these years. These circumstances imply, then, that real public spending on education per inhabitant in Latin America fell by about 40 per cent, and in Africa by around two-thirds over the years 1980–7.

Thus, the reduction in the flow of public resources to education has been sharp in Latin America over the last decade, but in Sub-Saharan Africa it has been truly horrendous. These reductions are, of course, a combined result of falls in the quantity of educational services provided per inhabitant, and of declines in the cost per unit of service provision. Wherever enrolments have grown less quickly than the school-age population—as in much of Africa at primary level—a decline in the quantitative availability of schooling has resulted. The process which has brought widespread cost-reductions in education, however, is more complex, and has been delivered mainly by broad changes in macro-economic, rather than merely in educational, policies. In Africa, as in Latin America, the large currency devaluations which have been introduced as part of economic-adjustment programmes have often been associated with sharp, and often extreme, falls in the real value of salaries in the public sector, including, of course, those of schoolteachers. Salary decline—an intended consequence of most adjustment programmes—has typically been engineered by holding the rates of nominal salary increases below the accelerating, devaluation-induced rates of inflation. As a result, in much of Sub-Saharan Africa, and in many countries of Latin America, wage- and salary-earners were, by the late 1980s receiving far lower real earnings than they would have had a decade earlier.[10] These circum- stances have been a major factor in reducing the costs of education provision. However, in many countries they have also brought strongly negative consequences for the morale of the teaching service. As will become clear later, the aim of reducing the unit costs of education is laudable; but the ways in which this has actually been achieved, particu- larly in Africa in recent years, have often been counter-productive: they have massively undermined the quality of service provision, and have sometimes threatened the very viability of the whole schooling process.

The above trends have, of course, affected all levels of education. There is some evidence, however, that secondary and tertiary systems have been more protected, throughout these years of recession and adjustment, than primary schooling. Table 1.1 indicates that, in a quantitative sense, the growth rates of secondary and tertiary levels proceeded at twice that of primary schooling throughout the 1980s, in all the developing-country regions. Indeed, Sub-Saharan Africa managed to maintain faster rates of growth at these levels than Asia and Latin America, even during the recent years of economic decline. More crucially, in each of the developing regions shown in Table 1.1, the post- 1980 fall in the rate of growth of primary enrolments has been larger, relative to earlier growth rates, than the reductions at secondary and tertiary levels. Does this suggest that the austerity measures have par- ticularly affected the base of the system—that secondary and tertiary expansion has proceeded at the cost of basic education in these parts of the world?

It is difficult to provide a general answer. Not surprisingly, countries have responded to the need to reduce public expenditures—including those on education—differently. Table 1.5, for example, shows unit

[10] Estimates of the extent of recent real-wage decline in these regions are given in Colclough (1991: 206).

TABLE 1.5. *Public recurrent expenditure per pupil in Sub-Saharan Africa,
1970–83 (constant 1983 dollars)*[a]

Country group	No. of Countries	Primary			Secondary			Tertiary		
		1970	1980	1983	1970	1980	1983	1970	1980	1983
Low-income semi-arid	6	105	51	49	262	158	168	2,791	2,313	1,929
Index		100	49	47	100	60	64	100	83	69
Low-income other	19	50	36	31	173	109	119	2,811	2,315	2,006
Index		100	72	62	100	63	69	100	82	71
Middle-income oil-importers	9	74	129	121	612	609	456	3,585	3,116	3,456
Index		100	174	164	100	99	75	100	87	96

[a] All data in this table are population-weighted mean values.
Source: World Bank (1988*a*, Tables A.17, A.18, A.19).

expenditures for thirty-four countries in Sub-Saharan Africa to 1983, time-series data for other countries and for later years not being available on a comparable basis. It is interesting, and perhaps surprising, to note that in the nine middle-income countries shown in the table public spending per pupil at primary level had actually risen by 64 per cent over 1970–83, whereas unit expenditures at secondary and tertiary levels had fallen over the same period. In these countries, then, primary schooling appeared to be doing rather well, compared with the higher levels of the system. One should note, however, that in some of these middle-income States, including Zambia and Ivory Coast, the economic record was sharply worse after 1983 than before, and unit expenditures at primary level fell heavily in real terms after that date. More recent data for the middle-income group of countries would probably, therefore, tell a somewhat different story.

By contrast, in the other countries shown in Table 1.5 public expenditures per student fell strongly, at each educational level, and ended the period at around two-thirds, or less, of their 1970 values. In these twenty-five low-income countries tertiary education appears to have been affected least, whilst primary schooling sustained the greatest proportional cuts in expenditure per pupil. It should be recalled that many of the world's poorest countries are in this group. It also includes some of those with the weakest primary systems, in terms of both quality and capacity. Here, then, it is reasonable to conclude that excessive resource starvation has occurred: in these countries, primary schooling has been relatively more affected than have the higher levels of the system. It is ironic to note that these are precisely the countries where improvements to the quality and availability of primary schooling are most especially needed.

In summary, then, we can say that the record of educational expansion in developing countries, since 1960, has been mixed. On the one hand, school systems have expanded at much higher rates than those that were contemplated, even in those optimistic times. On the other hand, the achieved rates of enrolment growth have still been substantially lower than would have been necessary to deliver schooling for all children of primary school-age. This result stems partly from population growth having proceeded more rapidly than was projected in the 1960s, and partly from many of the available school places being occupied by children who were beyond the officially designated primary-school age-group.

Thus, the deceleration in the rate of enrolment growth after 1975–80, which occurred throughout the developing world, was not primarily caused by widespread attainment of UPE, in the sense of universal attendance by children of the relevant ages. Notwithstanding the fact that mean GERs in developing countries had risen to around 100 by 1987, about one-quarter of children of primary-school-age remained out of school in that year. Furthermore, those countries with the sharpest reductions in primary enrolment growth were the African countries which, as a group, remained furthest from achieving universal enrolment.

The major influence upon the changing pattern of enrolment growth was, then, neither the completion of the task in hand, nor even a shift of priorities away from education towards other recipients of state spending. Rather, it was the result of recession and generalized economic decline. This was the *force majeure* which led to a compression of public budgets and a reduction in the per capita availability of public services in a large number of developing countries, but particularly in those of Africa and Latin America. It is difficult to generalize about the incidence and effects of these expenditure reductions. Outcomes were critically influenced by the political process which has differed between States. In some countries, expenditures were constrained across all sectors. In others, the ways in which the cuts were implemented appears to have seriously damaged the effectiveness of social services. Within education, primary schooling has sometimes been hit more than the higher levels, and sometimes not. Although the evidence is not conclusive, there does appear to have been a tendency amongst the poorer African nations to cut expenditures per pupil at primary level more sharply than those at other levels of education. In general, the expectation must be that those activities serving the least powerful or influential sections of the population will be most vulnerable to expenditure reduction during times of economic decline.

There is great danger here, not just for the individuals so affected, but for the future prosperity of society as a whole. Primary schooling is an enormously powerful investment, the prospective benefits from which would typically justify its receiving more rather than less public expenditure during times of recession and adjustment. It is to a brief review of the evidence for this statement that we now turn.

3. Primary Schooling: The Economic and Social Rationale

First, one should ask why it is that particular justification for the importance of investing in primary schooling—at least up to levels which provide access to it for all children—is required at all. After all, it brings obvious consumption benefits, and is demanded by most families, on behalf of their children, in and for itself. Furthermore, it has, since 1948, been formally accepted as a universal human right, the provision of which should be ensured by national governments. Yet until comparatively recently its advocacy by the aid community has been muted. Until the mid-1970s international organizations and aid agencies gave very little attention to primary schooling. It was not thought a suitable target for development aid partly because its provision was viewed to be a domestic matter, partly because its economic benefits seemed to be intangible and would, in any case, be gained only over the long term, and partly because, whatever the nature of those benefits, they were thought unlikely to generate foreign exchange in any direct sense. More fundamentally, the idea that expenditures upon primary schooling constituted investment, perhaps as much as did spending upon infrastructure, was slow to catch on. The human capital revolution of the 1960s had established the investment case for the higher branches of school/college systems. But at the primary-school level both argument and evidence seemed to be much more shaky.

As a symptom of the strength of these attitudes, one should note that the World Bank, which, by 1991, had become the most important source of external finance to the education sector in developing countries, had made no loans for primary schooling during the 1960s. The first stirring of interest came between 1970 and 1974, when they accounted for 5 per cent of total educational loans, and they still remained at a mere 14 per cent over 1975–8 (World Bank 1980, Table 7). The policies of the bilateral donors followed a similar pattern, with their first support to primary education being extended during the 1970s.

3.1. The mistaken emphasis upon parallel systems of 'basic' schooling

In spite of these stirrings of interest, however, aid agencies still did not fully accept, even in the mid-1970s, that existing primary systems adequately served economic objectives. What many believed to be needed was, instead of an educational experience in primary schools dictated by the academic curricula and requirements of the secondary schools, something more relevant to the majority of children whose lives and livelihoods would be spent in self-employment or peasant production. This raised an older idea, that of 'basic education', in a new form. In a policy paper setting out a new approach to educational lending (World Bank 1974) the Bank pledged future support for new programmes of 'basic' education. These were to be a 'supplement not a rival to the formal (primary) education system . . . intended to provide a functional, flexible and low-cost education for those whom the formal system cannot yet reach or has already passed by' (ibid. 29). It was believed that many developing countries with low primary-enrolment ratios were too poor to secure universal access to primary schooling. Aid agencies would therefore support shorter, cheaper alternatives, which focused upon providing skills which would be useful to rural populations. The idea was to concentrate upon those aspects of the primary curriculum which did lead to the formation of economically useful skills—such as literacy and numeracy—and to add others which might support productive self-employment in primarily rural communities. Thus, rather than placing emphasis upon helping developing countries to universalize existing primary systems, it was believed to be more functional and cost-effective to provide a specially designed programme which would improve equity by giving some education to those presently excluded, and, it was hoped, deliver somewhat higher returns, for the investments made, than would conventional primary schooling.

These initiatives, although well intentioned, were mistaken. The great weakness of education programmes set up in parallel with, and using different curricula from primary schooling, is that their graduates are unlikely to be able—no matter how well they have performed—subsequently to progress through to secondary or higher levels of education. Thus, the proposed reforms could easily have become mechanisms for legitimizing existing inequalities in society rather than means for their mitigation. Equally, they appeared to ignore some important lessons from history: for example, the main reason for the eventual failure of the Gandhian Basic Education movement in India—which is the world's largest experiment to date with parallel primary systems—was precisely that parents were not prepared to continue to support a movement which, notwithstanding the laudability of its stated aims, militated against the possibility of their sons or daughters gaining access to higher levels of formal education, and thus to the potential economic rewards which that allowed.[11]

[11] The following quotation summarizes the conclusion of one detailed evaluation of the Gandhian Basic Education movement: 'A fundamental weakness of the Basic school system was lack of client motivation . . . The slow progress towards Basic Education in most states thus undermined support for Gandhi's educational legacy. Instead there developed a

The World Bank, and the advocates of this form of basic education more generally, received a substantial amount of academic criticism on these, and other grounds (Williams 1975). It is salutary, therefore, that by the time its third education policy paper was published (World Bank 1980), the Bank's stated commitment to basic education as an alternative to primary schooling had become much less evident. Although the basic education concept was by no means abandoned, it was used increasingly frequently either as a synonym for primary schooling, or as a collective noun referring to all first-level education (whether for young children, youths, or indeed adults who had never attended formal schools). By the same token, the Bank's lending commitments to conventional primary schooling were set to increase to up to one-quarter of all educational lending during the early 1980s.

This apparent change of heart did not occur only by default of the basic education idea. It was also informed by the growing amount of evidence which demonstrated that primary schools were truly productive in a strictly economic sense, and that they affected people's behaviour in ways which supported a wide range of development goals.

3.2. The returns to schooling

The evidence took some time to emerge, in part because there are a number of inherent difficulties facing researchers who seek to provide evidence about schooling's productive effects. The first, for those who have focused their enquiries upon the formal sector, is that identifying the output of different workers in a production process is not as easy as it might seem. As a proxy for productivity differences, the earnings of workers have been used to calculate the private and social returns associated with different levels of education. The results are summarized in Table 1.6.

These studies have consistently indicated that the social returns to primary schooling (which range between 18 and 35 per cent in each of the southern continents) are considerably greater than both those at higher educational levels and those associated with most industrial projects. Private returns are substantially higher than social rates, because many of the direct costs of education are met by the State, and, once again, the highest rates of return are associated with primary schooling. This can be interpreted to mean that too much money is being spent on the higher levels of the system and not enough resources are going to primary

general antipathy towards Basic schooling, since graduates of Basic schools had for some years no clear rights of access to high school classes preparing for the matriculation examination—the key to higher education or middle level employment and to upward social mobility for rural children' (Sinclair with Lillis 1980: 59–60). See also Colclough (1976) for examples from other countries which suggest similar lessons.

TABLE 1.6. *Average social and private rates of return to education in the developing world*[a]

Region	Social			Private		
	Primary	Secondary	Higher	Primary	Secondary	Higher
Africa	27	19	14	45	28	33
Asia	18	14	12	34	15	18
Latin America	35	19	16	61	28	26

[a] Samples include studies from between 8 and 12 countries from each region for social rates of return, and between 5 and 9 countries from each region for private rates of return.
Source: Schultz (1991, Table 2.1), derived from Psacharopoulos (1973, 1985*b*).

schooling. It also suggests that primary schooling may be a better investment than that in many other sectors of the economy.

The interpretation of these results is hampered by the fact that there are a range of technical and methodological problems that typically surround the calculation of rates of return to education.[12] The first problem is that they are based upon calculations using market wages unadjusted for unemployment. They would closely reflect productivity differences only if the markets for products and labour worked perfectly, which they do not. In countries where wage legislation, or other factors, caused wages at the minimum to be higher than the social opportunity costs of labour, one may expect the rates of return to be biased upwards at primary relative to higher levels. But this outcome is dependent upon whether or not wages at higher levels were similarly biased upwards—perhaps because of the influence of public service pay scales—and upon the influence of the wage structure upon the cost side of the calculations as well as the benefit side. In such cases, the introduction of shadow wages and of the probabilities of being openly unemployed—which latter are generally higher for the more educated[13]—would tend to strengthen rather than weaken the profitability of primary schooling relative to other educational levels.

[12] In addition to those mentioned in the text, estimation biases arise from the available studies not capturing differences in ability, in the quality of schools attended, and in parental backgrounds, for workers in the selected samples. These omissions will tend to give some upward bias to the estimated returns to schooling. But there is no reason to suppose that removal of these biases would change the present reported ranking of returns by educational level. Indeed one would expect the reverse to be the case, owing to the likely correlation between each of these three attributes, and the level of schooling which people attain. A summary of 'best practice' methods, and of the technical shortcomings underlying many existing rate of return estimates is given by Schultz (1991).

[13] It may seem paradoxical that this statement is consistent with the fact that education to higher levels increases the probability of finding a paid job in the formal sector in most developing countries. The point is that the more educated who do not succeed in finding a job are more likely to do no productive work (because they are more likely to be able to afford that state) than the less educated who similarly fail.

A second problem is that the available studies estimate the *average* returns to different levels of schooling, whereas it is evidence on their *marginal* returns which is actually required. In circumstances where hiring standards rise over time, the job access (and consequent wage eligibility) of leavers from each part of the education system falls. In these circumstances, the marginal rates of return to each level of schooling would be less than their average rates. For the same reasons, the ranking of the marginal rates could also change: if, in some countries, the present wage-earning prospects for primary leavers were little different from those with no education (unlike people who left primary school five to ten years ago or more) the marginal rate of return to primary schooling would be lower than those associated with higher levels of schooling, even if a higher ranking was suggested by calculations based upon average wage rates.

Knight and Sabot (1990: 274–7) investigated the marginal rates of return to primary schooling in Kenya and Tanzania for the late 1970s. They show that, in both countries, marginal rates of return were lower than average rates, and that, in Kenya, but not in Tanzania, the difference was significant enough to change the ranking. In Kenya, then, average rates of return to schooling were highest for the primary level, but, on the basis of marginal rates, secondary schooling seemed just to have had the edge.

Whether the ranking of returns to education to each level would, in general, remain robust if marginal rates were used depends upon the changing balance of supply and demand in the market for educated labour in each country. This is an empirical question, the answer to which will differ between States, and concerning which very little direct evidence is available. However, one trend associated with economic recession and adjustment during the 1980s, will have tended to strengthen the reported ranking of returns to different levels of schooling. Most of the research findings on rates of return to education are derived from surveys conducted prior to 1980. Yet since then substantial real-wage reductions have occurred, particularly in Latin America and Africa, which were also associated with sharp reductions in the earnings differentials between more- and less-educated workers.

For example, in eight African countries having available data, the differential between salaries earned by university graduates and by secondary school-leavers fell by one-quarter between 1980 and 1988, and by one-third during the period 1975–88 (Colclough 1991: 207).[14] These trends will have lowered rates of return to schooling overall, particularly those for higher education which, in Africa, may have been reduced by as much as one-third of the levels reported in Table 1.6. However, since it is income differentials which determine the difference between the benefit

---

[14] See also Ch. 4, Sect. 2, below.

streams for educational investments at each level, these changes suggest that the reported ranking of the average rates of return to primary and higher levels of schooling will, if anything, be stronger by consequence. Thus, the primacy, within the education sector, of economic returns to primary schooling may well prove to have been robust over the past decade.

The final interpretative problem is that, no matter how strong the correlations appear to be between larger quantities of educated labour and higher output (or earnings), explanations which link these outcomes to factors other than merely education remain plausible. This is not the place to review the competing theories relating education to work.[15] For present purposes it is sufficient to note that most such correlations are consistent with the views both that schooling does make people more productive owing to increased cognitive ability, or to the non-cognitive attitudes and behaviour which schooling inculcates, and that it does not do so—merely sorting out (or 'screening') those who are clever (and likely to have the greatest productive potential) from those who are not.

These contradictory interpretations have not yet been finally settled, although a substantial amount of new evidence and argument which represents a powerful attack on 'hard' versions of the screening hypothesis, is provided by Knight and Sabot (1990).[16] Notwithstanding the state of that debate, it is limited, in its relevance, to relationships between education and work in the formal sector of the economy. It is the growing evidence of the productivity of education outside this sector which has tended to be most influential in recent years, and to shift the balance of professional opinion sharply in favour of primary schooling.

3.3 Other market and non-market effects

There is growing evidence that primary schooling improves productivity in rural and urban self-employment. As regards agricultural production, one might expect that education may enhance output in at least three different ways.[17] The first, or 'worker' effect, concerns the extent to which more education allows producers to increase output with given

---

[15] See Colclough (1982) and Hinchliffe (1987), where short accounts can be found.

[16] Using separate measures for each of the relevant variables, the authors show that, whereas the direct returns to reasoning ability in the labour market are small and the returns to years of schooling are moderate, the returns to cognitive achievement appear to be large. The critical evidence here is that, for both primary- and secondary-leavers taken separately, high achievers earn much more than low achievers, and the predicted wage of primary-completers who scored in the top third of their group is nearly as high as that of secondary-completers who scored in the bottom third of theirs. The authors conclude that, in both Kenya and Tanzania, how much one learns in primary or secondary school has a substantial influence on performance at work. See Knight and Sabot (1990: 64–77).

[17] These distinctions were first suggested by Welch (1970).

inputs—for example in cases where literacy or numeracy are important skills for those producing the product in question. In addition, one might expect that workers would, as a result of education, allocate existing inputs more efficiently, and that they may be more skilled at selecting new types of input for given production goals. These three effects of education—the worker, input-allocation, and input-selection effects—have been tested in a range of different settings, and evidence is growing for the separate importance of each of them (Welch 1970; Pudasaini 1983).

These, and other studies, demonstrate that primary schooling has a positive effect upon the agricultural output of small farmers. Evidence from thirteen low-income countries shows that four years of schooling were associated with increased farm output of about 8 per cent, after keeping land, capital, and labour-time constant (Lockheed *et al.* 1980). The positive impact of four years' schooling (compared with none) was higher than this in 'modernizing' environments, that is, where complementary investments in better roads, or access to marketing facilities, fertilizer, and improved crop varieties were being made. Furthermore, surveys of the urban informal sector in, for example, Botswana, Nigeria, Colombia, Peru, and Thailand have indicated that primary schooling increases the propensity to participate in urban informal-sector work, and that, amongst such workers, there is a positive association between education and earnings. Schooling also appears to encourage—or facilitate—entrepreneurship. Evidence from Bolivia, Malaysia, Ghana, and Ivory Coast, for example, shows a correlation between firm size and the number of years of schooling of the owner. This relationship holds for both the primary and secondary spans of schooling (World Bank 1991*b*, Fig. 3.3). Thus, the impact of primary schooling on production in both the rural and urban informal sectors appears to be significant. It is not clear whether these benefits are lower or higher than those documented for the formal sector. However, at least as far as earnings from urban self-employment are concerned, there is evidence from Thailand that private returns to schooling are closely similar to those available from wage employment (Chiswick 1976).

Research has also shown that primary (and secondary) schooling is important in facilitating the demographic transition from very high to moderate rates of population growth (Cochrane 1979, 1988; Schultz 1991). This is so because the schooling of women not only increases their ability to regulate their fertility through contraception, but it is also associated with a rise in the age of marriage (and, therefore, reduced exposure to the risk of pregnancy) and an increase in the perceived costs of child-bearing—in part arising from the economic returns to schooling already discussed.

The association between increases in schooling of women and declines in the total fertility rate is strong. Although in some parts of the world unschooled women have slightly lower fertility than those with up to three years (possibly, as argued by Easterlin (1975), because of the separate impact of education on health, and therefore upon the ability to bear children), subsequently there is a monotonic decline in fertility for every additional year of schooling. Data from the World Fertility Survey indicate the strength of a decline in fertility associated with education: a comparison of women with up to three years and those with seven or more years of schooling reveals a reduction in total fertility rates by between two and three children for each of the African, Asian, and Latin American regions.[18] The negative relationship between these two variables appears to be stronger when schooling is widely spread amongst the population. The presence of these externalities obviously adds to the case for universalizing primary schooling.

Primary schooling also appears to improve health (Cochrane *et al.* 1980). The evidence shows that for households at given income levels, schooling increases their ability to improve the nutritional content of diets, and initiate earlier and more effective diagnosis of illness. One recent study, for example, shows that in Ghana an increase in the education of the household head from none to complete primary schooling is associated with a reduction in the household's calorie gap by an amount equal to one-fifth of a typical adult's daily calorie requirement (Kyereme and Thorbecke 1991).

There is a strong correlation across countries between life expectancy and literacy. Moreover, infant and child mortality are lower the higher the mother's level of schooling (O'Hara 1979; King and Hill 1991: 55). Children of more educated mothers tend to be better nourished, and there is evidence that they suffer illness less frequently and less severely than other children (Leslie and Cochrane 1979). Thus, there is good evidence that parents with greater amounts of primary schooling have healthier, longer-living children. It is safe to conclude that increasing the coverage of primary schooling—particularly for females—would have positive long-term effects upon family health.

Numeracy and literacy brought about by schooling are not only critical to the improvement of productivity at work and in the home, but also to the enhancement of satisfaction in leisure. Where illiteracy is widespread, people have only a restricted access to a wide range of consumption benefits provided by books, the popular media, and cultural pursuits. The extension and qualitative improvement of primary schooling thus brings direct welfare benefits which may be more significant to society than those associated with higher levels of schooling, once literacy has been attained. Of equal importance is that literacy in parents helps to ensure

---

[18] UN (1987: Tables 112–15).

the literacy of their children. Again the importance of female education must be emphasized: creating schooled and literate women is critically important as a means of enhancing both present and future human capabilities. There are substantial externalities here which narrow assessments of the benefits of schooling too frequently miss.

Finally, a number of studies show that general cognitive and non-cognitive change occurs more rapidly amongst younger than older children, and that the impact of environmental conditions upon increases in IQ are much greater for children aged 8 years or less than for those who are older (Bloom 1964). Thus, the cognitive benefits of primary schooling per dollar of expenditure are likely to be greater than those associated with expenditures at higher educational levels. Moreover, this would also imply that the cognitive benefits of high-quality secondary and tertiary education following on from low-quality primary schooling would be considerably smaller than those which one might expect from some reversal of this qualitative hierarchy.

4. Does Quality Count?

This last point raises a question of some importance to our study: does the quality of schooling matter, and, if so, how much? Is the main challenge that of enrolling all children in school, or do the schools have to be of a certain standard in order to achieve the benefits discussed above? The easy answer to this question is that, since the research results surveyed did not generally incorporate school-quality variables, the benefits would be accessible to those attending schooling of similar quality to the average in the studied countries. This, however, is not particularly helpful, since we know nothing about how closely typical of all developing countries was the quality of those schools. Moreover, since there are trade-offs between quantity and quality, it is important to establish whether quantitative expansion should still be pursued if its attainment were to require some reduction in average resource inputs. The question of quality is important precisely because rapid expansion might imply, in some countries, that past qualitative standards could not be maintained.

Not unexpectedly, whether or not schools with different resource inputs have a similarly differential impact upon the extent to which children learn or reason has been an issue to which educational researchers have returned time and again. What is surprising, however, is that the results of their research have typically suggested that school-related factors are of minor significance in accounting for differences in student outcomes. One of the first major reviews of the available evidence in the USA concluded that 'schools bring little influence to bear on a child's achieve-

ment that is independent of his background and general social context'
(Coleman *et al.* 1966). The authors judged that this very lack of an
independent effect means that the inequalities imposed on children by
their home, neighbourhood, and peer environment are carried along to
become the inequalities with which they confront life at the end of school.
These results appeared to be confirmed by Jencks's later work (1992),
and also—more surprising still—by the first International Evaluation of
Educational Achievement (IEA) studies, which investigated the factors
determining school achievement in twenty-three countries. In the latter
studies, school factors such as the type of school, the teacher's experience, and school equipment were not generally significant in predicting
achievement-test scores within countries. The home background of
the student, however—a composite of parental education, father's
occupation, the number of books in the home, and family size—was
significant.

In spite of the importance and influence of these studies they have been
heavily criticized on methodological and technical grounds. Those criti-
cisms will not be repeated here.[19] Of more interest to us is the question
as to whether their results could—even if technically sound—be accepted
as relevant for developing countries. The main point, for our purposes, is
that the first two studies employed data only from the USA, whilst the
IEA included only four poorer countries amongst their twenty-three case-
studies. Thus, these research results were mainly obtained from samples
of schools which, relative to most developing countries, were of uniformly
high quality. There are, of course, good and bad schools in the USA and
in developed countries more generally. But those at the bottom end of
the quality spectrum in these samples would not fall below the top
quartile of schools in most developing countries. It may be, therefore,
that improvements in teacher/pupil ratios, teacher qualifications, and the
quantity of books and equipment in schools, make little difference to
student achievement if the values for these variables are higher than a set
of critical minima not found in the USA, yet which lie well above the
mean levels found in most developing countries. In these circumstances,
the 'northern' school-effects literature may have little to say about the
likely impact of increased resource inputs upon student learning in the
primary schools of most developing countries.

There is now a growing amount of evidence which suggests that this
judgement is correct. Heyneman and Loxley (1983), for example, find
that school effects are significant determinants of achievement in a sample
of countries which included sixteen developing and thirteen industrialized
countries. They find that the absolute achievement levels of children in

---

[19] Those wishing to peruse the detailed arguments should consult McPartland and
Karweit (1979), Madaus (1979), and the summary given in Solmon (1987).

the poorer countries are lower, for given time spent at school, than in the richer group. The factors which influence these levels of achievement in the two groups are also significantly different. Specifically, their results suggest that the lower the per capita income of the country, the weaker the influence of socio-economic background, and the greater the effects of school and teacher quality on pupil achievement. It remains the case, however, that only a small amount of the total variance in achievement levels is explained by school effects (16 per cent), even in the LDC group. Nevertheless, this is significantly more than is explained by this variable in the richer countries, and it also represents a much higher proportion of the total amount of variance explained.

These modestly positive results concerning the impact of school quality on pupil achievement in developing countries are increasingly confirmed by other research. Critical variables affecting school quality appear to be teachers and textbooks.[20] Based upon an examination of thirty-two different studies, Husen *et al.* (1978) conclude that the qualifications, experience, knowledge, and level of education of teachers, and whether or not they are formally trained, all have a positive effect upon pupil achievement in developing countries. Studies have shown positive relationships between English language proficiency of teachers and student achievement in Uganda (Heyneman and Jamison 1980), and between the secondary-school success of teachers, and that of their own students in Iran, Pakistan, and elsewhere (reported by Lockheed *et al.* 1990: 41).

The positive impact upon pupils' achievement of providing more and better textbooks is also clear. For example, Heyneman *et al.* (1981) find a stronger and more consistent relationship between pupil achievement and the availability of books than between the former and other school-quality variables. Country studies from Nicaragua, the Philippines, Brazil, and elsewhere have also documented the important positive effects on student learning of increasing access to textbooks.[21] More generally, sixteen out of twenty-four studies completed since 1970 find that the availability of learning materials contributes significantly to student achievement (Fuller 1987: 261). On the other hand, mere availability does not guarantee that they will be used. There is evidence from many countries that textbook quality is poor and that they are often too difficult for the age-group at which they are aimed (Cope *et al.* 1989). For these reasons they may often have far less impact than they might on student learning. Improving the quality, as well as the quantity of textbooks should thus be a high priority for many countries.

---

[20] It is interesting and important to note that class-size does not appear to be a significant variable affecting student achievement—at least not for the typical ranges for class-size found in developing countries. See Ch. 4, Sect. 2, below.

[21] These country studies can be found in the following sources: Jamison *et al.* (1981); Heyneman *et al.* (1984); Armitage *et al.* (1986).

There are a large number of other detailed research results which are relevant to the case that quality counts. Some will be discussed later in this book, where they have a bearing upon particular policy choice.[22] However, those mentioned above appear to be most important in the context of the general argument. In summary, what they imply is that in countries where there are many schools of low quality, the returns to school improvements, in terms of cognitive achievements, are likely to be high—and considerably higher than similar investments made in countries where school quality is already relatively good. This, in turn, implies that there are diminishing returns to expenditures on school quality, at least over a certain range. Many developing countries, however, are at a much earlier stage than that—perhaps best characterized as the range (on a curve showing the relationship between inputs to and qualitatively ranked outputs from primary schooling) where there are increasing rather than constant or declining returns to additional expenditures. For many of the countries that are the subject of the present enquiry, therefore, we expect to find pressing reasons to improve both the quality as well as the quantity of primary-school provision.

5. The Private Demand for Primary Schooling

We have seen that the economic case for investment in primary schooling, based upon estimated social rates of return supplemented by a range of additional benefits arising from externalities, is strong. However, private returns are also high; indeed, as shown in Table 1.6, they are higher, in most developing countries, than the estimated social rates, owing to the substantial proportion of the direct costs of schooling which are met by governments. Furthermore, some of the externalities which are not measured in the calculations of returns—such as better health and nutrition—accrue as additional private benefits. In view of this high private pay-off, it may seem puzzling that an insufficient demand for schooling is, in many countries, an important factor which impedes progress towards UPE. Why, then, does this occur?

There appear to be a number of reasons. First, even where returns are high, the direct and indirect costs of school attendance may be too great for poor families to afford. Although most of the direct costs of primary schooling are met by the government, fees for books, sports equipment, uniforms, meals, and other items are common. Furthermore, the opportunity costs of school attendance—most usually those associated with forgoing child labour in the home or on the land—are much more strongly

---

[22] For a scholarly and very sensible review of the results and policy implications of many of these studies, see Lockheed and Verspoor (1990), esp. Ch. 3.

felt by poor households. The increased difficulty of meeting these private costs has partly caused the reductions, during the 1980s, of primary enrolments in Africa which were mentioned earlier. On the income side, there is evidence from a number of African (and Latin American) countries of an increase in the incidence of rural and urban poverty during the process of adjustment. On the cost side, many governments have had to introduce user fees in education in response to increased austerity, often as a condition of financial support from the international community. For example, in a sample of over fifty World Bank structural adjustment loans, one-fifth included conditions stipulating the raising, or introduction, of book and tuition fees. In Malawi, Zaïre, Mali, and Nigeria, their introduction was followed by reductions in school attendance (Stewart 1991: 19–21). Capital markets cannot provide an effective solution to this problem, since collateral is required, and risk-aversion is greater amongst the poor.

Second, many families do not know, or find it difficult to appraise, the net benefits of primary schooling. Although some of the relevant externalities do accrue as subsequent benefits to the individual, many households appear unaware of this. Even where such benefits are expected, the extent and value of improved agricultural productivity or of efficiency gains in child care, health, or even in the conduct of daily life (Schultz 1975), are much more difficult to anticipate than is the impact of schooling upon likely wage earnings in the market economy.

A third, and critically important point, however, is that the relevant decision-making unit for matters to do with primary-school attendance is the household—or, more accurately, the parents within it—and not the child. Thus, whereas rates of return to schooling compare the returns to the pupil with the costs to the parents, in reality the important issue is the perceived balance between the costs and benefits to the parents of sending their child to school. Since only some portion of the returns to schooling will accrue to parents, there may be perfectly rational (if regrettable) reasons for households appearing to underinvest in primary schooling, and thus for low demand impeding progress towards UPE, notwithstanding its apparently high economic returns.[23]

Finally, even if private rates of return are high, they may differ (or be perceived to differ) sharply within countries as between separate population groups, urban and rural areas, and boys and girls. Average returns based upon market wages presuppose mobility and an absence of discrimination in the labour market.[24] If these conditions did not hold, some

[23] These relationships are recognized in a growing body of empirical work investigating the influences on school enrolment in developing countries. Here, schooling is treated as subject to decisions by households, but its costs and benefits are differentially allocated amongst family members. See e.g. Rosenzweig and Schultz (1982); Hill and King (1991).

[24] More strictly, they presuppose that the probability of remaining unemployed is roughly equal for all leavers from a particular level of schooling.

members of the community would face quite different expected benefits from schooling than others. Of particular importance here is the different enrolment experiences of boys and girls: as demonstrated in Chapter 2, a majority of those who are out-of-school at primary level are female. Does this imply that returns to schooling are different for boys and girls, or that they are perceived to be so by their parents?

In fact, there is little systematic evidence to show that returns to schooling are lower for female members of the labour force than they are for men (Schultz 1991: 47–55). However, their labour-force participation rates are lower—both in general and in the market economy—which probably helps to explain why parents are more averse to investing in the education of their female children. In addition, there are a range of powerful customary reasons why parents tend to favour the education of sons over that of daughters in many countries. We return to a discussion of these matters in later chapters.

In summary, progress towards universal schooling can be impeded by low demand, as well as by an insufficient supply of school places being provided by the State. Public policies, however, are not constrained to affect only the supply of schooling, for they can influence demand in important ways. In this context, education policy itself is important, since measures to improve the quality of schooling increase retention rates and help to stimulate demand. In addition, however, changes in fiscal and labour market policies, in ways discussed later in this book, are often also required. In each country where enrolments remain low, the extent to which this is caused by specific combinations of supply and demand factors will need to be identified. This task is not easy. But it must be attempted if policies to deliver universal schooling are to be effectively designed.

6. Conclusion

Much of the talk, over the past thirty years, about targets for enrolments in primary schooling has been about the need for all countries to achieve UPE. The precise meaning of this, as an objective, has, however, been interpreted in a number of different ways. This chapter has suggested that the most common statistical criterion used to monitor its achievement—the incidence of GERs of 100 or more—is flawed. Although such values for the GER have now been very widely attained (and although the weighted average GER for all developing countries is now slightly more than 100) there remains a very large number of primary-age children out of school. Thus, the GER measures merely the aggregate capacity of school systems, irrespective of whether or not their school places are filled by the children who are meant to be there. The attainment of UPE, if this criterion is used, is not dependent upon whether or not all children have the opportunity to go to school.

In addition, UPE is silent about the quality of schooling which is available. Yet it is obvious that some schools in developing countries—those with no trained teachers, no textbooks except those held by the teachers for their own use, and with few other learning materials, are scarcely able to perform more than a child-minding role. We have suggested that the many benefits which accrue from primary schooling are not insensitive to its quality. It performs best when it is well resourced, and when it is supported by a broader environment which is conducive to its pupils' learning tasks. Thus, universalizing schooling of poor quality is unlikely to serve the interests of the next generation as well as its members could reasonably expect.

We shall refer in this book to a broader concept—that of schooling for all (SFA). This incorporates both a quantitative and a qualitative dimension. It requires the UPE be attained, but it goes beyond it by seeking to enrol all children of school age, whether or not others outside the official age-range are, or are not, enrolled. It also, however, embraces the notion of schooling of a minimum acceptable quality being available to all. We shall show that UPE, as conventionally measured, is within the reach of most countries in the world, but that SFA will be rather more elusive in at least two ways: first, it is difficult to define in an operational sense, because the criteria for its attainment are to some extent socially and culturally specific; second, it is more costly, and thus less easily attainable than UPE. Nevertheless, in what follows, we shall ask why progress towards it in many parts of the world has been slow, and when, and how, it might be attained.

2

Differential Progress towards Schooling for All: A Cross-Country Analysis

1. Introduction

Why is it that, more than forty years after the first UN declarations asserting an urgent need to secure universal primary schooling throughout the world, to which most countries were signatories, more than half of all developing countries have still not achieved this goal? This is the main question addressed in this chapter.

At the outset, it should be recognized that in one important sense there may be no answer which has general validity: since the achievement of schooling for all at primary level is heavily—and perhaps mainly—influenced by the priority attached by governments to the provision of schooling relative to other uses of public resources, the deeper reasons for its non-attainment may differ on a country-by-country basis. Thus the reasons for Zambia having sufficient school places to accommodate all its primary-school age-group, in contrast to Sierra Leone—at a similar level of per capita income to Zambia—which has enough for hardly more than half the age-group, may mainly concern the ways in which the domestic policies, history, culture, and politics of the two countries have resulted in the provision of sharply different schooling opportunities for their respective populations.

Acceptance of this view might imply that the most productive way to set about answering the question posed above would be via country case-studies, bearing in mind that explanations covering groups of countries couched in less than very general terms may be unlikely to hold. A time-series, case-by-case approach to this question thus has much to commend it, and that method is used later in this book in order to derive general lessons for policy from the experiences of several countries which have been amongst the more successful in achieving UPE.

At the same time, a more aggregated approach is also useful for the purpose of examining whether or not there are particular characteristics, or circumstances, which are shared by countries with high or low levels of primary enrolment. Are there attributes which seem to be commonly associated with failure to secure UPE? If so, their identification may point to the existence of particular constraints which would need to be overcome if it were rapidly to be achieved. Such an approach would certainly aid a process of description, and probably also provide *partial* explanations for the widespread failures to secure UPE, and more widely so, SFA at primary level in the developing world.

2. Definitions of UPE and SFA

As indicated in Chapter 1, the achievement of 'schooling for all' has both quantitative and qualitative dimensions. Any acceptable definition needs to embrace not merely the proportion of eligible children attending school, but also the nature and quality of schooling offered. The achievement of SFA is not, therefore, merely a matter of securing sufficient formal attendance at school, but also of ensuring that the material and human resources available in schools are sufficient to allow minimally acceptable learning to proceed. Nevertheless, in the present chapter we shall be concerned primarily with the quantitative aspects of SFA, and with identifying some commonly shared characteristics associated with progress towards it.

In a quantitative sense, the capacity to provide SFA is proxied by the size of a country's gross primary enrolment ratio (GER), since, where this has reached 100 it is implied that the number of children attending primary school is equal to the size of the eligible age-group. However, because of the frequent incidence of repetition and, more generally, of over-age enrolment, the achievement of a GER of 100 is, in practice, not a sufficient condition even for the quantitative aspect of SFA to be achieved. The net enrolment ratio (NER), which indicates the actual proportion of primary-age children attending school, is arguably a more useful statistic for that purpose. But there are at least two reasons for preferring to use the GER. The first is practical—that the data on NERs are more unreliable and much less frequently available, covering less than two-thirds of the countries for which GERs are known (see Table A.1). Secondly, there is wide variation in the extent of over-age enrolment between countries. For example, in the mid-1980s, more than half of those attending primary schools in Mozambique, Haiti, Lesotho, and Colombia were outside the official age-range for primary attendance, whereas this was reported to be true of less than 5 per cent of the primary pupils in Korea, Sri Lanka, and Rwanda (Table A.1). Because these differences are so large, the NER seriously understates the number of primary-school places already available in some countries, though not in others. Since the GER is unaffected by the extent of over-age enrolment, it provides the best indicator of the comparative distribution of schooling opportunities around the world. It provides an index of the capacity of different countries to achieve SFA—even though, in many, policies affecting repetition and over-age enrolment would need to be sharply changed.

In this chapter, and throughout the book, we shall therefore refer separately to UPE and SFA. UPE is defined simply as 'the circumstance of having a primary GER of 100 or more'. SFA, on the other hand, is defined as 'the circumstance of having a school system in which all eligible children are enrolled in schools of at least minimally acceptable quality'. The latter would imply the attainment of NERs of around 95,[1] which, in turn, would require GERs of at least 100, unless repetition and over-age enrolment were reduced to insignificant proportions. UPE, on these definitions, is thus a necessary but not sufficient condition for the achievement of SFA.

3. Some Dimensions of the Problem

Amongst ninety-five developing countries having comparable data, more than half had GERs of less than 100 in 1986, and in thirty-seven of them less than 90 per cent of the eligible population attended primary school in that year. These, then, were the countries whose populations were the most disadvantaged, in terms of the quantitative goals of SFA. Enrolment ratios, together with a range of other salient characteristics of those thirty-seven countries, are shown in Table 2.1. A number of interesting and important points emerge.

First, the range of gross enrolment ratios shown is wide, varying from around 20 in Somalia and Mali, to over 80 in Mozambique, Egypt, Yemen Arab Republic, Nepal, and Bolivia, with the median value being 65. Thus, the typical enrolment challenge faced by the countries shown in the table is large: the data imply that in more than half of the countries shown, allowing for population growth, the total number of primary-school places available in 1986 would need to be doubled in order to accommodate, by the year 2000, all children of primary-school-age.[2]

---

[1] It is important to note that GERs with a value of less than 100 do not necessarily imply that SFA has not been achieved. The examples of a number of developed countries show that, as repetition and over-age enrolments are reduced, the gap between the GER and NER can shrink to negligible proportions, e.g. in Sweden and Norway there seems to be no measurable difference between these two statistics. In such circumstances GERs actually fall below 100. That is for a variety of reasons, including the sickness or disability of a small proportion of children, some parents choosing to abstain from sending their children to school, the late enrolment of some children in grade 1, i.e. subsequent to attaining the minimum age for school entry, etc. For these kinds of reason, both GERs and NERs in Italy, Belgium, Denmark, Sweden, and Norway lie in the range 95–99.

[2] Since this statement is based upon GERs actual age characteristics of those at school are unknown.

TABLE 2.1. *Countries with gross primary enrolment ratios of less than 90 in 1986: income, gender, debt, and expenditure*

	Primary level gross enrolment ratio (%)		Low-income countries (L)[a]	% Female to male primary enrolments 1986–8[b]	Debt-service ratio 1987	Public expenditure on education as % of total public spending		Annual rate of change in recurrent education expenditure (1980–4/5) per:	
	1980	1986				1986[b]	Rising or falling[c]	Teacher	Pupil
Sub-Saharan Africa									
Benin	64.0	64.0[d]	L	51.0	8.8				−5.2
Burkina Faso	18.0	31.0	L	59.0	6.6	21.0	F	−4.1	−5.2
Burundi	29.0	59.0	L	74.0	33.3	16.0[e]	F	−3.9	−12.1
Cent. African Rep.	71.0	66.0	L	62.0	12.0	17.0[e]	F	−4.4	−10.3
Chad	35.3	43.0[e]	L	40.0	2.7				
Ethiopia	35.0	36.0	L	61.0	29.5	10.0	F	0.5	3.3
Ghana	80.0	72.0		81.0	23.6			−3.3	1.4
Guinea	31.0	29.0	L	44.0	53.6[f]	15.0[e]			
Ivory Coast	74.0	70.0[e]		69.5	37.0	16.0[e]		−14.1	−8.3
Liberia	49.0	35.0[e]			3.3				
Malawi	60.0	65.0	L	81.0	22.9	9.0	F	−1.7	0.0
Mali	27.0	23.0	L	59.0	14.2	22.0	F		−3.9
Mauritania	37.0	51.0	L	69.0	23.0			1.6	−3.1
Mozambique	99.0	84.0	L	78.0	16.1				
Niger	27.0	29.0	L	54.0	39.4	23.0	R		
Nigeria	97.0	77.0[e]		78.6	13.1	12.0	R		
Rwanda	63.0	65.0	L	96.0	11.7	26.0	R	−1.9	4.8

Senegal	58.0	L	69.0	19.8			−16.2	−10.4
Sierra Leone	54.0[g]	L		5.3				
Somalia	15.0[e]	L	51.5	17.8	6.0	F		
Sudan	49.0	L	69.0	13.2			−3.0	−3.8
Tanzania	69.0	L	99.0	21.6	10.0	F	−4.6	−0.4
Uganda	70.0	L	83.0	10.1	22.0	R	−19.2	17.0
Zaïre	76.0[h]	L	81.0	18.2				
North Africa and Middle East								
Egypt	88.0	L	79.0	15.9	12.0	R		
Morocco	74.0		66.0	25.6	25.0	R	−3.2	0.3
Saudi Arabia	71.0		83.0		9.0	R		
Yemen Arab Rep.	86.0		28.0	20.1				−1.8
Yemen PDR	66.0[h]		36.0	25.8				
Asia and the Pacific								
Afghanistan	21.0	L	52.0		4.0	F	28.9	32.6
Bangladesh	60.0	L	71.3	18.3	10.0	R	14.1	17.3
Nepal	82.0[e]	L	45.0	9.4	11.0[e]	F	0.2	2.7
Pakistan	44.0[e]	L	55.0	19.1	5.0	n/c	4.4	−9.8
Papua New Guinea	70.0[i]	L	85.0	37.5				
Latin America and Caribbean								
Bolivia	87.0		88.0	41.6	20.0	F		
El Salvador	79.0[h]		105.0	21.4	18.0	F	12.9	7.9
Guatemala	76.0		85.0	31.2	12.0	F		

[a] Countries with per capita GNP of less than $US460 in 1986; [b] latest available year; [c] F: falling over previous 5 years; R: rising over previous 5 years; n/c: no change; [d] data are an average of 1985 and 1987 figures; [e] data are for 1985; [f] data are for 1982; [g] data are for 1986; [h] data are for 1983; [i] data are for 1987.

Sources: GER and expenditure data, Unesco (1989): low-income countries, World Bank (1988b); female/male enrolments, UNDP (1990); debt-service ratio, World Bank (1989a).

Secondly, the acute enrolment challenge is predominantly a low-income phenomenon: twenty-four of these countries (65 per cent) are low-income economies, having per capita incomes smaller than the equivalent of $US460 in 1986. They represent 65 per cent of all low-income States, and, excluding India and China, they account for 52 per cent of the population of this group of countries. It may be significant that of the remaining eleven middle-income countries on the list, nine are highly indebted nations, each with debt-service ratios in excess of 20 per cent of export revenues. Thirdly, the enrolment challenge is also concentrated amongst the countries of Sub-Saharan Africa (SSA). Twenty-four of the countries shown in the table are from that region, all except three of them being classified as low-income, and they include more than half of its population. On a population-weighted basis, however, the problem is more evenly distributed between SSA and South Asia, owing to the large 'school-age' populations of Bangladesh and Pakistan. Fourthly, the problem of low GERs appears to be disproportionately one of low female enrolments. With the exception of El Salvador, in every other country shown in Table 2.1 the female GER is less than that for males—often significantly so. A calculation of the (unweighted) average ratio between male and female GERs reveals that in the countries shown, the proportion of the eligible girls enrolled in primary schools is typically only 68 per cent that of the boys.[3]

The table also allows investigation of some simple dynamic characteristics of education systems in the countries shown. It is startling to notice that in sixteen (43 per cent) of the countries the GER actually declined between 1980 and 1986, which almost certainly implies that access to schooling has deteriorated over the past decade.[4] The GER *can* decline as a result of elimination of over-age enrolment, but this is less likely to be the explanation in countries which are far from providing universal access to schooling. Eleven of the sixteen countries with declining enrolment ratios were low-income economies, and twelve of them were in SSA.

The proportion of the government budget spent on education appears to be, on average, 14.6 per cent—about the same as the unweighted mean value for all low- and middle-income economies reported for 1985.[5] Thus, the reason for low enrolments at primary level in these countries does not, in general, appear to be that inadequate relative priority has been attached to spending on education (although spending priorities

---

[3] Furthermore, Table A.1 shows that, whereas there are 28 countries in which the male GER is <90, there are 39 countries where this is so for the female GER.

[4] The list comprises: Central African Republic, Ivory Coast, Mali, Guinea, Ghana, Liberia, Tanzania, Mozambique, Nigeria, Somalia, Sudan, Zaïre, Morocco, Afghanistan, Bangladesh, and Nepal.

[5] Lockheed and Verspoor (1990: Table 15).

within education may be part of the problem). On the other hand there are some countries where both GERs and public expenditures on education are unusually low. These include Malawi, Sierra Leone, Afghanistan, and Pakistan, where public spending priorities are partly to blame for low primary enrolments. It is worth noting, furthermore, that in thirteen of the twenty-one countries where data are available, the proportion of total public spending allocated to education had fallen over the previous five years. Not unexpectedly this feature seems to have been associated with cases where gross enrolment ratios had also fallen over the same period: reductions in the proportion of spending allocated to education had occurred in six out of nine countries where enrolment ratios fell, and where the data on both of these variables are available (see Table 2.1).

In about two-thirds of the countries shown in the table, expenditures per teacher and per pupil declined over the early 1980s. These trends are not unambiguous, since they could indicate either declines in the quality of schooling available (arising from smaller resource inputs) or improvements in efficiency (or both). In the case of the countries shown, however, the former outcome is the most likely—reflecting the increased economic stringency which governments and school systems were, in the early 1980s, having to face.

The quick and somewhat casual perusal of the data undertaken above is already suggestive. To what extent is the non-achievement of UPE strongly associated with poverty, adjustment, or debt? Are the recent reductions in the proportion of public spending going to education a significant contributory factor to deteriorating primary enrolment ratios? Why does Africa seem particularly unable (or unwilling) to secure UPE at primary level? Is it simply the relative poverty levels of African States, or are there grounds for thinking that other factors might be at work? To what extent is the problem of low enrolment ratios unequally shouldered by girls, and why? These are the main questions which are tackled in the statistical analysis which follows.

4. Determinants of the GER

The primary gross enrolment ratio is the relationship between total primary enrolments and the number of children of primary age. It is also possible, however, to define the GER in terms of the costs of schooling and the expenditures which society chooses to allocate to it. In principle, if expenditures on primary schooling rose, and if the costs per pupil remained unchanged, the proportion of pupils enrolled would also rise. In other words,

$$\text{GER} = x/ac, \tag{1}$$

where x = the proportion of GNP spent on primary schooling, c = primary unit costs as a proportion of per capita income, and a = the proportion of the population of primary school-age.

A more formal derivation of the above equation is given in the Appendix to this chapter. The equation states that increases in the proportion of national income allocated to primary schooling will result in increases in the GER, provided that the proportion of the population of school-going age and the relative costs per child enrolled remain unchanged or increase less rapidly. Since the value of a is likely to be constant over short periods of time, the critical condition for an increase in the GER would normally be that the rate of growth of x should be greater than that of c.[6]

It will be useful, for what follows, to take this analysis a small step further by distinguishing between expenditures incurred by the State and by private households. The proportion of GNP spent on primary schooling, x, comprises expenditures by government, x_g, and by the private sector, x_p. Similarly so, for expenditures per pupil. Here, total unit costs, c, comprise those provided by the government, c_g—for example the per pupil costs of teachers, learning materials, etc.—and those provided by households, c_p—for example, the costs per pupil of school fees, uniforms, school exercise books, and other privately financed schooling costs. So, the first equation can be extended, as follows:

$$GER = (x_g + x_p)/a(c_g + c_p). \tag{2}$$

Again, the Appendix to this chapter provides more details.

This second equation suggests that the proportion of national income spent by government on primary schooling influences the GER in more complicated ways than is often supposed. It is intuitively obvious that increases in public spending on primary schooling may merely increase expenditures per child rather than total enrolments. But the equation shows that this can occur in at least two ways. On the one hand a government may intend that result: perhaps the quality of schooling needs improvement; perhaps teachers secure an improved pay deal; perhaps the government does not view expansion of the system so importantly as spending more on those already enrolled. On the other hand, even if some increase in enrolment were intended by the government, a rise in public spending might be met by a similar fall in expenditures on schooling by private households. In this case public spending would merely act as a substitute for private spending, leading to an unintended rise in unit expenditures by government and little or no change in total enrol-

[6] Whether this holds in practice, i.e. whether the relationship with GER is positive for x, and negative for c when the values for the other variables in the identity are, in each case, not controlled, remain empirically testable questions to which we return later in this chapter.

ments. We shall return to the relationships between state and household expenditures on primary schooling in a later section of this chapter. Meanwhile it should be noted that increased spending on primary schooling by the State need not translate into higher enrolment ratios—that increases in x_g may lead to higher values for c_g (or, in some circumstances, to higher values for a)[7] rather than to higher GERs.

5. Public Spending and the Attainment of SFA: A Schema

What then is the relationship between levels of public spending and primary enrolment ratios around the world? More specifically, is there evidence for the suggestion made at the outset of this chapter—that the achievement of SFA is primarily influenced by the priority attached by governments to the provision of schooling relative to other uses of public resources? Or are there other natural or structural characteristics of countries which conspire to prevent its achievement, and about which one can generalize? The preceding analysis indicates that these questions cannot be tackled simply by inspecting public expenditures on primary schooling expressed as a proportion of either the public budget or GNP. This is so because, in cases where high values for these expenditures were associated with the provision of high-quality schooling for a minority of the age-group, the commitment to achieving SFA would be judged to be low. Thus, conclusions about the extent to which different States appear committed to achieving SFA need, at minimum, to reflect an assessment of the values of x_g, c_g, and a in each case.

In order to launch ourselves on that particular road, Table 2.2 sets out eight possible combinations of values for GER, x_g and c_g, and suggests the degree of public commitment to the achievement of SFA which each of these might imply. Like all schematic approaches this involves some oversimplification. In particular, the table assumes that the behaviour of private households is such as to accommodate rather than neutralize government action. Nevertheless some useful deductions can be made.

Considering first the four cases with low GER values, we see that only in the first of these can one clearly say that the public commitment to provision of primary schooling is low and that the remedy is to increase public spending thereon. In cases 3 and 4 commitment would also appear to be low, but solutions are dependent upon reductions in publicly incurred unit costs, in addition to (in case 3 but not case 4) expenditure

---

[7] This assertion is not meant to imply a new theory of population; rather that the value of a is partly administratively determined, and can be changed by altering the duration of the primary cycle (and thus the age-range which it covers). Thus, if the length of the cycle were increased, a and x_g would both rise, giving higher enrolments, yet with possibly an unchanged, or an even lower GER than before.

TABLE 2.2. *Gross enrolment ratios and public expenditure on primary schooling: a schematic approach to assessing state commitment to SFA*

National values[a] for:			Implied level of commitment to SFA	Likely policy changes required
$x_g{}^b$	$c_g{}^b$	GER[b]		
1. Low	Low	Low	Low	Increase public spending on primary
2. High	Low	Low	High but resource-constrained	Seek aid-inflows
3. Low	High	Low	Low but cost-restrained	Increase public spending on primary but reduce unit costs
4. High	High	Low	Probably low, but cost- and resource-constrained	Reduce unit costs
5. Low	Low	High	Uncertain: quality may be low	May need to increase spending on primary
6. High	Low	High	High, but quality may be low	Aid may be needed to support quality
7. Low	High	High	High	No change needed
8. High	High	High	High	Assess priorities in secondary/tertiary education

Notes: [a] 'Low' and 'high' values may be defined relative to international mean values, or means for country groups.
[b] x_g = public recurrent expenditures on primary schooling as a percentage of GNP; c_g = public recurrent expenditures on primary schooling per primary student as a percentage of GNP per capita; GER = primary gross enrolment ratio.

measures. Case 2, on the other hand, indicates an apparently high commitment to SFA, but an inability to achieve it owing to resource constraints. Assuming that efficiency reforms within education were already in place, aid would here be needed in order to increase the GER.

The second group of cases comprises those with high GERs. Whilst the quantitative targets of SFA are here achieved, attention would be needed in cases 5 and 6 to improve school quality. In the former, increased public spending is indicated, but in the latter the government is likely to be resource-constrained and aid may be required to secure qualitative improvements. Only in case 7 is no change in the public stance on primary schooling implied: here SFA with high per capita resource inputs has been achieved at relatively low GNP cost. The higher costs incurred in achieving the same results in case 8 raise questions about whether the balance in educational investment between primary and other branches of education is appropriate.

The stylized facts in Table 2.2 thus indicate that the 'priority attached by governments to the provision of schooling relative to other uses of public resources' is at best only part of the explanation for the continued non-achievement of SFA in many countries. They raise the possibility that such countries include those which are cost-constrained (in the sense that the publicly incurred unit costs are so high that, even with 'adequate' allocation of GNP by government to primary schooling, underenrolment would still result), those which are resource-constrained (in the sense of having already high expenditures relative to GNP), as well as those which simply need to spend more on primary provision. This suggests that solutions in many countries will need to include mixtures of fiscal and educational reforms, together with a reassessment of expenditure priorities, supported by concessional resource transfers from abroad. This, then, moves us some distance from the view that high or low levels of public spending on primary schooling necessarily indicate similar levels of commitment to the achievement of SFA: it is the start, rather than the end of the story.

5.1. Countries with low commitment to SFA

The time has come to put flesh on some of these bones. Tables 2.3 and 2.4 provide information on a range of relevant variables for fifty-five developing countries where data on x_g, c_g, and a can also be derived. The groups shown comprise 71 per cent of all countries with GNP per capita of less than \$2,000 in 1986. 'Low' and 'high' values for the expenditure and cost variables are assigned according to whether or not the value for each variable in each country was less than or more than the relevant mean value for all countries in the sample. The similar apportionment of GER categories is based upon a critical value for this variable of 90, for reasons indicated in the earlier text discussion of Table 2.1.

Of the fifty-five countries for which we have public expenditure data, twenty-three have 'low' enrolment ratios, in the sense that their GER values were less than 90 in 1986. They are shown in Table 2.3, and account for almost two-thirds of all such countries as listed in Table 2.1. They are ranked in ascending order of the publicly incurred unit costs of primary schooling, expressed as a proportion of GNP per capita, c_g. Those shown in the first part of the table are low-cost cases in that they each have c_g values which are less than the mean for all fifty-five countries in the sample. Inspection of the second column of the table shows that they have values for public expenditure on primary schooling expressed as a proportion of GNP, x_g, which are also low: only in Malawi and Bolivia did x_g reach the sample mean value of 1.6 and in most of the other ten countries shown public spending on primary schooling was substantially lower than this. This group of countries seems therefore to

TABLE 2.3. *Countries with GNP per capita less than $US2,000 and GER less than 90: public expenditures on primary schooling and related characteristics, 1986*

	c_g[a]	x_g[a]	a[a]	GER[a]	GNP per capita	% female to male enrolment	Defence expenditure % of GNP	Av. teacher's salary as a multiple of GNP/capita	Debt-service ratio	x_g required for GER = 100%[a]
Low-cost cases										
Nigeria	1.8	0.2	17.4	77.0	640	78.6	1.0		13.3	0.3
Uganda	2.1	0.3	19.6	70.0	230	83.0	4.2		10.1	0.4
Pakistan	3.8	0.3	17.7	44.0	350	55.0	6.7		26.7	0.7
Bangladesh	4.8	0.4	14.7	60.0	160	71.3	1.5	2.1	26.9	0.7
Guatemala	5.4	0.7	16.7	76.0	930	85.0	1.2	1.7	29.0	0.9
El Salvador	7.1	1.4	24.3	79.0	820	105.0	3.7		21.3	1.8
Tanzania	7.3	1.0	19.4	69.0	250	99.0	3.3	3.0	23.5	1.4
Nepal	8.0	0.9	13.0	82.0	160	45.0	1.5	4.3	9.4	1.1
Bolivia	8.6	1.6	21.0	87.0	600	88.0	2.4	2.6	33.5	1.8
Ghana	9.6	1.1	16.4	72.0	390	81.0	0.9	2.0	46.6	1.5
Malawi	11.7	1.6	21.3	65.0	150	81.0	2.3	5.8	35.8	2.5
Burundi	12.5	1.2	15.8	59.0	240	74.0	3.5	7.2	37.4	2.0
No.	12	12	12	12	12	12	12	8	12	
Mean	6.9	0.9	18.1	70.0	410.0	78.8	2.7	3.6	26.1	
WM[a]	4.4	0.5	17.0	63.9	376.4	72.0	2.9	2.7	22.7	

High-cost cases

Rwanda	15.2	2.2	22.0	65.0	290	96.0	1.9	10.4	13.3	3.4
Morocco	16.6	1.6	13.3	74.0	590	66.0	5.1	5.7	31.6	2.2
Ivory Coast	17.7	2.0	16.2	70.0	730	69.5	1.2	7.8	40.9	2.9
Burkina Faso	18.4	0.9	15.6	31.0	151	59.0	3.0	12.7	8.1	2.9
Mauritania	19.6	1.6	16.3	51.0	420	69.0	4.9	13.7	25.8	3.1
Liberia	25.6	0.9	9.9	35.0	460		2.2	2.7		2.6
Cent. African Rep.	28.4	3.0	15.7	66.0	290	62.0	1.7	6.9	14.1	4.5
Ethiopia	34.2	2.2	17.7	36.0	120	61.0	8.6	12.6	33.4	6.1
Yemen Arab Rep.	36.5	3.3	10.4	86.0	550	28.0	6.8		19.6	3.8
Sudan	37.3	2.9	16.0	49.0	320	69.0	5.9		10.0	5.9
Mali	41.2	1.5	15.6	23.0	150	59.0	2.4	13.7	16.0	6.5
No.	11	11	11	11	11	10	11	9	10	
Mean	26.4	2.0	15.3	53.3	370.1	63.8	4.0	9.6	21.3	
WM[a]	28.9	2.1	16.0	50.5	321.3	63.7	5.6	10.4	25.1	
Means for LDCs with GNP per capita of less than $US2,000										
No.	55	55	55	55	55	54	55	43	53	
Mean	13.0	1.6	16.0	89.1	738.3	86.1	3.9	4.5	24.3	
WM[a]	8.9	1.1	13.2	101.1	529.5	81.8	4.4	3.7	22.4	

Notes: [a] c_g = public recurrent expenditures on primary schooling per primary student as % of GNP per capita; x_g = public recurrent expenditures on primary schooling as % of GNP; a = the population eligible to attend primary school as a proportion of the total population; WM = population weighted mean. All data are for 1986 except teacher's salaries which are for 1985, and debt-service, 1987.

Sources: See Technical Appendix.

TABLE 2.4. *Countries with GNP per capita less than $US2,000 and GER greater than 90: public expenditures on primary schooling and related characteristics, 1986*

	c_g^a	x_g^a	a^a	GER	GNP per capita	% female to male enrolment	Defence expenditure % of GNP	Av. teacher's salary as a multiple of GNP/capita	Debt-service ratio
Low-cost cases									
Paraguay	2.3	0.4	15.0	102.0	1,000	95.0	1.0		28.0
Peru	2.8	0.5	15.4	122.0	1,090	96.0	6.5	1.3	11.9
Dominican Rep.	3.6	0.7	19.4	101.0	710	104.0	1.4	1.3	17.0
Mexico	4.1	0.8	15.7	119.0	1,860	97.0	0.6	0.9	40.1
Haiti	4.4	0.6	15.1	95.0	330	87.0	1.5	1.4	13.8
China	5.2	0.7	9.7	129.0	300	89.0	5.9		8.6
Turkey	6.9	0.9	11.3	115.0	1,110	93.0	4.9	0.2	36.0
Lesotho	7.4	1.5	17.2	115.0	370	125.0	1.8	3.2	2.1
Ecuador	7.9	1.5	15.8	118.0	1,160	98.0	1.6	2.0	33.8
Colombia	8.0	1.1	12.1	114.0	1,230	103.0	1.0	2.2	35.1
Philippines	8.4	1.3	15.0	107.0	560	102.0	1.7		38.5
Uruguay	9.4	1.1	10.8	110.0	1,900	98.0	2.4	1.0	37.4
Brazil	9.6	1.8	18.0	103.0	1,810	91.7	0.9		41.9
Togo	9.7	1.7	17.0	102.0	250	63.0	3.2	6.3	19.9
India	10.7	1.2	11.8	98.0	290	72.0	3.5	3.6	29.0
Mauritius	10.8	1.5	12.9	107.0	1,200	102.0	0.2	0.9	10.6
Cuba	11.9	1.2	9.3	105.0	1,999	93.0	7.4		0.0
Costa Rica	12.2	1.8	14.9	98.0	1,480	97.0	0.6	3.2	21.9
Syria	12.4	2.5	18.0	111.0	1,570	90.0	14.7	2.6	20.4
Tunisia	12.4	2.2	15.5	117.0	1,140	85.0	6.2	3.9	28.5

Iran	12.5	2.0	14.4	110.0	1,637	86.0	20.0	3.5	27.1
Madagascar	12.9	1.6	10.2	121.0	230	95.0	2.4		21
No.	22	22	22	22	22	22	22	16	
Mean	8.4	1.3	14.3	110.0	1,055.7	93.7	4.1	2.3	23.9
WM[a]	7.9	1.0	11.8	113.7	563.8	84.3	4.7	3.0	21.8
High-cost cases									
Jamaica	13.4	1.8	12.8	105.0	840	102.0	1.5	3.4	42.0
Honduras	13.4	2.4	17.0	106.0	740	104.0	5.9	4.2	34.8
Zimbabwe	13.4	4.6	25.3	136.0	620	97.0	5.0	6.6	33.9
Zambia	13.7	2.7	20.3	97.0	300	90.0	3.2	6.1	16.3
Nicaragua	14.1	2.3	16.7	98.0	790	111.0	16.0	4.5	10.8
Kenya	14.6	3.3	23.5	97.0	300	95.0	2.4	4.6	41.7
Chile	15.8	2.7	16.0	105.0	1,320	98.0	3.6	2.0	36.5
Botswana	15.9	3.4	18.9	112.0	840	105.0	2.3	2.3	3.6
Thailand	17.8	2.4	14.2	96.0	810	100.1	4.0	2.3	21.0
Malaysia	21.8	3.0	13.7	101.0	1,830	100.0	6.1	3.2	20.4
No.	10	10	10	10	10	10	10	10	10
Mean	15.4	2.9	17.8	105.3	839.0	100.2	5.0	3.9	26.1
WM[a]	16.4	2.9	17.7	101.4	799.1	98.5	4.3	3.6	27.5
Means for LDCs with GNP per capita of less than $US2,000									
No.	55	55	55	55	55	54	55	43	53
Mean	13.0	1.6	16.0	89.1	738.3	86.1	3.9	4.5	24.3
WM[a]	8.9	1.1	13.2	101.1	529.5	81.8	4.4	3.7	22.4

Notes: [a] c_g = public recurrent expenditures on primary schooling per primary student as % of GNP per capita; x_g = public recurrent expenditures on primary schooling as % of GNP; a = the population eligible to attend primary school as a proportion of the total population; WM = population weighted mean. All data are for 1986 except teacher's salaries which are for 1985, and debt-service, 1987.

Sources: See Technical Appendix.

fall clearly into the first of the schematic categories set out in Table 2.2: they each have low GERs, and they seem constrained neither by high unit nor total expenditures.

Before accepting this conclusion, however, it seems necessary on a priori grounds to establish whether there were any identifiable high and irreducible prior (non-educational) claims on government spending in these countries. The most important types of expenditure in this category are debt-service payments and, somewhat more debatably, defence spending. The latter category of expenditure is not necessarily discretionary because in some countries, part—and often a large part—of defence spending is needed to sustain a military machine which is actively engaged. But in many others, there are important opportunities to shift expenditures from the military to other sectors. For countries in each of these categories, therefore, examination of military budgets is of interest. Accordingly, the table provides comparative data on recent levels of defence expenditure and on debt-service payments (columns 8 and 9).

It can be seen that in the first group of countries, the mean values for defence spending as a proportion of GNP are considerably lower than the mean for all fifty-five countries in the sample, and also that their debt-service ratios are not significantly higher than the sample mean value. It is true that Burundi, Malawi, and Ghana are highly indebted, and that Pakistan devotes a particularly high share of GNP to defence spending. But these magnitudes do not themselves explain low social expenditures, as witnessed by the cases of Kenya and Nicaragua (Table 2.4) which incur unusually high debt and defence expenditures, respectively, but which also make substantial allocations to primary schooling. This first group of countries, then, is not unduly besieged by either debt or war (that is, not more so than are other low- and middle-income countries—considerable though those magnitudes are). There is, therefore, no evidence to suggest that such phenomena could explain why public expenditures on primary schooling should here be significantly lower than elsewhere in the developing world.

As shown in the final column of the table, at present cost levels, UPE could be achieved in this first group of countries by allocating 2 per cent or less of GNP to public spending on primary schooling (except Malawi, where it would need 2.5 per cent). Indeed in Nigeria, Pakistan, and Bangladesh, the most populous countries in the group, and where enrolment ratios are low, UPE would require public spending on primary schooling equivalent to much less than 1 per cent of GNP. Thus, these governments seem demonstrably to have a low commitment to the achievement of UPE and SFA, and the major policy priority is here to increase public spending on primary provision: with a fairly small change in fiscal stance and priorities, it appears from these data that UPE, at least, could easily be achieved.

This is not the place to attempt an explanation of why particular governments demonstrate lower commitment to the achievement of UPE and SFA than others. The range of variables which determine such outcomes is large. As indicated in the introduction to this chapter, they will reflect the history, culture, and politics of each country, and most will be unmeasurable in any sensible quantitative sense, save via their combined determination of the value of x/ac.

Nevertheless, one of the ways in which these variables are likely to influence the value of x_g (and, indeed, of x_p) is through the revealed attitudes of society towards the education of girls. This, in many parts of the world, is judged to be of lower importance than that of boys. Whatever the cause of these beliefs, those countries which are seen to place low importance upon the education of girls can be thought to demonstrate a lower commitment, other things being equal, to achieving SFA than countries which do not do so. An indicator of this aspect of commitment would therefore be the ratio between the gross enrolment ratios for females and males. Equal treatment in schooling provision amongst the sexes would imply a value for this ratio of around unity. Values substantially less than one would provide prima-facie evidence of a bias against the provision of education for girls, and, thus, lower commitment to achieving SFA, for given cost/income levels, than in countries where the ratio was closer to unity.

The sixth column in the table shows the female/male primary enrolment ratio in 1986, which provides a close proxy for the ratio of the two separate enrolment ratios. It is here preferred since the data from which it is calculated are more accurate and more universally available than those from which the separate ratios can be derived. It can be seen that there is indeed a bias against female enrolments, and that this is more pronounced in the first group of countries shown in Table 2.3 than in developing countries as a whole (both mean and weighted mean values of the proportions of female to male enrolments are 7 to 10 percentage points lower, in this group, than the means for all LDCs in the sample). The bias is particularly strong in Pakistan and Nepal, where the low GERs are particularly influenced by underenrolment of girls. But it is not limited to those cases. This evidence therefore provides indication of a link between the lack of achievement of UPE and the presence of discriminatory attitudes towards female education.

5.2. Countries with low commitment but high costs

The remaining countries with low enrolment ratios shown in the second part of Table 2.3 are rather different from the first group in terms of cost and expenditure characteristics. Here, average publicly incurred relative unit costs, c_g, are more than twice as high as the LDC mean, and the average x_g value is 25 per cent higher than that for all LDCs in the sample. These eleven countries are also poorer than the first group of countries shown in the table (with a mean GNP per capita of only half the LDC average) and they have considerably lower primary enrolment ratios (mean GER of 53, compared with 70 for the first group shown). In most of these countries both cost and resource constraints are already binding, in the senses previously defined.

It is of some significance that all of these countries are from Africa, and that a large number are Francophone. An important clue to under-standing the reasons for their high unit costs is given by the seventh column of the table. This indicates the generally high level of primary-teachers' salaries, relative to per capita incomes, which are paid in these countries. The ratio of (unweighted) mean values for this variable is 2.7 when compared to that for the first group of countries in the table, and 2.1 compared to that for all LDCs in the sample. Thus the relative cost burden per primary teacher is more than twice 'normal' levels in these eleven countries (Liberia being the single case amongst the group where it is reported to be lower than the LDC average). Since unit costs are determined by the teacher/pupil ratio multiplied by the sum of average wage and non-wage costs per teacher, and because the last element of this multiplier is typically very small, the high relative costs per teacher reported in Table 2.3 largely explain the sharply higher primary unit costs which these governments incur.

There are some States in this group where there is clear space (judged by the levels achieved by other developing countries) for increased public expenditures on primary schooling. These include Mali, Liberia, and Burkina Faso, where the x_g values are in each case less than its unweighted mean value for all LDCs. But, owing to the high levels of public ex-penditures per student, together with the low enrolment ratios presently attained, most of the countries in this group would nevertheless require some reduction in c_g if UPE were to be achieved within tolerable bounds for public spending. It can be seen from the final column of the table that the typical required values for x_g in order to achieve UPE at existing cost levels are large. Morocco, with a required x_g value of 2.2, is perhaps the only case which could be judged to be within relatively easy reach. Elsewhere, the range varies from 2.6 in Liberia to 6.5 in Mali. Even including Morocco, the average x_g value for the whole group of eleven countries would need to be 4.0 if UPE were to be achieved at present cost levels. This would amount to 2.5 times the present average x_g value for all LDCs. Zimbabwe is the only developing country which has achieved an x_g of this magnitude and, as will be shown later in this book, the rather special circumstances of the Zimbabwe case imply that it is unlikely to be generalizable—in this, as in some other respects.

As with the first group of countries shown in the table, the average levels of defence expenditures and debt-service ratios are not high in comparison with those for all LDCs. Nevertheless, inspection of the list of countries included in the second group reveals that at least in some individual cases, these factors have undoubted significance in explaining low participation in schooling. In some countries, already poor rural populations have been further ravaged by drought—Mali, Burkina Faso—which elsewhere has also interacted with the effects of war— Sudan, Ethiopia—to a terrible extent. Although in these latter two cases the data do show high levels of defence spending by the State, it is probably not so much the 'crowding out' of social expenditures, as much as the present inability of people to send their children to schools, even where these exist, which here is having a dominant influence upon primary enrolments.

A final important characteristic of this second group of low GER countries is the significantly smaller proportion of girls enrolled in primary schools, than in both the first group of countries shown and than in all LDCs taken together. The weighted means show that here, only 64 per cent of pupils are girls, which compares with 72 per cent for the remaining countries with low enrolment ratios and 82 per cent for all LDCs. Thus the association between low total and low female enrolments, to which we have already alluded, is further strengthened by these data: they show that underenrolment at primary level is disproportionately shouldered by girls.

5.3. Countries with higher commitment but where quality is often low

Table 2.4, in similar fashion to the preceding one, sets out expenditure and other correlates of GERs for those developing countries were UPE has been effectively achieved. The first part of the table shows those countries with c_g values which are lower than the LDC mean. It can be seen that in most cases the x_g values are also low, with only five governments spending more than the LDC unweighted average of 1.6 per cent of GNP on primary schooling. Most of these countries therefore can be grouped under the fifth heading of Table 2.2, i.e. States where there is room for further increases in public expenditure in order to increase the quality of primary provision. This is particularly so in the poorer countries such as India and China (see case-study, Chapter 3), where unit expenditures by government are relatively low, and where the benefits of the schooling experience for many children—in particular, for the progeny of the poorest groups—are severely constrained as a result.

In the second part of the table ten countries are shown where the commitment to achieve UPE, and perhaps also SFA, appears, on the basis of the data shown, to be particularly strong. In each of these cases, the values of both c_g and x_g are higher than the LDC means—and often substantially so. UPE has here been achieved by attaching high priority to the expansion of primary schooling within the budgetary process. They include countries at each end of the income spectrum, some of which have pursued capitalist strategies and others which have followed socialist development paths. At first sight these countries might be thought to belong clearly to group 8 in the earlier schematic Table 2.2. Some do so belong. However, more information is needed than that provided in Table 2.4 in order properly to judge the quality of schooling which is generally available in each country. Jamaica, for example, does not clearly belong in this group since both its cost and expenditure variables are close to the mean values. Furthermore, although the publicly funded unit costs are high in the other countries in the group, the average values shown are not able to indicate the distribution of resources between different regions, localities, or schools. Thus, the Zimbabwe case—notwithstanding its high publicly financed unit costs—is one where there remains a substantial need for further primary expenditure in order to increase the quality of schooling available, particularly in the disadvantaged areas of the country (see Chapter 3). These kinds of problem remain hidden in the absence of more disaggregated data than those shown.

There is an additional reason why the data on publicly funded unit costs may not—where they have high values—unfailingly indicate the attainment of relatively high school quality. It is that, for purely technical reasons, the values of c_g and x_g are co-determined in countries where UPE is close to being achieved. Since there is a tendency for the GER to have a natural ceiling at values between 100 and 120 (determined by the extent of over-age or under-age enrolment in each primary system) public expenditures increasingly have to be translated into higher unit expenditures (for given values of a) rather than higher GER values, as the ceiling is approached. By the same token, to the extent that the ceiling is constrained (for example at values lower than 100) by private households abstaining from sending their children to school, high public unit costs may in such cases partially reflect a frustration of attempts by the State to increase enrolments rather than a deliberate strategy to improve school quality.

5.4. The influence of population size

A final general comment about the data in Tables 2.3 and 2.4 is merited. This concerns the observed values for the size of the school-age population relative to total population. It will be remembered that this is the parameter a from equations 1 and 2, as set out in the preceding section. Clearly, for given levels of income and unit costs of schooling, those countries with higher rates of population growth (and, thus, proportionately larger school-age populations) will face a greater relative per capita cost in achieving UPE and SFA than other countries. Here, the contrasts can be strong. For example, in developed market economies, with zero or even negative population growth, those aged 6–11 years typically represent 5 to 8 per cent of the population as a whole. This compares with 12 per cent in China (a proportion which is falling sharply as the impact of low population growth rates continue to be felt), 13 per cent in India, and over 18 per cent in many of the African economies which still have high population growth rates.

Values for *a* shown in the tables are adjusted for the actual length of schooling in each country. Since the effects of these adjustments are not themselves correlated with differences in the size of the age-groups, strong contrasts in the magnitude of this parameter can be seen. For example, the comparable task faced by China or Cuba, with less than 10 per cent of the population eligible to go to primary school, is somewhat less than half that faced by Kenya, Zimbabwe, El Salvador, Malawi, and Bolivia. Thus the relative cost burden of achieving UPE and SFA can vary, in per capita terms, by as much as 100 per cent between countries with low and those with high growth rates of population. This indicates the enormous importance of population policy as a means of achieving and maintaining UPE and SFA. It is an obvious, but often neglected, point that fertility control is potentially much more powerful, in cost terms, than are more direct measures of educational reform in providing all children with access to schools. The two sets of policies also have interactive effects, as Chapter 1 has indicated.

5.5. Preliminary conclusions

It is appropriate to conclude this section by returning to some of the questions posed earlier in this chapter. The attempt to examine the characteristics associated with failure by some countries to secure UPE and SFA is clearly worth while. Although the successful models provided by some of the poorest countries demonstrate that UPE should, given appropriate commitment, be universally achievable, the analysis has indicated that the constraints faced by different countries are diverse, and that a rather wide range of policy reforms will need to be applied.

Our analysis has shown that the non-achievement of UPE is greater amongst the poorer countries, and that it is particularly concentrated in Africa: seventeen of the twenty-three low GER cases examined above were African. As regards causes, we have shown that low levels of public spending upon primary schooling are partly—but only partly—to blame: in 40 per cent of the countries with low enrolment ratios and for which we have expenditure data, the allocation of the same proportion of GNP to public spending on primary schooling as is currently spent, on average, across all LDCs, would be capable of delivering UPE. This, however, assumes both that the demand side would be facilitatory in response to increased government spending and that unit expenditures by government remained unchanged, neither of which may, in fact, hold.

The evidence shows that high levels of debt-service and defence commitments are not particularly strongly associated with failure to achieve UPE. Although such expenditures are a contributory factor in the case of one or two countries, those with low GERs do not generally face greater commitments in these areas than other States.

There are, however, two other phenomena which appear to be rather strongly associated with a failure to achieve UPE. The first of these is the existence of unequal access to schooling by girls and boys. We have shown that the ratio of female to male primary enrolments is significantly lower in countries with low GERs than in other countries. The existence of discriminatory attitudes towards the schooling of girls is informed partly by custom and culture. Traditional attitudes often do not encourage the education of girls. It is common for the private benefits to the family of schooling to be perceived as being greater for sons than for daughters. This may often be true, given the different labour-market roles of boys and girls in poor rural societies, and the different values these have to their parents. But from the perspective of the individual girls and boys, there is almost certainly no such inequality in the distribution of private benefits (particularly so in cases where primary schooling is terminal). And from the perspective of society, the differential is reversed, since there is a substantially higher social benefit to be obtained from the education of girls, given their greater long-term impact on the stock and quality of a nation's human resources.

The second phenomenon which is associated with failure to achieve UPE is the incidence of high publicly financed unit costs of schooling. Up to half of the countries with GERs lower than 90 appear to be cost-constrained in the sense that UPE could only be achieved, at current cost levels, by allocating an exceptionally high proportion of GNP to public expenditures on primary schooling. All of the countries in this group are African, and in many, the evidence suggests that one important contributory factor is the relatively high level of teachers' salaries. Whatever the cause, however, reductions in public unit expenditures may well be needed in these countries if UPE and SFA are to be achieved. As demonstrated in Chapters 3 and 4, this need not involve reductions in the levels of teachers' salaries themselves.

6. Multivariate Analysis of the Influences on the Achievement of UPE

The tabular analysis, presented above, of the public expenditure determinants of UPE and their correlates, is useful in allowing broad generalizations to be drawn across countries and, indeed, in inviting the inspection of country-level data. We now know more about why some countries have achieved UPE, and why others have not, than we did at the outset of this chapter. However, the tables allow assessment of the independent importance of a particular variable (i.e. after controlling for the influence of other variables) to only a limited extent. Answers to problems such as the extent to which African countries are different from others, at given levels of per capita income, or of x_g or c_g values, require a more formal multivariate analysis.

This is undertaken below. Since the material is more technically demanding than that provided thus far, the conclusions of the empirical analysis which now follows are summarized in a non-technical fashion at the end of the present chapter (Section 7). The main points relevant to the argument of the rest of the book are mentioned there. If they are read, the present section may be skipped by the general reader without undue loss.

6.1. The variables

It is clear from equation (2) that the basic form for the GER identity is non-linear, its log transformation being as follows:

$$\log \text{GER} = \log(x_g + x_p) - \log a - \log(c_g + c_p). \tag{3}$$

As we have seen, it is possible to obtain good estimates for the values of GER, x_g, c_g, and a. However, data on expenditures made by private households on primary schooling are not available on a cross-country basis. Thus, direct estimates for x_p and c_p cannot be obtained. In addition, since equations (1) and (2) are identities, no single estimating equation should include all of the GER, a, x_g, and c_g variables, since GER would thereby be completely determined, and there would be little point in estimating it.

The analysis which is reported below employs data from eighty-two countries, which include all those for which information on public expenditure on primary schooling can be obtained. Of these, sixty-seven are countries from low- and middle-income groups. These latter include all the fifty-five countries set out in Tables 2.3 and 2.4, together with a further twelve middle-income countries which had per capita incomes in excess of $2,000 in 1986.

The basic result to be derived concerns the extent to which the achievement of UPE varies across countries, in association with other determining characteristics. Thus, the dependent variable is GER. It will be remembered that this is defined as total primary enrolments divided by the population of school-going age. The latter differs for each country according to the length of primary schooling. However, owing to the fact that this statistic does not exclude over-age (or under-age) enrolments, the GER is not constrained to a maximum value of 100. Indeed as Tables 2.3 and 2.4 indicate, values for the GER in excess of 115–120 are not uncommon, particularly in middle-income countries. The question arose, therefore, as to whether the values for GER should always be entered as their actual values (i.e. gross of over-age enrolment), or whether a ceiling value at, or close to 100 should be imposed. The latter seemed the most sensible course, since, for the purposes of the present analysis, we are primarily interested in investigating the differences between those countries which have achieved UPE and those which have not, rather than between those which pursue different policies for repetition and over-age enrolment. Accordingly a ceiling value for GER of 105 has been used. This value is compatible with having sufficient school places for all the eligible age-group, together with a small allowance for repetition.

It was, however, felt necessary to check whether or not the introduction of a ceiling value for GER produced biased results—for example, by introducing unacceptable levels of heteroscedasticity in the estimated equations. Accordingly, the regressions were run for both capped and uncapped versions of GER and the results were compared. They were not qualitatively different in any important respect, and both sets of results support similar deductions. Nevertheless, the correlation coefficients and significance levels of the equations using the capped version of GER as the dependent variable were uniformly slightly higher than those using the uncapped version. The distributions of residuals associated with the capped version were sometimes slightly worse, but not unacceptably so. Thus, the results of the analysis using the capped version of GER are shown in what follows. It should be emphasized, however, that the choice of this version of the GER variable does not affect the conclusions that are drawn from the empirical analysis which follows. Apart from this, the variables included in the analysis are the same as those used in Tables 2.3 and 2.4, and have been defined in the ways indicated in those tables. In every case the log transformation has been used.

The correlation matrix for all the variables used in the analysis, for the full sample of eighty-two countries is shown as Table 2.5. It should be noticed that the signs for the coefficients between GER and each of the independent variables are all as one would expect on a priori grounds. There appear to be positive relationships between GER and GNP per capita, the female/male enrolment ratio, and x_g, and negative relationships between GER and a, c_g, and whether or not the country is in Africa.

The proportion of Muslims in the population is also used as an additional variable in this analysis. The reason for this is that the earlier tabular analysis revealed an apparently strong association between low GERs and low female enrolments. It was expected that the causes of

TABLE 2.5. *Correlation matrix: 82 countries*

Correlations	LogGER	LGER	Log$a$	LogPCY	Logc_g	Logx_g	LogISLAM	LogF/M	AFRICA
LogGER	1.000	-0.9870**	-0.3150*	0.5489**	-0.2033	0.0463	-0.4013**	0.5880*	-0.4662**
LGER	0.9870**	1.0000	-0.2988**	0.5083**	-0.2086	0.0529	-0.3960**	0.5937**	-0.5011**
Log$a$	-0.3150*	-0.2988**	1.0000	-0.6695**	-0.1587	0.1457	0.1973	-0.1619	0.4701**
LogPCY	0.5489**	0.5083**	-0.6695**	1.0000	0.1020	0.0205	-0.3001*	0.5216**	-0.5893**
Logc_g	-0.2033	-0.2086	-0.1587	0.1020	1.0000	0.8849**	0.1760	-0.1248	0.1585
Logx_g	0.0463	0.0529	0.1457	0.0205	0.8849**	1.0000	0.1096	0.0348	0.1805
LogISLAM	-0.4013**	-0.3960**	0.1973	-0.3001*	0.1760	0.1096	1.0000	-0.4823**	0.4041**
LogF/M	0.5880*	0.5937**	-0.1619	0.5216**	-0.1248	0.0348	-0.4823**	1.0000	-0.3027*
AFRICA	-0.4662**	-0.5011**	0.4701**	-0.5893**	0.1585	0.1805	0.4041**	-0.3027*	1.0000

Notes: all variables are log (base 10) transformations from their original form as given below:

LGER = gross enrolment ratio 1986.

LogGER = gross enrolment ratio 1986 with a ceiling at 105%.

Log$a$ = the population eligible to attend primary school as a proportion of the total population 1986.

LogPCY = GNP per capita 1986.

Logc_g = public recurrent expenditures on primary schooling per primary student as % of GNP per capita 1986.

Logx_g = public recurrent expenditures on primary schooling as % of GNP 1986.

LogISLAM = Muslim population as % of total population 1977.

LogF/M = female enrolment as % of male enrolment 1986.

AFRICA = a dummy variable assigning '1' for African LDCs and '0' for all other countries.

1-tailed signif: * 0.10   ** 0.01

TABLE 2.6a. *Determinants of the gross enrolment ratio: regression results for all countries in the sample*[a]

	Sample size	R^2	F-value	Coefficients and t-values (in that order)							
				Constant	a	x_g	c_g	PCY	ISLAM	AFRICA	F/M
(a)	82	0.36	12.5	1.50	0.10			0.10	-0.03	-0.06	
				8.50	1.00			3.40	-2.10	-1.90	
(b)	82	0.45	14.2	0.85	-0.01			0.04	-0.01	-0.07	0.50
				3.20	-0.06			1.15	-0.52	-2.40	3.60
(c)	82	0.09	4.8	2.30	-0.29	0.04					
				21.40	-3.10	0.90					
(d)	82	0.36	10.2	1.60	0.09	0.03		0.09	-0.03	-0.07	
				8.50	0.82	0.96		3.02	-2.17	-2.00	
(e)	82	0.144	7.8	2.39	-0.31		-0.09				
				20.69	-3.42		-2.49				
(f)	82	0.385	11.2	1.63	0.08		-0.07	0.10	-0.03	-0.04	
				8.90	0.72		-1.95	3.65	-1.80	-1.35	

[a]The dependent variable is the gross enrolment ratio (GER) with a ceiling value set at 105. All are double-log regressions.
R^2 = adjusted R squared.
GER = gross enrolment ratio 1986.
a = the population eligible to attend primary school as a proportion of the total population 1986.
x_g = public recurrent expenditure on primary schooling as % of GNP 1986.
c_g = public recurrent expenditure on primary schooling per primary student as % of GNP per capita 1986.
PCY = GNP per capita 1986.
ISLAM = Muslim population as % of total population 1977.
AFRICA = dummy variable assigning '1' for African LDCs and '0' for all other countries.
F/M = females as % of male enrolments 1986.

TABLE 2.6b. Determinants of the gross enrolment ratio: regression results for developing countries in the sample[a]

	Sample size	R^2	F-value	Coefficients and t-values (in that order)							
				Constant	a	x_g	c_g	PCY	ISLAM	AFRICA	F/M
(a)	67	0.4	12.0	1.60	-0.08			0.14	-0.04	-0.02	
				7.70	-0.55			4.09	-2.48	-0.62	
(b)	67	0.47	12.7	0.98	-0.18			0.08	-0.02	-0.04	0.49
				3.36	-1.28			2.08	-0.99	-1.11	3.06
(c)	67	0.05	2.7	2.30	-0.36	0.05					
				12.30	-2.23	0.96					
(d)	67	0.39	9.5	1.70	-0.09	0.02		0.14	-0.04	-0.03	
				7.60	-0.60	0.48		3.70	-2.46	-0.73	
(e)	67	0.11	5.3	2.46	-0.36		-0.11				
				12.91	-2.32		-2.40				
(f)	67	0.44	11.2	1.73	-0.12		-0.09	0.16	-0.04	0.00	
				8.27	-0.85		-2.28	4.54	-2.32	0.00	

[a] The dependent variable is the gross enrolment ratio (GER) with a ceiling set at 105. All are double-log regressions.

R^2 = adjusted R squared.
GER = gross enrolment ratio 1986.
a = the population eligible to attend primary school as a proportion of the total population 1986.
x_g = public recurrent expenditure on primary schooling as % of GNP 1986.
c_g = public recurrent expenditure on primary schooling per primary student as % of GNP per capita 1986.
PCY = GNP per capita 1986.
ISLAM = Muslim population as % of total population 1977.
AFRICA = dummy variable assigning '1' for African LDCs and '0' for all other countries.
F/M = females as % of male enrolments 1986.

TABLE 2.6c. Determinants of the gross enrolment ratio: regression results for African countries in the sample[a]

	Sample size[a]	R^2	F-value	Coefficients and t-values (in that order)							
				Constant	a	x_g	c_g	PCY	ISLAM	AFRICA	F/M
(a)	25	0.4	6.3	0.88	0.07			0.37	−0.08		
				1.70	0.18			4.15	−2.05		
(b)	25	0.58	9.1	−0.62	−0.10			0.24	−0.02		1.06
				−0.96	−0.34			2.68	−0.67		3.10
(c)	25	−0.06	0.4	1.70	0.11	0.09					
				3.05	0.24	0.75					
(d)	25	0.37	4.6	0.90	0.05	0.03		0.37	−0.07		
				1.70	0.14	0.27		3.99	−1.93		
(e)	25	0.14	3.0	2.11	0.02		−0.26				
				3.97	0.05		−2.40				
(f)	25	0.47	6.2	1.30	−0.03		−0.17	0.33	−0.07		
				2.50	−0.10		−1.90	3.70	−2.03		

[a] The dependent variable is the gross enrolment ratio (GER) with a ceiling at 105. All are double-log regressions.
R^2 = adjusted R squared.
GER = gross enrolment ratio 1986.
a = the population eligible to attend primary school as a proportion of the total population 1986.
x_g = public recurrent expenditure on primary schooling as % of GNP 1986.
c_g = public recurrent expenditure on primary schooling per primary student as % of GNP per capita 1986.
PCY = GNP per capita 1986.
ISLAM = Muslim population as % of total population 1977.
AFRICA = dummy variable assigning '1' for African LDCs and '0' for all other countries.
F/M = females as % of male enrolments 1986.

discrimination against the schooling of girls were partly economic and partly cultural. In order to test for this, it is necessary to find proxies for cultural differences between societies. This is not easy, but the incidence of Islam, as a cultural variable, suggested itself partly because the low GER States are ones in which the proportion of Muslims in the population is significantly higher, on average, than in the higher GER States. For example, the Muslim population as a proportion of the total is almost three times as great in the twenty-three low GER countries shown in Table 2.3, as in the fifty-five countries shown in that and the following table taken together. It seemed important, therefore, to explore whether or not this cultural variable had any explanatory power in the matter of low female enrolments, quite separately from the influence of poverty. This seems likely from Table 2.5, which indicates that the coefficients between Islam, GER, and the proportion of girls enrolled at primary level are each negative and significant. The coefficient with per capita income, however, whilst negative, is much weaker.

It is also interesting to note from Table 2.5 that, although GER is fully determined by the combined values of a, x_g, and c_g, their separate correlation coefficients with GER are generally low. Only the a variable achieves significance at the 10 per cent level, its negative coefficient indicating that those countries with relatively large school-age populations tend to have lower GERs. It should be noted, however, that this may, in turn, reflect the indirect effects of per capita income, which is strongly positively correlated with GER, and with which a is itself negatively correlated.

The effects of introducing a maximum value for the GER can also be seen from the correlation matrix, where both capped (LogGER) and uncapped (LogGER) versions of this variable are shown. In general the result of capping is to increase most of the simple correlation coefficients between the dependent and independent variables. As expected, the factors influencing the extent of over-age enrolment are different from those which influence the extent to which UPE can be achieved.

6.2 The results

The results of the more important regressions using the full sample of countries are summarized in Tables 2.6*a*–2.6*c*. Three groups of countries are shown, comprising all countries, developing countries, and African countries, respectively. The results of six separate regression equations are presented, labelled (a)–(f), for each group. For each of the independent variables, the regression coefficient and the *t*-statistic are shown in vertical order. The intercept is also shown, together with its *t*-statistic in each case. The results for each of the equations will be

discussed in turn, calling attention, where necessary, to differences between the results for each group of countries.

We know from our earlier tabular analysis that low primary-enrolment
ratios are found mainly amongst the poorer countries of the world. We
also know, however, that rates of population growth are inversely related
to per capita income, and that thus the proportion of the population of
school-going age will be larger in poorer countries. To what extent is the
former fact a reflection of the latter? The results for the first equation
shown in Table 2.6 shed some light on this question. They indicate that,
after controlling for differences in the relative size of the school age-
group, there remains a strong positive relationship between GER and per
capita income within religion/continental groupings. This is as we would
expect: countries which are very poor are likely to find the provision of
schooling opportunities for a given proportion of the population more
difficult than those which are not. In terms of equation (1), if GER =
x/ac, and if we know (from Table 2.5) that GER is a positive function,
and a a negative function, of per capita income, it follows that x/c must
rise with PCY. Lower per capita income, for given cost levels, increases
the value of c, and thus reduces GER for given values of a and x.
Equally, countries with higher per capita (and household) incomes can
afford to spend a greater proportion of their income on schooling. Thus,
not only is it the case that absolute expenditures on primary schooling
increase with per capita income, but also that the latter variable may
reasonably be taken (with others, as indicated below) as a proxy for x/c,
and, indeed, for x_p/c_p, where either x_g or c_g is controlled.[8]

The coefficients for Africa and Islam are, as expected, negative—
although only in the 'all country' case is that for Africa statistically
significant at the 10 per cent level. These results are important. They
show that even after controlling for a and per capita income, both the
proportion of the population which is Muslim, and whether or not the
country is in Africa, exert separately identifiable and cumulative negative
influences on the primary enrolment ratio. Thus, being African or being
Muslim seems to be associated with having a lower commitment to UPE.
These variables are henceforth used as cost/expenditure proxies in the
same way as, and in conjunction with, PCY.

[8] Per capita income, and, indeed, the other proxy variables employed in the statistical
analyses, in fact act as proxies for the excluded variables from the identity. Thus, their
measured significance derives from their correlations with these excluded variables.
However, where either x_g or c_g singly appear as variables in an equation, it follows from the
identities that the proxies measure the influence not only of the excluded public-sector cost
or expenditure variable, but also of the changing balance between private expenditures and
costs. This can be seen from the following: since, from (2), $x_g/c_g = x_p/c_p$, it follows that $c_g =$
$c_p \cdot x_g/x_p$. Thus, if x_g were, in a statistical sense, held constant, x_p/c_p would vary inversely
with the excluded c_g. Accordingly, a variable which served as a proxy for one of these
terms would become a proxy for the inverse of the other. Using similar logic, it can be
shown that, if c_g were held constant, x_p/c_p would vary directly with the excluded x_g.

How might these relationships be explained? Building upon the conclusions of our earlier tabular analysis, the second equation in Table 2.6 investigates the impact of adding the ratio between female and male enrolments to the list of variables investigated in the first equation. A major change in the results can be seen. The F/M variable is highly significant, and its beta values (not shown in the table) indicate that it is considerably more important than is log per capita income which, in the 'all country' case, is even rendered insignificant.

Of equal interest is the fact that Islam no longer retains significance in any of the three groups of countries. This suggests a number of conclusions. First, the Islam variable, which was important in equation (a), appears to have served as a proxy for variations in the F/M enrolment ratio. It attained significance there because it indicated discrimination against girls attending school, which tended to hold down the GER for given values of the other variables. This, of course, does not imply that the incidence of Islamic beliefs or culture necessarily implies systematic discrimination against the education of girls, even amongst poor States. The cases of Malaysia, Turkey, Syria, and Tanzania, all of which had, in 1986, per capita incomes of less than $US2,000 and large Muslim populations, and yet where female primary enrolments are closely similar to those of males, serve to make the point. Equally, low F/M ratios are not confined exclusively to States with large Muslim populations, as illustrated by the cases of Nepal and the Central African Republic in Table 2.3, where the Muslim population represents no more than 5 per cent of the total, in each case. Thus, equation (b), where the Islam variable no longer retains significance, shows that there are other countries where discrimination against the schooling of girls also occurs: although Islam is an important cultural variable in this context, it by no means provides the whole explanation for variations in F/M. The direct measure of the latter provides a stronger explanation for the variance of GER, with r^2 rising sharply in each case—particularly in the results for Africa, where it is increased by 45 per cent, from 0.4 to 0.58.

It should be noted that the value of the F/M ratio could vary between zero and infinity, with the extremes implying that only males and only females were enrolled, respectively. Values greater than 100 would indicate discrimination in favour of the enrolment of girls. Such cases are rare, but do exist. In a world which did not discriminate between the schooling of girls and boys, one would expect there to be no relationship between the extent of progress towards SFA, and the observed ratio between female and male GERs. There is, nevertheless, a risk of bias in using F/M as an explanatory variable for variations in GER. This, since for values of GER greater than 50, the minimum possible value for F/M becomes non-zero, and rises with GER. Thus the degree of explanatory power conferred by F/M may be partly (but not necessarily) a function of this constraint. Accordingly, in later models, we continue to use Islam and Africa as proxies for the sex ratio of enrolments bias, and other continental-specific downward influences on the level of the GER.

The third set of equations shown take log a and log x_g as the independent variables. It can be seen that the coefficient on the latter variable is positive, but not significant for each of the groups of countries. Thus there is no significant relationship between the proportion of GNP spent by States on primary schooling and the GER. The explanation for this is partly that a constant value for x_g represents very different absolute sums in low- and high-income countries. But it is also partly due to the existence of the trade-off shown by equation (2), for any increase in public spending on primary schooling, between expanding enrolments and raising the expenditures per primary child. As indicated by the high positive correlation between x_g and c_g shown in Table 2.4, increased values for public expenditures often tend to be (and have to be once SFA is reached) translated into increased unit expenditures rather than higher enrolments.

It should be remembered, however, that if increases in public spending on primary schooling are to increase enrolments, there are requirements for changes in household behaviour which must be satisfied. To the extent that there are private costs of schooling, increases in enrolments would increase private expenditures, unless privately incurred unit costs were to decline in full compensation. Perhaps, then, it is that private behaviour is not responsive to changes in public expenditures—that households are not prepared to change their educational expenditures, thereby preventing increased public spending from affecting the GER.

In order to test this, the fourth set of equations reported in Table 2.6 reintroduce per capita income, Islam, and Africa as additional determining variables. Recalling the identity GER $= x_g/a \cdot c_g = x_p/a \cdot c_p$, it follows that the positive coefficient shown for per capita income implies that, with x_g and a controlled, higher per capita income is associated with lower c_g values. Equally, the negative coefficients for Islam and Africa show that given values for x_g and per capita income generate lower GERs in African than in non-African countries and in those with proportionately smaller Islamic populations. This means that, in Africa, and in countries with greater proportions of Muslims, publicly funded unit costs of primary schooling are proportionately greater than elsewhere.

There could be a number of reasons why the publicly financed unit costs of primary schooling rise less quickly than per capita income. On the one hand, it could be that teachers become relatively cheaper as incomes rise, and as educated workers become less scarce, thereby allowing reductions in the values of both c_g and c_p. This seems to be particularly likely in Africa, explaining both the larger coefficient for the PCY variable in the fourth equation for the African group, and the negative coefficient for the Africa dummy in the other cases. On the other hand it could be that as private households become richer, the proportion of income spent upon schooling rises, allowing c_g to fall.

Both of these explanations would imply changes in the value of the ratio between private expenditures and privately funded unit costs (x_p/c_p). As indicated earlier, this also follows from our finding that c_g falls as per capita income rises when x_g is controlled.[9] Furthermore, a comparison of the results of equations (c) and (d) reveals that the size of the regression coefficient on x_g falls with the introduction of the proxy variables in each of the country groups: reducing the variability of the ratio for private expenditures via the proxies does, therefore, reduce the impact of public spending on the size of the GER, in the ways expected. We can say therefore that the reason for x_g not having a significant independent effect upon GER does not arise from the rigidity of x_p/c_p. However, since we have no separate evidence to indicate the ways in which private expenditures and costs independently move in response to increases in x_g, it remains possible that there is some resistance from private households to meeting the costs of higher enrolments, and that this prevents increases in public expenditures on primary schooling from being translated into enrolment gains as strongly as would otherwise be the case.

In the same manner as before, the final pair of equations investigates the relationships between GER, unit expenditures, and other variables. It can be seen from the first of these that, as expected, there is a negative relationship between GER and c_g, after controlling for values of a, and that in this case significance levels are high even in the absence of x_g. Does this imply that reductions in publicly incurred unit costs provide a fairly ready means to increase GER not only in principle, but also in practice? Perhaps so; but a moment's thought indicates that, just as was the case with the numerator of the identity, autonomous changes in elements of the denominator which are designed to increase GER may be frustrated in that endeavour in a number of ways.

The critical issue is the extent to which the reductions in publicly incurred unit costs affect those met by private households. By way of illustration, let us assume that publicly funded unit costs fell by 10 per cent, following the introduction of double-shift arrangements in government primary schools. This would permit an increase in enrolments of around 11 per cent, with no increase in state spending. But in order for that to be achieved, either privately funded unit costs would have to fall by the same amount, or private expenditures would have to rise in order to finance the higher costs of the new higher levels of enrolments. Yet, in the case of this particular reform, it is doubtful that private unit costs would fall (see below, and Chapter 4). Accordingly, if households were

[9] See n. 7.

unwilling to increase their expenditures, total public spending on primary schooling would be constrained by the lack of private demand, and x_g would fall below its previous level. The reductions in publicly funded unit costs would thus be translated into budgetary savings rather than increased enrolments.

More formally, it follows from the identity equations that if c_g falls, c_p would also need to fall by an exactly similar proportion if an increase in GER were to be achieved with no increase in x_p. In circumstances of a less than proportional fall in c_p, if the value of x_p did not rise—or insufficiently so—then x_g would have to fall below its previous level, and the opportunity to increase GER to the extent promised by the cost reductions in the public sector would be frustrated.

Some types of educational reform are, in principle, capable of reducing unit expenditures for both the State and private households at the same time, but whether they do so in practice is a different matter. For example, reductions in the level of teachers' salaries, in the prescribed length of the school year, in the teacher/pupil ratio—in other words, those reforms which are capable of affecting the general structure of the system and its cost parameters—are all changes which may reduce both the private and public costs of schooling. Nevertheless, in general, the unit cost reductions flowing from such reforms are likely to be much smaller for private households than for the government. Here there are three main considerations. First, within the state school system, there is generally a division of responsibility between parents and government for meeting different constituents of total costs. Teachers' salaries are usually met by the State, whereas if parents are required to contribute to direct costs this is more likely to be for textbooks, materials, sports items, even maintenance of school buildings rather than salary costs. Whatever the division of funding responsibilities between the two parties, the fact that they do, generally, pay for different items implies that the government, in seeking to reduce its own unit costs would be unlikely to affect the levels of private unit costs—for any given level of enrolments—unless this were an entirely explicit aim of policy. Second, the impact of declines in public expenditures per pupil in the case of 'private' schools (which, notwithstanding their designation, are usually recipients of state subsidies) is more likely to increase private unit costs—to meet the cost of services or subsidies withdrawn—than to reduce them.

Finally, there are important types of reform which are deliberately designed not to result in concomitant reductions in private unit expenditures. These comprise all those which shift costs to the users of the services concerned. There are many such reforms, but examples include introduction of, or increases in, the level of charges made for school meals, tuition, or boarding fees. These reduce the unit costs of schooling to the government, but, far from reducing those shouldered by private households, they actually increase them by an equivalent amount. In such circumstances, therefore, the level of x_p would need to rise both in order to meet the new higher private unit costs, and to accommodate the increased total costs implied by a higher GER.

In summary, therefore, we can conclude that there is no automatic link between the levels of publicly and privately incurred unit costs of schooling. Nevertheless, unless deliberately designed otherwise, policies to reduce public expenditures per pupil are likely to leave privately incurred unit costs either unchanged or higher than they were previously. In such circumstances, as the GER identities make clear, if the demand response were such that households were unwilling to increase the proportion of their income which they devote to primary schooling the net result of cost reductions by government would be to reduce x_g rather than to increase GER.

An attempt is made in the final equation shown in Table 2.6 to clarify these matters by introducing the income, Islam, and Africa variables as proxies both for x_g and for the private expenditure/cost ratio.[10] If the above arguments are sound, it follows that with a fall in c_g, and with c_p being more likely to rise or remain constant than to fall, the required increase in the ratio x_p/c_p, which is needed to achieve a higher GER, would call for increases in private expenditures on schooling. The negative coefficient for c_g revealed by each of the equations (e) in Table 2.6 already suggests that state actions to increase GER via cost reductions are not, in general, fully undermined by private households. However, a stronger test is provided by the equations (f).

These show that, for given levels of public expenditure per pupil, as per capita incomes rise, so do public expenditures on primary schooling as a proportion of GNP (the excluded variable), in order to produce higher GERs. They also show that x_g, for given levels of per capita income and publicly financed unit costs, varies inversely with the proportion of the population which is Islamic. These relationships emerge particularly strongly in the developing-country group. Whether or not a country is in

[10] See also n. 7. Separate data are available from international published sources for the proportion of total enrolments which are in private rather than state schools. Such information is available for 72 of the 82 countries included in our regressions. These data were used to provide a separate proxy for private expenditures. They were included as an additional determining variable in each of equations (c), (d), (e), and (f). The estimated coefficients for private schooling each had zero values, and no increase in explanatory power was achieved in any of the models tested for any of the groups of countries. There are reasons to believe that these data on the incidence of private schooling are unreliable. There is, however, another reason for the non-significance of this variable. It is that—somewhat counter-intuitively—the incidence of private schooling is an inadequate proxy for the magnitude of private expenditures on primary schooling: many public systems depend upon private financing to an extent which varies strongly from case to case, whilst state subsidies imply that many private schools are by no means wholly financed by households. There is no compelling reason to suppose, therefore, that the extent and pattern of private financial support is directly related to the incidence of 'private' schools.

Africa, on the other hand, does not significantly affect the size of x_g within income and religious groups.

For the same reasons as before, these results also indicate that the x_p/c_p ratio rises with per capita income and falls with the proportion of Muslims for given levels of public expenditures per pupil. Thus, total household expenditures on primary schooling increase faster than private expenditures per pupil as incomes rise.

It can be seen that reducing the variation in the x_p/c_p ratio, via the proxies, leads to a reduction in the size of the negative coefficient on c_g, as between the results for equations (e) and (f). This is particularly marked in Africa, where the coefficient changes from -0.26 to -0.17 with the introduction of the proxies. Since this implies that the GER increases to a greater extent when the private expenditure/cost ratio is, in a statistical sense, uncontrolled, we can conclude that private households appear willing to increase expenditures in response to reductions in publicly financed unit costs. Although this conclusion cannot be demonstrated to hold in the absence of separate data on the incidence of private unit expenditures, there can be a presumption for its general validity on the grounds stated above. These results, therefore, suggest that there is some elasticity in the supply of private expenditures on primary schooling.

It is, of course, important to emphasize that demand relationships cannot be validly derived from cross-section data. The above analysis is no exception to this rule. The cost and income-distribution circumstances of each country are different. It is therefore necessary to be circumspect before assuming that evidence based on cross-section data has predictive value for the results of particular policy changes within one country. Take, for example, the results for Africa. These show that, across the continent, a 10 per cent fall in c_g is associated with a 2.6 per cent increase in GER (in each case, for values around their mean levels). They also show that the rise in GER is only 1.7 per cent if per capita income and the proportion of Muslims in the population are controlled. Thus, it seems reasonable to conclude that GER increases more rapidly in response to unit cost reductions by government when there is per capita income growth than without it—owing to the increased capacity of private households to meet higher primary expenditures.

Nevertheless, the unit cost levels which are measured above are the means of different combinations of cost parameters in each country. These therefore reflect different class-sizes, teacher/pupil ratios, and teachers' earnings as well as differences between the extent to which these and other costs are split between the government and private households. Thus the reduced c_g values associated with higher GERs must be interpreted as reductions of an average mix of these cost parameters in ways which reflect their typical structure across Africa at the present time. This evidence cannot be taken to imply that increases in enrolments financed by reductions in publicly financed unit costs will always be accommodated by private households. Securing progress towards SFA by these means will depend strongly on how the cost reductions are achieved, upon the proportion of unit costs presently financed by the government and by private households, respectively, and upon whether or not household incomes are static or rising during the period covered by the reforms.

The final important issue which is clarified by the regression analysis reported in Table 2.6 concerns the nature of the 'Africa effect', initially detected in Table 2.1. What is it, then, about being in Africa, which leads to a GER which, as revealed by equation (b) for the 'all-country' group, is only 85 per cent of the level of other countries, at given levels of female/male enrolments, per capita income, and school-eligible population?[11] Equation (d), which introduces the x_g variable shows that it is not explained by lower levels of public spending on primary schooling, since the size of the negative coefficient remains unchanged from equation (b). Similar results can be seen by comparing the same two equations for the LDC group. They are weaker, however, in that both the coefficients and the levels of significance associated with them are much lower. Nevertheless, the results show a detectable difference between African and other developing countries in the sample, which is not significantly changed by the introduction of x_g.

The impact of introducing the c_g variable is much stronger, however. In the 'all country' case the negative coefficient is reduced from -0.07 to -0.04, implying a reduction in the Africa/non-Africa differential from 15 to about 9 per cent, whilst in the case of the developing-country group the coefficient is reduced to zero. Thus, one may conclude that the lower GERs for Africa, after allowing for differences in income, school-eligible population, and the cultural influences proxied by the Islam variable, are largely explained by higher expenditures per pupil which are met by African governments. This conclusion is further strengthened by the separate regressions shown for the Africa group: the elasticity of substitution between c_g and GER (given by the regression coefficient on c_g) is more than twice as high as those for all countries and for LDCs separately (compare equations (e) and (f) in each case). This implies that a given proportional fall in publicly incurred unit expenditures can be expected to have twice the relative impact upon mean GER within Africa as it would outside that continent.

Taken at face value, these results seem to imply that strategies to

[11] The (negative) regression coefficient for Africa indicates the extent to which the estimated regression surface for African countries is lower than that for non-African countries, i.e. it is equal to log (GER non-Africa) − log (GER Africa), or log (GER non-Africa/GER Africa). The Africa/non-Africa GER ratios given in the text are in each case the inverse of the antilogarithm of the regression coefficient.

reduce the public unit costs of primary schooling, relative to per capita income, are a high priority in Sub-Saharan Africa, and will need to be an important ingredient in policies to achieve SFA in that region. Our earlier analysis indicated that this was likely to be so in at least some countries of West and Central Africa, where average salaries of teachers represented, in the mid-1980s, a particularly heavy burden relative to other countries— both within Africa and beyond. There are, however, other reasons for the incidence of high values for c_g in Africa which modify these conclusions in important ways.

Africa has had the greatest relative shortage of educated workers of any of the southern continents. Furthermore, as we have seen in this chapter, African nations still account for the majority of the most educationally disadvantaged countries. In these circumstances it is to be expected that the average cost of teachers—typically the most numerous group amongst educated professional workers—relative to per capita incomes, would be higher than elsewhere. This circumstance was aggravated in many countries by the heavy overvaluation of exchange rates, which led to particularly high costs (when expressed in terms of foreign exchange) in the labour-intensive service sectors such as educa- tion. For these reasons, it is not surprising that the levels of c_g in Africa are high—nor that the countries where it is highest include some of those which could least afford further to increase access to schooling.

Secondly, and probably no less important, at the level of the household both the attitudes towards and the private abilities to finance primary schooling in Africa have themselves been negatively influenced by the continent's economic demise. Throughout SSA, rural and urban popula- tions are poorer than they were. They can afford the direct cost of schooling less easily, and they need the labour of their children to finance the household economy more than they did during the 1970s. Labour- market conditions have deteriorated, and the chances of using primary schooling to gain access to the formal sector are lower than at any time since independence. Finally, in many countries the direct costs of school attendance for households have risen as aspects of state spending are devolved to service-users—often at the behest of the international financial institutions—as part of the public-sector response to austerity, recession, and adjustment.

All of this has meant that, in a number of African countries, the private demand for primary schooling has been declining. Tanzania provides one of the more extreme examples, where the GER declined from 93 to 69 between 1980 and 1986. But it is by no means unique, as the cases of Mozambique, Sudan, and Zaïre, shown in Table 2.1, indicate. This has a number of consequences for our present analysis. First, to the extent that state expenditures on primary schooling, in aggregate, remain unchanged—or at least fall less quickly than enrolments—the effect is to increase the value of c_g. Thus the importance of this variable in explaining low enrolment ratios in Africa is likely to be, at least in part, a consequence of the declining private demand discussed above. Second, and more obviously, measures to reduce the level of c_g may still be needed in such circumstances, but they could hardly be expected to lead to increased values for GER. If anything, they risk reducing it still further, unless extreme care is taken to avoid concomitant upward pressure on the levels of c_p. Thus, in such countries, the move to SFA is unlikely to be possible without stimulating private demand for primary schooling—most obviously by reducing the actual or perceived levels of private costs. Finally, it remains the case that some African countries are facing public unit costs which are genuinely too high, as indicated in the earlier discussion of Table 2.3. However, low private demand interacts with this phenomenon, in ways which complicate and extend the possible explanations for the significance of the c_g variable, as identified in the regression analysis discussed above. Clearly, a range of reforms are relevant in African circumstances which will vary according to conditions in each individual country.

7. Summary and Conclusions

We have shown in this chapter that a number of important characteristics are systematically associated with the non-achievement of UPE around the world. As often happens in economics, they can usefully be thought of in terms of supply-side and demand-side factors. In most countries elements of both are present. Understanding their relative importance is necessary for effective policy design.

We have shown that countries with low GERs tend to have low per capita incomes. On the supply side, this is partly because poorer countries have higher rates of population growth, and thus proportionately larger school-age populations. Thus, the size of the educational task facing them is greater than in richer countries. Nevertheless, even after allowing for these different population characteristics, poorer countries still have a smaller proportion of children at school.

Low per capita income affects the capacity of governments to finance and deliver schooling, which causes its supply to be more restricted in low-income States. Provided that the relationship between costs and incomes is not constant across countries, the proportion of public spending needed for UPE would tend to be greater in poorer societies. This effect of low income is likely to be particularly important in the very poorest countries, or where incomes are in decline, as in much of Sub-Saharan Africa in recent years.

Nevertheless, irrespective of low incomes, it is possible to characterize

about half of the countries with low GERs as having low commitment to
the provision of schooling for all. In these countries, which include
Nigeria, Pakistan, Bangladesh, Nepal, Bolivia, and some others, it would
be possible, at present cost levels, to achieve UPE with amounts of public
spending on primary schooling equivalent to less than 2 per cent of
GNP—an amount which should be relatively easy to reach.

In the other countries with low GERs, however, including many in
west and central Africa, achieving UPE would prove difficult at present
cost levels. It would require public expenditures on primary schooling
equivalent to between 3 and 7 per cent of GNP, which is too high a
proportion for most such States to countenance. Cost reductions would
here need to be sought. We have demonstrated that in Africa GERs are
only 85 per cent of their levels in other developing countries, after
allowing for differences in income and school-age population size. This
difference disappears, however, if the unit costs of primary schooling are
also controlled. Moreover, a given proportionate fall in publicly financed
unit costs has twice the positive impact upon mean GER values within
Africa that it has outside that continent. For all these reasons, cost-
reduction strategies will be needed for this second group of low GER
countries, if UPE is to be achieved.

Contrary to popular view, variation in the amount spent by governments on primary schooling, expressed as a proportion of GNP, does not,
unassisted, explain a significant amount of variance in the level of GERs.
This is for three main reasons. First, given proportions of GNP represent
very different absolute amounts in low- and high-income countries;
second, higher expenditures on primary schooling are often translated
into increased expenditures per pupil rather than larger enrolments;
third, school systems differ in the extent to which they are publicly
and privately financed. Equally, debt-service commitments and defence
expenditures are not significantly related to the non-achievement of UPE
in any general sense. Nevertheless, as indicated above, our case-by-case
examination of the data did identify a number of countries where low
public expenditures appear to be a key variable in explaining low primary
enrolments, in some of which, recent levels of defence and/or debt-
service expenditures were high enough to present a formidable obstacle
to increased social spending.

The attainment of UPE and SFA, however, are critically influenced not
only by the supply of school places, but also by the demand for them by
private households. It may be that the perceived benefits of schooling are
lower in poorer States, and that this accounts for the observed relationship between low per capita incomes and low GERs. Equally, low household incomes reduce the ability of individuals to meet both the direct and
indirect costs of schooling, which reduces demand. In that connection we
have documented the very strong relationship between the incidence of

low GERs and an underenrolment of girls. This suggests that the net benefits of educating girls—as perceived by their parents—tend to be lower in poorer countries, which partly accounts for their failure to reach UPE.

Yet, even within per capita income groupings, variations in the proportion of girls enrolled explain a significant part of the variance of GERs. It seems then that it is not just the market-place, but also custom and culture which are important determinants. In some societies there are dominant customary attitudes which affect the role of women, and their education, separately from the economic benefits which schooling brings (although the latter are mediated, in important ways, by the former). We find, for example, that, in low- and middle-income countries, the proportion of Muslims in the population is significantly associated with low GERs, after allowing for differences in per capita incomes, and that the main manifestation of this is the lower proportion of female primary enrolments amongst such communities. The point here is not whether or not Islam *per se* discourages the education of the girl-child—indeed there is no evidence, from the Koran or elsewhere, that that is the case. Rather, it is that customary and cultural influences in Islamic (and other) societies help to determine the level of female enrolments, in addition to economic ones, and that these, in turn, are a further cause of low GERs.

The proper diagnosis of constraints—be they demand- or supply-side problems—has important implications for policy. For example, our cross-country analysis has shown that the higher are the publicly incurred unit costs of primary schooling relative to per capita income, the lower is the GER. Cost-reduction would therefore need to be part of any general strategy to increase primary enrolments sharply. However, there are ways in which the expansion strategies of States wishing to achieve UPE and SFA via cost-reduction, may be frustrated by private behaviour. It is obvious that GERs will not rise if parents decide not to enrol more of their children. What is often overlooked, however, is that household behaviour needs to be directly supportive, rather than merely permissive, if SFA is to be achieved. Policies to reduce public expenditures per pupil, given the ways in which school systems are typically financed, are likely to leave privately incurred unit costs either unchanged, or even higher than they were before. Thus, cost-reduction strategies by the public sector as a means of achieving increased enrolments will usually depend upon increased levels of household expenditure being forthcoming if they are to succeed.

In fact, our empirical results provide some modest encouragement for the view that attempts to increase the efficiency of primary schooling, or to divert public funds from other uses, would, in general, elicit additional resources from private households. Nevertheless, the success of such policies would always depend upon the context in which they were applied. Success would be unlikely, for example, in cases of severe per capita income decline (as in Tanzania), or where policies to reduce public costs sharply raised those which were faced by private households. In many of the countries suffering from severe recession, deliberate policies to stimulate the demand for schooling, by reducing its private costs, would also be required.

It is now appropriate to ask how these trade-offs have been accommodated in particular countries, and whether there are other general lessons to be learned from States which have had some success in the early achievement of UPE. These questions are tackled in the next chapter, which presents studies of six countries, in most of which the quantitative—albeit not necessarily the qualitative—aims of SFA have been attained.

Appendix
The Cost and Expenditure Determinants of the Gross Enrolment Ratio

This Appendix shows how equations (1) and (2), used in Chapter 2, are derived. The gross enrolment ratio is the relationship between total primary enrolments and the number of children of primary age. It is also possible, however, to define the GER in terms of the costs of schooling and the expenditures which society chooses to allocate to it. Consider the following:

Let E = primary enrolments,
   X = recurrent expenditures made by society on primary schooling,
   C = the recurrent cost per primary pupil,
   Y = GNP,
 PCY = GNP per capita,
   x = the proportion of GNP spent on primary schooling,
   c = primary unit costs as a proportion of per capita income,
   P = population, and
   a = the proportion of the population of primary-school age.
Now,

$$E = X/C = x \cdot Y/c \cdot \text{PCY} = x \cdot P/c.$$

Thus,

$$E/P = x/c,$$

and

$$\text{GER} = E/aP = x/ac. \qquad (A.1)$$

Thus, from the point of view of costs and expenditures, the GER can be seen to be equivalent to the proportion of GNP spent on primary schooling, x, divided by the product of the proportion of the population of school-going age, a, and primary unit costs as a proportion of per capita income, c.

In addition, however, it is important for analytic purposes to distinguish between those expenditures on primary schooling which are made by the State and those which are made by private households. By extending the above notation,

Let x_g = public expenditure on primary schooling as a proportion of GNP,
   x_p = private expenditure on primary schooling as a proportion of GNP,
   c_g = public expenditure per primary pupil as a proportion of GNP per capita,
and
   c_p = private expenditure per primary pupil as a proportion of GNP per capita.

A Cross-Country Analysis

Thus,

$$x = x_g + x_p,$$
$$c = c_g + c_p,$$

and, since $x_g/c_g = x_p/c_p$, by definition,

$$\text{GER} = x_g/ac_g = x_p/ac_p = (x_g + x_p) \, / \, a(c_g + c_p). \tag{A.2}$$

3

Case-Studies of Educational Reforms

1. Introduction

We now turn to an examination of experience with educational reform. As shown in the last chapter, although low primary enrolments are more usually found amongst the poorer countries, exceptions to the rule are frequent. Equally, it seems that simple measures of public 'commitment' to UPE, such as the proportion of GNP spent upon primary schooling by the State, are not decisive in picking out countries with high enrolments. The reality is more complex. It is the interaction between these and a range of other variables, including the public and private costs of schooling, and the ideologies which inform private behaviour, which determine UPE outcomes. An important question thus concerns the extent to which changes in public policy can affect these variables in ways supportive of UPE and SFA. This is the central question addressed in this chapter.

Six countries are selected for particular study. In four of them UPE has already been attained, two being low-income countries (China and Sri Lanka) and two being from the middle-income group (Zimbabwe and Colombia). In the remaining countries—Ghana (low income) and Senegal (middle income)—GERs remain less than 100. However, in all six countries important educational reforms have recently been introduced, with the intention of achieving universal access to higher-quality primary schooling. In China and Zimbabwe the reforms became the vehicle for the rapid achievement of UPE. In Sri Lanka and Colombia, they helped to consolidate the enrolment gains of the past by improving the quality of primary schooling, particularly in rural areas, and increasing net enrolments towards SFA levels. In Senegal and Ghana, they refocused policy on the base of the system and provided the means of increasing primary enrolments at much lower costs than hitherto. Finally, each of the African cases, together with Colombia, experienced severe economic difficulties during the 1980s. Their lessons are therefore particularly important for many of the poorer countries which remain far from achieving SFA: they show that a great amount can be achieved, even where public revenues are in decline.

2. China: Towards SFA—Insights from the People's Republic

Since 1949 the People's Republic of China has made impressive gains in educational development—primary enrolments increased from around 24.4 million to about 125 million by 1988, giving a GER well in excess of 100. The number of primary schools increased from 347,000 to 793,000. At the junior secondary level[1] enrolments increased from about 1 million to about 40 million over the same period, and the number of schools rose from about 3,000 to 75,000. The proportion of school-age children actually attending primary school has climbed from less than 50 per cent in 1952 to exceed 90 per cent during the 1980s. Adult literacy is approaching 70 per cent. This record of achievement is outstanding. China has a population in excess of 1.1 billion and is one of the poorest developing countries, yet in 1991 its ranking on the UNDP's Human Resource Development Index was comparable with that of much richer countries (UNDP 1991).

China has therefore been able to achieve UPE despite having the largest number of children to enrol, 80 per cent of whom live in rural areas, and notwithstanding a turbulent sequence of political upheavals and natural disasters. Although some of these experiences are specific to China's cultural and political circumstances this case-study highlights those which provide more general lessons for SFA policy.

Four questions are addressed. First, what are the main factors that have enabled China to approach UPE at relatively low public cost, relative to government expenditure and GNP? Second, what is the framework that has defined recent primary education policy and promoted its achievement? Third, what mechanisms are being used to generate additional resources for primary schooling and how effective are these? Fourth, what kinds of organizational reforms have been introduced to provide incentives for teachers, and to improve internal efficiency and school quality?

2.1. The approach to UPE

The quantitative development of primary schooling in China is summarized in Table 3.1. Enrolments probably peaked during the cultural revolution (1966–76), although this is uncertain because the collection of statistics was suspended for most of that period. Subsequently, enrolments declined owing to lower rates of population growth. The student/qualified teacher ratio in 1988 was about 23:1. Net enrolment ratios were claimed to

---

[1] Junior secondary schooling starts in grade 6 or 7 depending on location and usually lasts for 3 years.

TABLE 3.1. *Basic statistics for primary schools in China (in units of 10,000)*

	No. of schools	Entrants	Graduates	Enrolment	Teachers[a]	School-age pop.	Net enrol. ratio
1949	34.7	680	65	2,439	83.6		
1952						6,642	49.2
1957	54.7	1,249	498	6,128	188.4	8,078	61.7
1965	168.2[b]	3,296	668	11,621	385.7	11,603	84.7
1978	94.9	3,315	2,288	14,624	522.6	12,131	94.0
1985	83.2	2,298	1,999	13,370	537.7	10,362	95.9
1988	79.3	2,123	1,930	12,536	550.1	9,656	97.2

[a] Full-time teachers.
[b] By the mid-1960s virtually every village had a school but many of these had only one unqualified teacher and were without proper buildings.
Source: SIHRD 1991 (Tables 4.1 and 4.2).

be between 95 and 100 per cent.[2] Over 45 per cent of primary-school students were female.[3]

China devotes about 3 per cent of GNP and only about 6 per cent of its public budget to education. Table 3.2 compares China's educational expenditure with that of other low-income countries. What, then, are the main factors that have enabled China to achieve UPE at cost levels which require much lower budgetary allocations to education than is typical in other developing countries?

The first reason is that a significant amount of expenditure is not provided directly by central government but is financed from lower tiers of the administrative authorities[4] and from community revenue generation. This expenditure does not appear consistently in national accounts, and explains why it is that the proportion of GNP allocated to education is not significantly different from other countries, yet the reported proportion of public spending so allocated is very much lower (Table 3.2). Recent estimates suggest that, if all administrative levels were included, the percentage of the national budget allocated to education

[2] Net enrolment ratios given by other sources differ from those in Table 3.1. UNDP (1991) suggests 100 for 1986–8; the World Bank (Lockheed and Verspoor 1990) suggests 79.9 for 1980 and 93.1 for 1985. These differences are due to the unreliability of some data used in aggregation, e.g. for the size of the primary age-group, and the technical difficulties arising from the different lengths of, and ages of entry to, primary schooling in different parts of China. Nevertheless, it is reasonable to assume that net enrolment ratios are in excess of 90.
[3] Republic of China (1989: 15) claims females to be 45% of total enrolment at primary level in 1988; the World Bank (Lockheed and Verspoor 1991: 189) give a figure of 41% and UNDP (1991) give 47.5% for 1987–8.
[4] These include provincial, prefectural, municipal, county, and district levels.

TABLE 3.2. *Educational expenditure as a percentage of GNP and total government expenditure in China*

	1970		1975		1980		1985	
	%GNP	%Govt. exp.	%GNP	%Govt. exp.	%GNP	%Govt. exp.	%GNP	%Govt. exp.
China	1.3	2.9	1.8	4.2	2.5	n/a	2.7	6.1
Low-income countries median	3.2	16.2	2.8	15.0	3.1	12.7	3.2	15.3
Low-income countries mean[a]	3.1	11.4	3.2	12.1	3.1	9.4	2.9	12.5

[a] Excluding China and India.

Sources: Lockheed and Verspoor (1990: 221).

would rise to about 11 per cent for 1987 (World Bank 1989c). As many as 45 per cent of teachers were 'public supported' in 1987 (Lofstedt 1990: 111),[5] paid predominantly from locally generated revenue which fell outside the normal budget.

The second factor is that teachers' salaries in China are both absolutely and relatively very low. The typical teacher's salary in 1991 was about $US30–40 per month, providing an annual income comparable to GNP per capita. In low-income countries as a whole, primary teachers' salaries have a median value 6.1 times GNP per capita and the mean is 4.9 times. Largely as a result of relatively low teachers' salaries, average public expenditure per child in 1988 was about 60 yuan (about $US15) which was about 5 per cent of GNP/capita (Republic of China 1989: 15). This compares with a mean of 13.5 per cent for low-income countries. Thus higher enrolment ratios are possible than is feasible in countries where teachers' salaries, and unit costs, are much greater multiples of GNP per capita.[6] This remains the case despite the fact that China allocates a relatively low proportion of total educational expenditure to primary education (28.6 per cent compared to a low-income country mean of 46.6 per cent).

Third, population growth rates have fallen from 2.2 per cent (1965–80) to 1.2 per cent (1980–7) and are projected to remain at this low level into the next century (World Bank 1989a: 214). More particularly the annual

---

[5] These 'public-supported' teachers include minban teachers (who are paid by local communities and not by the national government) and other categories. They are often, but not always, underqualified and are paid lower salaries than government teachers.

[6] But see Ch. 4 on the importance of extending this analysis to include the effects of different mixes of employment in agriculture in the economy.

TABLE 3.3. *Projected school-age population, and primary enrolments in China,*
1983–2000

	7-year-olds	Population 7–12 yrs	Total enrolment
1983	20	144	136
1988	17	113	101
1990	17	111	99
1995	16	91	88
2000	15	94	94

Source: World Bank (1984*a*: Annexe C1, Table 1.1).

rate of growth of the 6–11-year-old age-group declined from 3.3 per cent
(1965–75) to 0.6 per cent (1975–80). Over 1980–5 the age-group actually
fell by about 4 per cent per year. This contraction was a direct result of
family planning and of China's 'one child' policy. The 6–11-year-old age-
group is now expected to grow at only 0.8 per cent per year for the rest
of the decade. With the exception of some small island States, only
those developing countries experiencing the devastation of war (e.g.,
Kampuchea, Lebanon) have seen a comparable shrinkage in the size of
the primary-age cohort, and, for low-income countries as a whole, projected annual population growth rates to the year 2000 remain at around
3.0 per cent (Lockheed and Verspoor 1990: 165).

The effects of demographic changes can be seen from Table 3.3. Under
this projection, undertaken by the World Bank in the early 1980s, the
effect of a decline in the size of the 7-year-old age-cohort would result in
a decrease in the number of 7–12-year-olds by 50 million and a decline in
total enrolments by 42 million in the year 2000. This would enable total
enrolment to match the size of the age-group, i.e. GER 100, with 70 per
cent less places than in 1983. A comparison of Table 3.3 with Table 3.1
shows that enrolments have declined more slowly than was anticipated (in
1988 there were 125 million enrolled as against 101 million projected).
Nevertheless, this example demonstrates the importance of low population growth in limiting the additional expenditure that will arise from
universalizing access. Under constant unit cost assumptions a shrinking
cohort will necessarily reduce total costs.

2.2. The framework for primary-education policy

After 1976 the government of China committed itself to the achievement of the Four Modernizations—of industry, agriculture, defence, and
science and technology. Each policy area had educational implications
and emphasis was initially given to those for higher education, which had

been largely closed down during the Cultural Revolution, and clearly demanded priority. Nevertheless, by the early 1980s a new emphasis was beginning to be placed on primary education as it became clear that modernization depended on raising the educational level of the mass of the working population (Lewin and Xu 1989). The reform process catalysed by these events included new arrangements for curriculum development, the supply of books, teacher training, examination reform, school administration, and many other innovations.

The formal basis for the new policies on basic education can be found in the Provisional Regulations on the Basic Requirements for Universalizing Primary Education (1983), the Reform of China's Educational Structure (1985), and the Law of Compulsory Education (1986). This legislation consolidated practices which were being introduced experimentally in different parts of China throughout the early 1980s. They committed China to achieving nine years of compulsory education throughout the country. Three time-scales were agreed. In those areas that were already approaching universalization in the coastal provinces and the economically advantaged areas, the year 1990 was set as a goal. In most of the rest of China the target was 1995. However, in some educationally and economically deprived areas, mostly around the borders of China populated mainly by minority groups, no target was specified, but improvements were expected by early in the next century.

The regulations require all areas to develop their own detailed plans for the implementation of the policy. They also establish targets for rates of enrolment, retention, and graduation. Legislation exists on most aspects of basic education policy which includes explicit performance indicators against which progress is to be assessed. National criteria for universalizing basic nine-year education (Republic of China 1989) include:

- 93 per cent enrolment of school-age children in primary schools.
- An annual retention rate of at least 97 per cent for each grade (retention is defined as the ratio of enrolments at the end of the year to those at the beginning).
- Graduation rates for the final year of primary school above 95 per cent for urban schools, above 90 per cent in the better-off rural areas, and 80 per cent elsewhere.
- Enrolment rates for 12–15-year-old children of more than 95 per cent (using enrolments in any grade).
- Criteria for the elimination of illiteracy.[7]

---

[7] These require that the rural population learn to use 1,500 Chinese characters, while workers, government employees, and urban residents should learn 2,000. The targets for literacy campaigns are to bring the number of literates to more than 85% of the 15–40-year-old group in rural areas and over 90% in the urban areas and to eliminate illiteracy amongst 15–40-year-olds by the end of the century or shortly afterwards.

These criteria are widely publicized and administrators at all levels are aware of them. The national criteria are supplemented by a range of targets defined at Provincial level and below. Examples of such targets include the following: the elimination of dangerous buildings; the provision of classrooms for every class and of sufficient desks and chairs for all students; the provision of adequate accommodation, playground space, equipment, laboratories, library space and books, and of teaching staff for all major and minor subjects; the attainment, by at least 60 per cent of teachers, of teacher-training or higher-education qualifications; the replacement or upgrading of all those currently underqualified; the prohibition of the employment of those who have not completed nine years of schooling; and the local collection of resources for schools.

Though the targets are clearly specified, progress towards some of them is difficult to assess as a result of the unreliability of aggregated data and the use of non-standard definitions. In many areas there remains uncertainty about the size of the school-going age-group. This is partly a result of poor record-keeping and may also arise from the late registration of some births.[8] Retention rates, as normally defined, do not account for those students that enrol one year but do not return the next. One result of introducing the targets for promotion, which are locally set for each grade, has been that repetition rates have fallen as it has become less acceptable to delay promotion. This is increasing the internal efficiency of the school system as automatic promotion becomes more common.

It is probably unique, internationally, to find legislation that prohibits employment for those who have not completed nine years of schooling.[9] In China, this covers workers in general, and not just members of the teaching profession. The effectiveness of the enforcement of this policy is difficult to gauge. It is applied in some more developed areas where secondary-school enrolment ratios are relatively high. It is easiest to enforce in factory employment, and is difficult if not impossible to apply to agricultural work.

The significance of the framework for primary-education policy is that it is explicit and widely publicized. Popularization campaigns have been mounted to extend knowledge of the targets beyond those directly involved in school administration to gain community support. At the local level targets are prioritized. Thus the elimination of dangerous buildings is usually very high on the agenda, whilst the upgrading of untrained teachers is being tackled less rapidly. The targets also have considerable political authority behind them and are prominent in periodic reviews of

[8] In rural areas, second and subsequent children may not be registered at birth. Most become registered at later dates but they may not be entered in the statistics for the appropriate year. This can lead to errors in the calculation of enrolment ratios.

[9] This is usually interpreted as meaning nine years of attendance, rather than completing grade 9.

administrative effectiveness at different levels. Local officials have the responsibility for ensuring that progress is made towards the targets.

2.3. Providing the resources for schools

Under the new arrangements designed to promote basic education primary schools derive their income from five main sources. First, the national government, county, or municipality provides a block grant based on the number of students enrolled. Government teachers' salaries are paid directly from these funds. Buildings and equipment may also be provided.

Second, local education taxes are levied on industry and other economic enterprises by local authorities, who also have the responsibility for disbursing the money. The nature of the tax and the rates paid vary in different locations. A typical arrangement would be a 5 per cent levy on the profits, before taxes, of rural businesses, and a 2 per cent turnover tax on urban factories. In some cases a levy is applied on the construction of buildings based on their floor area, with an additional recurrent levy on maintenance and equipment cost of urban buildings.

Third, People's Education Funds have been established, usually based on an income tax paid by state employees. In some cases this tax is paid by other workers, including farmers. It is generally collected at the rate of about 2 per cent of gross salary for every employee, although the rate may sometimes be progressive.

Fourth, many schools are linked to factories or other productive enterprises with which they have shared management. There are no fixed rules about the amount of support available. In general it will be dependent on profitability in particular years, the generosity of the local leadership concerning how much to allocate to schools as opposed to other types of investment, and on the performance of the school.

Fifth, a Social Fund administered at the district level may exist which accumulates donations from individuals and organizations that wish to support the schools.

Other sources of school income include kindergarten fees—some schools organize pre-school provision for which parents have to pay and/or after-school provision for younger children of working mothers. In a town this might generate 5 yuan per month per child. Though there are no tuition fees, many schools levy registration fees and miscellaneous charges of between 1 yuan and 10 yuan per term at primary rising to higher levels in secondary schools.[10]

---

[10] The Chinese currency is the yuan. It steadily depreciated over the 1980s from a value of 1.5 yuan per $US in 1980, to 2.9 in 1985, and 4.8 in 1990. These are average official rates for each calendar year (IMF 1991).

TABLE 3.4. *An example of school financing from Tongxian*
(in millions of Chinese yuan)

	Central funds	Education tax	People's Education Fund[a]	School factories	Social Fund
1987	26.80	4.11	5.0	0.77	
1988	25.60	6.10	6.0	3.73	
1989	27.89	7.28	7.0	6.28	5.0[b]

[a] These are estimates. The total collection of People's Education Funds for the period 1987–9 was 18 m. yuan but yearly figures were not available. Collections were increasing over the period.
[b] This is an estimate, based upon a reported figure of 2.48 m. yuan over 6 months in 1989.
Source: Lewin *et al.* (1991).

Some indication of the scale of these various sources of funding at the county level can be given from Tongxian, a county in the top 10 per cent of income per capita. Since the new system of local responsibility for raising finance dates from 1986, figures are only available after that date. The growing proportion of funds raised from outside the central budget is striking and this is common in other parts of China (SIHRD 1991). It can be seen from Table 3.4 that, by 1989, almost half of all school finance was being generated outside the central budget in Tongxian. In Ansai, near Yanan, one of the 300 poorest counties, the figure was closer to 30 per cent (Lewin *et al.* 1991).

The balance between state and local funds can vary greatly within counties. This can be seen from the comparison of two districts in Tongxian shown in Table 3.5. The income from the central budget is about 230 yuan per student in both districts. Non-budget income is about 700 yuan per student in Xiji and 20 yuan per student in Dadushe. In the former non-budget income is 75 per cent of the total; in the latter it is a mere 8 per cent. This, it will be remembered, is in a rich county close to Beijing in two districts that are not geographically far from each other. The problem of disparities in non-budget revenue between districts is therefore a serious issue which is likely to exacerbate differences in provision as greater proportions of school finance come to depend on contributions and local taxes.

There are several other important resource-allocation issues. First, the distribution of the public budget between elementary and secondary education is unbalanced. It is not uncommon to find expenditure on secondary being greater than that on primary despite much smaller numbers of students being enrolled.[11] Expenditure per student on

---

[11] Unit expenditures in primary education appear to be about thirty per cent of those in secondary and only two per cent of those in higher education.

TABLE 3.5. *Total revenue for 1989: Xiji and Dadushe*
(yuan per student)

	Xiji	Dadushe
Central budget		
State revenue	203	194
County revenue	28	35
Total budget	231	229
Non-budget income		
Education tax	205	10
People's Education Fund[a]	9	8
School factories	45	0
Social Fund	423	0.4
Registration fee	11	2
Total non-budget	693	20
GRAND TOTAL	924	249

[a] This is normally collected as a tax based on a percentage of salary of government employees. In Dadushe, it is generated by a 10-yuan fee levied directly on students.

Source: Lewin *et al.* (1991: 28).

primary from the public budget alone in Xiji is about 128 yuan whilst it is about 173 yuan in Dadushe. The unit costs at lower secondary are 452 yuan and 383 yuan respectively. The differences can be much greater[12]— in Ansai county in Shaanxi province, the gap between the expenditures per pupil at secondary and primary school increased from a ratio of 5:1 to over 8:1 between 1985 and 1991, despite the emphasis placed on primary education.

Second, financial allocations for books and equipment tend to be very low—seldom more than 2 per cent of total expenditure. The consequence of this is that most rural schools have very little in the way of state-provided learning resources. Textbooks are widely available, however, since they are usually purchased by parents. In the poorest areas teachers may buy books for their students from their own income since parents are too poor to afford them. The financial allocation system contributes to the problems of rural schools. In Ansai, school-operating budgets are provided by the State at the rate of 100 yuan per government teacher in post. However most rural schools have only a small proportion of such teachers—one-third or less of the total—whereas in most town schools all teachers are paid by the government. Thus the operating budget

[12] If non-budget income is taken into account, the differences will increase over and above any variations resulting from the allocation of public expenditure.

generated by this system varies greatly between schools, with unfortunate distributive consequences.

Third, differences in total recurrent unit costs are largely dependent on teachers' salaries. Government primary schoolteachers in 1991 earned about 170–200 yuan per month on average. Other teachers, on the other hand, often had much lower incomes. In Ansai, where 66 per cent of the teachers were 'public supported' their average income was 79 yuan, although they also received a grain allowance. In more developed areas, like Tongxian, less than 20 per cent of teachers are likely to be public supported, and in cities and towns there is virtually none.

Fourth, there is reason to believe that in some areas repetition rates are much higher than those which are officially reported. Although the average repetition rate claimed in Ansai is about 5 per cent, there are schools where more than 50 per cent of grade 4 students have repeated at least once in their school career. The data suggest that no more than 30 per cent of students complete primary school within six years in Ansai, resulting more from high rates of repetition than of drop-out. Thus, considerably more than six student-years are needed for each primary school graduate in this area, even though the average claimed nationally is six and a half years.

A final point concerns the relationship between student/teacher ratios, class-sizes, and teachers' workloads. Teacher/class ratios at primary level generally vary between 1:1 and 2:1. The lower levels are found in incomplete primary and small rural schools which may have only one teacher per class. In cities higher levels are not uncommon. At lower secondary level the ratio is frequently around 2:1 and may reach 3:1 in especially favoured schools. Primary student/teacher ratios average about 23:1 which is much less than the mean for low-income countries of 39 in 1985 (Lockheed and Verspoor 1990: 197). There are approximately thirty teaching periods per week in primary schools and teaching loads of about 15–20 periods are common in urban areas. At secondary level teaching loads are lower—perhaps 12–15 periods per week. There are great variations in class-size—45–50 students is common in cities and towns and densely populated rural areas; in more sparsely populated rural areas 15–25 is more common. Most principals and vice-principals do not teach, and non-teaching administrative staff may be a sizeable proportion (15–25 per cent) of the total staff in medium and large schools, especially at secondary level. By international standards this level of teacher-utilization is low—if teachers had larger teaching loads fewer trained teachers would be needed and/or class-sizes could be smaller. Since most teachers repeat lessons in parallel classes in the same grade, preparation time for lessons would not necessarily increase greatly. The position is not quite as simple as it appears since many teachers do have duties which extend beyond those associated with full-time teachers in other countries, e.g. home visiting, extensive extra-curricular activities, organizing in-service work, and taking part in political work. Nevertheless, the efficiency with which trained teachers are used could be increased, especially in secondary schools where teacher/class ratios are high. There may be more scope for multigrade teaching to increase the utilization rate of trained teachers in rural areas where class sizes are small.

2.4. Organizational reforms to support improvements in school quality

During the 1980s several steps were taken to improve primary teachers' motivation and performance. The status of primary schools had fallen, they were at the lower end of the salary range for public sector employees, and opportunities for earning additional incomes were very limited. In addition, teachers were rewarded primarily on the basis of seniority. This did not reward performance directly and led to frustration and dissatisfaction amongst younger teachers, especially as teacher turnover is low as a result of the Chinese employment system.

Salary awards have improved the situation, and, by 1990 in many areas, teachers ranked in the top half of public sector salary-earners. Some fringe benefits, including health care and travel concessions, were introduced. A structural reform of salaries was introduced in a number of urban areas whereby teachers' basic salary could be enhanced by the payment of bonuses linked to teaching load, years of experience, and the performance of teachers and their pupils.

Although details differ, typically about one-third of total remuneration is derived from the basic salary, a half from the teaching period allowance, and one-sixth from bonus and experience payments. Within each area all teachers receive the basic rate appropriate to their post.[13] The bonuses relate to the performance of the students in the school and may be distributed at a flat rate across all teachers, or allocated differentially to those who perform well. Judgements on teachers' performance are made on a number of criteria. These include assessments of lesson-preparation notes, the marking of students' books, involvement in in-service work, classroom teaching, examination results, and evidence from supervisory and inspection reports. Additional allowances may also be given for special responsibilities.

In 1988 about 70 per cent of primary schoolteachers had reached the minimum educational level stipulated by government for qualified teachers and about one-third of lower-secondary teachers were fully qualified. Extensive arrangements have been made for upgrading teachers

---

[13] Government teachers are paid on three main grades–senior, middle, and junior. The bulk of teachers are in the junior grade. Senior teachers have similar salaries to university lecturers.

through in-service programmes, both full time and part time, at a rate of about 100,000 per year. These arrangements, coupled with attrition and replacement by new teachers, are intended to ensure that all teachers are trained by about the year 2000. In-service training is delivered through a number of channels. Teachers who are underqualified are identified and divided into those who require small amounts of additional training, those who require formal courses, and those unlikely to become qualified. A combination of locally based in-service training requiring minimal release time and full upgrading courses leading to qualifications equivalent to those of new teachers is available to the first two categories of teacher. Teachers' guides are provided with most curriculum materials and these are used by study groups at school and local level to improve teaching and learning methods. Teaching and research groups are formally constituted at school and local levels and have responsibilities for in-service support. Professional journals exist for all major subjects and have a wide circulation.

As in several other countries, primary schools in most rural areas of China fall under the administrative responsibility and professional leadership of a central school. A cluster typically contains ten to twenty schools. Central primary schools usually have two principals. One takes responsibility for the day-to-day running of the central primary school, and the other has overall responsibility for the development of the cluster. Teachers in the central school lead groups for the development of teaching in the different grades and are allocated time for these duties. In-service activities are arranged periodically for all teachers in the cluster and all primary-school principals will meet regularly. There are difficulties in the functioning of school clusters. For example, central schools tend to concentrate on building up their own resources at the expense of other schools, and some communities are unwilling to provide resources that may be distributed to other schools in the cluster. Principals are accountable for the cluster of schools as a whole, however, and without the cluster system, overconcentration might be even greater.

2.5. Conclusion

This case-study has explored some aspects of China's recent experience in implementing primary-education policy. In summary the following points stand out. First, it is clear that the resource demands for the universalization of primary education are heavily influenced by recent demographic trends. The overall need for additional school places at primary level is modest because the age-cohorts entering schools are shrinking. The position of the economically deprived parts of China, where enrolment ratios are lower, is different—here new school places will be needed. However the resources required are not great given China's relatively low unit costs. Teachers' salaries are a relatively small proportion of GNP per capita when compared to other developing countries. This, taken together with other parameters, greatly reduces the public cost of universalizing basic education.

Second, devolution of responsibility to the local level for primary-school development has been accompanied by increasing emphasis on the generation of resources from the community. A wide range of instruments is used, including local taxes, fees, and voluntary contributions. These sources of income now account for large parts of the recurrent resources available to primary schools. This has had the effect of widening the gap in expenditure per student between rich and poor areas. The existence of large numbers of non-government teachers in poor areas further contributes to the disparities in educational investment per child.

Third, the national policy framework for primary education is unusually detailed. It has set public targets for enrolment, retention, and graduation rates and has been accompanied by the development of Provincial and local criteria that may include the elimination of dangerous buildings, the provision of adequate classroom space and teachers, and discourage the employment of students with less than nine years' experience of schooling. The targets are widely publicized and local authorities are accountable for their achievement. Although data limitations make it difficult to assess progress in meeting the targets, the latter have nevertheless provided a focus for efforts to improve provision.

Fourth, teachers' salaries have been increased relative to other public-sector employees. In some areas salaries have been restructured to relate them to performance. This has provided incentives for effective teachers and appears to have benefited school management. In-service training and upgrading courses have been introduced to improve educational quality. New patterns of school organization have been adopted in many rural areas. In these the responsibility for the development of clusters of relatively poor schools falls to central primary schools. However, an examination of teaching loads, class-size, and student/teacher ratios suggests there may be scope for the more efficient use of trained teachers, at least in the larger schools, in more densely populated areas, and in secondary schools, where unit costs are highest. In rural schools where class-sizes tend to be small, there may still be scope for some further school amalgamation and/or the more widespread use of multigrade teaching to make better use of teachers' time.

In conclusion China has an impressive record of achievement in primary education. As a low-income country with a very large population it has succeeded in enrolling a large proportion of students in school, reducing repetition and drop-out, and taking steps to improve quality. Finally, in principle, many of the policy measures discussed in this case-study are of potential interest to other countries. Though the Chinese social, economic, and political context is unique, the framework for primary-education policy currently in place, the methods used to generate financial resources, the structural reform of teachers' salaries, and new patterns of school organization each have potential applications elsewhere.

3. Zimbabwe: Rapid Achievement of UPE, but at what Cost for Quality?

Zimbabwe is a country which has doubled its GER at primary level from around 60 to more than 120 within ten years of achieving independence, and almost all those who are in the primary-school age-group are now enrolled. It has been transformed from a country in which resources for education were profoundly maldistributed, and heavily concentrated in favour of the white community, to one in which there is open access to education for all racial groups, where primary schooling is compulsory, and where all who wish to do so can proceed to secondary schooling after completing Grade 7. This case-study examines how this has been achieved. It shows that Zimbabwe has much to teach other countries which are trying to achieve SFA. There are, however, positive and negative lessons. Whilst the quantitative impact of education policy has been remarkable, its effects upon the quality of schooling have been less than satisfactory. The ways in which these unintended consequences could have been avoided in Zimbabwe are explored.

3.1. The main educational reforms

In 1980/1, within a year of independence, the new government of Zimbabwe introduced a set of educational reforms designed to redress the disparities and inequalities inherited from the colonial regime. The earlier dual system of education, which had given whites access to the best schools via a system of school zoning, was abolished. Racial integration was introduced in all schools. Tuition fees were abolished at primary level, and primary schooling became formally compulsory for all children of primary school-age. Tuition fees were retained at secondary level. However, all pupils who had completed primary schooling were given the option of attending up to four years of secondary schooling.

These changes had an immediate and major impact upon school enrolments. As shown in Table 3.6, enrolments at both primary and secondary levels doubled over the two years 1979–81. Accordingly, UPE at primary level was achieved very quickly, and after 1981 primary enrolment growth, which averaged 3.5 per cent per year over the years to 1989, was determined mainly by the rate of growth of the primary age-group. At secondary level, starting from a much smaller base, rapid growth continued over the decade 1979–89, with a more than tenfold increase in

TABLE 3.6. *Schools and enrolments in Zimbabwe,*
1979–1989

Year	Primary		Secondary	
	Schools	Enrolments	Schools	Enrolments
1979	2,401	819,600	177	66,200
1980	3,161	1,236,000	197	74,300
1981	3,689	1,715,200	694	148,700
1985	4,234	2,216,900	1,215	482,000
1989	4,501	2,269,000	1,502	695,600

Sources: Govt. of Zimbabwe (1979–89).

enrolments. Tertiary education also expanded rapidly: the university in Harare quadrupled in size to more than 9,000 students over the decade to 1989; and at the polytechnic and the technical colleges student numbers rose from 3,000 to around 14,000 over the same period.

Such a pace of expansion would have been exceedingly difficult to manage in any country. In Zimbabwe, proceeding as it did from the legacy of a colonial government which had been completely hostile to the idea of universal access to schooling, there were neither plans nor sufficient resources available to aid its implementation. There was, accordingly, an urgent need for policies to maximize the efficiency of resource use—particularly school buildings and teachers—to increase rapidly the supply of teachers, to reduce the unit costs of schooling in order to contain the budgetary impact of expansion, and to explore alternative means of generating resources to sustain it.

In order to improve the utilization of existing buildings and equipment two major reforms were introduced. First, a system known locally as 'hot seating' was introduced into all urban and some rural schools. This is essentially a double-session system, whereby schools accommodate two different populations of pupils each day. It differs from other double-shift arrangements in that two sets of teachers, rather than just one set, are employed. It therefore makes more efficient use of existing classrooms, whilst leaving the teacher/pupil ratio unchanged. Secondly, automatic promotion was introduced throughout primary and the first four years of secondary schooling. By reducing the length of time taken for the average pupil to progress through school, and for any given level of total costs, it allows a higher proportion of the eligible age-group to be enrolled in school.

The main way of increasing teacher supply in response to the massive build-up of enrolments was to employ untrained teachers, particularly at primary level. Although many were well motivated, their low levels of basic schooling proved to be a constraint on achieving qualitative improvement in many schools. This remained a major problem throughout the 1980s, and even by 1990 almost half of the primary schoolteachers then employed had received no formal teacher training.

The second way of increasing teacher supply was via an accelerated teacher education programme introduced in 1981. The Zimbabwe Integrated National Teacher Education Course (ZINTEC) was a low-cost approach to help alleviate the massive shortage of trained teachers. Although the course lasted four years, only the first and last terms of this period were spent at college, with the remainder of the time being spent teaching in the schools. This programme expanded rapidly, and at its peak in the mid-1980s, there were five regional centres having a total of around 3,000 graduates annually. Subsequently the programme contracted—not because it proved unsatisfactory, but mainly because its consequences could not be afforded from a budgetary point of view, owing to the links between salaries and the training qualification of teachers.

Reductions in the unit costs of schooling were secured in a number of ways. First, class-sizes were standardized throughout the system which involved increasing the size of classes in many of the more privileged schools. Secondly, resources were allocated to schools—for payment of teachers' salaries and purchase of school books and equipment—strictly on the basis of the number of pupils enrolled. These per capita grants set a maximum for the publicly funded unit costs, which varied from school to school only with the seniority and level of qualifications of the teaching staff employed. Thirdly, the curriculum was reformed: the number of subjects, and the topics within them were rationalized; examinations were localized; science teaching at secondary level was improved and made more cost-effective by the design of science 'kits' which enabled the teaching of science to proceed even in the absence of a laboratory, running water, electricity, or a trained teacher. Finally, vocational subjects were introduced throughout the system, but particularly so at secondary level. This was intended to provide more appropriate education for youngsters about to join the labour market. It was hoped (notwithstanding the rather discouraging experience in other African countries with vocational education at secondary level) that it would encourage the formation of useful skills, enhance the productivity of the labour force, and, in some cases, reduce educational costs by producing marketable goods and services in the schools.

In some ways the most influential reform introduced by the new government in 1980 concerned the new arrangements for the financing of the education system. For reasons which will be indicated later, it was

TABLE 3.7. *Summary of financing mechanisms for primary and secondary schooling in Zimbabwe, 1989/90*[a]

Type of school	Items provided and financed by government	Items provided by 'responsible authorities'	Items provided/ financed by parents/community
Govt. primary	Salaries of all staff Maintenance All other materials and running expenses		Construction of school buildings and provision of building materials General purpose fees $Z1.50– $Z27 p.a. Voluntary additional community support
Non-Govt. primary	Salaries of teaching staff Per capita grant: $Z17.35 per child (average)	Maintenance Salaries of non-teachers Furniture, equipment, textbooks Running expenses of schools	Construction of school buildings and provision of building materials General purpose fees, building fund, sports fees Voluntary additional community support
Govt. secondary	Construction of school buildings and provision of building materials Maintenance Salaries of all staff All other materials and running expenses		Fees: $Z135 tuition p.a.; $Z510 boarding p.a. General purpose fees $Z6– $Z36 p.a. Voluntary additional community support

clear that the government would be unable to fund a substantial part of the additional costs involved in the move to UPE, particularly in the light of its wish also to universalize access to secondary schooling within a very short period of time. Accordingly, the government deliberately devolved a considerable part of the responsibility for planning, financing, and implementing the expansion of the school system to local communities and households. Without this, the doubling of the number of primary schools and the eightfold increase in the number of secondary schools that occurred during the 1980s would not have been achieved. The detailed

TABLE 3.7. (cont'd)

Type of school	Items provided and financed by government	Items provided by 'responsible authorities'	Items provided/ financed by parents/community
Non-Govt. secondary	Building grants to cover up to 5% of costs of construction of buildings and materials Salaries of teaching staff Per capita grant: $Z15 per child	Maintenance Salaries of non-teachers Furniture, equipment, textbooks Running expenses of schools	95% of construction costs and materials for school buildings Fees: $Z60–$Z3,000 tuition p.a.; $Z300–$Z8,000 boarding p.a. General purpose fees, building fund, sports fees $Z6–$Z36 p.a.

[a] The value of the Zimbabwe dollar declined from $US1.6 in 1980 to $US0.6 in 1985 and $US0.4 in 1990. These are average official rates for each calendar year (IMF 1991).

Sources: Interviews with officials from the Ministry of Education and Culture, Govt. of Zimbabwe; Statutory Instrument No. 243 of 1989, Govt. of Zimbabwe; Education Act (No. 5 of 1987), Govt. of Zimbabwe; interviews with schools' personnel, Zimbabwe.

financing arrangements which were adopted at primary and secondary levels are of importance to the general theme of this book. Each of these are summarized, for both government and non-government schools, in Table 3.7, and they will now be briefly described.

3.2. Primary schooling

It is often stated that primary schooling in Zimbabwe is free to the individual, or his parents. This derives, historically, from the abolition of tuition fees at primary level shortly after independence. Although this act certainly made primary schooling cheaper for many families, it dit not, by any means, succeed in making it free.

As regards government primary schools, after 1980 parents and communities became responsible for constructing all school buildings and for the supply or purchase of the building materials. The government, on the other hand, held responsibility for maintaining the buildings, for paying the salaries of all school staff, for providing all teaching materials and other consumables, and for meeting the running expenses of the schools.

The financing of extra-curricular activities became the responsibility of the parents. Headmasters were required to establish a 'general purpose fund', contributions towards which, in 1990, ranged from $Z1.5 to a permitted maximum of $Z27 per year per child.[14] This was expected to finance sports activities, and other cultural, physical, or intellectual pursuits beyond the confines of the formal curriculum.

In the case of non-government primary schools (comprising over 90 per cent of the total number of primary schools), the task of school management is delegated to a 'responsible authority'—usually, though not always, the individual or organization under whose auspices the school was originally established. In these cases the division of financial responsibilities is somewhat different. The parents or local community again have to construct the schools themselves, including provision of building materials. Central government pays the salaries of the teaching staff. But the responsible authorities have to provide the furniture, equipment, and textbooks in the schools, pay the salaries of non-teaching staff, if any, maintain the buildings, and cover the running costs of the schools.

These expenses are met in two main ways. First, the parents pay fees to the responsible authorities for these purposes. Most non-government primary schools maintain a 'building fund', into which parents are expected to pay fees each year. Their level varies from school to school, but in 1990 minimum annual payments were around $Z5 per child, and maxima were about $Z20. In addition, parents usually were required to pay a 'sports fee' of between $Z1 and $Z6 per year. 'General purpose fund' fees can accommodate the difference between building and sports fund charges and the permitted maxima of $Z27 in fees annually, per child. Clearly, in non-government schools less of the parents' contributions to the general purpose funds are available for extra-curricular activities than is the case in government schools.

The second main source of funds for the responsible authorities is a grant to each non-government primary school, linked to the number of pupils enrolled in each year of study. This 'per capita grant' stood, in 1990, at an average of $Z17.35 per pupil—although the rates were lower for younger children, and higher in the upper grades—of which the responsible authorities kept 10 per cent as a contribution to their own administrative expenses. The per capita grant was intended to supply the pupils with exercise books and textbooks, and buy all other teaching materials needed to run the school. As we shall see, it has been severely inadequate for these purposes.

3.3. Secondary schooling

A similar distinction to that at primary level is made between government and non-government secondary schools. In the case of the former, just

---

[14] The value of the Zimbabwe dollar declined from $US1.6 in 1980 to $US0.6 in 1985 and $US0.4 in 1990. These are average official rates for each calendar year (IMF 1991).

as at primary level, the government pays for the salaries of all staff, and meets the costs of maintenance, teaching materials, and running expenses. Unlike the situation in government primary schools, however, the government takes responsibility for the full costs of constructing the school buildings at its own secondary schools. Furthermore, tuition fees are also charged. These fees were, in 1990, $Z135 for day-students and $Z510 for boarders, per year. These were in addition to general purpose fund contributions, which varied between a minimum of $Z6 and a maximum of $Z36 per year per child, and which were used for the same purposes as at primary level.

In the secondary non-government schools financial arrangements are different. As at primary level, a strong degree of community support is expected by the government. Here, however, 95 per cent (rather than all) of the costs of building the facilities have to be met by the parents or the communities themselves, with the other 5 per cent being provided by the government. The State also pays the salaries to the teachers, as at primary level. The responsible authorities—most usually, a district council, mission, farm, mine, or private foundation—arrange for the purchase of furniture, equipment, and textbooks, pay the salaries of the non-teaching staff, and cover the maintenance and running costs of the schools. Just as at primary level the non-government secondary schools receive a per capita grant—which is supposed to fund the purchase of books and teaching materials—which, in 1990, stood at $Z15 per pupil per year (subject to a 10 per cent deduction by the responsible authority, as at primary level).

In addition to these sources of funds, however, the non-government secondary schools charge tuition fees, the levels of which varied between $Z60 and $Z190 for district council day-schools, $Z315–900 for mission boarding-schools, $Z315–3,000 for the 'trust' day-schools, and $Z2,500–8,000 for the 'trust' boarding-schools. Clearly, with resource inputs per student, which at the extremes differ by a factor of 50 for day-schools, the educational experience of children in different kinds of secondary school varies enormously.

3.4. Problems arising from the modes of financing adopted

The methods of financing described above have led to the emergence of a number of pervasive problems in the pattern of provision of education in Zimbabwe. The government is presented with a paradox arising from its own success. The major achievement, of course, is the enormous expansion of access to schooling documented earlier. The promises which were given during the immediate pre-independence period in terms of providing universal access to schooling have been kept—to an extent which most observers did not believe possible. But the ways in which this was achieved have led to a pattern of provision which is highly unequal, and which discriminates much more strongly in favour of the richer groups in society than is compatible with the longer-term social and economic objectives of the government. There are a number of dimensions to this problem.

First, the heavy dependence upon individuals, families, and communities for the provision of facilities, equipment, and materials, through fees and voluntary contributions at both secondary and primary levels, has led to a highly differentiated structure of schooling which is itself strongly correlated with the incomes of parents. For example, a field-trip to some of the more disadvantaged border areas of the country revealed that there were still, in 1990, many pupils learning under self-help shades which leaked when it rained (see Colclough *et al.* 1990: 94). Logs, supported by bricks or stones, served as chairs for the pupils. Most of the blackboards needed painting, and what was written on them was hardly legible. On some of the former commercial farms, old tobacco barns and storerooms served as classrooms, with little effort having been made to transform them for their new uses. There were primary schools where up to nine teachers shared a three-bedroom house, and those who were married were often forced to live apart from their families. These facilities contrasted sharply with those typically available in the urban centres.

As regards materials support, those schools dependent only upon the per capita grant from government found it insufficient to purchase the books and equipment needed. During the same field-trip in 1990, one primary head indicated that his pupils needed two exercise books per term for each of six subjects taught. The cost of each exercise book was $Z0.77, which for all, would amount to some $Z27.72 per pupil per year. Even one exercise book per term for each subject would amount to $Z13.86, which would almost exhaust the average per capita grant of $Z15.62 (after deduction of the 10 per cent service charge payable to the responsible authority). This would have left less than $Z2 per year per pupil to finance the cost of textbooks and other learning materials needed for each child. This was completely inadequate, and accounts for the widespread sharing of textbooks between many children which is found throughout the non-government primary-school system. It is common for five or more children to share one textbook, and there are many cases of classes where the only available texts are held by the teacher. Thus, unless parents are able and willing to supplement school resources by buying additional materials, the quality of the education available to their children is seriously affected.

The situation has been further complicated by the fact that many families find themselves unable to pay the non-tuition fees that are expected at primary level. The sense in which it is true that primary schooling is free is that those who are unable to pay the fees are not expelled from school, as happens at secondary level. Although this policy is surely right, its effects have been perverse. Many rural non-government schools appear to be able to collect only about half of the amount in fees that parents are expected to pay. Since these monies are not made up by central government, the result has been that the resource base of the school is further undermined, with the available funds (excluding the per capita grant) being required to accommodate the needs of up to twice as many pupils as intended.

At secondary level the pressures on the poor are even more intense. On the one hand the main reason for the non-participation in secondary schooling by 20 per cent of the age-group, is that their parents cannot afford to pay the school fees. This was cited as the main explanation for low continuation rates from Grade 7 to Form 1 by teachers in a sample of eighteen rural schools visited in 1990 (Colclough *et al*. 1990: 83). On the other hand the per capita grant provided by the government has been, at $Z15, lower than that for the primary sector, yet the cost of textbooks and materials at secondary level is considerably more. For schools in poor areas, where parents cannot afford to pay large fees, the schools have therefore been faced with a difficult choice: either to charge high fees yet not be able to enrol many of the eligible pupils in their catchment area, or to charge fees that are affordable for most families, but which will be incapable of generating sufficient resources to enable the school to provide a reasonable education for the pupils enrolled.

There are two other aspects of the system of financing primary and secondary education which have further strengthened the resource bias in favour of schools which serve the richer communities. First, all schools receive the same per capita grants, irrespective of whether they are already well resourced from high fees charged, and afforded, by the parents. Secondly, the practice of paying the actual salary bill for teachers in post (subject to a quota on the number of teachers, determined by a target teacher/pupil ratio at each level) has meant that those schools with the most experienced and the best-qualified teachers receive the highest subsidies per pupil. Since such schools are usually in urban centres, and are already well resourced (these are the schools that can attract the best teachers), the best schools, accessible only to the children of the richer families, receive the highest per capita subsidies from the State.

In summary, we can say that the present system of financing primary and secondary education in Zimbabwe has had very unfortunate consequences for equity. The children of the poorest 20 per cent of households do not generally go to secondary school. Furthermore many of them can only attend primary school because their parents are able to avoid paying the fees. This reduces the quality of schooling available both to themselves and to others in the same schools whose parents are able to pay. Thus, for those who do go to school the quality of their education is

TABLE 3.8. *Public expenditures in Zimbabwe: education and total,*
1979/80–1988/9 ($Zm.)

	1979/80	1980/1	1983/4	1988/9
Education				
1 Recurrent	119.0	216.9	455.9	1,012.6
2 Capital	3.4	6.1	24.5	27.0
3 Total	122.4	223.0	480.4	1,039.6
Total				
4 Recurrent	828.3	958.7	2,232.7	4,437.1
5 Capital	54.9	65.8	208.0	523.0
6 Appropriations	143.2	177.7	425.4	1,167.0
7 Total	1,026.4	1,202.2	2,866.1	6,127.2
Proportions				
1/4 (%)	14.4	22.6	20.4	22.8
3/7 (%)	11.9	19.1	16.8	17.0
6/7 (%)	14.0	14.8	14.8	19.0

Sources: Govt. of Zimbabwe (1984–9; 1987; Tables 7.6 and 7.7; and 1989).

strongly correlated with their household incomes and with the prosperity of their local community. Those schools in areas where families cannot afford either to pay high fees, or to provide voluntary monetary contributions, are seriously disadvantaged in comparison with better-off communities. All of this institutionalizes the privileged access of the richer groups to good-quality education, to better prospects for promotion to higher levels of education, and thence to the better jobs in the labour market. The critical question, therefore, is whether anything could have been done by government to alleviate these circumstances, bearing in mind that the pubic resources available were severely constrained. It is to a consideration of this question that we now turn.

3.5. Public expenditure on education, 1980–90

Broadly speaking, whether or not more could have been done by the government to improve the quality of primary schooling in the large number of schools serving poor communities depends upon whether the resources available for primary schooling could have been increased, or whether its costs could have been reduced.

As to the former, the expansion programme at primary and secondary levels proved to be so expensive that it is very unlikely that yet more resources could have been found from the public purse. The impact of enrolment increases upon total costs was very strong within a year of independence having been gained. At the same time the salaries of

TABLE 3.9. *Public expenditures on education in Zimbabwe, 1979/80–1988/9 and unit costs by level ($Zm.)*

	1979/80	1980/1	1983/4	1988/9
Total recurrent ed. (nominal)	119.0	216.9	455.9	1,012.6
High income CPI[a]	100.0	114.6	117.7	290.6
Total recurrent ed. (real)	119.0	189.3	256.6	348.5
Primary recurrent (nominal)	72.2	145.0	282.0	550.5
Primary recurrent (real)	72.2	126.5	158.7	189.4
Enrolments (000)[b]	1,236	1,715	2,132	2,267
Real unit costs	58	74	74	84
Secondary recurrent (nominal)	34.9	46.6	106.6	309.6
Secondary recurrent (real)	36.9	60.7	60.0	106.5
Enrolments (000)	74	169	416	696
Real unit costs	470	360	144	153

[a] Weighted average value for last calendar year mentioned in each column.
[b] As at January for last calendar year mentioned in each column.
Source: Govt. of Zimbabwe (1979–89, 1989, 1990).

African teachers rose sharply, as the earlier practice of salary discrimination between blacks and whites was abandoned. Accordingly, as shown in Table 3.8, public spending on education doubled between 1979/80 and 1980/1. It rose from 14 per cent to almost 23 per cent of total recurrent expenditures, and from 12 per cent to 19 per cent of total government spending in that year. The proportion of total spending allocated to education fell back slightly to around 17 per cent in 1983/4, where it remained during the rest of the 1980s. That record is remarkable, given that statutory appropriations (which include debt service) increased from 14 per cent to 19 per cent of total spending over those years. Unlike the situation in many other countries facing a rising debt burden, education spending actually managed to capture an enhanced proportion of the non-debt-service recurrent spending at this time. Not only did government expenditure on education increase in relative terms over the 1980s, but its absolute real rate of increase was very marked. As shown in Table 3.9, the real value of educational spending almost tripled over the nine years to 1988/9, representing an average annual rate growth of 12.7 per cent. This was much faster than the real growth of public spending as a whole which averaged 8 per cent per year over the same period.

Thus, whatever criterion is used, education appears to have been given extremely high priority in public spending in Zimbabwe after independence had been gained. It is important to note that out of fifty-nine low- and middle-income countries for which data are available, only fifteen (25 per cent) allocated a greater proportion of total budgetary resources to educational expenditure than Zimbabwe in the mid-1980s (Lockheed and Verspoor 1990: Table 15). The weighted average proportion of government spending devoted to education in such countries in 1987 was around 12 per cent (World Bank 1989*a*: Table 11). These comparisons, whilst not decisive, indicate that Zimbabwe would probably have found it extremely difficult to have allocated a higher proportion of public spending to education than it did in the late 1980s, except, perhaps, for short periods of time.

The second question concerns whether or not the unit costs of schooling might have been reduced, thereby to secure budgetary savings. A sharply different pattern for the evolution of real unit costs at primary and secondary levels is revealed by Table 3.9: although primary unit costs rose steeply in the first year of independence, and again in the late 1980s, those at secondary level fell sharply, and consistently throughout the period. What explains these differences?

At primary level the sharp increase in unit costs in 1980/1 was caused mainly by the upward revision in the salaries of African teachers, mentioned earlier, which increased average earnings in the education sector by 53 per cent between 1979 and 1980.[15] The cost increases later on came mainly from the increased proportion of trained teachers emerging from the ZINTEC scheme, and the impact which this brought for average teacher earnings. Ultimately such cost increases could not be afforded, and the scheme had to be much reduced. Nevertheless, the real increases in unit costs at primary level were somewhat lower than those of average teacher earnings over the whole decade, as a result of the series of cost-saving education reforms introduced by the government, discussed earlier.

The main reason for the very different cost experience at secondary level is that, unlike the case of primary schooling, most secondary enrolments prior to independence comprised children of settler families who were attending very high-cost schools. The sharp restructuring of access for black children, and the much lower per capita expenditures which were associated with the rapid expansion of secondary-school facilities, resulted in secondary unit costs declining sharply in the early 1980s. The fact that those unit costs subsequently remained stable reflects the tight control which was maintained by the Ministry of Education and Culture over pupil/teacher ratios and other critical cost factors at the school level. Although this must be a matter of judgement, it is difficult to see how more favourable unit costs outcomes could have been achieved. The reduction in the costs of secondary schooling were dramatic. At primary level, unit costs increased somewhat, notwithstanding the introduction of

---

[15] See Govt. of Zimbabwe (1989: Tables 7.1 and 8.1).

efficiency reforms, following from the salary increases associated with the ending of racial discrimination in the teaching profession. On political grounds there was little room for manœuvre over the extent to which salary costs could have been further contained. To the extent that costs increased, these were probably a necessary and justifiable consequence of Zimbabwe's historical legacy.

3.6. Conclusion

Zimbabwe achieved a massive increase in enrolments throughout the school/university system over the 1980s, and UPE was reached. This was a consequence of introducing substantial reforms to the structure and financing of education: schooling became compulsory, repetition was abolished, and new low-cost teacher-training schemes were introduced, there was a sharp increase in untrained teachers, pupil/teacher ratios were increased, communities were required to finance a large part of educational costs, yet real public spending on education also tripled, reflecting a substantial increase in the priority allocated to education in total public spending. But in spite of these impressive quantitative achievements, the quality of schooling remained extremely variable, and the particular mode of subsidy/fee incidence used to finance the system discriminated strongly against the poorer communities. The result was a system of bad schools for the poor majority and good schools for the rich.

If these unfortunate consequences were to have been avoided, however, the alternative policy choices available to the government were very limited. As has been shown, strong measures to reduce the unit costs of schooling were introduced. Measures further to increase the intensity of teacher-use or lower their average costs would have jeopardized the quality of schooling even more.[16] Equally, there was little chance of increasing public spending on education beyond the 22 per cent of the budget which it already consumed. Although there were ways of increasing resources for education via tax reforms of various kinds, their impact would have been marginal rather than fundamental in this already heavily taxed economy (World Bank 1987).

In fact, it is difficult to avoid the conclusion that education in Zimbabwe expanded more quickly than was consistent with effective and equitable management. The real question concerns secondary schooling. If, for example, secondary enrolments had increased only fivefold, rather than almost tenfold, over the decade to 1988/9, the savings to government of

---

[16] Class-sizes were already high; the proportion of untrained teachers was large; and the earnings of primary and secondary schoolteachers as a multiple of income per capita was 5.6 in 1983, i.e. after the salary increases of the early 1980s. The average for SSA as a whole, in the same year, was 5.3 (World Bank 1988*a*: Table A23) suggesting that, by international standards, teachers' earnings were not excessive.

$Z150 m. in that year would have amounted to more than 28 per cent of recurrent expenditures on primary schooling (see Table 3.9). Cumulated over the decade these savings would have represented a very substantial potential means of tackling the qualitative problems in a primary system, and, therefore, of improving the capacities of pupils who would subsequently progress into secondary school. Thus, although education policy in Zimbabwe has been pursued with tremendous energy and imagination, it has only been a qualified success. It was probably a mistake to expand all levels of education very rapidly at the same time. A more measured approach—giving early priority to achieving SFA at primary level and providing open access to secondary schooling at a rather later date—would, ultimately, have been a more equitable and efficient strategy.

4. Sri Lanka: Beyond UPE in a Low-Income Country

Sri Lanka has an impressive record of educational provision. Although it is a low-income country with a GNP per capita of about $430 (1989), it had gross enrolment ratios of 103 at primary, 66 at secondary, and 4 at tertiary level by the mid-1980s. Primary gross enrolment ratios of more than 90 were first achieved in the 1960s. Since independence in 1947, Sri Lanka has consistently ranked high on indices of social development. Its rank on the UNDP Human Development Index (a combination of performance on life expectancy, literacy, and real GDP per capita) is similar to that of countries with much higher incomes, e.g. Democratic Republic of Korea, Peru, Syria, and Thailand, all of which have a GNP per capita over $1,000 (UNDP 1991: 122).

These achievements have been the consequence of consistent policy to provide free education at all levels. Schooling facilities are widely distributed throughout the island and children of primary-school age rarely have to travel more than 4 km. to attend school. It is significant that higher-education enrolments have always constituted a small proportion of the total. Though unit costs in the universities vary between ten and thirty times those in the school system, depending on the subject, a policy of restricted growth has limited the proportion of the national education budget allocated to higher education. The quality of education has been enhanced by a free textbook scheme for all children in grades 1 to 11[17]

---

[17] Under the old nomenclature primary schools comprised kindergarten and grades 1–5, secondary schools covered grades 6–10, and upper secondary included grades 11 and 12. In the 1980s kindergarten became year 1, primary schooling extended from years 1–5, junior secondary from years 6–11, and senior secondary included years 12 and 13. The nomenclature used in this case-study follows this more recent pattern.

introduced in 1979, innovative curriculum development at all levels since the 1960s, and high-quality teacher training and in-service programmes.

This case-study explores recent experience in trying to sustain the gains of the past and extend schooling for all to the remaining parts of the primary age-cohort. It focuses on three main questions of general relevance to SFA. First, how efficient and equitable is the current deployment of teaching resources and how might changes contribute towards improved quality and access? Second, what role can a donor play in supporting enrolment growth and improved achievement in educationally deprived areas? Third, what scope exists for using cost-recovery mechanisms to help finance improvements in teaching and learning?

4.1. Background

There are about 9,600 schools in Sri Lanka and a total of approximately 3.9 million students are enrolled. Unusually, education is provided in two language media, Sinhala and Tamil, from grade 1 to university degree level. Government schools are divided into types and there is no clear division between primary and secondary schools (see Table 3.10). Type 3 schools cater for the early grades; type 1 and 2 schools include both lower and higher grades. Non-selective schooling is available up to grade 11. National selection examinations control access to grades 12 and 13 and to higher education.

In addition to government schools, basic education is provided in *pirivenas* (temple schools) and in private schools, most of which cater for urban middle-class children. Collectively these account for a small proportion of total enrolment. Enrolments in the school system have grown from 2.8 million in 1971 to 3.9 million in 1988. The number of schools grew by about 10 per cent whilst enrolments increased by about 40 per cent. Primary enrolments (grades 1–5) expanded slowly from about 1.8 million to 2 million over this period. Enrolments above grade 8 increased from 378,000 to 985,000, representing 13.5 per cent of the total in 1971 and 25 per cent by 1988. Thus enrolment growth has been concentrated above grade 8 as would be expected from the early progress made towards high gross enrolment ratios in primary grades.[18] Repetition rates have remained high, particularly in the primary grades (years 1–5), where rates of about 9 per cent have been typical. Although repetition falls to less than 5 per cent between grades 8 and 10, over 40 per cent of students repeat O level in grade 11 and about 60 per cent of A-level students typically repeat grade 13. Overall, these high rates of repetition are a significant source of internal inefficiency.

[18] Technical difficulties arise in calculating the growth rates at different levels as a result of changes in the length of the school system, the age of entry, and the treatment of kindergarten classes. The estimates we have made try to take these into account.

TABLE 3.10. *Distribution of government schools in*
Sri Lanka by type, 1988

Coverage		No.	%
Single-teacher schools		520	5
(up to grade 5 or less)			
Type 3	Grades 1–5	3,480	36
Type 2	Grades 1–11	3,915	41
Type 1[a]	Grades 1–13	1,520	17
TOTAL		9,635	

[a] Type 1 schools are divided into three categories—Type 1a:
all subject streams and boarding facilities; Type 1b: all
subject streams; Type 1c: arts and commerce streams only.
Source: World Bank (1989*d*: 7).

TABLE 3.11. *Unit costs in Sri Lankan schools*

	1977	1980	1983	1986	1989
Unit cost	1,064	874	917	1,029	1,038

Note: Costs are shown in constant 1987 rupees. The value of
the rupee was $US0.034 in 1987. This is the official average
rate for the calendar year, as given by IMF 1991.
Source: World Bank (1989*d*: 49).

The cumulative drop-out rate was estimated at 11.6 per cent for grades
1–5, and 18.6 per cent for grades 6–8 in 1987. Thus about 88 per cent of
the entry cohort reach grade 5, 71 per cent reach grade 8, and 16 per cent
successfully complete grade 11 passing at a level sufficient to enter A-
level classes (World Bank 1989*d*: 8). There are wide disparities in the
amount of schooling received by children from different income groups.
Estimates of drop-out in a sample of thirty schools in an economically
deprived area suggest that in twelve of the schools less than half the grade
1 entrants completed grade 5 (Baker 1986: 249). In urban schools, by
contrast drop-out rates are generally very low at primary level. School-
avoidance rates correlate with family income and are greatest amongst
the poorest households (Govt. of Sri Lanka 1984).

The expansion of the education system and the provision of free education was sustained from 1965 to 1975 by allocating between 10 and 15 per
cent of public expenditure to education. In the late 1970s the proportion
of government expenditure allocated to education was reduced and, by
the 1980s, had stabilized a little above 8 per cent. This reduction was not

TABLE 3.12. *Average values and range of variation in student/teacher ratios between districts by grade in Sri Lanka, early 1980s*

	Mean	Range[a]	Standard deviation
Grade 1–5[b]	34.6	28–48	6.83
Grade 6–11	20.4	18–25	2.43
Grade 12–13	13.0	10–21	2.50

[a] Range indicates the lowest and highest district-level average values.
[b] Using the nomenclature described in n. 17.
Source: Ariyadasa *et al.* (1986: 31).

TABLE 3.13. *Average values and range of variation in student/teacher ratios between districts by type of school in Sri Lanka, early 1980s*

	Student/Teacher			Student/Trained teacher		
	Average	Range	Standard deviation	Average	Range	Standard deviation
Type 1	25	22–33	2.83	44	38–60	5.44
Type 2	27	24–41	6.79	45	34–74	11.07
Type 3	32	23–52	7.19	45	32–128	18.18

Source: Ariyadasa *et al.* (1986: 32–3).

reflected in reduced expenditure per child (see Table 3.11) as the size of the total government budget increased as a proportion of GNP. This increase was a consequence of large commitments to development in other sectors, e.g. the Mahaweli Irrigation scheme and the Million Houses Program. Educational expenditure as a proportion of GNP has been fairly stable at about 3 per cent of GNP throughout the 1980s.

4.2. The use of resources

First, we consider the equity and efficiency of resource use and their implications for strategies to achieve SFA. Here, there are two particular issues of general interest—the distribution of teachers and the utilization of their time. Differences in average student/teacher ratios by grades and by school type, and the range of their variation is shown in Tables 3.12 and 3.13.

Student/teacher ratios for 1989 (World Bank 1989*d*: 55) suggest few improvements since the early 1980s, and it also seems unlikely that the dispersion around the mean has diminished significantly. The implication of these tables is that student/teacher ratios are greatest in the lower grades, and that the extreme values may be very high. Since average salaries of primary-grade teachers are lower than those at secondary level differences in expenditure per student will be greater than the ratios alone suggest.

These overall differences conceal the pattern of the distribution of teachers between grades within schools. Two main factors are at work. First, class-sizes tend to be smaller in the higher grades of primary school, especially in the rural areas, mainly because of the cumulative effects of drop-out. Second, in schools which have grades above primary, specialist teachers are employed for particular subjects and may teach relatively small classes of students who have survived beyond grade 5. They may therefore be underloaded, in the sense that they have a similar number of classes but far fewer students than colleagues in lower grades. There is considerable community pressure on many Type 3 schools to extend enrolments beyond grade 5 and to become recognized as Type 2 schools despite having few students reaching grade 6 and above. One result is that it is possible to find schools where class-size in grade 1 may exceed sixty whilst class size in grade 8 and above may be less than twenty. Thus grade 1 children experience much higher student/teacher ratios than, say, grade 8 students. It is reasonable to argue that at least part of the problem of higher repetition rates in the early grades is related to less-intensive contact with teachers.

There are other indications of disparities which reduce internal efficiency. Recurrent expenditure per child between educational districts varied by 1.7:1 in 1985. Non-salary recurrent expenditure per child varied even more—in six districts it was less than one-third that of Colombo which had the greatest allocations. Districts with lower recurrent expenditure per child also tend to be those where completion rates are lowest. Completion rates for the primary grades in different districts varied from more than 90 per cent to less than 50 per cent (Ariyadasa *et al.* 1986: 37).

The essential points are, therefore, that the provision of resources is lower in the primary grades and that there are substantial disparities between districts in both teachers and recurrent expenditure per student. This seems perverse from the point of view of an SFA policy, especially if, as seems likely, those schools with the highest rates of repetition and drop-out are also those with high student/teacher ratios and low recurrent support per child. Enhancing inputs to these schools could pay large dividends in terms of SFA.

The utilization of teachers' time is also problematic. The reasons for this lie both in the working of the school calendar and in the number of teaching days actually available. The official school year is about 180 days and it is on this basis that the primary school curriculum is planned. All schools, and particularly rural schools, are subject to events that diminish the number of teaching days utilized. The start of teaching is often delayed by the problems of registering new and old students who may not all arrive on the first day of term. Teaching may also be disrupted by the late arrival of teachers not living locally, organizing elaborate sports days, receiving official visitors, absenteeism in response to the economic demands upon children's (and increasingly teachers') time, and the suspension of normal teaching during public examination periods.

Formally, teachers, like other civil servants in Sri Lanka, have twenty-one days' casual leave and twenty days of sick-leave available annually. Many teachers make use of all or most of the casual leave days and a good number take all the sick-leave days available. When teachers are absent, especially in smaller schools, classes are often left without a teacher. One recent study (World Bank 1989*d*) estimated that classroom attendances by teachers are only 70 per cent of the level they would be if all teachers taught on all teaching days. Casual and sick-leave together, if fully taken, account for 22 per cent of the teaching days. Overrun absences alone accounted for 27.4 days per teacher (15 per cent of the total teaching days) in 1987. Baker's study of thirty schools indicated that teacher absenteeism was widespread—13 per cent of principals were absent from schools on the day of an unannounced visit; in one school half the teachers were not present and in another no teachers attended on one day with no notification to children or parents. This provides some illustration of the extent of the problem, though these may be extreme cases. Daily rates of student absenteeism varied between 10 per cent and 35 per cent in Baker's sample of schools showing that this is also a difficulty (Baker 1986: 229).

We can conclude that as many as 20 per cent of classes may be without a teacher on a particular day. In addition the number of normal teaching days over the year may be substantially less than the number assumed by the curriculum. Irregular attendance of teachers and students exacerbate the problem, especially in small rural schools, resulting in possible reductions of as much as 30–40 per cent in the teaching time experienced by students over a year. It must therefore be a priority to improve the management of schools in ways which promote their regular functioning and provide the full number of teaching days planned. There may also be some scope for curriculum redesign to reduce the learning difficulties that arise from irregular attendance where this seems unavoidable.

4.3. The role of foreign assistance

Sri Lanka has benefited from considerable inflows of international assistance and the magnitude of these, on a per capita basis, is amongst the highest in Asia. Official Development Assistance reached 7.5 per cent of GNP in 1987 (UNDP 1990: 165) which was exceeded only by Bangladesh and Bhutan. Though much of this assistance has been allocated to other sectors, the education sector has also benefited. In 1985 about 10 per cent of government spending on education and training was supported by external assistance, much of it to higher education (Lofstedt *et al.* 1985: 48). The emphasis of aid-supported basic-education projects has been on the more disadvantaged populations which have low enrolments and low levels of achievement.

It is instructive to consider one of these projects in order to illustrate some of the achievements, possibilities, and problems of external assistance. The Badulla Integrated Rural Development Project (BIRDP) includes an education component. In the first phase the Ministry of Education identified forty-two Tamil medium schools for a programme of development funded by the Swedish International Development Authority (SIDA). Literacy amongst Indian Tamils in the plantation area has been well below the national average (67 per cent compared to 87 per cent in 1981). Tamil medium plantation schools have the lowest primary and secondary enrolment rates in Sri Lanka. In 1984 less than a third of government teachers in plantation schools were trained and student/teacher ratios averaged 55:1. BIRDP was conceived to improve existing provision and increase enrolments, reduce repetition and drop-out, and to improve the process and content of formal schooling. It offers support for physical resources (buildings, furniture, equipment, learning materials) and includes a quality-improvement programme—the first of its kind in an IRDP. The quality-enhancement programme has four main elements: the reproduction and distribution of syllabi and curriculum material; the development of supplementary teaching and learning material; the in-service training of teachers and principals; and the development of supervision, information, and professional support systems (Little and Sivasithambaram 1991).

During the first phase of the project enrolments increased substantially in the Tamil medium project schools growing by 36 per cent from 4,607 in 1984 to 6,278 in 1988. Enrolment in all grades increased by about 10 per cent over this period nationally and the 6–11-year-old age-group as a whole increased in size at an annual rate of about 1 per cent (Lockheed and Verspoor 1990: 165). There is evidence that academic achievement increased in the project schools. Achievement tests were administered in mathematics and language in 1985 and 1987 to grade 4 students. Table 3.14 presents the results from these tests for the thirty-three schools that took part.

Improved performance was accompanied by an increase in the dispersion of scores as the number of students taking the tests grew. Since the maximum score on each test was 100 it is clear that the gains were

TABLE 3.14. *Grade 4 student achievement (marks out of 100) in Tamil language and mathematics in 1985 and 1987 in 33 project schools in Sri Lanka*

	1985	1987
Tamil language		
Mean Standard	16.70	27.76
deviation	11.38	20.63
No. in sample	352	526
Mathematics		
Mean	20.50	33.76
Standard deviation	13.19	18.87
No. in sample	352	526

Note: In each case the difference between the means for 1985 and 1987 is significant at the 1% level.

Source: Little and Sivasithambaram (1991: 107).

achieved from a low base. Not all project schools showed an increase in performance—in fact five experienced a decline in mean score. Seven control schools drawn from plantations outside the project were also tested. Achievement in this matched group of schools showed no achievement gain over the 1985–7 period.

Some flavour of the changes that have taken place can be illustrated by the experience of one school in the project which developed rapidly (Little and Sivasithambaram 1991). In this case enrolment has grown more than threefold from 261 in 1984 to 811 in 1989. The number of teachers has increased from six to fifteen, reducing the teacher/pupil ratio from 77 : 1 to 50 : 1 (it had been as high as 177 : 1 in the 1970s). Despite the near doubling of the population of the school between 1985 and 1987, the mean achievement scores of the grade 4 students increased from 25.5 to 30.54 in Tamil and 27.16 to 34.13 in mathematics. Three children succeeded in passing the grade 5 national scholarship examination in 1989 though none had done so in previous years. One of the ironies of this school's performance is that in some respects its success has actually resulted in a deterioration of conditions. Thus the classroom space per student, which has a nationally recommended minimum of 10 sq. ft., fell from 6.2 sq. ft. in 1984 to 5.4 sq. ft. In this case the classroom building programme did not keep up with the enrolment growth.

Factors which seem to have been responsible for the success of this school include a period of intensive supervision and interest from the project staff, an active school development society, low teacher mobility, links with nearby schools, and an active principal. A follow-up study has been conducted of two other plantation schools, one which has greatly improved the achievement of its students and one which has not. The schools are similar in size, catchment, and location. The more success- ful school experienced greater enrolment growth, had a greater rate of growth of student attendance, a more stable staff, less leave taken by teachers, more in-service participation and greater supervisory support (Little *et al*. 1991: 27).

The total project costs in the first phase averaged around $US10 per student enrolled in the project area per year. These externally financed costs are marginal in the sense that they are additional to the expenditure allocated by the Ministry of Education. The recurrent expenditure of the Ministry has grown roughly in line with the increased enrolments, with some assistance from SIDA on a temporary basis for additional teachers to overcome short-term bottlenecks in providing additional salaries. About three-quarters of externally financed expenditure was on buildings and furniture, multiplying many times the normal allocations for these purposes. The remaining 25 per cent ($US2–3 per student) was used to support the quality-improvement programme. External finance for this enabled the setting up of new administrative and distribution systems and provided the small but essential amounts of money needed by the project for travel, subsistence, and materials development which could not easily be provided within the normal working procedures of the Ministry. The costs can be compared with the recurrent unit cost of general education (grades 1–13) in Sri Lanka which was 911 rupees ($US30) in 1988 (World Bank 1989*d*: 49). We estimate average recurrent unit costs for grade 1–5 to be of the order of 600 rupees ($US20) (school census data 1987). Buildings have been constructed to local standards and the costs per classroom are between $US2,000 and $US3,000. The project has imported very little equipment (the major item being a project vehicle) and has not provided extensive training programmes outside Sri Lanka.

There are several tentative inferences that can be drawn from the experience of the BIRDP. First the project has increased the enrolments in Tamil medium schools at a rate more than three times greater than general enrolment growth. It has also realized significant achievement gains amongst a marginalized population with relatively low enrolment rates.

Second, the investment in buildings and furniture has been an integral part of a programme to improve teaching and learning and increase enrolment. Support for the development and distribution of teaching materials, and for the supervisory, monitoring, and in-service activities has been critical to the achievements so far. The quality-improvement programme has played a major role in ensuring the regular functioning of schools so that their performance becomes more similar to those in other parts of Sri Lanka.

Third, the donor has been able to alleviate bottlenecks which have limited the development of the schools in the project area. Though the schools should receive the same per capita support from the government as other schools, their location and history has determined that their basic fabric and complement of teachers is often well below national standards. Selective intervention has meant that building work has been able to proceed much faster than would otherwise have been the case and the means for improving school infrastructure have been established at sustainable levels of cost.

4.4. Cost-recovery and improving teaching and learning

The third policy question asks what scope exists for using cost-recovery mechanisms to help finance improvements in teaching and learning? Throughout the 1980s schools in Sri Lanka have been encouraged to explore methods of mobilizing resources from the community to supplement those provided centrally, and by the recently established provincial governments. These resources may be in the form of money or community support in kind or both. The extent of community support varies widely and is difficult to quantify, as is shown by a recent study (BRIDGES 1988). From this it is clear that it depends very much on characteristics specific to communities and the individuals who catalyse such efforts. A little over half of the schools in Sri Lanka in 1988 seemed to have active school-development societies which organize most of the non-monetary community support that schools receive.

Data on money raised by schools give an insight into the financial aspects of the system and its limitations. There are three recognized mechanisms. First, facilities fees are levied in all schools up to a statutory maximum which is graded into three bands depending on the type of school. In 1988 the maxima were between 3 and 5 rupees per month per student. Exemption from fees can be obtained on grounds of low income. If fees are not paid sanctions are not generally enforced. Second, school-development societies can collect unrestricted amounts from the community. They usually levy small membership fees annually (2–5 rupees) and may organize special fund-raising events. Third, old boys' and girls' associations provide financial support but they tend to exist only in well-established schools that serve relatively wealthy communities.

Fees and contributions generated about 2.9 per cent of recurrent expenditure in 1984 (Ariyadasa *et al.* 1986: 38). Twenty-seven per cent of the total collected was raised by schools in Colombo which has only 2.6 per cent of the total number of schools and just over 6 per cent of enrolments; 1987 data from the school census suggest that the majority of schools raise less than 1 per cent of their recurrent budget in this way.

A reanalysis of data from a national sample of 252 schools (Lewin with Berstecher 1989) showed that facilities fees are collected only in about 63 per cent of schools. The collections averaged less than 10 rupees per child per year in 49 per cent of the schools compared to a theoretical maximum of between 24 and 40 rupees per child per year depending on the type of school. School-development society funds are collected by about 54 per cent of schools. In 36 per cent of the schools the average collected was less than 10 rupees per child per year. The number of old boys' and old girls' associations is small. In the sample only 2.5 per cent of schools had money in these accounts. Invariably these schools also had large facilities fees and school-development society accounts.

The distribution of income between schools is therefore highly skewed. A small number of schools collect amounts indicating that almost all students have paid the fees. The great majority collect half or less of the theoretical maximum. School-development society funds usually have an income of a few rupees per child per year but there were five well-known state schools in the sample that managed to exceed 100 rupees per child per year. Amongst a group of private schools not in the main sample, income appears to average more than 500 rupees per child per year in school-development society funds alone. Some school-development society balances run into tens of lakhs (millions of rupees) but most are of the order of several thousand rupees.

Patterns of expenditure from school funds are also skewed. Of the facilities fees collected nationally in 1986 12.8 per cent was allocated to salaries of temporary teaching staff and ancillary workers, 11.9 per cent to library resources, 23.7 per cent to school sports, 8.7 per cent to stationery, 6.9 per cent to renovation, 10.4 per cent to term tests, and the remainder was unclassified. For school-development society expenditure 3.0 per cent was allocated to library acquisitions, 36.6 per cent to buildings, 12.5 per cent to sports, and the remainder was unclassified. The largest allocations are directed towards sports activities where much of the disbursement is committed to special events and to supporting teams made up of children from the upper grades; large expenditures are also incurred in producing test material for examination classes in grades 11 and 13. Building projects are most commonly supported from school-development society funds.

Fee income is not intended to supplement the recurrent costs of teachers' salaries, though some temporary staff are paid from such resources where they exist. It is meant for non-salary recurrent expenses and building projects. Most schools covering the primary grades have a nominal budget for non-salary recurrent expenses of the order of a few hundred rupees or less. Non-salary costs—maintenance, equipment, and furniture, utilities—are paid from central funds through provincial and district budgets. The free textbook programme is a national scheme which ensures the widespread availability of basic class-texts. Beyond this, however, the system is often unable to support the other needs of schools.

Lengthy delays are common in obtaining furniture and equipment such that it is often inadequate, basic services can be unreliable, and consumable material is very scarce since it has to be provided largely by the school, its teachers, or the students. In these circumstances non-salary income, if wisely spent, can make all the difference between a sterile classroom and one where curiosity and productive study are encouraged. The problem in Sri Lanka, as in many other developing countries, is how to ensure that schools have realistic amounts of money available at school level to meet needs specific to their circumstances.

It is clear that though significant sums are being raised the revenue generated is very unevenly distributed among schools. Indeed between a third and a half of schools appear to have little or no money in the relevant accounts. The problem of non-collection is greatest in Type 3 schools. These are the schools in which physical deprivation is greatest, teacher/student ratios often highest, school avoidance most frequent, and learning materials in shortest supply. Moreover, patterns of expenditure of money raised from the community appear to favour the needs of students in higher grades. It follows that further emphasis on cost recovery through the mechanisms described above is not likely to benefit those schools which are in greatest need. On the contrary it is likely to widen the gap in conditions between them and other schools. The implication is not that these mechanisms should be abandoned, since they can generate useful additional resources, rather that complementary measures are needed to ensure that schools serving poor communities where contributions cannot be collected are adequately supported through other means.

4.5. Conclusion

Sri Lanka has an impressive record of achievement in providing schooling to the great majority of its primary-age population. Nevertheless problems remain and this case-study has drawn attention to three policy areas where there are lessons of general applicability.

First, it is clear that the internal efficiency of the system remains low. The distribution of teaching resources is very uneven and is almost certainly a contributory factor to high repetition and drop-out rates which are concentrated in particular types of schools. Reducing the variation in student/teacher ratios between districts and schools would incur few extra costs but could bring learning gains. It would certainly be more equitable. There is also evidence of the underutilization of teaching resources. It may be feasible to introduce gradual changes in conditions of service so as to encourage higher teacher-attendance rates, possibly coupled with modest extra payments. More effective supervision and professional support might also improve school administration to the point where fewer days were lost as a result of organizational shortcomings.

Second, foreign assistance has a role to play in promoting increased enrolments and improvements in teaching and learning. The small example we have given illustrates the benefits of combining support for buildings, furniture, and equipment with quality-improvement programmes. It also shows that donor assistance can be important in overcoming bottlenecks. By focusing on an educationally deprived population it indicates that considerable progress towards SFA can result from selective interventions.

Finally, our analysis of fee-generating schemes to support school expenditures suggests that it would be unsound to place more emphasis on these until there are mechanisms to ensure that schools which cannot or do not generate income in this way are not unduly disadvantaged as a result. The schools with the greatest needs to improve their physical and educational quality are those with the least capacity to raise such additional resources. They are also the schools which tend to have the least favourable staffing ratios and working conditions. A commitment to SFA requires positive discrimination in favour of the most deprived schools.

5. Ghana: Educational Restructuring for Greater Efficiency

5.1. The setting

Until the mid-1970s, Ghana had one of the most developed and effective educational systems in Africa. It was, however, unusually protracted, and its costs, accordingly, were high. Primary schooling was free and compulsory (in law, although not in practice) for all pupils aged 5–11 years. Five years of secondary schooling led to O levels, a further two years, for those who stayed the course, led to A levels, and a further three to a university degree. As is common elsewhere, children left at various defined points in the system, for other forms of post-school training, or for the world of work.

The unusual aspect of this structure, however, was that, at the end of primary schooling, very few pupils succeeded in passing the Common Entrance Examination (CEE), which regulated entry to the secondary schools. Most pupils proceeded from primary to 'middle' schools, there to receive up to four years of post-primary schooling, during which time they might have several further attempts to pass the CEE. Typically, there were places at secondary school for less than 10 per cent of the age-cohort, which implied that competition for entry was fierce. Accordingly, most secondary-school pupils had already attended three or even four years of middle schooling prior to being selected for the secondary course. Since their years in middle school carried no credit, all secondary pupils had to attend for the full five years. By consequence, it was not unusual for students to have had seventeen years of schooling in primary, middle, and secondary schools prior to being admitted to university.[19]

The result was a high level of student attainment at secondary schools and at the universities, particularly in comparison with most other countries of SSA. However, the system was extremely expensive, and was an obvious candidate for reform. This had been attempted on various occasions during the 1970s without success.[20] But it was made inevitable by the severity of economic recession which Ghana experienced towards the end of that decade.

In common with many other African States at that time, the economy sustained a series of external shocks. The difficulties caused by domestic mismanagement of the economy were exacerbated by the sharp increases in petroleum prices in 1973 and again in 1978, and by a sustained fall in the prices of Ghana's major exports. In addition, the need to absorb over one million Ghanaians who unexpectedly returned from Nigeria contributed to the country's economic problems. By consequence, between 1970 and 1982 real per capita income fell by 30 per cent, import volumes dropped by one-third, and real export earnings fell by 52 per cent. Domestic savings and investment declined from their 1970 levels of 12 and 14 per cent of GDP, respectively, to insignificant proportions by 1982. Meanwhile, inflation was running at about 40 per cent per annum over the period. Over these twelve years only Chad and Uganda experienced a faster rate of economic decline than Ghana.[21] At the outset of the 1980s, therefore, the country was in a state of economic collapse.

These circumstances brought serious problems for the quality of education. Educational expenditure by the State fell in both relative and absolute terms, and amounted to only 3 per cent of GDP in 1985 compared with over 6 per cent in 1976. As the total amount of real resources for education shrank, their distribution became increasingly skewed towards high-cost urban schools serving the interests of a small proportion of the population.

[19] Further details of this structure, and of its consequences can be found in ILO (1981: 96–103).

[20] The most notable earlier attempt at reform was that which led to the report of the National Consultative Committee on Education Finance (Govt. of Ghana 1975). This committee, which had been set up by the Ministry of Education in 1974 had been instructed 'to find ways and means of reducing education expenditure . . . without detracting from the efficiency of the educational system or find fresh revenue sources for educational expenditure without burdening the citizens unduly'. A very wide range of recommendations was made, including the reduction of the length of schooling, the elimination of many subsidies, particularly for boarding at secondary and tertiary levels, and the introduction of student loans. The White Paper on Education published later in 1975 (no. 5/75) chose to ignore most of the committee's recommendations.

[21] A statistical summary of Ghana's progress over the years 1970–82, in comparison with that of other countries, can be found in the World Development Indicators tables of World Bank (1984*b*).

Due to declining salaries, trained teachers were leaving the profession, and had to be replaced by untrained personnel. It was estimated that, in the early 1980s, untrained teaching staff as a proportion of the total represented 51 per cent of primary and 25 per cent of middle school-teachers. Further, there appeared to be a lack of control over hiring practices resulting in the employment of excessive numbers of teachers and auxiliary staff, which contributed to high unit costs. Education materials, essential texts, and library books were often unavailable due to the lack of foreign exchange. The existing facilities were run down owing to unplanned cuts in maintenance expenditures. The system became increasingly overcrowded owing to the suspension of construction expenditures by the State.

In view of these pressures, it is not surprising to find that the quantitative picture also deteriorated: enrolments stagnated or declined at all levels of the system after 1980. The gross enrolment ratio at primary level fell from a peak of 80 in 1980 to around 70 by 1987, whilst at secondary level the ratio also declined slightly from its 1980 peak of 41. The absolute levels of university enrolments remained constant over those years.

Lack of effective planning was evident in many areas of the sector with no ceilings being applied to the provision of physical facilities, spatial requirements, teacher allocation, or financing. For example, an early government policy decision had been to provide secondary and tertiary boarding facilities in order to enable students from diverse tribal backgrounds to study together. By 1985, over 10 per cent of the budget for secondary and tertiary education was devoted directly to a food subsidy for students, and to the direct and indirect costs of boarding at those levels. Clearly, priorities had become seriously derailed.

5.2. The policy response

The Provisional National Defence Council, constituted when Flt. Lt. Jerry Rawlings took power in December 1981, had introduced an economic recovery programme (ERP) in 1983. During its first phase (1983–6) there was a strong emphasis on the economic sectors, using conventional macroeconomic instruments to liberalize the economy and to encourage resources to shift from traders to producers and from urban to rural areas. The second phase, however, covering the period 1986–8, placed much greater emphasis on the social sectors, including education.

Following extensive discussions with the World Bank, an adjustment credit was secured and a programme of educational reforms was introduced in 1987. The key objectives were to expand access to primary schools, to improve educational quality and efficiency, to improve the equity and efficiency of educational financing, and to strengthen the systems of planning and educational administration. In order to realize these objectives, a number of important changes have occurred. The government initiated a major restructuring of the education system, which involved the abolition of middle schools, and reducing the maximum length of the pre-university cycle from seventeen to thirteen years. During its introduction over the years 1987 to 1992, savings made were reallocated mainly to primary education, thereby generating resources to finance its further expansion. The school year was lengthened from thirty-six to forty weeks, partly to offset the time lost.

One of the main initiatives to improve the pedagogic efficiency of the school system has focused upon the junior secondary schools, which replaced middle schools, and now occupy grades 7–9. A considerable amount of attention was given to a redesign of the curriculum, with the intentions of making it more consistent with Ghanaian social and economic conditions, and of maximizing the use of local resources, thereby to reduce unit costs. This included some shift towards vocationalization of the junior secondary schools' curriculum, in recognition of the fact that most leavers from Grade 9 would be destined for self-employment of one kind or another.

By 1991, it seemed that much had been achieved. The JSS curriculum had been elaborated and introduced into schools, and teachers' guides for science instruction and for practice in the use of hand-tools had been developed. Almost all new junior secondary schools had, by 1990, received the new texts, science kits, science tools, and stationery. Reflecting this, educational expenditure on non-salary items increased from 2.8 per cent in 1986 to 3.1 per cent in 1987, and the planned provision rose to 8.5 per cent by 1988.

A National Planning and Implementation Committee was established to take responsibility for the training of JSS teachers. A modular post-middle-school teacher-training programme for upgrading untrained teachers was adapted to cater for O-level certificate-holders. In addition, since the government had announced that all untrained teachers would have to have received upgrade training by 1995 or face dismissal, the Ghana Organization of Teachers established evening classes to assist in skills upgrading. In order to attract good candidates into the teaching profession, allowances were introduced for trainee teachers, and, since many JSS teachers would be teaching two shifts, a double-shift allowance of 60 per cent of base pay was introduced. Implementation of the vocational curriculum, however, proved to be more difficult, mainly because there were insufficient trained technical teachers for the new vocational courses.

The equity and efficiency of resource use were improved by several measures. A task force in the Ministry of Finance and Economic Planning announced recurrent expenditure ceilings which were to be used in the preparation of the budget for 1989. Those for education were based upon specified maxima for teachers and non-teaching staff, equipment and material allowances, textbooks and allocations of space per pupil for each of the different types and levels of education.

Additional measures intended to improve efficiency included: freezing the number of teachers until such time as an audit of staff could be completed, to determine real need; reducing the number of non-teaching staff at secondary and tertiary level institutions by between 20 and 30 per cent; converting urban primary and remaining middle schools to double-shift operations; increasing students' share in recurrent expenditures by charging both a book-use fee and the full costs of lodging and feeding at secondary and tertiary institutions; and stimulating community involvement in constructing and running local schools. Progress with implementing these measures is briefly reviewed below.

A census in 1986 of all students and staff in secondary institutions uncovered many irregularities, including the existence of more non-teaching staff than there were posts established for them. In response, a reduction of 8,500 non-teaching staff at the secondary level was achieved. The total number of teachers' posts was frozen, and was properly reflected in a reduction of student intakes to the teachers' colleges.

The government introduced a textbook-user fee from primary class 3 upwards which, in 1990, stood at 120 cedis per year, or about $US0.43 per student; the Canadian International Development Agency provided funding for paper to print texts. Pupils now had to pay for all stationery items and exercise books, which were sold through the schools. A revolving fund was established solely for the provision of textbooks and stationery to first-cycle schools.

At post-primary levels, there was also a substantial decrease in government subsidies. By 1990, secondary and tertiary students had to meet the full costs of texts (for secondary students, this was about 3,000 cedis or $US10.80 per student) and exercise books.[22] The feeding subsidy for secondary and tertiary students had been reduced, if not eliminated (representing a saving of $US0.36 per student per day for the former and of $US0.72 per student per day for the latter).[23] The government had not, by 1990, made much progress in eliminating the boarding subsidy, although it had announced that no new boarding-schools were to be constructed, and some boarding facilities had already been converted to day facilities.

Prior to the reform, many communities had lost interest in assisting education. But a new enthusiasm was detected, particularly in the southern half of the country, where parents had traditionally assigned

---

[22] The value of the cedi declined from $US0.18 in 1985 to about $US0.03 in 1990. These are average official rates for each calendar year, as reported in IMF (1991).

[23] The sense in which a subsidy for food remained is that it was supplied to schools at 1988 prices rather than current prices (Toye 1991: 9).

even greater value to education than was typical elsewhere. This may have been because the benefits of the reforms were very widely publicized, and supported by people at the top of the political system. Indeed, the President himself was so strongly supportive that the JSSs came to be known as 'Jerry's Special Schools'.

Communities were expected to help provide school facilities either by raising funds or by directly providing materials and labour. At the primary level, they were responsible for school construction. In that connection a new scheme, whereby the government provided prefabricated roofs made it easier for the communities to build schools in their areas. At the junior secondary level, communities have willingly met their obligation to provide workshops. On the other hand, schools and their communities are reported not to have been too successful in developing income-generating schemes (World Bank 1986*b*). This is attributable in part to the fact that teachers, understandably, are usually not well prepared for the role of entrepreneur.

5.3. Conclusion

Ghana's education reforms were intended to concentrate an increasing proportion of available educational resources on the nine years of basic education. The main intention was to secure universal access to higher-quality primary schooling. These goals were to be financed mainly by a restructuring of the education system, as well as by the cost-savings realized from improving efficiency at all educational levels.

Although it is still early days, the initial experience with the reforms has been highly promising. Primary enrolments increased by 11 per cent in 1989 and by 7 per cent the following year (comfortably exceeding the planned rates of 5 per cent), whilst the education budget had, by 1989, only slightly exceeded its pre-reform level of 3.3 per cent of GNP in 1986.[24] Overall, unit costs at the primary level decreased from an already low figure of $US25 in 1984 to $US21.60 in 1988. They increased slightly for secondary schooling, from $US119 in 1984 to $US129.60 in 1988. Both of these sets of figures are impressive, given that teacher salaries were raised in 1986, just prior to the reform. Clear cost-savings have been achieved in several areas, including reducing overstaffing, introducing user fees for textbooks, and reducing food subsidies at secondary and tertiary levels.

Apart from facilitating much wider access to schooling, Ghana's new approach to education aims to provide children with literacy skills both in their own, a second Ghanaian language, and in English, practical

---

[24] Recurrent education expenditures increased to 3.6 per cent of GNP in 1989, compared to 3.3% in 1986 (World Bank 1988*b*: Table 23; 1991*b*: Table 11).

familiarity with modern farming methods and with using simple tools, practical mathematical skills, and positive attitudes to hard work and to national development. It is not yet clear to what extent these particular goals will be achieved. Nevertheless, the reforms have demonstrated that a determined approach to restructuring can release substantial resources with which to improve the quality and availability of primary schooling. Not all countries face such strong opportunities to reduce the length of their school cycle as Ghana. But in many, the same principles could be used to reallocate resources between different levels of the school/university system and to reduce both total and unit costs.

6. Senegal: Double-Shifting and Reductions in Unit Costs

6.1. The setting

Senegal's recent economic performance is all too familiar in Sub-Saharan Africa. Chronic drought, increasing oil prices, falling export prices, especially for groundnuts, rising interest rates, and poor domestic financial and investment policies led to the emergence of severe economic problems in the late 1970s. By 1980, the economy was in sharp decline, and real per capita income was reported to be lower than it had been in 1965.

As regards education, Senegal in 1980 ranked in the bottom third of low-income African countries for adult literacy (28 per cent) and the GER at primary level was, at 46 per cent, amongst the lowest in the region. In addition, educational opportunity was unequally distributed: over 60 per cent of children of primary school-age lived in rural areas, but they only accounted for 37 per cent of enrolments. Rural children had fewer facilities available to them and intake in some areas occurred only once every second or third year.

The internal efficiency of primary education was low and declining. The pass rate for the primary-level completion examination had fallen from 59 per cent in 1966 to 42 per cent in 1983. Factors which adversely affected the quality of primary schooling included: widespread shortages of trained teachers; a poorly trained inspectorate without the physical means to conduct school visits, and without the authority to impose sanctions for unsatisfactory teacher performance; shortages of textbooks and teacher guides, that, even when available, were often not relevant to the children's environment and learning requirements; serious overcrowding of urban classrooms (by 1983/4, 27 per cent of urban classrooms had between 70 and 120 students); and inadequate physical facilities, with 50 per cent of the classrooms lacking a sufficient number of student benches and about 25 per cent of the classrooms being in a state of disrepair.

Judging from the government's budgetary history, these circumstances were not simply the result of inadequate priority being assigned to education. Public expenditures on education grew rapidly over the years: in 1965, recurrent expenditure on education had accounted for less than 1 per cent of GNP, but by the early 1980s this had climbed to almost 5 per cent. Between 1974 and 1981, the proportion of government expenditure allocated to education was maintained at more than 20 per cent.

The problems confronting education in Senegal were much more the product of high unit costs than of low public expenditures. In the mid-1980s, the unit costs of primary schooling in Senegal were in excess of $100, and were amongst the highest in Africa. As in a number of other West African nations, these costs were mainly due to the country's relatively high salaries for teachers. In 1980, for example, the ratio between average salaries and GDP per capita was 12 for teachers and 9 for assistant teachers (World Bank 1983)—in part a product of the strong political position of the teachers' unions. Other factors contributing to high unit costs included low student/teacher ratios in rural areas, and excessive administrative staff/teacher ratios.

Costs were also excessive in other parts of the education system. In 1985, university fellowships comprised 25 per cent of the higher education budget and indirect subsidies (meals, lodging, transport, etc.) accounted for a further 9 per cent. Sixty per cent of all university students received fellowships or other financial assistance. But over half of the fellowship budget was awarded to about 2,000 students studying abroad, the per capita cost of which was about five times that at the local university. Internal efficiency of higher education was also low: only one out of five students graduated and the average graduate took over seven years to complete the four-year cycle. Finally, most public service employee training institutions (including teacher-training colleges) had very low student/teacher ratios, resulting in high unit costs.

6.2. The policy response

In 1980, the government, in co-operation with the World Bank, initiated a programme of structural adjustment in response to the economic crisis. The primary goal of the programme was stated as being to improve the management of public resources through sectoral reforms designed to ensure a more efficient allocation and use of resources.

Proposals for educational reform began to be aired the following year, when the government convened a national debate on the state of education in the country. The initial detailed work was conducted by a National Commission for the Reform of Education and Training (CNREF), which submitted its proposals to the government in mid-1984. These covered a very wide range of issues, including the length, structure, and curricula of the proposed system, together with matters of pedagogy, religion, language, and culture. The proposals of most interest here concern the ways in which resources for primary schooling were to be mobilized. They are discussed and assessed in what follows.

The fundamental objective of the education reform programme, which was embarked upon in 1985, was to increase both the quality of, and enrolments in, primary schooling. The government aimed to achieve this objective in three main ways. First, the unit costs of education were to be reduced by making more efficient use of teachers and facilities. Second, primary-school construction costs were to be cut. Third, education expenditures at post-primary levels were to be strictly controlled; funds thereby released would be reallocated to primary schooling. The government's goal was to keep education's share of the recurrent budget at its 1985/6 level. To what extent have these aims been achieved?

Reductions in unit costs were to be sought in a number of different ways. The average salary cost of teachers was to be reduced by changing the balance between teachers and assistant teachers. In 1985 the ratio between these grades stood at 100:89. By 1988, owing to changes in recruitment policy for teacher trainees, this had fallen to 100:127, with consequent benefits for unit costs.

In order to reduce the overhead cost burden, the Ministry of National Education intended to redeploy 400 administrators from their present jobs in secondary schools and from the inspectorate to the teaching service (Mondon and Thelot 1989: 41). In the event, by June 1988, fully 1,260 administrators had been redeployed as primary teachers. This was substantially more than had been planned, and it secured a 10 per cent increase in the teaching force at primary level with no net cost to the recurrent budget.

The most important means of securing a reduction in unit costs, however, was to be by introducing double-shift systems in urban primary schools and multigrade systems in rural areas. Overcrowded classrooms for grades 1–4 were to be reorganized into two shifts of twenty hours per week each, in place of the previous twenty-seven hours per week. The school year would be extended to compensate and specialized curricula would be developed. This was expected to reduce investment costs per new student by 50 per cent, and also to reduce recurrent costs significantly.

A pilot programme had first been introduced in sixty-one classrooms in 1982. The method employed at that time was to utilize one classroom for two separate classes each day. There was a separate teacher for each class. In this way, the use of classroom space was optimized. It was reported that educational quality was holding up well under this system. In fact, compared to the results in traditional classrooms, students in the new system generally achieved higher test scores in reading, writing, and maths—probably reflecting the lower student/teacher ratios in double-shift schools.

Although problems were identified during the pilot project,[25] it was in general judged a success, and expansion was planned. But there was to be an important change in the approach used. Under the new system the same teacher would take both the morning and afternoon sessions in each class. Teachers under this system would now teach for forty hours per week instead of the previous twenty-seven hours, and they were to receive an additional 25 per cent of their base salary in payment for the extra hours worked. It can easily be shown that these arrangements provide extra savings on recurrent costs of about 15 per cent in comparison with the earlier double-shift model.

As it has transpired, this approach to double-shifting (one classroom with one teacher who successively teaches two different classes) is probably the most important of the reforms introduced in Senegal. It was introduced in 712 urban classes (substantially more than the seventy-five classes which had earlier been planned) and multigrade teaching was introduced into 142 classes (again, well in excess of the initial target of twenty-five). As a result, by 1988, 14 per cent of primary students were enrolled in double-shift classes and 1.4 per cent were in multigrade classes. Given teacher/pupil ratios of 1:46, and a 50 per cent increase in the contact hours of teachers under this scheme, it follows that these measures alone offered access to some 40,000 new pupils, with savings of 580 teachers (equivalent to some 5 per cent of the teaching force) and of 786 classrooms. Unpublished documentation from the World Bank shows that the combined impact of the redeployment of administrators, discussed earlier, together with the introduction of double-shifting allowed an increase in primary enrolments of 11 per cent (56,000 pupils) between 1985/6 and 1987/8, with only a 2 per cent increase in the teaching force (World Bank 1988c: Annexe 1). Class-sizes also benefited, particularly in urban areas, where they were reduced from upwards of seventy children to the more manageable sizes of forty to fifty pupils per class.

A critical question, of course, is whether or not these changes have been associated with any decline in the quality of education offered by primary schools in Senegal. Assessments thus far seem to be positive. The results of the first phase of double-shifting have been evaluated by a French consultancy firm, working in collaboration with the National Pedagogic Institute in Senegal (Aubret 1989). The authors studied thirty-two classrooms, of which half were in double-shift and half in single-shift classes. The study indicated no noticeable drop in quality for students in the double-shift classes: tests covering attainments in maths and French

[25] These mainly concerned negative reactions from parents whose daily schedule had to adjust to the new school times.

suggested that students in double-shift classes performed as well as those in single-shift classes.

An equally important conclusion of the study was that test results appeared actually to be higher in classes taught by assistant teachers than in those classes taught by full teachers in both double- and single-shift classes. This seems to vindicate the government's strategy of achieving economies in salary costs via changes in the structure of employment towards more assistant teachers.

Nevertheless, the study revealed that parents and teachers continued to think poorly of the system; most thought that the standard of education under double-shift arrangements was weak. This was, at least in part, a reflection of the speed with which the double-shift arrangements were introduced. Not all teachers were able to participate in the specialized training programmes before they began their teaching duties, nor did all receive the necessary teacher guides for the new curriculum. In particular, the accelerated introduction of double-shifting did not allow the government properly to address the negative image of this system among parents and teachers. These lessons will be important to the government during the intended extension of double-shift and multigrade systems nationwide.

We should now return to some consideration of the other ways in which the State's objective of increasing access to higher-quality primary schooling was pursued. As regards the reduction of primary-school construction costs, the government's plan was to employ an intermediate technology using fired brick and/or ram-pressed cement-earth brick, as an alternative to conventional construction methods. This intermediate technology was judged preferable because its labour-intensive characteristics would reduce capital costs, it could help to develop construction technology and services at the regional level, and it would facilitate community participation in construction programmes. As to the latter, communities were expected to provide the local materials and contribute 50 per cent of the unskilled labour. It was estimated that this would reduce the cost per place for each student by about one-third.

In the event, the introduction of double-shifting in urban areas was so successful that large numbers of new classrooms were needed to meet the growing enrolments in the fifth and sixth grades (which remained on a single-shift basis). By 1990, 100 classrooms had been built in urban areas, and 125 in rural areas. The impact upon costs appears to have been substantial. In 1988, for example, the cost per classroom in urban areas had been reduced from about 7 million to 4 million CFA francs.[26] This

---

[26] The average official exchange rate for the CFA franc in 1988 was $US0.0034 (IMF 1991). Thus, in dollar terms, the cost per classroom was reduced from $US24,000 to $US14,000 by these reforms. In comparison with other African countries, therefore, the cost of urban classrooms remained high.

was in spite of the amount of urban community support being less than expected, which resulted in large contractors performing much of the construction work. In the rural areas, however, the impact upon costs was greater, with the average cost per classroom falling to about 2.4 million CFA francs.

The third, and final aim of the government in this area of policy was to restrict sharply the growth of expenditures upon post-primary education and training. Here, progress was more limited. The scholarship budget, which provides support for overseas students, was cut by 2.5 per cent in real terms in 1988. The government, influenced by growing student unrest at home, was content with reductions which were substantially less than the 8 per cent that had been planned.

As regards higher education within the country, the government succeeded in reducing expenditures for campus services by its planned 14.5 per cent, and the recurrent costs of Dakar University were contained to a 1.3 per cent annual growth during the years 1985–1988. But the cost-recovery methods, which had earlier been proposed, to help finance higher education have not been introduced. Equally, the planned ceilings for growth in recurrent expenditure in secondary and higher education appear to have been either forgotten or overlooked.

6.3. Conclusion

In summary, the experience of educational reform in Senegal has been fruitful. The main characteristic preventing rapid moves towards UPE and SFA had been the extremely high levels of unit costs throughout the system. The redeployment of educational administrators to teaching posts, and the policy of using more junior and less qualified teachers at much lower cost, each hold promise for other countries needing to secure financial savings during their progress to SFA. Furthermore, the new policy of double-shifting, seen both as a response to overcrowding in schools and as additional means of increasing enrolments for apparently small financial and educational costs, is likely to be a relevant model for more general application in other countries.

7. Colombia: Cost-Effectiveness and the Quality of Rural Schools

7.1. The setting

Colombia has made great strides in the provision of primary education. The primary GER increased from 77 in 1960 to 114 in 1985, so that UPE, as conventionally measured, was achieved. However, primary schooling was extremely inefficient, with high rates of repetition and drop-out being widespread. By consequence, the net enrolment ratio was estimated in 1985 to be only 73, indicating that large numbers of eligible children still did not attend school. Colombia in fact provides an extreme case of a country where enrolments in the mid-1980s were high, but where SFA, in both its quantitative and qualitative senses, remained far from being achieved.[27] This case-study examines the government's attempts to remedy this circumstance. It focuses upon a novel set of reforms which appear to have reduced costs and increased both enrolments and school quality in the rural areas of Colombia, and which have important lessons for other countries attempting to achieve SFA.

Rural residents in Colombia have faced much more restricted opportunities to attend schools of reasonable quality than have those living in the urban centres. For example, in the early 1980s, the urban primary NER was about 90, whereas that in the rural areas was around 65. Nearly half of all rural schools did not offer all five primary grades. Furthermore, only about one in five rural children completed primary school, whereas in urban schools more than half of the age-cohort finished the full five-year cycle. By consequence, it took twenty-one student-years to produce a single rural graduate from grade 5. In financial terms, a rural primary graduate cost society about $US1,700 in 1980, rather than the $US400 which would have been needed in an efficient system.[28]

The low internal efficiency of rural education was directly related to the paucity of resources available to rural schools. There were acute shortages of teachers, those available were undertrained, two-thirds of rural children had no textbooks, and both physical facilities and supplies of school equipment were rudimentary. Although the curriculum was designed to be taught by teachers who were assigned to only one grade, more than two-thirds of rural primary schools were multigrade schools and had only one or two teachers in total. There were insufficient incentives for teachers to take up rural residence: whilst hundreds of rural schools remained closed owing to teacher shortage, there was excess demand for teaching jobs in the cities. Finally, academic schedules were

---

[27] The justification for the quantitative aspect of this statement derives from the fact that in Colombia the reported value for the NER in 1986 was less than two-thirds that of the GER at primary level. There are only 3 countries where the difference between these two statistics is known to have been larger: in Lesotho the NER/GER ratio was 0.62 in 1986; and in Mozambique and Haiti it was 0.58 in each case in the same year. In these 4 countries, then, there is a greater incidence of primary enrolments amongst children outside the official age-range than is the case in other countries. However, amongst these cases, only in Colombia and Lesotho were primary GERs greater than 100 in 1986. Thus, amongst those countries which had achieved UPE (as conventionally measured), Colombia and Lesotho are the two countries in which the quantitative aspects of SFA were, in 1986, furthest from being achieved. The relevant data are shown in Table A.1. Evidence for the qualitative deficiencies of rural primary schooling is given in the text.

[28] These statistics are from World Bank (1982).

rigid, and were reported not to take account of the special needs for rural pupils to help with agricultural and other chores.

7.2. The policy response

7.2.1. *The Unitary School Programme*

Serious attempts to improve the quality of rural education in Colombia have been made over many years. An early approach was the Unitary School Programme, upon which later reforms were based. This was conceived by Unesco in the early 1960s and had been intended to provide a complete primary school education in regions with low population density. It had the following characteristics: only one teacher was required in each school, whose main function was to help children to teach themselves rather than to give lessons in the traditional sense; children were to be allowed to advance at their own pace; teaching materials were designed so as to allow a teacher to work with several groups of pupils at once; the key elements were 'instructional cards', or subject guides, which gave more autonomy in learning to the pupil, and also allowed children leave to participate in agricultural chores, later to re-enter the learning programme. These methods were intended to make it possible for one teacher to supervise five grades of primary schooling in each school.

Colombian educational authorities experimented with this approach, under Unesco guidance, throughout the 1960s and early 1970s. However, it was never wholly successful. The central problems, which made it impossible to generalize the programme throughout rural areas in Colombia, were that, although it dealt with the learning process at the level of the child, it failed to address the fundamental concurrent changes needed in the national curriculum, in teacher-training methods, and in the local supervision of the system, for the programme to be a success.[29]

7.2.2. *The introduction of Escuela Nueva*

Escuela Nueva (or 'new school programme') began in 1975, and built upon the experience with Unitary Schools. It incorporated a number of features which were designed to tackle the earlier problems. The main differences in this new approach are outlined below.

A new curriculum was designed which allowed the possibility of teachers making their own adjustments, in line with local circumstances. Class organization also became more flexible: popularly elected student leaders were to assist the teachers in group work, and help the teacher to

---

[29] For a fuller account of the reasons for the demise of the Unitary School Programme, see Colbert and Arboleda (1990) and the references cited therein.

handle up to five grades simultaneously. Classrooms were redesigned to allow groups of students separate space in which to work on particular assignments, with only occasional direct help from the teacher. The new curriculum promoted practical problem-solving experiences rather than rote learning. Continuous assessment and evaluation procedures required demonstrated competence at each stage, before the student could progress to the next level; the criterion for advancement in the programme became the ability to apply knowledge within the community rather than the performance of pupils in knowledge tests. The likelihood of student absences during peak periods of agricultural activity was recognized. This enabled drop-out to be reduced and children to resume their studies without repeating grades.

One of the reasons for the failure of the Unitary Schools was that teachers had been given little training in the methods which they were expected to use. This matter was treated much more seriously in the Escuela Nueva programme. In addition to initial training, teachers attended training workshops during the school year which covered the philosophy and content of the programme, school organization, the production and use of simple teaching aids, and student evaluation. Increased salary incentives for rural teachers were attached to their completion of the in-service training programme and to the successful introduction of Escuela Nueva methods in their schools.

Links between school and community were strongly emphasized. Teachers were encouraged to acquire a thorough knowledge of the community, and to use local materials in class. Students gained some understanding of their culture through folksongs, myths, and stories which are retold by local people. The schools served as a conduit for health, sanitation, and nutrition information; and were often built by members of the local communitity, who also retained an important role in school management.

One of the critical shortcomings of the Unitary Schools programme stemmed from the fact that no structures were created to provide administrative support or supervision at the local level. In the words of an early assessment from the World Bank, 'the absence of a local administrative framework means that assistance for and control over schools and teachers outside the departmental capital city, and especially in remote areas, are minimal' (World Bank 1982). Under Escuela Nueva, decentralized strategies for implementing the innovation were promoted. Essentially, central authorities retained responsibility for the design of the programme and for providing practical support, whereas training and implementation became the responsibility of regional and local officials. Departmental supervisors were trained in programme content and pedagogy and made frequent and regular school visits. The number of supervisors was increased in order to meet these requirements.

In summary, the Escuela Nueva programme can be seen as having four major aims. First, it sought to provide the full five-year primary course in all rural areas through multigrade teaching methods. Second, it aimed to improve the internal efficiency of rural education: the increased relevance and flexibility of the curriculum, the new evaluation procedures, and the provision of the full five-year course were expected to reduce drop-out rates and to make repetition unnecessary. Third, the improved inputs, such as the new curriculum, and the provision of better teachers, educational materials, supervision services, and physical infrastructure were expected to enhance student-learning. Finally, the approach would reduce the expenditures on teachers and materials, in comparison with the conventional model of schooling. Here, the main saving was that each rural school no longer required five teachers for five separate classrooms.

A number of evaluation studies of the Escuela Nueva programme have been conducted. These (e.g. Rodriguez 1982), have been generally positive. The results of one of the most comprehensive of these evaluations are worth reporting. This study, which compared 168 Escuela Nueva schools with sixty traditional rural primary schools (each with five grades and with one teacher for each class), was undertaken in 1987 for the Ministry of Education (Castillo and Rojas 1988). It compared the creativity, self-esteem, self-evaluation of civic and social development, and achievement levels in mathematics and Spanish of students from the two sets of schools. The study concluded that self-esteem levels were similar for the two groups, though in terms of civic and social behaviour Escuela Nueva was rated higher. Of considerable importance, however, is that the Escuela Nueva students scored consistently higher in academic achievement tests (third-graders were tested for mathematics performance and fifth-graders for mathematics and Spanish).

The evaluation also noted that 90 per cent of the teachers believed that Escuela Nueva was superior to other traditional rural schools. Other positive aspects were a reported increased participation by teachers in community activities, and by parents in school activities and in children's work assignments. As regards internal efficiency, little difference in drop-out rates was detected between the two programmes. Repetition rates were difficult to measure, since each student in the Escuela Nueva advances at his or her own pace. However, students' subjective assessment as to whether or not they had fallen behind their other classmates was used as a proxy. By this measure, 47 per cent of Escuela Nueva and 57 per cent of traditional school students reported that they had repeated one or more years of schooling.

The government of Colombia has a stated commitment to raising the overall quality of primary education and to universalizing access to it. On the basis of the positive assessments of Escuela Nueva, the government initiated a third phase for its expansion, which began in 1988. The intention was, and, in 1991, remained, to extend the Escuela Nueva programme to all rural schools in Colombia.

7.3. Conclusion

Many middle-income countries, like Colombia, have managed to provide relatively high-quality primary education to the majority of the children living in urban and suburban areas, but have more difficulty in extending high-quality schooling to children in rural areas. Low population densities in the relevant age-groups, and the difficulty of attracting skilled teachers and administrators to rural areas, are common problems. Rates of drop-out and repetition are generally higher in rural areas, partly owing to the greater non-school-related demands on children's time.

Colombia's Escuela Nueva is an exceptional innovation that goes some way towards overcoming these problems. In that sense other countries could usefully reflect upon its results. It appears to be successful primarily because it is a low-cost programme that is capable of delivering education of good quality. Cost-effectiveness is gained by increasing the student/teacher ratio in rural areas. Quality is improved (or at least does not seem to be particularly threatened) through the use of specially developed pedagogical materials designed for multigrade classes, together with carefully planned teacher training and follow-up activities. The curriculum appears to be successful in encouraging both community involvement in the school's endeavours, and support for local educational initiatives. Finally, the more flexible attendance requirements, whereby children can rejoin the system after periods of absence, appears to be more suited to the realities of rural life than are those of the traditional schools. In consequence, the private demand for schooling from rural households in Colombia remains high.

There are, of course, some obvious dangers with the approach. There must be some limit to the extent to which the quality of schooling can be improved, or indeed preserved, in multigrade settings. Whilst Escuela Nueva may represent a cheaper and higher-quality alternative to more traditional rural primary schools, as presently resourced in Colombia, the question for the longer term must be the extent to which the programme is able to offer schooling of similar quality to that available in urban centres. It is that comparison which will ultimately demonstrate its effectiveness, and, indeed, determine whether or not the programme remains acceptable to rural communities.

4

Policy Options for Increasing Access to Schooling

1. Introduction

The case-studies discussed in the previous chapter have shown that in some countries which are poor, and where initial enrolment levels are very low, UPE can still be attained over comparatively short periods of time if a determined and imaginative approach to policy change is adopted. The present chapter draws lessons from this experience, and integrates it with evidence gleaned from the wider research literature. The aim is to review the policy choices facing States which, although fiscally constrained, wish seriously to address the challenge of securing schooling for all.

In principle, state capacity to provide more and better primary schooling can be enhanced in two main ways: first, by improving the efficiency with which resources are used, thereby allowing increased output for given levels of cost; and second, by generating additional resources for use in the primary system. There is a complication, in that both the quantity and the quality of educational provision are critical variables in establishing the 'value' of the product delivered by schools—a conjunction fully recognized by the definition of SFA proposed in Chapter 2. Thus, measures to reduce costs may often reduce quality, and, therefore, the value of the product. This problem can also be present where measures are taken to raise additional resources for schooling. For example, some cost-recovery policies may result in reduced private expenditures upon school inputs, such as textbooks, which are important to maintaining the quality of schooling. The potential trade-off between the achievement of budgetary savings and maintenance of school quality must, therefore, be confronted in assessing the extent to which particular reform measures can improve the efficiency of, or enhance resources available for, primary schooling.

Accordingly, in what follows, types of policy reform are identified which increase state capacity to provide universal access, whilst at the same time giving greatest benefit (or doing least harm) to the quality of schooling. The discussion is organized in four sections, which correspond

TABLE 4.1. *Public expenditure per student on education and net enrolment ratios, major world regions, around 1980*[a]

	Public expenditure per student as % of per capita GNP			Net enrolment ratio (%)			No. of countries included
	Primary	Secondary	Higher	Primary	Secondary	Higher	
Anglophone Africa	18	50	920	77	17	1.2	16
Francophone Africa	29	143	804	46	14	2.4	18
South Asia	8	18	119	71	19	4.4	4
East Asia and Pacific	11	20	118	87	43	9.1	6
Latin America	9	26	88	90	44	12.0	19
Middle East and North Africa	2	28	150	82	36	9.4	11
Developing countries	14	41	370	75	23	6.9	74
Developed countries	22	24	49	100	80	21.0	20

[a] Differences between data in this table and those in Table 1.3 are mainly due to the smaller number of countries from which the NERs are derived in this case.

Source: World Bank (1986a: Table 9).

to the main objectives of the relevant categories of policy change. The objectives are those of reducing the unit costs of schooling, of reducing total costs per school-leaver by changing the organization and length of the school cycle, of redistributing expenditures so that more are directed towards primary schooling, and of raising additional financial resources for education in general, and for primary schooling in particular. Policies which hold promise in pursuit of these objectives will be discussed in turn.

2. Policies to Reduce the Unit Costs of Schooling

We know from Chapter 2 that if unit costs, i.e. total recurrent spending on education, per pupil enrolled, by government and private households, are reduced, *ceteris paribus*, enrolments will rise.[1] Important policy questions for the attainment of UPE, therefore, are whether there is scope for unit costs to be reduced, and, if so, how this may be done.

Table 4.1 indicates the extent to which publicly incurred unit costs vary at different levels of education and in different parts of the world. It shows that, in developing countries, the unit costs of primary schooling relative to per capita incomes are lower than in richer countries, whereas at secondary and tertiary levels the reverse is generally the case. The enormously high costs of providing secondary and tertiary education relative to primary—particularly in Africa—are plain. These cost differentials imply that, in Africa, one-fifth of total public educational spending provides higher education for only 2 per cent of the age-group. More generally, primary schooling captures less than half of all educational expenditures even though it is the only part of the system—particularly in low-income States—which most people have the chance to join.

It should be noted that these unit cost differences are open to a number of interpretations. Since they relate only to public expenditures, it is possible that the introduction of private household expenditures would change the picture. For example, the lower unit costs, relative to per capita incomes, of primary schooling in developing countries may result from private households meeting a greater proportion of its direct costs than is typically the case in richer countries. Nevertheless, allowing for these private expenditures would reduce, but by no means remove the enormous cost differentials between higher and primary/secondary schooling within developing countries: even if household expenditures accounted for two-thirds of the direct costs of primary schooling (which

---

[1] The *ceteris paribus* conditions here are that expenditures on schooling as a proportion of GNP and the proportion of the population of school-going age remain unchanged. These are the variables x and a, respectively, in the notation of Ch. 2.

would be unusually high),[2] the average unit cost differential between higher education and primary schooling would still be about 9:1, whereas in richer countries, as the table indicates, it is scarcely more than 2:1. These observations suggest that the main priority for seeking reductions in the unit costs of education are at higher levels of the system rather than at primary level: taking an international comparative perspective, the publicly incurred unit costs of higher education, and, to some extent, those of secondary schools, seem to be too high in developing countries, whilst those at primary level seem, if anything, too low.

There are other reasons for being sceptical of the need to seek cost reductions at primary level. Although the target of UPE may be satisfied by securing sufficient formal attendance at school, that of SFA requires that both quantitative and qualitative criteria be met. In particular, for the latter, the material and human resources available to schools need to be sufficient to promote minimally acceptable standards of learning. It is clear that in a very large number of countries these qualitative criteria cannot be said to have been met. In part this is because expenditures per pupil have been insufficient to provide schooling of adequate quality. In such cases, reductions in unit costs are surely likely to be the opposite of what is required.

Although both of the above points are sound, they do not undermine the validity of investigating whether there is scope for reducing unit costs on efficiency grounds, even if, on balance, and in order to secure schooling of better quality, they would need to be increased. The important question is whether there are any constituents of unit costs which could be reduced with little or no damage to the quality of schooling— thereby to help finance other cost increases which may be separately required.

It is well known that the two items which dominate the determination of the unit costs of education are the earnings of teachers and the size of the teacher/pupil ratio. Since, at the school-level, salary costs typically account for around 90 per cent of recurrent expenditures, it is sensible to begin with some discussion of teachers' earnings.

2.1. The average earnings of teachers

Salary levels. It has often been argued that the levels of teachers' salaries in developing countries are too high, and must be reduced as part of a strategy to reduce unit educational costs. It is true that over the years

---

[2] A recent estimate of the proportion of education costs incurred by private households in India puts it at about one-third of the total (Tilak 1991). Indian public expenditures on education, relative to GNP, are low (see Table 6.5, below). This, therefore probably represents an 'upper bound' estimate for developing countries in general. No separate evidence is available on differences in household expenditures at each level of schooling.

1960–75 teachers' earnings often increased considerably faster than those of other groups. This was partly a result of the power of the (large and rapidly growing) profession in many countries. But it was, rather more so, a result of an upgrading of the qualifications of the profession—to which levels of remuneration were often explicitly linked—and of a much faster expansion of secondary and tertiary education, wherein the most highly paid teachers were concentrated, than of primary schooling. The budgetary implications of these structural changes were unfortunate, but they do not, *per se* provide a convincing case for salary reductions.

Some commentators point out that the ratio of average teachers' salaries to per capita income is often very high in the poorest countries.[3] This too, is a misleading indicator: it is as likely to reflect the different proportions of the population dependent upon agricultural self-employment—and, thus, structural differences amongst countries—as it is the absolute or relative wage differentials between them. It is, for example, easy to show that exactly similar absolute levels of wages and per capita agricultural product would produce widely different wage/per capita income ratios as between countries not so dependent and those highly dependent on agriculture. The more instructive comparisons, therefore, are between teachers' salaries and per capita agricultural product on the one hand, and the salaries earned by 'similar' workers in other sectors of the economy on the other.

As regards the latter, wages in the teaching profession in most countries are determined in the context of established differentials with other professions. Although there may be some flexibility for raising or lowering salaries earned by one group, the extent to which this can be achieved without generating equal or compensatory pressures from or for other groups is usually fairly limited. Thus the issue of teachers' salaries cannot usually be addressed separately from that of the level of wages and salaries more generally.

In this regard, recent changes in many low-income and adjusting countries are beginning to make the argument that wages are too high seem absurd. Average real wages outside agriculture began falling in Latin America and in Sub-Saharan Africa from the mid-1970s onwards. In Latin America, although Brazil, Argentina, and Colombia registered significant gains in real wages over the years 1971–84, there were sharp falls in Bolivia, Mexico, Paraguay, Peru, Uruguay, and Venezuela over the same period. In SSA the situation was much worse. Wages have fallen in almost every country for which data are available, and in some cases (Ghana, Tanzania, Sierra Leone, Zambia) dramatically so. By

---

[3] e.g. a recent World Bank report on Education in Sub-Saharan Africa observes that, for primary teachers around 1980, the ratio of average salaries to per capita income was 2.4 in Latin America, 2.6 in Asia, but it was 5.6 in the 22 SSA countries for which data were available (World Bank 1988*a*: 46).

consequence, average real wages in SSA were typically halved between 1970 and 1985.[4]

Teachers have been able to mount little defence against these trends. Indeed, in so far as public servants have often taken the brunt of salary decline, the earnings loss for teachers will have been rather greater than the average figures indicated above would suggest. For example, for fourteen African countries having available data, average real starting salaries for primary teachers in 1985 stood at only 46 per cent of their values in 1975.[5] Table 2.1 also confirms that, in SSA, the impact of salary decline in the teaching profession has been particularly strong: unit costs of teachers declined in twelve of the fourteen SSA countries having comparable data for the early 1980s, often by considerable proportions. These changes, of course, also reflect changes in materials and other support costs; but, given the large size of the reductions, they mainly reflect real salary decline. In current circumstances, many countries have experienced such a sharp reduction in teacher morale and efficiency that the major operational question is not whether, but how, to *increase* the real value of wages and salaries—even at the cost of having to reduce the numbers of those currently employed.

At secondary and tertiary levels, there may be still some scope for achieving cost-savings via salary compression between teachers at different levels of the hierarchy. It must be noted, however, that the long-established trend of reducing earnings differentials between jobs at the top and bottom of the formal sector (classified according to either occupation or educational qualifications held or required) has accelerated during these recent years of decline in earnings. For example, in eight African countries for which data are available, the differential between the starting salaries for university graduates in the public sector, as compared with those for secondary school-leavers, fell by an average annual rate of 2.3 per cent between 1970 and 1975, and by a rate of 5.5 per cent between 1975 and 1986. Thus, the pace at which differentials were eroded in these countries more than doubled after 1975.[6] Again, teachers have been similarly affected, with starting salaries for the higher teachers' grades falling more sharply, in real terms, than those of primary teachers.[7] All of this implies that whilst some further compres-

---

[4] Evidence for this statement is shown in Colclough (1991: Table 9.2).

[5] The countries included in this calculation are Benin, Central African Republic, Ethiopia, Gambia, Kenya, Mauritania, Morocco, Niger, Nigeria, Sierra Leone, Somalia, Sudan, Tanzania, and Togo. The statistic reported is the simple unweighted average of real salary declines in each country. Calculated from Tibi (1990: Table 5).

[6] The countries included are Botswana, Gambia, Ghana, Kenya, Malawi, Sierra Leone, Tanzania, and Zambia. These results have been calculated from data shown in Colclough (1991: Table 9.3).

[7] For the 14 African countries mentioned in n. 5 the starting salaries for higher teachers had fallen, by 1985, to only 37% of their 1975 values, compared to 46% for primary teachers (Tibi 1990: Table 5).

sion may be possible via a decline in real earnings for more senior grades, many (though not all) countries had, by 1990, already moved in this direction as strongly as was compatible with minimal standards of teacher efficiency and morale.

Structural change. Allowing salaries to decline is not the only means of reducing the amount which the average teacher is paid. This can also be done by changing the structure of the profession towards a more intensive use of lower-cost personnel. This is a much more promising area for reform and there are various ways of achieving it. In countries where salaries are tied to education or training qualifications it may be possible to reduce the average education/training background of the profession without significantly affecting teacher quality or performance. As indicated in Chapter 3, the government of Senegal has progressively increased the proportion of 'assistant teachers' over the last few years. This is reported to have contributed to a reduction in unit costs with no noticeable negative impact upon teaching quality. Colombia was also able to reduce teacher costs in similar ways, by increasing the roles of 'teacher helpers' in the Escuela Nueva programme. Not all countries are in a position to introduce such reforms. They would often be inappropriate for those in which the proportion of untrained or insufficiently educated teachers is already large. Elsewhere, however, there do seem to be potential savings to be made.

In addition, there is scope, in many education systems, to redeploy staff in ways which reduce overheads. In Ghana more than 5,700 non-teaching staff were removed from the payroll in 1986; this was equivalent to more than 20 per cent of non-teachers at secondary/tertiary level, and to more than 5 per cent of the total teaching force, bringing significant unit cost savings. Senegal, too, redeployed 1,260 administrative staff into the teaching force—which would be possible in other countries where educational administrators are also qualified teachers. These experiences, then, provide useful lessons for countries with low GERs, where a number of similar reforms could be tried.

2.2. Teacher/pupil ratios

The second major way of reducing the unit costs of schooling is by using teachers more intensively. About half of the Sub-Saharan African countries for which data are available had pupil/teacher ratios of 37 or less at primary and 23 or less at secondary levels in the mid-1980s. Where salaries are a high proportion of recurrent costs, a 20 per cent increase in this ratio—from, say, 35 to 42 at primary, and from 23 to 28 at secondary —brings an almost exactly similar budgetary saving. Here, then, there appears to be significant scope for reductions in unit costs.

Multiple shifts. One way of making more intensive use of teachers is to introduce some form of multiple-shift schooling. Under such systems two or more entirely separate groups of pupils can be accommodated for regular teaching during the same term, week, or day in the same school. The most common of such approaches, the double-shift system, involves one group of pupils attending in the mornings and a second group using these same facilities in the afternoons. But there are many other variants.

Whether teachers' salary costs are reduced depends upon the particular system used. If each shift required a different set of teachers (as in Singapore) there would be no savings in total salary costs of teachers. Alternatively, if teachers were paid for the work they do pro rata, salary costs would again be unaffected, but the number of teachers required— and, thus, expenditures upon classrooms, staff housing, and teacher training—would be much reduced in comparison with single-session arrangements. Again, if teachers were paid more for two sessions than for one, but at a lower hourly rate (as in Senegal, where those teaching the second shift receive a 25 per cent supplement to their basic salaries for a 48 per cent increase in hours worked, or as in Ghana, where a 60 per cent allowance for double-shift teaching is paid), savings in both the number of teachers and in the salary bill could be achieved.

As regards recurrent costs more generally, double-shift schooling also usually achieves economies in the employment of clerks, cleaners, main-tenance, and security workers. These and other recurrent costs are not halved by double-shift methods, since the more heavy use of plant involves higher maintenance expenditure than in the case of single-shift arrangements. Nevertheless savings here can still be significant.

The most substantial source of cost-reductions from double-shift teaching is in the area of capital costs. Here, major savings in the costs of land, equipment, libraries, laboratories, and classrooms can be made. For example, Zambia's extensive use of double and triple shifts allowed its capital costs at primary level to be almost halved (Bray 1989: 32). This, however, was exceptional since there are a range of reasons why moving to a double-shift system would not reduce costs by half. Nevertheless, in Jamaica and Malaysia, notwithstanding the extra maintenance costs involved, and somewhat lower average school enrolments in the after-noons, savings in capital costs of 32 per cent and 25 per cent, respectively, were obtained.

Although the balance of the above observations is fairly strongly positive, there is, of course, a range of economic costs that attend the introduction of double-shift schooling: parents have to look after their children during the shift which they do not attend, the costs of which, in the market-place, may be substantial. Tutors are sometimes privately retained in order to compensate for the short day that double-shifts usually imply. Finally, there are a range of risks to the quality of schooling which double-shift methods bring: the school is usually more tense and hurried—both breaks and teaching time are reduced; teachers, particularly those who have already taught a morning session, may often be tired and therefore able to offer only an impeded service; preparation and marking time is squeezed, management costs, and inefficiencies, rise the more difficult the conditions become. Perhaps most significantly for SFA policies, it is the younger children who tend to be allocated to the afternoon sessions which are generally less attractive to teachers.

Nevertheless these, and other problems are not decisive. There is in fact very little concrete evidence to suggest that double-shifts (and their associated reduced learning time-inputs) have any significant impact upon the cognitive achievements of children. Early studies in Malaysia (Beebout 1972) and Chile (Farrell and Schiefelbein 1974) found no significant association between the level of academic performance and the number of shifts in which a school was daily utilized, except where the physical facilities were not adequately designed to accommodate double-shift teaching. The experiment reported on in our case-study of Senegal is also positive in this respect. Here, more than 14 per cent of primary-school pupils were enrolled in double-shift classes by 1988. This had allowed an 11 per cent increase in enrolments with only a 2 per cent increase in the teaching force. An evaluation of the experience in 1989 showed, on the basis of language and mathematics tests, that the move to double-shift teaching had not been associated with a reduction in school quality.

It is possible that reducing the attendance obligations of pupils more generally may provide a further way of increasing pupil/teacher ratios. However, shortening the number of weeks in the school year is probably associated with declines in quality, except where gross inefficiencies or teacher absenteeism are already prevalent. By contrast, evidence from Venezuela suggests that reductions in the number of hours per day is probably not so clearly associated with qualitative decline (at least down to about six hours per day). Part-day attendance—as in double-shift schooling—tends to reduce the opportunity costs of schooling for poorer households, who may have to depend partially on child labour. For all of these reasons an increase in the incidence of double-shift teaching represents one of the more promising means of reducing pupil/teacher ratios in many countries.

Increasing class-size. The final means of using teachers more intensively is via increases in the size of classes. Research in some developed countries shows that variations in class-size from twenty-five to forty students have no consistent effect on the performance of children in achievement tests (Thorndike 1973; Simmons and Alexander 1980; Fuller 1987). At primary level, classes of up to forty-five children are judged to be tolerable—if undesirable—where costs dictate this. Whatever the reported average figure for class-size at the national level, however,

there is always a wide dispersion around the mean. Obviously attempts
to raise class-size should focus upon those schools with the smallest
number of children per class, whilst reducing, wherever possible, the
number of overcrowded classes.

Sometimes, within individual schools there are opportunities for a more
rational utilization of teaching staff. For example, as indicated in Chapter
3, there are some Sri Lankan schools in which the pupil/teacher ratio
declines from 60 to 20 between grades 1 and 8. This skewed utilization
of teaching resources is common elsewhere, yet concealed by the presentation of aggregate data at system rather than school level. Often, of
course, low population density in rural areas prevents easy increases in
class-size, whereas overcrowding is a frequent problem in urban centres.
School mapping, and the rationalization of facilities can help to tackle
this. But in some countries the geographical distribution of the population
of school age does present an important constraint on the effectiveness of
these measures.

2.3. Improving internal efficiency

The counterpart to using teachers more intensively is achieving a more
effective use of *pupil* time. The costs per graduate from each level of
the school system are increased the longer it takes the average child
to graduate. Reductions in this average time-span—by reducing the
incidence of early leaving and repetition of grades—thereby reduce total
costs per graduate.

In all systems there are defined points at which children leave school.
In most developing countries, such leaving points include the end of the
primary, lower secondary, senior secondary, and tertiary cycles. Children
who leave school at points other than these are often described as 'drop-
outs'. Yet whether their 'drop-out' is indeed more wasteful than that of
children leaving at one of the established exit points is debatable. It is
only so if the benefits of schooling accrue not on a pro rata basis for each
year attended, but if they are more than proportionately bunched at the
end of each particular cycle. This may be plausible for some—but by no
means all—curricula, but particularly for skills which, like literacy and
numeracy, take several years to acquire. At higher points in the primary
cycle where, it is to be hoped, basic skills have been acquired, it is the
social principle of SFA, rather than the principle of economic efficiency,
which is countermanded by subsequent drop-out.

In twenty-five low-income countries of SSA 13 per cent of primary-
school pupils and 10 per cent of secondary-school pupils are repeaters
(data are for 1983, World Bank 1988*a*: 136). But the range across
countries is very wide—from one-third of primary-school pupils in
Mali, Togo, Central African Republic and over one-fifth in Benin,

Guinea-Bissau, Guinea, and Mozambique, to close to zero in Tanzania, Zimbabwe, Ghana, and Zambia where policies of automatic promotion prevail. This range demonstrates the opportunity: the number of children given the chance to attend primary school could be increased by over 20 per cent in six of the first seven African countries mentioned above, simply by abolishing repetition.[8] Furthermore, in the average SSA country this reform would be capable of pushing net enrolment ratios up from their present two-thirds to around three-quarters without any increase in educational costs.

The impact of abolishing repetition on learning achievement within education remains controversial. Clearly, *some* small level of repetition allows slow learners with special problems to be diagnosed and helped. But the standards adopted for securing progression within the system should not be set at a level which is inappropriate for a significant number of students in each grade. There is no doubt that repetition rates should be reduced in most of those countries which are currently far from achieving SFA. In most such countries savings of at least 5 per cent of recurrent spending on education would result, without substantial costs to the quality of schooling being incurred.

2.4. Capital costs

Capital expenditures on education in low-income and adjusting countries have fallen during the 1980s—much more sharply so than recurrent expenditures on education in real terms. But this has primarily been a function of budgetary constraints, and only rarely because of savings in capital costs.

Comparative data on construction costs in education are scanty and unreliable. However the experience of a number of countries demonstrates that, by using local rather than imported materials, and by using low-cost, low-maintenance construction teachnology considerable savings can be made. For example, as a result of these kinds of innovation, together with increasing the involvement of local communities in construction work, Senegal has reduced capital costs by 40 per cent—albeit from a very high base—since 1985.

2.5. Boarding- versus day-schools

Both capital and recurrent costs can be affected by a number of the reforms discussed above: multiple-shift schooling, reductions in teacher requirements and repetition rates each reduce both recurrent and capital

---

[8] These countries comprise all those with gross repetition rates in excess of 20%, with the exception of Togo, where the primary GER already exceeds 100%.

costs of schooling. A final important means of achieving such cost-reductions would be reducing the incidence of boarding-schools—particularly at secondary level. Recent evidence from Malawi shows that the annualized capital and recurrent costs per pupil of boarding-schools are more than twice as high as those of day-schools. For Somalia the differential appears to be as great as 3.5 (World Bank 1988*a*: 60). Ironically boarding is particularly prevalent in the countries that can afford it least. Thus quite a high proportion of the most educationally disadvantaged countries shown in Table 2.1 provide boarding facilities for a significant proportion of secondary students. The main reason is that where a fairly small proportion of primary-leavers continue to secondary school, it is frequently not possible to provide cost-effective day secondary schools in rural areas. Living away from home is therefore necessary if children from rural households are to gain access to secondary school.

To some extent, then, high secondary costs in poorer countries are an inevitable consequence of their lower secondary enrolment ratios. Whilst this situation cannot be changed overnight, care is needed to reduce dependence upon boarding as secondary education expands and as day-provision becomes increasingly viable. Eligibility for boarding status should be sharply restricted to those from isolated communities: children from urban households should not, under normal circumstances, be allowed to board at public expense.

3. Policies on the Length and Organization of the School Cycle

It is obvious that, other things being equal, the longer are the primary, secondary, and tertiary cycles of education, the greater will be their costs. The organization of teaching and learning also have direct consequences for the levels of investment needed to support each cycle. The range of policy options which affect these parameters needs to be explored. As before, the main task is to identify reforms which offer increased efficiency without compromising educational quality. Those identified as having most significance can be broadly classified under the following heads:

- Changes in the length of different educational cycles
- Changes in the age of entry to formal schooling
- Organizational and pedagogical reforms
- Developing links between education and productive work.

There is no single, optimal set of structural and organizational reforms which all countries should adopt. Historical circumstances and present socio-economic contexts vary, and constrain the room to manœuvre in different ways. National priorities and values are heterogeneous and lead to different judgements on appropriate policy. Nevertheless the fact that there are wide differences between countries in the length and organization of their school systems indicates that there *are* important choices to be made.

3.1. The length of the formal cycle

The most common length of the primary cycle in both developing and developed countries is six years and there is an extreme range of three to nine years. The length of the secondary schooling varies over a similar range and six years is also the most common value (Unesco 1989: Table 3.1). Usually, those countries with the shortest primary cycles have the longest secondary cycles and vice versa. A small number of countries, e.g. Sri Lanka, do not separate primary and secondary schooling and provide eight to ten years of non-selective basic education. Further and higher education ranges from two to six or more years, with a wide variation of patterns at degree and sub-degree levels. Francophone Sub-Saharan African countries tend to have longer tertiary cycles than do the Anglophone ones.

These general patterns conceal considerable diversity. For example, it is quite common for parallel systems to exist at secondary and tertiary level with different curricular specialisms (technical, vocational, etc.) which differ in length from the main cycle. A number of systems have special arrangements that vary the length of schooling for particular population groups, e.g. to cater for the need to transfer to a different medium of instruction as with the 'remove' class[9] in Malaysia. Other countries have different cycle lengths in different regions. In China, for example, most urban primary schools taught a six-year course in 1990, yet in many rural areas primary schooling of five years' duration remained common.

As regards the primary cycle, excessive length usually leads to lower internal efficiency. In long cycles, student motivation tends to be lower in the middle grades and the incidence of repetition is higher. Further, the propensity to drop out is positively related to previous repetition. Repetition leads to differences between the official length of the first cycle and the average length of time actually taken by students to complete it. Recent estimates (Berstecher and Carr-Hill 1990: 37) indicate that for twenty-five African countries with five-year primary cycles, the average completion time was less than five and a half years in only three cases, and it exceeded six years in a further thirteen cases. Perhaps more alarmingly these averages increased in twelve African countries between 1980 and 1986/7. By contrast the difference between the official

---

[9] The remove class allows students from Tamil and Chinese medium schools to transfer to secondary schools which all teach in Bahasa Malaysia, the national language. It adds an extra year.

and actual durations of primary schooling tends to be lower in other regions, where, also, rates of repetition have been falling.

Internal efficiency is also compromised by high drop-out rates, since these increase the number of student places required for a given number of primary-school completers. Less than three-quarters of a cohort typically survive to grade 5 in twenty-eight of fifty-seven developing countries for which there are data (Berstecher and Carr-Hill 1990: 110). Again, survival rates deteriorated in about half of these countries during the early 1980s, and particularly so in Africa.

The extent to which the length of a cycle affects student achievement is difficult to determine. Data from the International Association for the Evaluation of Educational Achievement (IEA) science studies (Postlethwaite and Wiley 1991) indicate that, internationally, there is no simple correlation between longer cycles and higher student achievement in science subjects. This does not of course imply that shortening a cycle length within a system will have no effect on achievement since cross-national studies of this kind are subject to many technical limitations (see Chapter 1). Nevertheless it is quite possible that achievement levels could be maintained, at lower cost, if measures to increase both the effectiveness of teaching and the time spent learning within the school year were introduced simultaneously with reductions in the cycle length. Ultimately, a judgement about the appropriate length of primary schooling is not simply an economic one—it depends on the educational aims of the cycle and on the probability of most students achieving them within a given number of years.

Questions concerning the appropriate length of secondary education have to be examined in relation to the length of other cycles. The most common length of primary and secondary cycles, taken together, is twelve years. The most costly situations arise where long primary cycles are coupled with long secondary and tertiary cycles. For example, as indicated in Chapter 3, Ghana had, until the late 1980s, a pathway through the formal system to university entry that could last as many as seventeen years. This was standardized at thirteen years, with the intention of reallocating the savings made to primary education.

In a number of the countries with high gross enrolment ratios an eight-to-ten-year basic education cycle, with no selection examinations, is increasingly common. This raises the important question as to whether the incorporation of some post-primary grades into primary schools would be better than retaining the widespread practice of transferring students to separate junior secondary schools. The latter generally have higher unit costs—sometimes substantially so (Table 4.1). In most systems a change of school is associated with significant reductions in grade-specific enrolment ratios. This arises both from deliberate restrictions on the transition rate from primary to secondary, and from drop-out precipitated by the additional costs and greater travelling distances generally associated with attendance at junior secondary school.

Curricular and pedagogic concerns are relevant to the choice of strategy. Organizational differences between primary and junior secondary schools may be small (for example, it is common to find subject-based curricula with roughly similar time-allocations at both primary and junior secondary level). It could be argued that this favours the lower-cost strategy of extending primary enrolments upwards within the same schools. However, there may be legitimate needs for more specialized facilities in junior secondary grades, e.g. in science and other practical subjects, indicating that efficiency can be enhanced by providing these in secondary schools where their use can be shared with older students. In practice, such facilities are often reserved for upper secondary students alone, resulting in underutilization. Whichever model is selected, it needs to be consistent with the curricula used and the physical facilities available.

In summary, the main structural issue to resolve is whether the current length of the primary cycle is appropriate, both absolutely, and in relation to higher levels of schooling. Six years is the most common length for primary schooling and this seems to be the minimum needed to gain the range of benefits associated with its successful completion. The impact of the large differentials in unit costs at different education levels, discussed earlier, is magnified the greater are the durations of secondary and tertiary cycles. Where secondary cycles last longer than six years, particularly when preceded by long primary cycles, there is a prima-facie case for reducing them. Furthermore, if their length reflects poor achievement by primary-school students the case is strengthened, since more is likely to be gained by shifting investment from secondary to improve the quality of primary schooling. Finally, where tertiary cycles last much longer than three years, the extent to which public subsidy bolsters private rather than social benefits needs to be examined.

3.2. The age of entry to primary school

In most countries, children enter primary school aged 6 years (Table 4.2). Africa has the highest proportion of systems with an entry age of 7 years. These ages are effectively minima since over-age entry is not uncommon, although under-age entry also occurs where the cycle officially starts at 7 or 8. To what extent does this represent best practice, from the perspectives of both educational and cost implications?

The age of entry is falling in many countries. This is occurring partly because of success in reducing over-age entry and partly as a result of the development of pre-school facilities. The latter are often financed at the household (as in Sri Lanka) or community (as in parts of China) levels—

Policy Options

TABLE 4.2. *Age of entry into primary school in developing countries*

	Age of entry (years)			
	5	6	7	8
Africa	3	24	17	1
Asia	5	18	6	1
Arab countries		17	4	
Latin America and Caribbean	15	22	7	
Oceania	6	12	2	

Source: Unesco (1989: Table 3.1).

although somewhat less frequently they are provided by the State (as in Malaysia). Consequently, pre-schools are more usually found in urban and relatively wealthy areas and in middle-income rather than low-income countries. The unweighted mean enrolment in pre-school classes was 3 per cent in low-income countries, 7 per cent in middle-income, and 22 per cent in upper-middle-income countries in 1980. In all cases it had been growing over the previous decade (Lockheed and Verspoor 1990: 253).

The educational significance of the age of entry depends partly on the quality of the educational environment outside the school. This has many dimensions, including child-rearing practices, the levels of educational activity in the home, the availability of informal pre-school groups, and the existence of opportunities to learn outside the home. Many studies of cognitive development indicate the importance of early learning experiences for subsequent development and provide a compelling case for low entry ages to structured learning. The periods of greatest plasticity in intellectual development occur at the youngest ages and this is where the greatest gains appear to take place. Young children require less expensive learning materials and fewer specialized physical facilities than do older children. Differences in learning achievement between poor rural children from educationally disadvantaged backgrounds and their more favoured peers increase over time. Thus, providing equitable and early access to primary schooling is likely to lessen the cumulative differences that would otherwise emerge in learning achievement. If school effects have greater influence upon academic achievement than do out-of-school factors, the case for early enrolment is further strengthened.

Lower ages of entry obviously imply longer enrolment before children reach the age where they can enter the labour market. This may imply extensions of the primary-school cycle and increase the total costs of its completion. Nevertheless, current trends in both policy and practice are towards reductions in the school entry-age. Attempts to increase the age of entry have generally proved unpopular with parents, as in Sri Lanka, where it was raised, in 1972, from 5 to 6 years, with the non-selective cycle being shortened from 10 to 9 years. This policy lasted until 1977, when a new government again reduced the entry age to 5 years, in the face of widespread popular dissatisfaction.

In general, reducing the entry-age to below 6 years is probably pre-mature in countries where GERs remain well short of 100. Unless resources are increasing, the net effect could easily be to reduce further the GER over the primary cycle as a whole. The challenge is how to reduce equitably the entry-age, perhaps by utilizing community resources —via play-groups and informally organized kindergártens—without adding to the pressure on resources. Raising the entry-age in order to reduce costs is educationally unattractive, and in most countries is likely to prove politically unacceptable.

3.3. Organizational and pedagogic reforms

Ways of providing primary education vary widely. Which organizational and pedagogical reforms offer the most cost-effective means of improving internal efficiency? Three sets of observations provide the context for tackling this question.

First, the number of school days is far from constant between countries. For example, in the twenty-three IEA science study countries (Postlethwaite and Wiley 1991) the annual number of teaching days for 10-year-olds varied from 158 in Ghana to 220 in Korea—a difference of nearly 40 per cent. Since daily teaching hours also vary independently, the range of instructional time formally available to students may differ, certainly by a factor of two and probably by more. For example, the length of the teaching year in the twenty-three IEA countries varied between 672 hours (Hungary) and 1,134 hours (Nigeria) with a modal value around 950 hours. Teaching loads are also unevenly distributed—in some countries these may exceed 30 hours a week in double-shift schools with the majority of this time being spent in contact with children; in others teaching loads of three or four periods a day are common, amounting to between 10 and 15 hours teaching per week. Teacher/ class ratios span a range from less than one to as much as 2.5:1 in more favoured institutions. The number of non-teaching staff on school payrolls also varies from minimal allocations, to numbers that can be comparable with the number of teachers. These facts indicate that there are opportunities to reduce unit costs through a reconsideration of working practices. In some countries, teacher productivity is much lower than in others.

Second, far fewer days may actually be available for teaching than those which are allocated. The actual number of normal teaching days in rural primary schools may be anywhere from 70 to 90 per cent of the official number. The reasons commonly include: the loss of teaching days at the beginning of school terms for registration of new and returning students, school refurbishment/cleaning etc.; the use of a week or more for administering public examinations when normal teaching is disrupted (particularly in schools with secondary grades); special school events—sports days, school exhibitions, official visitors; extended public holidays; and leave and teacher absenteeism.

Teachers are often used very inefficiently (see Chapter 3, Sri Lanka case-study). Clearly higher teacher attendance coupled with full utilization of teaching days would significantly increase the hours of instruction available and might reduce the number of teachers needed.[10] It should also improve student achievement assuming there is some relationship between the latter and the amount of teaching received. Where student absenteeism is high, curriculum planning which assumes that school experience is not necessarily continuous would also bring benefits.[11]

Third, the organization of teaching and learning typically involves students remaining in whole class-groups during all teaching hours. The amount of time spent by students working without direct supervision during school hours is usually small. Where this happens, it is more often a product of teacher absenteeism than of design. Yet much useful learning can be achieved without the continuous presence of a teacher. Opportunities to use peer-group learning, self-study, and older children as guides for younger ones, are insufficiently taken up. Practice differs greatly in the extent to which community resources are mobilized to supervise and assist with learning.

Many countries have experimented with projects that seek to enhance access and maintain quality through changes in the organization of teaching and learning. Project Impact is one of the most well known of these. From its origins in the Philippines and Indonesia derivatives have spread to Malaysia, Jamaica, Liberia, and Bangladesh. The project uses

---

[10] Community teachers in the Bangladesh Rural Advancement Committee (BRAC) non-formal primary-education project have very low absenteeism despite being in poor rural communities. The administrative arrangements are such that unexplained absences result in loss of pay; when they occur substitute community teachers are utilized (Lovell and Fatema 1989).

[11] Seasonal absenteeism is common in rural areas during planting and harvest times. The deleterious effects of this on student achievement can be lessened if learning is planned in discrete 'blocks'—as in the Colombian case discussed in Chapter 3—so as to allow students to leave and rejoin school at later dates.

self-instructional material and involves older children in the teaching process. The original goals of Project Impact included raising student/ teacher ratios to 150:1 or more, thereby making considerable savings on teachers' salaries, the largest element of primary costs. Though it is clear that these projects have had many positive outcomes, savings have generally been much less than were originally anticipated. In the Philippines, for example, arrangements for financing schools encouraged the hiring of fewer teachers and investment in more self-instructional materials. But the projected savings, amounting to 40 per cent of the budgetary costs, did not materialize. The main problem was that there was little incentive to generate such savings, because they produced no financial benefits to the schools that made them. In the Liberian project average school sizes did not increase to levels where there would have been significant economies of scale. Indeed the evidence suggests that the unit costs for project schools exceeded those for ordinary schools. In Indonesia, too, the savings gained were much less than had been initially planned (Cummings 1986).

The evaluation of the Impact projects indicates that learning achievement does not necessarily suffer if reductions are made in the time students spend with trained teachers provided that self-instruction and peer-learning opportunities are used as a substitute. There are many other projects which change the organization and delivery of teaching in order to reach out-of-school children. Several of these have succeded in reducing unit costs by employing educated members of the local community, who are given short introductory training courses and paid rates lower than government teachers. Two examples of this are the Banglandesh Rural Advancement Committee's non-formal primary-education project and the Shiksha Karmi project in Rajasthan. In both of these, achievement levels are comparable with, or better than, those in government schools in the same areas (Lovell and Fatema 1989; Anandalakshmy *et al.* 1991). Such experiments can make a useful overall contribution to improved access and quality. In some cases this can be achieved at less cost than would otherwise be the case. However, where novel delivery systems are in competition with normal government schools, the latter are usually preferred by parents.

Finally, many mass education systems are based on the assumption of linear progression through successive grades where what is taught and learned in one year is extended and deepened at the next. In principle this cumulative model of learning ought to result in higher and higher levels of achievement through the school system. The evidence from achievement studies and from the examination performance of students in many countries is disquieting. Failure to master large proportions of the curriculum is widespread, as demonstrated by the significant number of students whose score on multiple-choice tests would be obtainable by chance, even after several years of instruction. In the IEA science study the bottom 20 per cent of 14-year-old students in Ghana, Nigeria, the Philippines, and Zimbabwe scored at little more than these levels (Postlethwaite and Wiley 1991: 79). It would not be surprising to find similar results at younger ages. It is reported that mathematics achievement in a sample of Sri Lankan schools at grades 6 and 7 is little better than that in grade 5 when similar test items are administered. Achievement data require careful interpretation, but examiners from many countries would not be surprised by these results. If curricula in higher grades are based on the assumption of mastery of the lower levels, of which many students have at best a poor grasp, then later learning problems are inevitable. Far from being progressive, learning may become more of a cycle of cumulative ignorance where, at each level, a smaller proportion of what is supposed to be learned has actually been mastered.

In many countries there are subjects which are passed by only small proportions of candidates—sometimes as few as 10–20 per cent—after completing an educational cycle. Where the assessment tests are technically well conceived, the problems must reside in a combination of ineffective teaching and unrealistic curriculum goals. In such circumstances curricular goals are needed which are within reach of the majority of children with typical teachers and schools. The learning outcomes that are judged essential for all, or most, of the school population can thus be emphasized, and resources can be focused upon their achievement. Contrary to popular opinion, curriculum development of this kind, which emphasizes the mastery of particular learning goals, does not lower standards. On the contrary, setting goals that are demonstrably unattainable to the majority is itself often the cause of poor performance. The level of achievement of the most able students can be protected through the introduction of 'express promotion' streams which, incidentally, would result in a release of school places that could be made available to those not currently enrolled. Curricular reforms of the kinds suggested above are a precondition for successful implementation of automatic promotion. They are an important part of SFA strategy since they would increase internal efficiency by reducing repetition and lower the costs per primary school graduate. They also offer the prospect of quality improvement through the more widespread achievement of the learning goals that are set.

Individually none of the organizational and pedagogic innovations discussed here is likely sharply to reduce the costs of delivering primary education at reasonable quality. However, many could facilitate the more efficient use of existing resources. In different combinations, and depending on starting conditions, they offer the prospect of significant increases in access and achievement, whilst maintaining quality and without escalating costs.

3.4. Developing links between education and productive work

The enhancement of links between schooling and work is commonly advocated to reduce the costs of schooling and to increase its relevance. To what extent are such methods successful?

There are two main types of scheme. In the first, students undertake production activities as part of the normal curriculum and thereby contribute to the costs of their education in kind or through the sale of items produced. Innovations of this general kind have several limitations, amongst which the most important are:

- Students and parents may oppose the allocation of time to production activities if this is seen to damage performance in competitive examinations which give access to modern-sector jobs.
- The school environment typically precludes some activities, e.g. production of artefacts for sale depends on materials, tools, and an accessible market; agricultural production depends on the availability of suitable land (Gustafsson 1985).
- Production linked to education is likely to be less efficient than commercial production; it therefore has to be subsidized (directly or through discounting labour costs), or protected.
- Scarce production skills have an economic value and skilled practitioners may be unwilling to share these with others or see their market undermined (Lewin and Little 1984).
- Too much emphasis on production may lead to the subordination of learning to repetitive manufacturing tasks which provide little coherent skill-acquisition (as in Zambia; see Chunga 1991).

The vocational school fallacy propounded by Foster (1965) remains a powerful explanation of the limits to which vocationalization and 'education with production' innovations can be pushed. In many of the least-developed countries schooling is seen as a conduit through which scarce opportunities for modern sector employment are regulated. The symptoms of what Ronald Dore has termed the Diploma Disease (Dore 1976; Oxenham 1984) which accompany excess demand for access are not easily neutralized by appeals to eschew academic schooling in favour of acquiring vocational skills for which the rewards are much less attractive. Linking education with production is difficult to sustain in situations where selection pressures retain a dominant influence over the curriculum (see, for example, the analysis of the development of the Seychelles National Youth Service since 1978 in Haffenden 1991). It is difficult to strike a balance between academic and production activities, although some projects, for example the Secondary School Community Education project in Papua New Guinea, have been more successful than others (Vulliamy 1983). Nevertheless, in some circumstances, production can make a modest but significant contribution to the costs of schooling (see Komba and Temu 1987; Bray 1988; Swartland and Taylor 1988). Advocates of such policies argue that students, particularly at secondary level, have an obligation to contribute to the administration, maintenance, and development of the schools from which they benefit and that the expression of this obligation brings educational as well as financial benefits.

A second model is provided by work-experience schemes which reduce the time spent in school by some students, whilst shifting responsibility for their supervision and training to other organizations that benefit from their work. Savings occur if needed tasks within the public sector are performed at costs less than the market wage. Though there may be an element of cost-shifting in these circumstances the fact that useful work is undertaken offsets this. Educational benefits may also be gained for less than the cost of full-time schooling. Work experience of this kind is generally thought to contribute to character-building and national unity, to transmit useful skills and to assist community development.

Community service schemes that provide opportunities for older students to work as unqualified teachers, or as teacher assistants in primary schools, can help where there is a shortage of teachers. Though such students may not be as effective as trained teachers there are many support roles that they can play (practising reading, supervising self-study, assisting with marking, organizing creative activity and sports). This can release the time of trained teachers for important pedagogical tasks needing training and experience. Such opportunities may also attract more students into teaching, helping them both to start developing teaching skills and to adjust to the world of work. To the extent that they are paid less than trained teachers there are cost advantages, as in the case of Senegal discussed in Chapter 3. Since they assist rather than replace full-time teachers they need not be seen as a threat to teachers' pay and conditions of service.

The linking of education and production is a reform which is more suitable for secondary than primary schooling. The more time that is allocated to work-experience, the less will be available for basic learning goals, which, already at primary level, many students fail to reach. Older students can make useful contributions to the costs of schooling but such contributions will always be limited by the balance that has to be struck between production and training (World Bank 1991: 57).

4. Redistribution of Expenditure

Progress towards SFA requires policy measures that redirect resources towards primary education. This is especially so in the most economically disadvantaged countries in which recession and increased debt have introduced severe constraints on the growth of public spending and in which present financial allocations are a small part of what is needed. Five categories of redistribution need consideration: between sectors, delivery systems, higher and lower educational levels, types of institution, and types of expenditure. Which of these are a priority in pursuing SFA and how can they best be encouraged?

4.1. Redistribution between sectors

The first issue concerns the priority assigned to education in total public spending. The evidence suggests that for a substantial group of countries, especially those in Sub-Saharan Africa, educational expenditure as a percentage of the national budget has declined more often than it has increased over the last decade. Over the period 1972–86 more than twice as many low- and middle-income countries reduced than increased the proportion of government expenditure on education[12] (Hallak 1990: 27). Moreover this tendency was stronger in the education sector than in any other. It appears that military expenditures have not suffered in the same ways, the more so since they are often thought to be under-measured by national accounts. In countries with GERs below 90, ten out of twelve have experienced a decline in proportional allocations to education (Table 2.1) though it is in these countries that the needs for increases might be thought greatest. Though this group of countries has proportional allocations above the mean for all developing countries, low or even negative growth in real public spending has often reduced the value of educational expenditure. Thus, there have been sharp reductions in the flow of public resources to education in Latin America over the last decade and severe declines in Sub-Saharan Africa (Tables 1.4 and 1.5).

Two central dimensions of the policy debate concern debt-service payments and military allocations. In a good number of countries the squeeze on educational spending—absolutely and as a proportion of the national budget—has been linked to the escalation of debt-service payments. These have put pressure on the public expenditure base available for social-sector spending. The World Bank Development Reports indicate increased allocations given to 'other expenditure' in national budgets over the 1980s. In substantial part this reflects the increased burden of debt-servicing. Indeed debt-servicing as a proportion of export earnings has grown sharply in the majority of developing countries since 1980. We have seen (Chapter 2) that a causal relationship, though plausible in some

---

[12] Declines in the proportion of government expenditure taken alone do not necessarily indicate real reduction in expenditure per student since these will also depend on changes in the relative share of GNP that public expenditure represents. Nevertheless the downward trend reported above is striking. Ch. 2 has shown that unit expenditures by governments have been falling in many of the countries with GERs of less than 90.

countries, does not appear consistently across countries—those with the highest debt-service ratios are not necessarily those allocating less to educational expenditure. Nevertheless the debt burden on developing countries continues to siphon off as much as $170 billion a year (UNDP 1991: 79)—amounts that are vastly greater than the costs we later estimate for the external assistance needed for SFA. Thus relatively small concessions or debt swaps for human development could have a major impact on national budgetary allocations, particularly in the most indebted countries.

More than 30 developing countries were involved in armed conflicts in the late 1980s with the effects often spreading well beyond their borders. In those countries most severely affected there are likely to have been substantial negative effects on GDP growth and on the level of non-defence-related public-sector spending. A recent study argues that twenty-one out of fifty-three African States have experienced war as one of the largest factors in suppressing economic growth, comparable only to the effects of decline in the terms of trade. This has resulted in a decline in GDP growth in Southern Africa from an otherwise attainable 5–6 per cent to an actual 2–3 per cent per year, i.e. less than the rate of population growth in many cases (Green 1991). There are examples from Asia and Latin America which suggest similar trends. In Sri Lanka government spending on development projects has been truncated whilst civil disorder persists, drawing attention to other deleterious effects of violent strife. The range of effects includes dislocation of investment, destruction of infrastructure and physical facilities, reallocation of skilled and trained staff away from the social sectors, and the neglect of medium-term planning and policy review. All these circumstances inevitably contribute to undermining the morale and professional commitment of teaching staff, one of the most fragile and critical commodities of all.

As with debt, there is no simple relationship between defence spending and educational investment. It is widely recognized that current levels of defence provision are often excessive when measured against plausible needs. It is not uncommon in South Asia and Sub-Saharan Africa to find the proportion of GNP allocated to the military reaching two or three times that allocated to education (UNDP 1991: 82) and that military expenditure has been rising much faster than the national budget as a whole. This must result in a diversion of resources from other purposes and this problem has to be addressed in any coherent discussion of the resource needs of SFA, especially in those situations where external assistance is requested.

Thus, there is no simple global picture concerning the sectoral distribution of resources and the share allocated to education. What pertains in particular countries is a product of a combination of the willingness to support education *vis-à-vis* other sectors and the ability to do so, especially where austerity has become a recurrent feature of public-expenditure bargaining (Lewin 1987: 26). Which of these is dominant, willingness or ability, in the decisions to allocate a particular share of public expenditure to education will vary from country to country. Where there is evidence of low proportional allocations the temptation is to conclude that commitments to SFA are largely cosmetic and that the first task is to transform the policy-making environment so that espoused priorities are reflected in allocations. The only exceptions will be where there really are irreducible forward commitments that prevent this. Even in these cases the two most commonly cited obstacles—debt-servicing and defence needs—are open to scrutiny to see whether there really is room to manœuvre. When allocations are relatively high, yet SFA is elusive, the reasons will lie either in the internal distribution of the education budget (favouring higher levels of education), or in the low and possibly declining absolute levels of expenditure resulting from more general economic collapse. In the latter case external assistance seems unavoidable, in the former educational policy re-evaluation is needed to redirect resources to basic education.

In sum every effort must be made to restore budgetary provision for education at least to former levels in those countries where it has fallen. As our later simulations show, the provision of SFA will require budgetary allocations well in excess of the present levels in those countries furthest from SFA targets. Thus external assistance to promote SFA should be conceived in forms that protect educational investment within the broader context of structural adjustment and development planning.

4.2. Redistribution within the education sector between different delivery systems

Though much has been written about the prospects for enrolling more students outside conventional formal school systems there is little reliable evidence on the experience of this. Non-formal and out-of-school programmes are notoriously difficult to cost. Their forms are very varied, sources of support may be extremely diverse and include non-monetary contributions of uncertain value, successful completion rates and achievement data are usually not available, the programmes themselves are often transient, and target groups are often not clearly defined. Studies which have tried to compare the cost-effectiveness of adult education programmes have run into irresolvable problems arising from these factors (e.g. Carr-Hill and Lintott 1984).

There is some evidence on the cost-effectiveness of distance-learning. This is a widely promoted alternative delivery system, and includes open university systems, correspondence colleges, and radio learning. In most cases, however, these have not supplanted the formal systems that exist alongside them; rather they are complementary, satisfying demand that cannot be met through existing institutions. Sixteen distance-teaching projects, about half of which are at tertiary level, are reviewed in a recent study (Perraton 1986). Open University programmes usually have lower costs per graduate than conventional universities. Amongst the secondary-level programmes reviewed, several were more expensive per completed graduate than normal schools, although the majority were cheaper. Completion rates are crucial to these calculations, yet these are often not easy to discover. These studies indicate that well-designed and implemented distance-learning can offer lower unit costs, but savings that accrue are almost invariably made at post-primary levels.

There are a wide range of methods through which young learners can acquire useful knowledge out-of-school. Informal apprenticeship is common and many countries have institutionalized community-based education programmes that, to a greater or lesser extent, shadow the formal system (Lewin and Jones 1985). However, these are rarely given high priority by governments, since they have less political visibility than the formal system. Employers may also be wary of supporting large-scale schemes unless they have some guarantee that those trained will use their skills within the sponsoring enterprise. Where skills are job-specific these kinds of scheme seem to be most successful. But, as with distance-education, such opportunities occur mainly at post-primary level. Where training programmes are in direct competition with established primary schools the effective demand for them tends to be weak.

There are exceptions to this general perspective. The Bangladesh Rural Advancement Committee (BRAC) has run a non-formal primary education programme since 1985. This focuses on children who have been deprived of access to normal primary schools as a result of poverty, and it particularly encourages girls to enrol. By 1989 2,500 schools were functioning and a further 2,000 were planned. These schools offer a three-year programme for 8- to 10-year-olds and a two-year programme for 11- to 14-year-olds. There are no tuition fees. Teachers for these schools are recruited from local communities and given twelve days' initial training followed by monthly training sessions. They are paid a stipend of about $US10 month (1989) which is about one-third of that for a government teacher. Preliminary evaluations (Lovell and Fatema 1989) suggest that the cost per student is about $US15 per year, excluding the contributions that communities make to the maintenance of classroom facilities and the opportunity costs arising from school attendance. Four international donors have supplemented the internal resources of BRAC. The drop-out of students appears to be very low (1 to 2 per cent annually) and about 95 per cent of those following the programme for 8- to 10-year-olds subsequently enter grade 4 of government primary schools. Evidence suggests that achievement levels are comparable with those of students in government schools. These features are probably critical to its success and popularity with parents. However this demonstrates that it is possible for alternative systems to work effectively at low cost with students who would otherwise not be enrolled. However, it remains to be seen whether the extension of the project to a much larger scale will prove viable. BRAC schools are not replacing normal provision, but supplementing it for groups to whom it has not been available.

In those countries experiencing the most intractable recessionary pressures, and in those where the SFA challenge is greatest, spending on formal education, and, in particular, on salaries, is likely to absorb an increasing share of the total budget. Substantial growth in government resources for non-formal education and non-traditional educational delivery systems is therefore unlikely. This does not preclude growth in non-government support for these programmes, or external assistance to them. Where there are substantial cost advantages in adopting new delivery methods they should be explored if they make SFA more afford-able. However, these may be most realistically regarded as attractive short-term interventions to meet special educational needs (especially for those currently not enrolled) rather than as system-level solutions that will lead to the replacement of formal schools.

4.3. Redistribution between levels within the cycle

Strategies aimed at limiting places at secondary and tertiary levels, or at reducing the level of subsidies to them, would seem to provide an obvious and attractive source of additional resources for primary schooling. However, care is needed in drawing conclusions from recent trends in allocations to different levels. In those countries which are approaching UPE, it is to be expected that the percentage of the budget allocated to higher levels will grow as a result of increased post-primary provision. Nevertheless, as shown in Chapter 1, the majority of developing countries, even those with low gross enrolment ratios, have experienced historically higher growth rates at secondary and tertiary levels than at primary over the twenty years from 1970 to 1990. This has inevitably resulted in relative shifts in resources towards the higher levels. Exceptions are countries like Malawi and Tanzania which have deliberately limited the supply of post-primary places and have resisted the pressures of excess demand, at least in so far as the publicly financed elements of the system are concerned.

Mingat and Tan (1985) attempt to measure the resources which would be released by reducing or eliminating subsidies at higher levels. Their study indicates that the scope for this is greater in Francophone Sub-Saharan African countries where unit cost differences are greatest. Using data from ten countries (eight of which are Francophone) they argue reductions in subsidies for higher education by 10 per cent would permit an increase in primary enrolments by about 2 per cent. Similar changes at secondary level would support an increase of 1.6 per cent in primary enrolments at the current unit cost levels. It is only when large reductions in subsidy and high levels of recovery of operating costs are introduced that substantial enrolment gains become possible. Thus if student subsidies were cut completely, GERs at primary could be improved by up to 18 points in some cases, though the average is much less than this. Removal of all subsidies at higher and secondary level and 100 per cent cost-recovery in higher education fails on its own to release enough resources for UPE in most of the countries studied. Part of the reason is that the countries with the smallest current primary enrolment levels also have the smallest absolute enrolments in higher education and therefore the lowest amounts of subsidy which can be transferred. Since unit cost ratios are much lower outside Africa the impact of subsidy withdrawal elsewhere is potentially less.

Worth-while transfers are possible however. In a system which allocated 20 per cent of its finance to tertiary education, and where 1 per cent of the age-cohort were enrolled, a reduction in the length of higher education by one year (and/or by combining some income-earning work-experience with study to achieve the same effect) could release about 4 per cent of the total education budget. This could facilitate as much as a 10 per cent increase in primary expenditures and enrolments. Chapter 3 has drawn attention to some countries (Senegal, Ghana) where transfers of this kind are being pursued.

One distributional issue which has commanded insufficient attention in the past, yet which has great relevance to policy for SFA, concerns resource allocations *within* schools. Where the same schools include both primary and secondary grades it is not uncommon to find disproportionate amounts of resources allocated to the teaching of the higher grades. Yet this is rarely detectable from published statistics, which hardly ever indicate the distribution of resources available to each grade of primary or secondary pupils separately. In practice, classes in higher grades tend to be smaller and therefore benefit from lower pupil/teacher ratios. They also have much higher proportions of qualified teachers. They tend to receive the benefit from investments in expensive equipment, for example in science subjects (Lewin 1991: 70). Skewed resource allocation towards higher grades also appears where cost-recovery mechanisms are in place. The probability is that most contributions are collected from students in lower grades (since this is where enrolments are greatest) but that expenditure is biased towards upper grades where public examinations are held. This invites analysis, grade by grade, of the differences in unit costs which result from allocation policy at the level of individual schools.

4.4. Redistribution between different types of institution

The policy issue here concerns the appropriate institutional mix at each educational level. The possibilities include public and private institutions, fee-paying or free places, community-supported schools, boarding- or day-schools, technical and vocational as opposed to general schools, and many others. Since some types of institution have higher unit costs than others, an important question concerns whether changing the mix can lower average unit costs and therefore provide more school places for the same investment.

The financial issues surrounding the encouragement of private schooling, levying fees, and increasing community contributions are taken up later in this chapter. At primary level non-specialized day institutions generally have the lowest costs and the case for specialized facilities is weakest. Boarding provision seems overgenerous except where geographical and demographic circumstances demand it. Similar arguments apply at secondary level (see Section 4.2).

The financial aspects of providing technical and vocational education, where unit costs tend to be higher than in general academic schools, have been the subject of an extensive debate. The complexities of measuring cost differentials are considerable and include difficulties with the treatment of direct and indirect costs, the rates of discount to apply to capital costs, social and private costs, and the appropriate unit of analysis— should this be teaching periods, the completed programme, or something else? (Cummings 1988). In Tanzania recurrent costs in the early 1980s were 19 per cent greater in agricultural schools than academic schools, 13 per cent greater in technical schools, and 9 per cent greater for commerce (Hinchliffe 1983). In Kenya industrial education subjects have had twice the staffing costs and five times the capital costs of normal subjects (Cummings *et al.* 1985). In Thailand unit costs in agricultural and technical colleges were 98 per cent and 54 per cent higher respectively than in other professional training-colleges (Tibi 1986). In the case of Colombia and Tanzania (Psacharopoulos 1985*a*) there is no compelling evidence that graduates from such institutions are valued in the labour market more highly than those attending academic schools, at least in terms of calculated rates of return. In similar situations there may be savings to be made by restricting the future growth of technical and vocational schools to those areas where there is no alternative way of meeting human-resource needs.

A final policy concern is the distribution of unit costs between nominally similar institutions at the same level. An example will serve to make the point. In some countries overstaffed schools coexist with other schools which are understaffed in the sense that they have fewer teachers than the number to which they are entitled. This sometimes occurs where urban schools are attractive teaching locations and where many teachers are spouses of salaried workers located in the towns. Where salaries are paid from a central budget overstaffed schools suffer no penalty for excess teachers. In contrast understaffed rural schools, with less attractive working conditions, may suffer the double penalty of higher teaching loads and class-sizes, and receive no benefit from the savings that are made on salaries as a result of their being understaffed. The consequence is that actual unit costs may vary between schools by a factor of 2:1 or more (see Chapter 3). Reducing these disparities is important for increasing internal efficiency and distributing quality more evenly. It may have only marginal implications for the salary bill as a whole.

4.5. Redistribution between types of expenditure

The final redistributive issue concerns the balance between different categories of expenditure—capital, salary recurrent, and non-salary recurrent. In developing countries the proportion of expenditure allocated to recurrent, and the proportion within that allocated to salaries, increased much more frequently than it decreased in the first part of the 1980s (Lewin 1987: 61). These trends were strongest in Sub-Saharan Africa. It is probable that the trend subsequently slowed, if only because, in many countries, salaries accounted for almost the whole of recurrent expenditures. Of course, the greater proportional importance of salary costs does not imply that salaries have increased in real terms. As Section 2.1 has shown, the opposite has often happened, most notably so in Sub-Saharan Africa.

Capital expenditures on education have also fallen to tiny amounts in many of the poorest countries, and in many others, those which occur are largely externally financed. Cancellation of new capital projects and investment programmes is usually one of the first responses to austerity. This, despite indications that the stock of buildings is stretched well beyond capacity in many countries (De Bosch *et al.* 1985).

It follows from what has been said above that expenditure on materials and other non-salary recurrent expenditure has fallen, sometimes to close to zero. This is a fairly universal feature of countries suffering from recession (Cornia 1984; Lewin 1987; Hallak 1990). Unesco data suggest that in all regions the proportion of educational budgets allocated to teaching materials diminished in the first part of the 1980s, more strongly in Sub-Saharan Africa than elsewhere. There, expenditure on educational materials represented about 1 per cent of the recurrent primary-school budget in 1983 (World Bank 1988*a*: 141) which was equivalent to about 60 US cents per child. Because of unequal distribution, for a good proportion of the school population it is safe to assume that such expenditures were negligible. This, despite well-known studies that indicate the strong relationship that exists between availability of textbooks and school achievement (Heyneman 1978; Fuller 1985). In recognition of this, some countries have taken steps to improve the supply of materials and increase their durability. The Philippines and Ghana are undertaking this in the context of structural adjustment and Sri Lanka has had an effective free textbook scheme for more than a decade.

The tendency to protect salary budgets at the expense of other types of recurrent expenditure has had several unfortunate consequences. These include the shortage of teaching materials, the depletion of professional support for teachers (in-service courses, advisory and inspection services), and increased reliance on non-government support. The first and second of these have undermined conditions in schools to such an extent that effective teaching has become difficult or impossible in many. The third consequence has had negative implications for equity and efficiency since the capacity to substitute community resources for those previously provided by government is unevenly distributed.

To conclude, some reconsideration of patterns of allocation in all the above ways is desirable in identifying policy options to promote SFA. To ignore the distributional issue is to endorse the current allocation of resources, which is often not consistent with attaching priority to the development of primary education. Savings are potentially available from rearranging the disposition of existing expenditures, and increased access to primary schooling can be achieved by such means. Such benefits, of course, can also be secured by directing additional resources towards those communities where SFA goals are furthest from being met. It is to a consideration of measures to raise additional resources that we now turn.

5. Raising Additional Financial Resources

5.1. Public versus private provision

Earlier sections of this chapter have indicated that the opportunities for reducing the unit costs of education, and for providing efficiency savings by restructuring school systems are significant, but that they are likely to provide only part of the 'solution' to the problem of universalizing access to primary schooling. Equally we have shown that although the under-provision of resources for education can sometimes be tackled by changing national spending priorities, it is not *usually* caused by governments giving too little importance to education relative to other sectors. The main problem faced by low-income and adjusting countries needing to raise educational expenditures is one of insufficient financial resources to support appropriate levels of spending across the whole range of public sector activities. Education has been squeezed by the needs to cap public spending and to finance rising debt-service obligations. But so too have expenditures in other sectors.

A critical question, therefore, is whether additional finance for education can be raised so as to permit the achievement of SFA, and, if so, how this could best be done. A number of advocates of educational policy reform, including some aid agencies and international financial institutions, have in recent years concluded that additional resources for education will have to come from private rather than public resources.

5.2. User-charges and private provision

There are three major arguments for the continued public provision of schooling. First, the benefits of education accrue not only to the individual, but also to society at large. Thus, without state provision some underinvestment in schooling would be likely, even amongst those who can afford to pay for it. Secondly, exclusion from school of those who are too poor to pay fees would involve efficiency losses arising from their unexploited human potential. Thirdly, private provision strengthens existing inequalities by giving privileged access to education—and, hence, higher future incomes—to those who are already amongst the better-off. These present a formidable list of dangers in the path of proposals to finance schooling privately.

These considerations have, throughout the twentieth century, led the majority of countries to move gradually away from dependence upon philanthropic and private funding sources towards the public provision of education. In recognition of some of the dangers of leaving the provision of schooling to the private market, the UN Declaration of Human Rights, in 1948, included free elementary education as one of its major goals. Later pronouncements of the UN have tended to extend the advocacy of free provision to include secondary, technical, and higher education for all who have the capacity to benefit therefrom. In this context, the recent advocacy of an increased dependence upon fees and the private provision of schooling is, at first sight, puzzling.

The fact is, however, that in a great many countries a mixture of public and private funding of schooling presently exists. Private schools and colleges are common, both in the forms of highly resourced, élite institutions, and as second-chance establishments for those who failed to gain or maintain access to the public system. The equity implications of these kinds of parallel system are usually unfortunate: if private schools are high quality relative to the public sector they tend to foster easy access to élite status; and if they are the reverse they tend not to offer social mobility for those who utilize them. Within the public sector, fees are fairly frequently charged, albeit not usually fully cost-covering. Also, they are often a higher proportion of unit costs at lower than they are at higher levels of schooling. This tends to have perverse equity and efficiency consequences in view of the small proportions and higher-income characteristics of the population enrolled at upper-secondary and tertiary levels.

The complexity of these circumstances belies the apparent simplicity of the case for free and universal schooling. Although arguments are made in defence of the greater efficiency of private schools in Colombia, Tanzania, Thailand, and elsewhere in the developing world (Psacharopoulos 1987a; Jimenez *et al.* 1988), the evidence remains weak, and at present appears dwarfed by the likely dimensions of their associated equity costs. Nevertheless the case for restructuring the *existing* balance of private provision and fee incidence in ways which improve equity and efficiency at no (or negative) net cost to the State is considerably stronger. This, to use the jargon of economics, is a type of 'second best' solution, which is cognizant of the need for financial stringency (or for the achievement of net savings) in the public sector.

In this context the introduction of cost-recovery measures at higher levels of education—particularly if they allowed fee reductions at school level—could have positive equity and efficiency consequences. Additional resources for the expansion of primary schooling could be generated, and the public subsidies to higher education, which at present mainly benefit the richer groups, would thereby be reduced. It would, of course, be necessary to ensure that the introduction of such fees did not reduce private returns to levels which led to absolute declines in tertiary enrolments. This would be a danger in some Sub-Saharan countries at the present time (Colclough 1991: 204–7). Equally, such changes are regressive to the extent that they prevent bright children from low-income households from continuing to pursue their studies. This problem is accepted by most advocates of charges, who seek mitigation of these costs—particularly at tertiary level—by the introduction of loans and/or scholarships in order to remove the bias against the poor.

5.3. Loans and scholarships

In principle, at least, loans schemes tackle both the problems of equity and of resource-generation very subtly. By shifting the costs of tertiary education to the direct beneficiaries, and by financing them out of future rather than present income, a desirable wedge is opened up between eligibility to attend and the present ability to pay. This would reduce the future net benefits of tertiary education, and, by providing machinery with which poor bright children can meet the present direct financial costs, both static and intergenerational equity would seem to be promoted by such a scheme.

Student loans schemes are widely used in Latin America and the Caribbean (twenty-nine countries), but they are not common elsewhere. Ghana, Tanzania, and Nigeria have experimented with loans to finance university students, and a new loans scheme was introduced in Zambia early in 1989. China, too, began to implement a loans scheme for some university students in the late 1980s. These countries remain exceptions outside Latin America. In practice, experience suggests that loans schemes confront a range of practical difficulties. They tend not to become self-financing, owing to high default rates on repayment, unemployment or abstention from the labour market, and high administrative costs (Woodhall 1983). Equally, they do not provide a source of additional public revenue which will rapidly become available, owing to the length of time needed for repayments to build up. Moreover, although loans schemes provide equity benefits in comparison with the net effects of user-charges, there are, of course, net equity costs in comparison with the present typical structure of subsidies. Since, under the present system of fee-free higher education, the poor, typically, do not enrol, student loans could only exacerbate this pattern. Thus, any net increase in the costs of tertiary attendance will cause the *de facto* inequities of access to increase further rather than the reverse. Since loans involve both higher perceived and higher actual personal costs than grants, far from their providing an escape whereby the pro-equity effects of user-charges can be captured, they rather appear to be an instrument whereby the present inequities of access to and provision of higher education—and possibly of lower levels also—would be further entrenched.

The only escape from this consequence would be to provide scholarships to promote access for the poor to higher levels of education, but this obviously further undermines the revenue-raising objectives of user fees. Is it then not possible to secure both revenue-raising and equity-promoting objectives at once?

5.4. Expanding the tax net

The traditional response to this dilemma would be to reassert a separation between the financing of and the determination of access to publicly provided services. This is partly—though by no means wholly—achieved via the fees, loans, and scholarships approach. A more thoroughgoing option is, of course, offered by the general tax system. There are a number of difficulties with this option, particularly for low-income and adjusting countries. First, it is widely believed that many countries in this category are approaching the limits of their taxable capacity. Incentives within the formal sector have been heavily undermined by the reduction of personal incomes associated with devaluation and other adjustment measures. In the early 1990s, the critical issue in many public sectors is how to raise disposable incomes so as to improve motivation and productivity at work rather than to contribute to their further decline via increasing marginal rates of tax. Equally, the need to restore lost output (both the value and the physical quantity thereof) cannot be addressed without restoring profitability. Measures to increase company taxation are, therefore, often judged to be inauspicious in the present environment.

These points have substance. However, we should recognize that to use them as arguments for cost-recovery via user fees is dangerous, since success with the latter would itself provide evidence for the existence of additional taxable capacity. Furthermore, countries are by no means equally affected by these incentive and capacity constraints. In many there remains scope for increases in tax (probably in the context of wider fiscal reforms), and such opportunities need to be considered on a country-by-country basis.

A second argument frequently cited against further dependence upon general taxation is that, at present, such systems are typically regressive. Yet this implies the need for advocacy of differential, in preference to equal changes in marginal rates, rather than that the tax instrument should be completely ignored. Finally, the argument that additional public revenues from general taxation would be used either to reduce public deficits, i.e. would not be spent, or to expand non-educational services (or to pay off debt) is not decisive: it seems just as likely—or unlikely—that, in response to higher revenues accruing from user fees, public expenditures on education would be compensatorily reduced. The political likelihood of either of these two sets of outcomes may not be significantly different from each other in many of the poorer countries. The total resources required to provide education for all in these countries are large. Increases in the tax base, and in the progressivity of the tax system will have to play an important part in raising the necessary resources in a good number of countries in this group.

5.5. New fiscal instruments

The design of new fiscal instruments for the purposes of raising additional educational finance has been largely ignored in the relevant literature. In this context a promising alternative to user fees and student loans schemes would be a payroll tax, levied upon employers, related to their employment of (or wage payments to) graduates from designated educational programmes. Payroll taxes have in fact been used in a number of countries as a means of financing vocational training. These have been broadly of two types. First, levy-grant schemes have been established in Ivory Coast, Kenya, Fiji, Singapore, Taiwan, and Tunisia. Typically the schemes tax employers in the private sector at rates varying between 1 and 2 per cent of their wage/salary bill. Rebates and grants can be claimed by firms undertaking 'approved' training of their own employees.

Of special interest for present purposes are revenue-raising schemes where tax revenues (again, usually derived from taxes in the range of 1–2 per cent of wage and salary costs) are earmarked to finance training provided by the State. Such a scheme was first introduced in Brazil in the early 1940s, and they are still mainly operative in Latin America, where fourteen countries have introduced them. In Sub-Saharan Africa, Zimbabwe has a well-established scheme. These have raised substantial revenues which have been used to build up national training systems, often providing a wide range of pre-employment training courses (a recent review of such schemes is provided by Whalley and Ziderman, 1989).

Arrangements such as these have not yet been used to finance educational (as opposed to training) programmes. Yet there are no decisive reasons to suggest that they would be inappropriate for those purposes. A recent analysis of a payroll tax levied on the wage bill for university graduate employees suggests that it would be superior to a student loans scheme as a means of raising additional educational finance in a number of important ways (Colclough 1990). It can be shown that the costs of the tax initially fall entirely on private employers, but they result in downward pressure upon graduate wages over the medium run. This, together with associated employment effects, would be useful in countries where university graduates remain in short supply, and where scarcity rents have been excessive. More significantly, there would be none of the equity costs associated with user fees or student loan schemes: although graduates do pay part of the cost of the tax via lower wages and employment (depending, in fact, upon the relevant demand elasticities in the skill markets for graduates) they are not actually aware of so doing. Thus, the disincentive effects of fees and loans for the progeny of poorer households are avoided. Finally, the revenue-generating potential of a payroll tax is greater than that of a student loans scheme: its financial impact is not heavily lagged, and for governments with high rates of time-preference (as in low-income and heavily indebted countries) it would usually prove to be a superior instrument on financial grounds. More work on this proposal is needed in a range of countries. But initial calculations for a number of African countries suggest that the net additional revenues which could be generated by a modest graduate payroll tax (of the order of 10 per cent) would be equivalent to between 5 and 10 per cent of the recurrent costs of primary schooling. This, then, represents a useful potential source of resources for primary-level expansion.

5.6. Community financing

A large number of countries have experimented with ways of passing some schooling costs to local communities. Rooted in traditions of self-help, such initiatives can often mobilize resources which otherwise would remain underutilized, and they can engender the further commitment of parents (in terms of both time and interest) to the schooling of their children. The most usual form of such community financing is the provision of labour and local materials, thereby to reduce the capital costs of school provision or expansion. There are examples, however, of teachers' salaries being paid partially or entirely by the community which they serve, and of school books and equipment—over and above some centrally provided minima—being similarly financed.

Although appealing from the perspective of the costs incurred by the State, such schemes have a number of associated problems. First, the full costs of community financing are rarely acknowledged or measured. There is a tendency to believe that labour provided by villagers has little or no associated opportunity cost. Yet unless great care is taken in the mobilization of such labour (including the timing *vis-à-vis* other demands) there will almost certainly be a cost in lost agricultural, or other, output, which it is wrong to ignore.

Secondly, passing schooling costs to the community is only slightly less inequitable than is passing them to the individual household via user fees. It can result, as in the cases of China and Zimbabwe discussed in Chapter 3, in a highly differentiated school-structure which closely reflects the relative prosperity of different communities and geographical areas.

Nevertheless, the devolution of responsibility for some aspects of schooling provision is less damaging than others. In general the provision of those aspects of the infrastructure, the quality of which are not likely to be causally associated with cognitive outcomes (some buildings, latrines, sports facilities) is less risky and inequitable than the devolution of responsibility for other items (teachers' salaries—and thus the proportion of teachers trained/untrained—school textbooks, and other learning materials) which are so associated.

Thus, provided that such approaches are used with care, some subsidy to the education budget can be provided by local communities without surrendering too much equity in the process. The costs should nevertheless be recognized. Although such services may be free goods from the perspective of the Ministry of Education, they are not free from that of the Ministry of Finance in terms of output, exports, and taxes forgone, still less so from that of society as a whole.

6. Conclusion

The analysis in this chapter has indicated that there are a wide range of educational and fiscal reforms which can be used in order to reduce the costs of education, to redistribute resources in ways which would be more supportive of primary schooling, and to raise additional resources to finance increased spending on education by the State.

Some of these reforms involve reorganizing existing practice in ways which would be more effective from an educational viewpoint, and in that sense they have few, if any, associated costs. Most of them, however, are not costless. In some cases, the trade-off would involve weighing the priority associated with different categories of expenditure, and therefore assigning values to the goals of UPE and SFA, as compared with those in other sectors, or within education itself. In other cases, as with some of the measures to reduce the unit costs of education, there would be threats to the quality of schooling, and in others there would be equity costs associated with the implementation of the reforms.

On the basis of these kinds of consideration, the next chapter selects a group of reforms which we consider likely to be most efficient from the standpoints of minimizing the costs of education and of raising additional resources whilst doing least damage to the quality of schooling, and to equality of access to it. In addition, we identify a further group of reforms which are designed to raise the quality of primary schooling well beyond the levels which at present characterize the school systems of most developing countries. The question then becomes whether or not such changes would be sufficient to bring UPE and SFA within reach for all countries in the developing world.

5

Modelling the Impact of Reforms:
Cost and Quality Issues

1. Introduction

As indicated in earlier chapters, UPE can no longer be considered to be
the main goal for the development of primary education. This is because
it fails to address the problems of low internal efficiency and poor educational quality. In a good number of school systems achieving UPE alone
would simply expand inefficient and low-quality provision. However, a
series of policy reforms, based on lessons derived from the analysis of
Chapters 3 and 4, appear to offer the opportunity of more efficient and
higher-quality schooling at an affordable cost. These include interventions
that could both save or transfer costs with minimal damage to quality,
as well as those which would directly enhance quality and ensure that
greater proportions of the 6–11-year-old age-group were enrolled.

This chapter therefore asks how, operationally, should schooling for all
(SFA) be defined in ways that would increase internal efficiency, improve
quality, and make the costs more affordable? Specifically, which policy
reforms offer the most promise in moving towards the goal of SFA? What
is the best way of simulating the cost implications of implementing these
reforms and how can we interpret the results?

2. The Operational Definition of SFA

We have argued (Chapter 1) that UPE, defined as the achievement of
GERs of 100, understates the problems of providing education for all
because it takes no account of the extent of over-age entry nor of rates
of repetition which are often high. Consequently, net enrolment ratios
(NERs) often fall well short of 100 even where UPE has been reached.
Furthermore, UPE is silent about the qualitative dimensions of educational development. Our definition of SFA, which, from Chapter 2, is
'the circumstance of having a school system in which all eligible children
are enrolled in schools of at least minimally acceptable quality', avoids
those pitfalls.

Nevertheless, a more operational definition of SFA is needed if its cost implications are to be explored for each country separately. Here, there are two main problems which have to be addressed. The first concerns the identification of a measurable enrolment criterion which would suit all circumstances. The attainment of NERs of around 95, whilst conceptually appropriate (see Chapter 2) turns out not to be useful operationally. This is because data for NERs are less widely available and much more inaccurate than those for GERs, partly because information on the ages of pupils is often not systematically collected.

Even if these data were available, however, estimates of cost based upon the achievement of NER targets would understate true costs to the extent that repetition and over-age enrolment remained in the system. It follows that the GER values associated with SFA have to be implicitly or explicitly assumed if the costs of the latter are to be assessed. Nevertheless, the use of the same GER for all countries also would not work: no single value is appropriate since the gap between the GER and NER depends on the interaction of a number of parameters, the values of which differ between countries.

Accordingly, the operational definition of SFA which we have adopted takes UPE (where GER equals 100) as the starting-point, and then requires reductions in rates of repetition by three-quarters of their current levels and in drop-out rates by one-half. These criteria do not explicitly require the elimination of over-age entry to primary schools, since, if its present incidence continued, the reduced rates of repetition and drop-out would still ensure that most students completed the cycle. Some possibility of over-age entry is in any case desirable—at least during the transitional period until SFA is reached—in countries with large numbers of out-of-school children of primary age.

This approach produces GERs at SFA which are typically between 100 and 110 depending on the starting conditions in different countries. This outcome is plausible: the fact that GERs at SFA exceed 100 by a modest margin, whilst repetition and drop-out are reduced, ensures that NERs would be greater than 90 in all but a few extreme cases, thus reasonably approximating the conditions where almost all children would actually be enrolled. This then provides a useful basis for estimating the enrolment consequences of achieving SFA in the circumstances facing each country.

The second problem concerns how best to measure, and cost, the difference between the mere expansion of existing primary systems to UPE levels, and the substantial qualitative improvement necessary, in most countries, for SFA to be achieved. This is not easy. Since each national education system both reflects and operates within a unique historical, cultural, and economic context, any single set of quality-enhancing policy reforms would obviously not be fully appropriate for all countries. On the other hand, the factors that might reasonably be relevant in each country could not possibly be assessed in every case. Some compromise is needed if the methods adopted are to be both useful and feasible. This has been tackled by developing a number of policy reforms, the application of which can be simulated for each country in ways which are, to some extent, responsive to a country's circumstances.

Thus, the quality-enhancing differences which separate SFA from UPE, in this approach, are the reductions in rates of repetition and drop-out already noted, the allocation of a minimum sum of resources per pupil for learning materials, and increased real expenditures upon teachers' salaries. As will be explained later, this package of measures is sensitive to the initial circumstances in each country. It identifies a minimum set of conditions necessary to satisfy the qualitative criteria of SFA, and, in that sense, completes its operational definition.

In addition to the quality-enhancing reforms, other policy changes are simulated which are designed to make SFA more attainable by reducing the cost-burden to the State. Although not part of the definition of SFA, their implementation would be critically important in a large number of countries if SFA is to be achieved. The full package of reforms adopted is discussed in more detail later in this chapter. They allow the development of an analytical approach which goes well beyond the otherwise trivial exercise of projecting the cost of increased enrolments on a pro rata basis. The next section explains the details of the approach used.

3. The Approach to the Simulations

The costs to the State of achieving UPE and SFA can be investigated in a number of dfferent ways. The simplest approach would be to inflate existing GERs to 100 over, say, a period of ten years, and compute on a pro rata basis the necessary increased expenditures. This, however, would seriously underestimate the total costs of UPE, since the implications of expansion at secondary level, imposed by achieving UPE, would be ignored. Equally, the impact of changing some of the parameters which determine unit costs could not easily be investigated.

Alternatively, the reasoning of Chapter 2, which provided the identity

$$\text{GER} = x_g/ac_g$$

could be utilized. Thus, x_g (public expenditure on primary schooling as a proportion of GNP) would be defined by the following equation for a GER of 100:

$$x_{g100} = \frac{\text{GER}_{100} \cdot x_{gc} \cdot c_{g100} \cdot a_{100}}{\text{GER}_c \cdot c_{gc} \cdot a_c}.$$

This[1] would allow changes in primary expenditure per pupil as a proportion of GNP, c_g, and in the proportion of the population of school-going age, a, to be taken into account. However, even here, changes in the value of c_g would have to be assumed rather than integrated analytically in the approach used. And if both c_g and a remained unchanged from current values the equation would reduce to:

$$x_{g100} = x_{gc} \cdot GER_{100}/GER_c.$$

This, of course, is the same as the first option discussed above. Neither of them could account for the knock-on consequences of expanded primary schooling nor of the cost-impact of policy reforms.

A much better approach is to utilize an enrolment-transition model to project school enrolments at all levels, so as to reach UPE and SFA over a given period of time. Recurrent costs can be calculated from the annual costs of servicing a school place for each category of student, multiplied by total enrolments. Capital costs can also be projected on the basis of demands for additional classroom space depending on the number of students to be accommodated in one classroom. This method can provide a flexible way of simulating growth in public expenditures, including those at secondary and tertiary levels.

This approach also allows the impact of a variety of policy reforms to be simulated. Thus, both enrolment parameters, e.g. primary enrolment ratios, repetition, promotion, drop-out, and transition rates by grade, and unit cost parameters, e.g. teachers' salaries, materials costs, administrative salaries, boarding costs, private enrolments, classroom building costs, can be manipulated independently. The effects on costs of different combinations of policy reform can thus be examined. This method provides an appropriate basis for comprehensive modelling.

The enrolment-transition model used was initially developed by Unesco,[2] and modified to suit our own purposes. In this model a spreadsheet is constructed showing enrolments by grade for primary, general secondary, technical and vocational schools, and teacher training. This is linked to another spreadsheet which itemizes unit costs associated with each level for teachers' salaries, ancillary staff, administrative and supervisory support, and learning materials. The two spreadsheets are linked to calculate capital and recurrent costs in future years. These may be compared to projections of the resources available, calculated on the

---

[1] Where GER_c = current GER; GER_{100} = GER of 100; x_{gc} = current public expenditure on primary education as a proportion of GNP; x_{g100} = public expenditure on primary education as a proportion of GNP where GER = 100; c_{gc} = current public expenditure per primary pupil as a proportion of GNP per capita; c_{g100} = public expenditure per primary pupil as a proportion of GNP per capita where GER = 100; a_c = the current proportion of the population which is of school age; a_{100} = the proportion of the population which is of school age when GER = 100.

[2] Further technical information on the model is given in the Technical Appendix and in Unesco (1990).

basis of assumptions about growth in the public budget and the share taken by education.

The model has been used to project costs over a fifteen-year period, for each level of education. With no change in the value of the initial parameters, increases in enrolments lead to pro rata increases in costs, as would be expected. However, the impact of policy reforms on these parameters can be isolated to explore their effects upon recurrent and capital costs, the distribution of expenditure between levels, and other expenditure outcomes.

4. Selection of Promising Reforms

The promising policy options identified from the analysis of Chapters 3 and 4 can be divided into three groups: 'cost-saving', 'cost-shifting', and 'quality-enhancing'. Inevitably there is some overlap between these categories, but they nevertheless provide a useful organizing structure for discussion. The advantages of each reform are considered below, as are the methods used to simulate their implementation. Cost-saving and cost-shifting reforms are defined first. These will be important for those countries which are presently furthest from achieving UPE or SFA and least able to afford either. In richer, or more educationally developed countries, these reforms may not be necessary from a financial point of view. But their efficiency benefits are still worthy of consideration. The quality-enhancing reforms are discussed subsequently. These are the reforms which are necessary to differentiate SFA from UPE.

4.1. Cost-saving reforms

A central problem in educationally disadvantaged countries with con-strained public-sector budgets is to find ways of providing more school places at lower total cost. The possibility of reducing teachers' salaries as a means of reducing unit costs has been rejected. We have argued that in many countries, especially in those most affected by poverty and recession, salaries have fallen below the levels necessary to retain qualified staff and to provide reasonable incentives for effective teaching (Chapter 4). Thus, it would, almost certainly, be counter-productive to contemplate any further reductions whatever the savings implied. The alternative is to focus on reforms that increase internal efficiency, in terms of the number of teachers required to support a given level of enrolment. Those reforms with the widest potential applicability are: introducing or extending double-shifting, allowing modest increases in the size of classes where these are low, and encouraging greater community participation in primary schools.

Double-shifting (Reform 1). The use of double-shifting in schools is widespread. Patterns vary considerably and include two schools using the same building in different shifts, different grades of the same school enrolled during mornings and afternoons, lengthened school days or weeks allowing overlapping shifts, and alternating day-attendance by different groups of students (Bray 1989: 16). The impact of any of these variants of double-shifting on recurrent costs depends predominantly on whether it places teachers in contact with more students. If the number of periods taught per day is greater, with a less than proportionate increase in salary costs, savings will accrue. There are examples where extending the amount of double-shifting has resulted in these kinds of benefit (Chapter 4).

This reform can have a substantial effect on costs without a necessary decline in quality. It operates directly on teachers' salaries per student, the largest element in recurrent costs, and does not necessarily change pupils' contact hours. It also has the virtue that it enables more students to be accommodated in the existing stock of classrooms. Some economies of scale can also arise through more intensive use of plant and a reduction in fixed overheads per student. Since it is essentially an organizational reform it can be implemented relatively speedily.

However, changes to established practices must be approached carefully, since this reform can be perceived by teachers as simply implying greater workloads, without concomitant increases in pay. It is preferable to see it in terms of increased productivity, where teaching time is released by increased teacher efficiency. In that regard, preparation time is not necessarily increased pro rata by increasing the number of lessons taught if these are of the same type. There is an additional marking load if each teacher has responsibilities for more students. But this can also represent a less than proportionate increase in workload if the opportunity is taken to increase the efficiency of assessment. For example, standardizing classroom tests, and/or collective setting of test papers is more efficient than individual setting. The careful re-using and sharing of teaching material from year to year also saves considerable teacher time and may also improve quality.

Although it is sometimes suggested that double-shift schools have a negative impact upon student achievement, the available evidence does not support this view (e.g. Hartley and Swanson 1984). There can be disadvantages for those who attend afternoon classes in countries where the climate is not congenial to study after midday. But this can be ameliorated by using a form of double-shifting that allows alternation of student groups between morning and afternoon school classes in different grades. Careful planning is also necessary to avoid obliging teachers to work unreasonably long hours in some versions of double-shifting.

Double-shifting reforms are introduced, in our analysis, via reductions in teacher/class ratios. It is assumed that these can be reduced by 15 per cent over ten years in primary and secondary schools. This has no effect on class-size, which remains the same. However, classroom building costs are reduced pro rata, since fewer new classrooms will be needed than would be the case without double-shifting. Of course, in some small schools double-shifting will not be possible as a result of low population density. However where schools exist and where local children are not enrolled, double-shifting can be a useful option.

In the first instance, the model assumes that no double-shifting exists. Of course, many systems already have a measure of double-shifting currently, but this does not vitiate our assumptions. The projections reflect relative changes in costs as a result of introducing reforms from an existing base. The implication is that whatever the current level of double-shifting, it is possible to increase this further to result in a 15 per cent reduction in the teacher/class ratio. Since there is in any case no reliable cross-country data on double-shifting this, in practice, is the only way to proceed.

Class-size (*Reform 2*). Increases in class-size reduce recurrent costs via increases in the pupil/teacher ratio. They also affect capital costs by reducing the number of new classrooms needed. This is a more familiar source of savings than double-shifting.

However, savings from this source bring attendant dangers. First, increasing class-sizes beyond the design specification of existing class-rooms is educationally counter-productive—overcrowding would result and furniture would be inadequate. Second, increases in the average class-size in most countries should be encouraged only if simultaneous measures are introduced to reduce the dispersion of class-size around its mean. Otherwise, the viability of teaching and learning in those schools which already have large classes would be undermined. Third, there are limits to the extent to which the size of classes can be increased in areas where population density is low. Fourth, increases in class-size obviously increase teaching loads and dilute students' access to teachers, although changes in teaching methods can reduce the attendant negative effects. Larger classes require different pedagogical and organizational skills and are often unpopular with teachers and parents for these reasons. Nevertheless, as indicated in Chapter 4, school achievement does not appear to be simply related to class-size, and in some cases, students in large classes outperform those in smaller ones (Fuller 1987: 276).

Thus, in many countries, careful increases in the average size of classes could release resources to enrol some of those currently out of school, or improve school quality, or both. These benefits can be gained where it is possible to consolidate small schools into larger units, combine under-enrolled classes to make up larger student groups, and use multigrade teaching methods to increase average class-size in low population density areas.

This reform has been modelled by assuming that current class-sizes can be increased by five pupils per class for all cases where the current average size is forty or below at primary and secondary levels, and thirty or below in teacher-training colleges and technical and vocational schools. This reform is implemented over a ten-year period and the values are subsequently held constant. Where current values exceed these limits the reform is not implemented. In practice, the dispersion of class-size around the mean should be reduced in those cases where it is large. This would have no net effect on student/teacher ratios, but it would bring equity benefits. It would also increase efficiency to the extent that the number of underenrolled classes were reduced.

Community participation (*Reform 3*). Encouraging the participation of ordinary people in the work of schools can reduce costs by making better use of the time of trained teachers. There are several ways in which this can occur. Most obviously parents, grandparents, or other relatives can help with tasks that do not require high levels of pedagogic skill. This already happens in many systems (Bray with Lillis 1988) where helpers from the community listen to children practising reading and writing, assist with self-study activities, and help organize extra-curricular activities. Teachers may need to organize and co-ordinate such contributions, so financial savings may not be exactly proportional to the amount of teaching time saved. Innovations of this kind require attention to curricular questions: Which learning activities do not require the time of trained teachers? How might learning tasks be modified to make them easier to supervise by untrained adults? These additional costs, however, can be modest compared with the amount of teacher-time saved.

Savings can also be secured by introducing school-leavers as temporary teaching assistants, often as part of national service schemes. School-leavers thereby acquire useful experience, contribute to national development, and save the time of trained teachers. Similarly teaching assistants, appointed from the community and paid at rates below those of trained teachers, can provide schooling at lower cost than conventional delivery methods, as in the Shiksha Karmi project and in BRAC (Chapter 4). Such teachers are more likely to remain in rural schools which are unpopular postings for teachers from other districts. More radical, but also possible, are schemes which use older pupils to work with younger pupils. Fourteen-year-olds benefit from contribution to the learning of younger children. Reading a story written by an older child and asking questions about it is one example of learning activity that can be of benefit to both the older and younger child. More use of peer-group learning, sibling assistance, and senior students can therefore generate savings in the time of trained teachers. The Child to Child programme, which operates in a large number of countries, illustrates some of these practices (Hawes 1988).

This reform, as implemented in our model, assumes that some combination of the strategies outlined above would reduce the unit cost of primary teachers by 10 per cent over ten years. If one period a day can be supervised, using community helpers or older children, about 15 per cent of the time of trained teachers would be saved. If this time were supervised by paid assistants remunerated at one-third of the salaries earned by teachers, the overall reduction in recurrent costs would be about 10 per cent. Of course, if assistance was unpaid the savings would be concomitantly greater. This calculation assumes that the opportunity costs of these reforms are negligible. This seems reasonable in the cases of those who are otherwise underemployed or of older students who are not yet active in the labour market. On the other hand, opportunity costs will sometimes be significant, and there may be a seasonal dimension which determines the most appropriate times of the year for contributions to the work of schools.

Reforms which involve community members more closely in the life of schools have other potential benefits. They could increase the willingness of the community to offer other kinds of support. They could help spread useful knowledge amongst adults as well as children, and provide valuable work-experience for some older children. In the present context, however, their strength lies in their ability to extend schooling opportunities, by increasing the number of students taught by a given number of trained teachers.

4.2. Cost-shifting reforms

The three policy reforms discussed above each reduce unit costs directly. There are others, however, which can shift some of the costs of education from the State to the users of the service. In this category, there are three reforms which are particularly promising. These are: allowing some growth in privately financed school places; recovering a proportion of the building costs of primary-school classrooms from the communities which use them; and freezing higher-education subsidies at current levels.

Privately financed school places (*Reform 4a*). There is ample evidence of the willingness of parents to spend money on the schooling of their children. The existence of official and unofficial fees and levies charged directly to parents, the extensive development of private tuition in many countries, the increasing numbers of private schools in some countries, and the successful fund-raising efforts of parent–teacher associations and school development societies all illustrate this. Thus, where it is not possible to increase public resources for education by other means, such as by increases in general taxation, it may be possible to shift some of the costs to communities or individuals.

Cost-recovery as a means of financing the mass of schools is unattractive. As argued in Chapter 4, it is invariably regressive and often divisive. However, in those countries where cost-recovery is one of the few feasible options for raising additional resources, it can be used as a selective rather than a universal mechanism. If the costs of some school places can be shifted from the public budget to communities and parents that have the ability and willingness to support them, resources for additional enrolments in other schools, serving less advantaged communities, would thereby be released.

At the simplest level a policy which allowed a regulated growth of private schooling would remove a proportion of enrolments from the public system and release places for new students. The first cost-shifting reform posits a 10 per cent decrease in unit costs over a decade, arising from an increase in enrolments in privately financed institutions. This is achieved by allowing private enrolment at primary level to increase from zero to 10 per cent, and from 5 to 15 per cent in secondary, technical, and vocational schools. We have assumed that 5 per cent of unit costs in private institutions fall on the public budget—a necessary adjustment given that teachers are generally trained at public expense and costs of curriculum development are often born centrally. As before, since we are concerned mainly with relative cost increases, the actual starting-point for private enrolments is not important; the implementation of this reform assumes merely that they can increase by the percentages stated.

There are, of course, dangers associated with this kind of reform. The encouragement of private schools may thwart national redistributive policies and diminish equitable access, as in Tanzania (Samoff 1990). Depending on how it is implemented it could result in flight from the public-school system by children of relatively wealthy parents, and possibly also by the better teachers. If this were so on a large scale it would impoverish public schools. It would also prove regressive if significant public subsidy were to be given to selective, effectively private, élite schools, notwithstanding the capacity of their clientele to support them as has happened in Zimbabwe. It could exacerbate differences in provision and educational opportunity, based purely on the ability to pay, or on the accident of which community students were born into, as appears to be the case in Sri Lanka.

There are a number of alternative methods of implementing this reform which would have a broadly similar impact on costs. These include levying fees related to family income; providing free schooling to those below a specified level of family income; generating scholarship funds from private money to sponsor places in the public-school system, and so on. None of these is preferable to the public financing of mass education systems. They are relevant both because private-school systems and fee-paying already exist on a large scale, and because their careful development could yield benefits for SFA policy. If this option were chosen it is clear that it should be designed so as not to increase the direct costs of schooling for children from very poor homes.

Reducing building costs (Reform 4b). A type of community support, for which there are many precedents, is the use of local resources to subsidize the costs of school building. This has a direct effect on capital costs. Schemes of this kind can take a number of forms, including cash donations, and the contribution of labour and/or materials. In many countries the government provides materials that are not readily available locally or have foreign exchange costs (such as roofs, cement, and furniture) and enlists the support of local contractors and labour to construct the schools. Such practices reduce the costs of commercially constructed premises considerably. If extended to the maintenance of buildings they can also reduce public (and sometimes total) non-salary recurrent costs.

Building costs vary according to the cost of land, labour, materials, and the design specification. Land-acquisition costs are influenced by local arrangements: in some countries communities are required to provide land for new schools; in others, land is compulsorily purchased at or below market rates. Labour may be commercially contracted or provided by the local community below its market cost. School building programmes using local labour can often provide welcome cash income for the local economy. Materials costs are often closely linked to the design specification, and can also vary widely. For example, secondary science laboratories vary in cost from about $US15,000 to as much as $US100,000 in eleven developing countries surveyed; equipment costs from $US3,000 to over $US50,000 (Caillods and Gottelman-Duret 1992). Self-evidently, low-cost designs using local materials are preferable both from a capital-cost and a maintenance point of view. It seems unlikely that either school quality or achievement gains are strongly related to building costs.

This reform is modelled by assuming that the average capital cost of primary classrooms will be halved over a five-year period. The costs of secondary school classrooms remain unchanged. These are less frequently constructed using community resources, although Kenya provides an exception to this rule (Lillis and Ayot 1988: 124). This reform also has equity implications, although less sharply so than with reform 4a. Problems typically arise on first introduction of the policy. Thenceforth, new schools are to be financed by local communities, whereas established schools only have to raise resources for additional classrooms. The burden therefore falls unevenly between disadvantaged areas with few schools and those areas which are already well provided. Differential public subsidies for schools in different locations may thus be required.

Freezing higher-education subsidies at current levels (Reform 5). There is a case for limiting subsidies to higher education in many educationally disadvantaged countries. Some level of subsidy is both necessary and desirable for political, economic, and social reasons. However, in many countries, careful analysis of the costs of higher education is needed: where subsidies are necessary they should be provided, but where they are essentially regressive, serving mainly private ends, they need to be progressively withdrawn. Since the unit costs of higher education are so much greater than those for primary schooling this reform has the potential to generate significant savings within the education budget (Chapter 4).

This reform is simulated by freezing public spending on higher education at its 1990 level, thus reducing the rate of growth of total public educational expenditure. This does not preclude the further growth in higher-education enrolments, financed by a combination of increased efficiency and greater private contributions. Within this framework, public subsidies could continue to favour faculties and institutions judged central to national development strategy.

The ease with which this reform could be achieved depends upon national circumstances. In principle, it is straightforward to freeze resource-allocation at current levels and create a planning climate where additional needs will be met outside the public purse. In practice, there would be resistance from groups with vested interests in maintaining public subsidies to higher education. The political choice is clear: equity and efficiency will often be best served by limiting such subsidies. But the extent to which this can be achieved will depend upon the political circumstances facing each country.

4.3. Quality-enhancing reforms

The achievement of SFA will require considerable improvements in the quality of primary schooling in most developing countries. These will be costly. In order to investigate their likely impact upon public expenditures, four quality-enhancing reforms have been simulated for each country. These comprise: increasing learning resources per student; increasing teachers' salaries; reducing repetition rates; and reducing rates of drop-out.

Increasing learning resources (*Reform 6*). The first quality-enhancing reform seeks to ensure that, at minimum, annual expenditures on learning resources equivalent to $US5 per child are made. That is a realistic figure for the majority of developing countries and sufficient to make a considerable impact on school quality when compared with existing levels (Chapters 3 and 4).

This reform addresses several problems. The first is that of chronic underfunding of non-salary budgets, especially in countries suffering from recession, where budgetary stringency has often increased the proportion of the recurrent budget allocated to salaries at the expense of other items. In the absence of sufficient textbooks, teaching aids, consumable materials, and school visits by supervisors, learning becomes compromised. Second, many countries have inefficient administrations which cannot ensure that those learning materials that do exist are present when and where needed. Third, even where learning materials do reach schools in sufficient quantity, many school budgets are too small to purchase supplementary books, writing material, wall charts, and classroom furniture, and maintain equipment and infrastructure. The need for these items can be determined only at school level since circumstances vary. Many cost little, but are important to the quality of learning.

Implicit in the specification of this reform is the need for careful planning to ensure that the allocations made for learning materials do result in benefits at school level. This may imply administrative reorganization to ensure schools have some recurrent budget to spend on materials directly and that distribution systems for materials succeed in reaching all schools. The reform is implemented at primary and secondary level in all cases where existing expenditure is less than $5, and not where it is greater.

Action of this kind has equity and efficiency benefits. As indicated in Chapter 1, the availability of learning materials has been shown to be positively associated with student achievement in a large number of studies. It is safe to assume that, at least until minimum thresholds have been exceeded, additional learning materials are a priority for improving school quality. Moreover, the provision of this minimum level of learning resources would reduce existing disparities between salary and non-salary spending per child.

Increasing teachers' salaries (Reform 7). Increases in teachers' salaries are incorporated in the policy reforms. These are vitally needed if the morale and quality of entrants to the profession are not to fall catastrophically. Recurrent costs are, of course, very sensitive to improvements in teachers' salaries. Increases are required which, on the one hand, do not provide an unsustainable burden on the budget but, on the other, recognize the appalling difficulties faced by teachers, particularly in the poorest and most educationally disadvantaged countries. Accordingly, this reform adopts a real salary growth of 15 per cent over a decade. More than this is often desirable, but its affordability in low-growth economies is questionable, particularly in economies where teachers' salaries are linked to other public-service pay scales. These increases are distributed smoothly over the ten-year period.

There is clearly an opportunity for the reform of salary structures in those countries which display anachronistic patterns, e.g. secondary teachers' salaries which stand at large multiples of those of primary teachers; large differentials based on initial qualification level rather than teaching performance or teaching-load. Salary reform could lead to greater incentives for high-performing teachers, for those posted in difficult schools and remote areas, and for those taking an unusual range of responsibilities which are discharged effectively. It must be recognized that such structural reforms are needed and that the salary increases simulated here will only partly tackle the problem of low productivity and morale.

Reducing repetition and drop-out (Reforms 8 and 9). Central to our definition of SFA is a substantial reduction in rates of repetition and drop-out. Each of these has different characteristics. High rates of repetition have the effect of slowing the flow of students through a school system and producing a higher level of enrolment than would otherwise be necessary for a given net enrolment ratio. Thus students who repeat, occupy places that might otherwise be occupied by those currently out of school. Repetition rates cannot be considered in isolation from promotion rates since repetition is a result of the conditions governing promotion. The two together define drop-out rates, since students who do not fall into either category leave the system. Reducing repetition, with drop-out staying constant, would lead to gains in internal efficiency since fewer school years would be needed to produce a primary-school completer.

Introducing automatic promotion—the simplest way to reduce repetition—therefore has considerable cost advantages. However, where repetition is high because students fail to meet standards for promotion to the next grade, promoting more students may exacerbate early drop-out as the work becomes progressively beyond the capabilities of such children. Curriculum-development activity is needed in association with automatic promotion, to allow curricular goals to be set at levels which are within reach of the great majority of children. Teaching groups may need reorganization to accommodate those learning at a much slower, or much faster, pace than others. Reforms of this kind have no effect on unit costs, except those arising from adjustments to the curriculum and the reorganization of teaching. The gap between gross and net enrolment ratios would close as repetition fell, satisfying a condition for the achievement of SFA.

However, SFA would be compromised if primary drop-out rates did not also decline. Although unit costs remain unchanged with reductions in drop-out, total costs (and GERs) increase in line with the growing numbers enrolled. This also has implications for enrolment at higher levels. The proportion of a cohort reaching the end of primary schooling increases as drop-out falls. Thus, even if transition rates from primary to secondary school remained constant there would be a substantial increase in secondary entrants beyond the underlying rate of population growth for the cohort as a whole, with a consequent increase in costs.

Mechanisms to reduce drop-out must depend upon an assessment of its causes. Those easiest to attack may be determined by curricular considerations. If scholastic failure leads to drop-out, more modest curricular expectations should reduce it. Curriculum reform designed to respond to automatic promotion policy may therefore have a double benefit if it also addresses learning difficulties that result in drop-out. Low household incomes are often strongly associated with the incidence of drop-out. The reforms proposed here cannot tackle this problem directly. But this serves to emphasize the condition, advanced earlier, that reforms should not increase the direct costs of schooling to low-income groups.

In the simulations these reforms are introduced in two stages. First, repetition is reduced by 75 per cent and promotion concomitantly increased over a ten-year period. Second, drop-out is reduced by 50 per cent and promotion increased concomitantly. Thus, with typical figures for Sub-Saharan Africa, annual repetition rates fall from 18 per cent to 4.5 per cent, and drop-out rates from 10 per cent to 5 per cent at primary level. Faster rates of reduction in repetition are selected, since it should be easier, in principle, to reduce them than drop-out rates in view of the causal factors involved.

Table 5.1 summarizes the specification for each of the reforms. These provide the basis for estimating the costs of SFA. The analysis balances

TABLE 5.1. *The nine reforms*

Cost-Saving
1. Reduce teacher/pupil ratio by 15% over 10 years as a result of the introduction of double-shifting at primary and secondary levels
2. Increase class-size by 5 pupils a class for all cases where the current value is 40 or less in primary and secondary schools, and 30 or less in teacher-training and vocational schools, over a 10-year period
3. Reduce primary teachers' unit costs by 10% over a 10-year period through increased use of self-study, teaching assistants, and community helpers

Cost-Shifting
4a. Decrease unit recurrent costs of primary and secondary schools by 10% over a 10-year period by increasing private contributions
4b. Decrease the capital costs of classroom construction at primary level by 50% over 5 years through increased community support
5. Freeze higher-education subsidies at current levels

Quality-Enhancing
6. Increase annual expenditures on learning resources to $5 per child over 5 years at all educational levels in those cases where they are less than $5
7. Increase teachers' salaries by 15% in real terms over a 10-year period
8. Reduce repetition rates to 25% of existing values at all levels over 10 years whilst keeping drop-out unchanged and allowing promotion rates to increase concomitantly
9. Reduce drop-out rates to 50% of existing values at all levels over 10 years and allow promotion rates to increase concomitantly

the quality-enhancing reforms with those that would make the package more affordable in countries facing severe financial constraints. The result would be higher quality and more efficient primary systems than could be achieved in the absence of the reforms. The gap between GERs and NERs would diminish such that those countries with GERs of 100 to 110 would have NERs in the low to mid-90s—as close an approach to full enrolment as can be expected over a 10–15-year period. Thus we are able to model beyond UPE towards SFA, and to explore both its costs and the ways in which it can be financed.

5. Introduction to the Simulation Model

The remainder of this chapter examines a simulation of a hypothetical Sub-Saharan African country in order to explain how the model works and to illustrate some of the conclusions that it can support. The main aims are, first, to review some of the more important assumptions made in the modelling and, second, to demonstrate the impact of the policy reforms on recurrent and capital costs incurred by movement towards SFA in the hypothetical country. This then illustrates the extent to which the reforms might assist in achieving that goal. The results of the national simulations and their implications are reported in Chapter 6.

Sub-Saharan Africa contains the majority of countries with low primary GERs and those where the financial problems of achieving UPE and SFA are greatest. It is informative, therefore, to construct an analogue of a typical Sub-Saharan education system. The SSA simulation models a system with primary and secondary cycles which each last six years. This is a common pattern. Technical and vocational education and teacher-training systems have many national variations. The simulation uses a representative version of these: both commence after three years of secondary education and last for three years. The SSA simulation uses the most recently available weighted mean data[3] for key parameters. These are used to construct a 1990-enrolment cohort for the simulated country, and a unit cost spreadsheet. The SSA simulation starts with an education system that has a GER of 69.5 and a population growth rate of 6–11-year-olds of 3.3 per cent. In both cases these are weighted means for all SSA countries. The other basic characteristics of the SSA simulation are indicated in Table 5.2. The Technical Appendix explains the assumptions made in constructing simulations.

It is important to remember that the SSA simulation is an analogue, representing what would be the case in a country where the parameters

---

[3] These are weighted by the size of the 6–11-year-old cohort. Where data sets are incomplete, or where there is variation in the countries on which data exist, arithmetic means have been used where these seem more plausible.

TABLE 5.2. *Baseline data used in SSA simulation*

Primary gross enrolment ratio (%)	69.5
Annual rate of growth of 6–11-year-olds 1990–2000 (%)	3.3
Primary	
Primary enrolments 1989/90	1,624,064
Pupil/teacher ratio	40 : 1
Repetition rate (average) (%)	18.2
Drop-out rate (average) (%)	10.3
Classroom building costs ($US)	3,500
Transition rate to secondary (%)	40.0
Secondary	
Pupil/teacher ratio	31.2 : 1
Repetition rate (average) (%)	17.5
Drop-out rate (average) (%)	11.0
Classroom building costs ($US)	6,500
Vocational	
Pupil/teacher ratio	15.9 : 1
Vocational pupils/general secondary pupils (%)	8.2
Classroom building costs ($US)	7,000
Teacher training	
Pupil/teacher ratio	17.5 : 1
Teacher-training pupils/general secondary pupils (%)	7.9
Classroom building costs ($US)	8,000
Financial variables	
Recurrent ed. exp./total rec. exp. (%)	16.1
Primary unit costs ($US)	38.2
Composition of recurrent primary expenditure*	
Salaries (%)	94.7
Teaching materials (%)	2.4
All other expenses (%)	2.9
Secondary unit costs ($US)	237
Composition of recurrent secondary expenditure*	
Salaries (%)	71.2
Teaching materials (%)	3.2
All other expenses (%)	25.6

Note: Data are means, weighted by the size of the 6–11-year-old population, except for those* which are based on arithmetic means. The most recently available data for Sub-Saharan Africa have been used to construct the values and are mainly from 1986. All financial data are in 1986 constant prices.

had the values shown. In each real country the values stand in a different relationship to each other, and consequently projections would show different outcomes to those illustrated.

The first step in running the simulation is to increase the enrolment

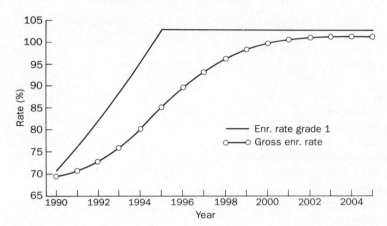

FIG. 5.1 *Enrolment rates required to achieve UPE by 2000 in a simulated African country*

rate in grade 1 to a level which allows the GER to reach 100 by 1999/2000. The GER is then maintained at this level until 2004/5. Fig. 5.1 illustrates the relationship between primary GER and the enrolment rate in grade 1 as the former rises from 69.5 to 100. Over this period the transition rate from primary grade 6 to the first year of secondary is held constant. In this condition the SSA simulation models the costs of providing enough places for all 6–11-year-olds, though of course repetition and over-age students will mean that NERs are less than 100. It is therefore equivalent to UPE under the conventional definition.

From this point the various reforms are introduced sequentially so that costs can be calculated for different types of reform at different points in time. The treatment given to the reforms in the simulation is *cumulative* —each reform-level adding to the effects of the previous one. This simplifies the discussion of the impact of the reforms and is consistent with our argument that, taken together, they are a reasonable set of conditions for the achievement of SFA in those countries which have scarce resources and are furthest from achieving GERs of 100. The individual effects of each reform are apparent from comparison of one reform-level with the next.

6. The Results of the SSA Simulation

Running the SSA simulation produces the pattern of results shown in Table 5.3 for enrolment growth, unit costs, expenditure, and the resources available.

TABLE 5.3. *Results of the SSA simulation*

	Projected position constant GER			Projected position in 1999/2000 at each reform level											
	1989/90	1999/2000	2004/5	UPE	1	2	3	4a	4b	5	6	7	8	9 SFA 1999/2000	SFA 2004/5
1. Primary enrolments															
1.1 1989/90 = 100	100	138	162	199	199	199	199	199	199	199	199	199	185	206	245
1.2 Grade 1–6 (millions)	1.52	2.24	2.64	3.23	3.23	3.23	3.23	3.23	3.23	3.23	3.23	3.23	3.00	3.35	3.98
2. Gross enrolment ratio															
2.1 (6–11-year-olds) (%)	69.5	69.5	69.5	100.0	100.0	100.0	100.0	100.0	100.0	100.0	100.0	100.0	92.8	103.6	104.6
3. Recurrent unit costs ($US)															
3.1 Primary	38	38	38	38	33	29	27	24	24	24	28	31	31	31	31
3.2 General secondary	226	226	226	226	201	201	201	180	180	180	180	198	198	198	198
3.3 Teacher training	356	356	356	356	317	282	282	282	282	282	282	309	309	309	309
3.4 Vocational	226	226	226	226	201	176	176	176	176	176	176	193	193	193	193
4. Expenditure ($USm.)															
4.1 Primary (cap.)	5	6	8	12	10	9	9	9	5	5	5	6	3	5	4
4.2 Secondary (cap.)	2	2	2	7	6	6	6	6	6	6	6	6	3	11	8
4.3 Higher educ. (cap.)	1	2	2	2	2	2	2	2	2	1	1	1	1	1	1
4.4 Total (cap.)	8	10	12	20	18	17	17	17	12	12	12	12	11	17	14
4.5 Primary (rec.)	62	86	101	124	106	95	86	78	78	78	90	101	94	105	124
4.6 Secondary (rec.)	76	105	123	114	101	100	100	91	91	91	91	100	94	118	196
4.7 Higher educ (rec.)	28	39	46	39	39	39	39	39	39	28	28	28	28	28	28
4.8 Total (rec.)	166	230	270	276	246	233	225	207	207	197	208	229	216	251	349
5. Resources ($USm.)															
5.1 Total pub. rec. res.	1,030	1,425	1,676	1,425	1,425	1,425	1,425	1,425	1,425	1,425	1,425	1,425	1,425	1,425	1,676
5.2 Total rec. education	166	230	270	230	230	230	230	230	230	230	230	230	230	230	270
5.3 Rec. ed. surplus/deficit	0	0	0	-47	-16	-4	5	22	22	33	21	1	14	-22	-79
5.4 % Tot. rec. res. req'd	16.1	16.1	16.1	19.4	17.3	16.4	15.8	14.6	14.6	13.8	14.6	16.1	15.1	17.6	20.8
5.5 % change in line 5.4		0	0	20.4	-11.0	-5.2	-3.6	-7.7	0	-5.2	6.1	9.8	-5.8	16.4	

Notes:

1. 4.1–4 Capital costs for each level
2. 4.5–8 Recurrent costs for each level
3. 5.1 Total public recurrent budget. This is allowed to grow at the rate of population growth.
4. 5.2 Total recurrent education budget. This is calculated on the assumption it remains a constant proportion of the total budget.
5. 5.3 Total recurrent education budget surplus/deficit (5.2−4.8).
6. 5.4 Total recurrent resources as % of total recurrent budget (5.2/5.1) ×100.
7. 5.5 Percentage change in line 5.4 when compared with previous column showing the impact of each reform on recurrent expenditure as a % of the education budget.
8. The first three columns show the position in different years if GER were held constant.
9. Column UPE and reforms 1–9 show the position in 1999/2000. Each column includes the previous reform level. Reading across each line shows the cumulative effect of reforms in 1999/2000.
10. Column SFA 2004/5 shows the position with all the reforms implemented in 2004/5.
11. Primary recurrent costs are the product of unit costs (3.1) and enrolments (1.2). Secondary recurrent costs (including teacher training and vocational/technical) are derived in the same way (data not shown). Higher education costs are projected from current values, initially at the rate of 6–11-year-old population growth.
12. Capital costs are calculated by enumerating enrolment growth between years, dividing by class-size, and multiplying by classroom costs.
13. Each reform has an impact on costs which depends on the characteristics of the reform (see text).

Table 5.3 can be understood first by reading down the columns. The first column (base 1989/90) contains initial values for the hypothetical system in 1989/90. The second and third columns show the position in 1999/2000 and 2004/5 if the GER were held constant. These data thus indicate the impact of population growth on enrolments and costs. The fourth column (UPE) illustrates the situation in 1999/2000 if GERs were to be increased to 100 with no reforms. The next ten columns, labelled 1–9, show the effects of the progressive implementation of the policy reforms that we have defined on costs, expenditure, and resources in the year 1999/2000. These outcomes are cumulative in the sense that each reform-level includes the effects of the previous ones. Column 9 includes all the reforms and therefore represents SFA in 1999/2000. SFA 2004/5 shows the position for SFA in 2004/5. As discussed earlier the reduction of repetition (reform 8) causes the GER to fall, but this is more than compensated by the increase associated with the addition of reform 9 (reducing drop-out). The final GER achieved in 1999/2000 is thus 103.6 in this simulation. For both UPE and SFA enrolments would have to double, approximately, over a ten-year period.

6.1. The impact of the SFA reforms

6.1.1. Recurrent and capital costs

Fig. 5.2 summarizes the relative impact of the reforms on recurrent costs as a multiple of expenditure in 1989/90 for each reform level leading to

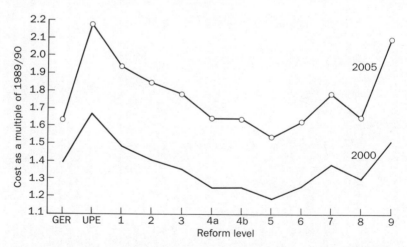

FIG. 5.2 *Impact of UPE and policy reforms on recurrent costs in a simulated African country*
Note: GER = Constant GER 69.5. UPE = GER of 100.

SFA. From this (and from Table 5.3, line 4.8) it can be seen that in the year 1999/2000 recurrent costs for UPE are 1.7 times greater than in 1989/90 and 1.5 times greater for SFA. By 2004/5 the recurrent costs of SFA have risen to 2.1 times those in 1989/90 for the unreformed system.[4]

It can be seen from the slope of the lines joining reform-levels that the reforms which reduce recurrent costs most sharply are double-shifting (reform 1) and shifting some costs to the community and individuals (reform 4a)—the steeper the gradient the greater the effect. Increasing class-size (reform 2) also has a marked effect. Total recurrent costs are also affected significantly by freezing higher-education subsidies (reform 5).

Providing minimum learning resources of $5 per child (reform 6) and increasing teachers' salaries (reform 7) result in steep increases in total costs. So also does reducing drop-out (reform 9). Reducing repetition (reform 8) appears to reduce total costs but does so as a result of increased efficiency (which temporarily lowers the GER) and is more than balanced by the effects of reducing drop-out (reform 9). The net impact of reducing drop-out rises sharply between 1999/2000 and 2004/5 (the gradient becomes steeper) as the reduced drop-out expands the size of the cohort enrolled, particularly at secondary level, where unit costs are higher.

Capital costs (Table 5.3, line 4.4) are different in nature to recurrent costs: they are derived from the rate of expansion of the system rather than from its absolute size. Thus, whilst the recurrent costs shown in Table 5.3 reflect the cost-impact of a given year's enrolments, the capital costs reflect the *change* in size of the enrolled cohort in the current as compared with the preceding year. Fig. 5.3 shows the pattern of increases in capital costs over 1990–2000. It can be seen that they more than double to 1995, remaining roughly constant thereafter. Primary costs decline after 1995, as the sharp build-up of enrolments necessary to reach UPE by 2000 falls off, but this is counterbalanced by the expansion at secondary level, which is necessary to maintain constant the transition rate from primary to secondary school. Ultimately capital costs will grow at the same rate as population growth, after the effects of reaching UPE and SFA have stabilized.

The initial rate of increase in total capital costs in the first period is greatly reduced by reform 4b, which halves primary classroom costs to the State. The introduction of double-shifting (reform 1) has a smaller effect. Reducing repetition and drop-out (reforms 8 and 9) taken together increase capital costs (see Table 5.3, line 4.4). All these results are, of course, sensitive to the capital costs associated with classroom building. If

---

[4] All costs and expenditures are in 1986 prices.

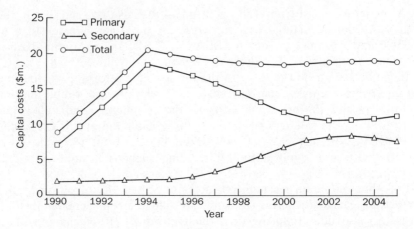

FIG. 5.3 *Impact on capital costs of achieving UPE by 2000 in a simulated African country*
Note: Secondary includes teacher training and vocational.

costs were greater than the values chosen, this would increase the capital expenditures needed, but the patterns over time would remain similar.[5]

6.1.2. Gaps between resources and costs

It is of central importance to establish the financial challenge posed by SFA. The magnitude of this depends both on the growth in costs and the growth in the government budget which is used to meet them. The SSA simulation assumes that real educational spending per person can be held constant at 1990 levels. Thus resources available are allowed to grow at the same rate as population growth.

One simple way of looking at the results is to examine line 5.4 of Table 5.3. This shows the proportion of the national budget that would have to be allocated to education to meet the costs generated by UPE and for each level of reform leading to SFA. Initially, the SSA simulation allocates 16.1 per cent of total public recurrent resources to education. This would have to rise, *ceteris paribus*, to 19.4 per cent for UPE in 1999/2000. SFA, with all the cost-saving and cost-shifting reforms, could be achieved at a somewhat lower cost (17.6 per cent of the public recurrent resources). However, by 2004/5 the costs of SFA have increased as the effects of enrolment growth and the various reforms work their way through. SFA 2004/5 would require 20.8 per cent of total public recurrent resources. This implies that the recurrent budget at this time

---

[5] This would be so unless the ratio between primary and secondary costs changed significantly from the values assumed.

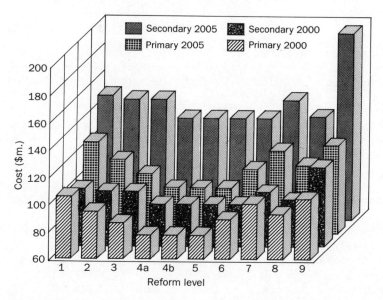

FIG. 5.4 *Primary and secondary recurrent costs in 2000 and 2005 in a simulated African country*

would need to be nearly 30 per cent greater than in 1989/90, expressed as a proportion of total recurrent expenditure. If economic growth fell below the level needed to maintain constant per capita expenditure on education, or if other changes created the same result, the increases needed would be greater. In the SSA simulation, with all the cost-saving and cost-shifting reforms implemented, SFA is always a cheaper option than unreformed UPE, although, as Chapter 6 shows, this will not necessarily be the case for every country in SSA.

6.1.3. The balance between primary and secondary costs

The balance of total recurrent costs between primary and secondary school systems is sensitive to the number of reforms implemented and it also changes over time. Fig. 5.4 shows this.

In 1999/2000 the total costs of the primary and secondary school systems are not dissimilar for all levels of reform. However, total secondary-school costs become greater than those for primary in 2004/5 as the cost-saving and cost-shifting reforms are completed (reforms 1–5). When all nine levels of reform are implemented secondary recurrent costs reach a value nearly 60 per cent greater than for primary. The growing dominance of secondary costs is the result of a combination of the expanded primary cohort transferring to secondary, the effects of reduced

TABLE 5.4. *The impact of increased transition rates*

A. Transition rate constant at 40%

Recurrent ($m.)	Base	UPE2000	SFA2000	UPE2005	SFA2005
Primary	62	124	105	147	124
Secondary	76	114	118	168	196
Higher	28	39	28	46	28
Total recurrent	166	276	251	361	349
% of Total recurrent resources needed[a]	16.11	19.40	17.63	21.56	20.82

B. Transition rate rising from 40 to 70% from 1989/90 to 2004/5

Recurrent ($m.)	Base	UPE2000	SFA2000	UPE2005	SFA2005
Primary	62	124	105	147	124
Secondary	76	160	169	295	348
Higher	28	38	28	45	28
Total recurrent	166	322	302	487	500
% of Total recurrent resources needed[a]	16.11	22.56	21.12	29.06	29.81

C. Transition rate constant at 40%. 6–11-year-old population growth rate falling from 3.3 to 1.4% from 1990 to 1995 and thereafter remaining constant.

Recurrent ($m.)	Base	UPE2000	SFA2000	UPE2005	SFA2005
Primary	62	106	90	116	97
Secondary	76	111	114	151	172
Higher	28	39	28	46	28
Total recurrent	166	256	232	313	297
% of Total recurrent resources needed[a]	16.11	18.00	16.30	18.64	17.77

[a] This assumes that total budgetary resources increase at the population growth rate.

drop-out increasing numbers entering and remaining in secondary, and the much higher unit costs of secondary schooling. Capital costs follow the same patterns. The implications are clear for countries which have similar ratios of enrolments and unit costs to those we have simulated. Though the cost burden of UPE and SFA falls at the primary level in the first instance, the bulk of resources will be needed at secondary level as time passes.

This situation may turn out to be more problematic than the simulation suggests. The SSA simulation employs a constant transition rate of 40 per cent from primary to secondary school as UPE and SFA are implemented. However, there are few countries where transition rates have remained constant when primary GERs have grown. Accordingly, Table 5.4 illustrates the cost-impact of a steady rise in the transition rate from 40 per cent in 1989/90, to 70 per cent in 2004/5.

The increase in secondary recurrent costs is very rapid when the transition rate rises. These become greater by 43 per cent for SFA 1999/2000 and 78 per cent for SFA 2004/5 when compared to costs with constant transition rates. The proportion of the recurrent budget allocated to education would have to rise from 16.1 per cent to 21 per cent for SFA 1999/2000 and would reach 30 per cent by SFA 2004/5 if transition rates increased as simulated. This translates into an 85 per cent increase in the proportion of the national budget needed to meet costs, compared to the 30 per cent increase necessary by 2004/5 for SFA if transition rates remained constant.

There is therefore a need to consider carefully the possible unintended consequences of UPE and SFA policy. If an emphasis on primary access and quality improvement is to be sustained the costs of secondary enrolments have to be contained. The first-order problem is how to bring secondary unit cost more closely in line with those at primary level. This suggests that additional reforms will be needed at secondary level which go beyond those included in our analysis.

6.2. Population growth

Over the medium term, and after the implementation of the policy reforms, the growing costs of SFA will be primarily influenced by the growth of the number of children aged 6–11 years. The sustainability of SFA is therefore directly linked to underlying population growth rates. If population growth amongst 6–11-year-olds fell to the levels projected in some sources for all low-income countries (a weighted mean of 1.4 per cent year by the year 2000 is suggested by Lockheed and Verspoor (1990: 166)) this could have a significant impact on costs.

The effects of declining population growth can be explored, using the SSA simulation. The lower part of Table 5.4 indicates the cost-impact of a reduction in the growth rate of 6-year-olds from 3.3 per cent per year to 1.4 per cent over the five years beginning in 1989/90. Comparison with the first part of the table shows that reducing the population growth rate reduces recurrent costs at primary by about 14 per cent for SFA in 1999/2000 and by 22 per cent for SFA in 2004/5. At secondary level the cost-reduction is about 3 per cent for SFA in 1999/2000 rising to 12 per cent for SFA in 2004/5. The effect on secondary expenditure is delayed by the length of time needed for the more slowly growing cohorts to reach secondary school. Overall the impact of reduced population growth is sufficient to reduce the cost of SFA in 2004/5 to about 17.8 per cent of public recurrent expenditure compared to 20.8 per cent with no reduction in population growth.

In the short term, reductions in population growth rate have a limited, but useful, impact on costs. Eventually, when the effects of the SFA reforms have worked their way through, the underlying growth rate in expenditure would return to the growth rate of the 6–11-year-old population—in this case 1.4 per cent rather than 3.3 per cent. In practice, reduced population growth arising from demographic trends initiated in the base year would only have substantial effects after ten years or more. Nevertheless, the effects are cumulative and ultimately extremely important in determining the long-term cost of sustaining SFA.

6.3. A note on quality-improvement

The SSA simulation indicates that, in the medium term, the costs of achieving SFA are similar to those for UPE. In other words, the net financial impact of reforms 1–9 is small: the cost savings finance the qualitative improvements, producing a desirable reallocation of given levels of expenditure. Although there will be further costs to incur, related to quality improvements over and above those that we have modelled, these need not be large. Part of the evidence for this assertion lies in the fact that school quality already varies widely in every system and is not correlated with cost in any simple fashion. In similar types of institution with similar pupils, examination pass rates vary strikingly; so do the reputations of schools for quality indicators other than examination results. Critical to these outcomes are effective school leadership, suitable buildings, an appropriate complement of adequately paid teachers, sufficient learning materials, and an efficient administrative system. Our simulations are designed to model the costs of providing the basic infrastructure of schooling, and the teachers needed to work within the school system. They therefore identify the major first-order costs of SFA. How well schools perform need not primarily depend on additional expenditure above this basic level.

Quality improvements across a system depend at least as much on distributional matters as they do on raising expenditures. More is likely to be gained in the pursuit of SFA by redirecting resources to marginalized institutions where the problems are most severe than by adopting policies which allocate resources independent of need. Thus, considerable quality-enhancement is probably already available within existing levels of expenditure if redistribution and more equitable resource allocation are goals to which there is genuine policy commitment.

7. Conclusions

This chapter has provided an operational definition of SFA which includes both enrolment targets and the specification of appropriate policy reforms. This definition has been used to develop a simulation model which can project the costs of UPE and SFA. The SSA simulation, presented above, illustrates how the model works. It leads to a number of tentative conclusions concerning the problems of achieving SFA. It is of course true that had different values been chosen for the simulation the results would have been different. Nevertheless the values chosen *are* plausible and are derived from data from Sub-Saharan African countries. What then do we learn from this analysis?

First, in typical African circumstances, substantial additional resources for education would be required to achieve UPE and SFA. Recurrent expenditure would have to double by 2005 in real terms. If per capita public expenditures remained constant in real terms, the proportion of the public budget allocated to education would have to increase by about 30 per cent if SFA were to be domestically financed.

Second, these estimates may yet be conservative since, where the growth rate of the economy falls below that of the population, the problems of financing SFA will be even more acute. Furthermore, if transition rates into secondary rose above current levels the proportion of the budget needed for education by 2005 would rise very sharply. In many of the poorest countries, such expenditures could probably not be financed solely from internal sources.

Third, in countries where all the cost-saving, cost-shifting, and quality-enhancing reforms are implemented, the simulation suggests that the costs of SFA would be no greater than those associated with achieving UPE without reforms. Thus, efficiency savings are capable of financing the improvements in quality which are required for SFA.

Fourth, the relative impact on recurrent costs of the different reforms simulated shows that the most cost-saving reforms are double-shifting (reform 1) and shifting some costs to the community and to individuals (reform 4a). Increasing class-size (reform 2) also has a marked effect. Total recurrent costs are reduced significantly by freezing higher-education subsidies (reform 5). All the quality-enhancing reforms have a strong upward impact on costs, especially the reduction in rates of drop-out.

Relative increases in capital costs are greater than for recurrent costs, but their absolute magnitudes are small, varying between 5 and 10 per cent of recurrent costs on the basis of the building costs we have assumed. Reducing the cost of primary classroom building (reform 4b) produces the greater savings along with the introduction of double-shifting (reform 1). Reducing drop-out (reform 9) is responsible for a considerable increase in capital costs, but is essential if SFA is to be attained.

Fifth, the initial cost-burden of SFA falls on primary education. Over time secondary costs become more important as increased numbers of primary students enter secondary schools where unit costs are substantially greater. Even when the transition rate to secondary is held constant this leads to secondary expenditure growing faster than primary beyond the short term. If transition rates were to increase, costs at secondary level would greatly exceed those of primary schooling by 2004/5. Careful consideration may need to be given to reforms at secondary level to make this cost-burden sustainable.

Sixth, population growth rates are critical to the long-term growth of costs. In the short term, costs are dominated by the move to SFA. If Sub-Saharan population growth rates were to come down to the mean projected for upper-middle-income countries recurrent costs would fall by at least 14 per cent by 2004/5 compared to their value if no reduction in population growth rate occurred.

Finally, it must be remembered that an improvement in the quality of schooling is not guaranteed by the reforms simulated. They provide a minimum indication of measures that may be needed. The reforms have been specified in ways which seek to limit the adverse effects on quality of the cost-saving and cost-shifting measures which may be necessary to bring the quality-enhancing reforms within reach. Most of the reforms have qualitative aspects which need consideration in identifying strategies for implementation, e.g. equitably introducing double-shifting, reducing the dispersion of class-sizes, designing learning materials to assist progression to higher grades and ensuring their proper distribution; coupling increases in teachers' salaries with reforms of the salary structure and conditions of service; introducing automatic promotion policies; discouraging drop-out through improved school quality and learning relevance. The reforms should therefore be seen as necessary but not sufficient conditions for quality improvement.

The above conclusions are illustrative of the range of insights generated by the simulation approach. The extent to which these have general applicability can only be established by conducting the analysis at the national level. This is undertaken in Chapter 6, which presents the results of a large number of national simulations. The costs of UPE and SFA across the developing world are estimated, and the extent to which these could be financed from domestic sources, with or without the assistance of educational and fiscal reform, is assessed.

6

Assessing the Costs and Financing of Schooling for All

1. Introduction

We have shown that a wide range of policy instruments can be used to increase primary enrolments, to reduce the public-sector costs of schooling, and to protect or enhance school quality. In the last chapter, a detailed specification of possible reforms—based upon the research results and case-studies reviewed earlier in the book—was presented. The magnitude of their cost-impact was illustrated, using a model of a simplified education system. This allowed some operational distinctions between UPE and SFA to be made, together with an initial appraisal of the simulated policy reforms in terms of their likely impact upon costs.

In the present chapter, the simulation framework is again employed. In this case, however, it is used in order to address two concrete sets of questions. First, what will be the likely financial costs for developing countries of achieving SFA over the next decade or so, and how do these compare with the costs of UPE? Secondly, how feasible do these targets actually look—that is, can we expect that developing countries will be able to reach SFA from their own resources? If so, to what extent, and in what ways would existing policies have to change? If not, to what extent, and in what ways would international support be required? These questions will be tackled in turn.

2. A Note on Method

It is necessary, by way of introduction, to say something about the methods we have employed, although most technical details are relegated to the Appendix. The discussion draws upon separate simulations of the resource implications of implementing UPE and SFA in all developing countries. In the cases of ninety-seven of these countries, national data were adequate to support separate simulations for each of them. The remaining sixty-five countries had insufficient data to support separate analyses, and were grouped together. These countries had a combined population of about 100 million people in the mid-1980s (some 2 per cent of the total for all developing countries), and mainly comprised those with populations of less than one million people.[1] Thus, the ninety-eight simulations reported upon in what follows cover all 162 low- and middle-income developing countries, as conventionally defined (World Bank 1989*a*).

The grade-transition model introduced in Chapter 5 has been used for these analyses. National data for the GER, school-age populations and their projected rates of growth, class-size, repetition and promotion rates, the length of the school-system, pupil/teacher ratios, recurrent expenditures, primary and secondary unit costs, and a range of other variables was separately used in each country's simulation.[2] These data were mainly for the year 1986, which was, for the majority of countries, the most recent available from international sources. Estimates of total primary enrolments in 1990 were derived from age-specific population projections, the existing length of the primary system, and the GER value for 1986, for each country. In each case, the model is used to derive, from these data, increased enrolments to the years 2000 and 2005, and their cost implications, both for UPE and for each of the cost/quality reforms leading to SFA. Alternative approaches could have been adopted but, for reasons set out in the Technical Appendix, this seemed to be the best.

It follows from the above that all estimates of costs generated by the methods used are in 1986 constant-price terms. Furthermore, the approach assumes that the reported GER values for 1986 remained constant over the following four years for the purpose of estimating school enrolments in 1990. As it happens, however, an update using 1990 values would be unlikely to generate a very different aggregate picture. The late 1980s were not years of growing prosperity for most lower-income countries. The widespread reductions in public expenditures per teacher and per student which occurred between 1980 and 1985 have been documented earlier in this book (Table 2.1). The continued currency depreciation and reductions in public expenditure necessitated by adjustment programmes in many lower-income countries imply that the same trends will have continued over the years 1986–90. Similarly, we have shown that in recent years progress towards UPE, as measured by increasing GERs, has not been steadily maintained. Table 2.1 indicated that for half of the most educationally disadvantaged countries (which therefore have most ground to make up) primary-level GERs either fell or remained unchanged, over the period 1980–86. For these reasons, the use of 1986 values for the cost and enrolment-ratio parameters is unlikely to be too

[1] Ten of these 65 countries, however—including Afghanistan, Kampuchea, South Africa, and Taiwan—had larger populations. In each of these cases sufficient data were not available to support separate simulations. Details can be found in the Technical Appendix.
[2] Where gaps for any of these data were found, a standard procedure was employed for their estimation. See the Technical Appendix for details.

restrictive. Data for 1990 will, when they emerge, obviously reveal differences, when compared with the detailed country outcomes estimated here. But the overall picture generated by our results is thought likely to remain robust.

A second general point to make is that the costs of moving to UPE and SFA, which are presented below, comprise those of the primary system itself, together with those arising from the associated expansion of the higher levels of education which primary expansion would subsequently bring. The analytic focus, however, is on primary schooling—its actual length, starting size, and costs in each country. We assume that, in all cases, the transition rate from primary to secondary school will remain unchanged over the period. Thus, the analysis does not imply any move towards the universalization of secondary schooling over the coming years, nor does it incorporate any such costs. Transition rates to teacher-training and vocational courses are also held constant. No separate data were available on the unit costs of these courses, so assumptions, linking these to unit costs at secondary level, had to be made. Similarly, recurrent expenditures upon higher education were treated as exogenous, equal to 20 per cent of total education spending by government in the base year, and increasing in absolute terms at the same rate of growth as that of the population aged 6–11 years.

Thus the costs of the education system simulated for each individual country are those associated with only part of the actual system which may exist. Total education expenditures are built up from the unit costs and total enrolments which are calculated for the simulated systems. These are expected to underestimate actual education budgets, in most cases, owing to the fact that post-secondary expenditures will be understated. This was an intended outcome, owing to our wish to capture the unavoidable, rather than the discretionary, consequences of primary expansion for the rest of the system.[3] By consequence, more interesting than the absolute size of expenditures estimated for 1990, is the change in these expenditures over time, both in absolute terms, and relative to those of the base year. These kinds of comparison and contrast will form the basis for much of our discussion.

3. UPE and SFA: Their Impact on Enrolments and Recurrent Costs

The cost and enrolment implications of achieving UPE and SFA in all low- and middle-income countries by the year 2000 are summarized in

---

[3] It could be argued that the expansion of secondary schooling implied by the maintenance of a constant transition rate is, in fact, discretionary. However, there are few countries where such rates have fallen (at least in 'normal' economic circumstances), even during periods of rapid primary expansion. The political reality, for most countries, is that constant, or gradually increasing, transition rates to secondary schooling are unavoidable.

TABLE 6.1. *The impact of UPE and SFA on annual costs and enrolments by major region (reforms selectively implemented)*[a]

	1990	2000	Cost-saving reforms			Cost-shifting reforms		Quality-enhancing reforms			2005			
	UPE No reforms	UPE No reforms	Double-shifting	Increase class-size	Teacher-helpers	Community financing	Freeze higher ed. subsidies	Increase materials	Teacher salaries	SFA Repetition & drop-out	UPE No reforms	Cost-saving	Cost-shifting	SFA
			1	2	3	4	5	6	7	8/9		1–3	1–5	1–9
Sub-Saharan Africa (n = 35)														
Primary enrolments (millions)	58.5	116.9	116.9	116.9	116.9	116.9	116.9	116.9	116.9	120.6	140.7	140.7	140.7	144.4
GER	69	100	100	100	100	100	100	100	100	104	102	102	102	106
Primary unit costs ($)	41	40	35	33	31	29	29	32	36	36	39	31	29	35
Annual recurrent ed. expend. ($bn.)	5.2	8.7	7.9	7.6	7.3	6.9	6.6	7.0	7.6	8.0	10.9	9.2	8.2	10.3
Other Africa (n = 4)														
Primary enrolments (millions)	14.4	19.7	19.7	19.7	19.7	19.7	19.7	19.7	19.7	19.5	21.8	21.8	21.8	21.6
GER	89	100	100	100	100	100	100	100	100	99	100	100	100	99
Primary unit costs ($)	129	127	112	99	92	84	84	86	96	95	128	93	85	96
Annual recurrent ed. expend. ($bn.)	4.2	5.5	5.0	4.6	4.5	4.2	4.0	4.0	4.4	4.4	6.2	5.1	4.4	4.9
India and China (n = 2)														
Primary enrolments (millions)	232.2	219.3	219.3	219.3	219.3	219.3	219.3	219.3	219.3	236.0	228.3	228.3	228.3	249.5
GER	117	100	100	100	100	100	100	100	100	108	100	100	100	110
Primary unit costs ($)	11	10	10	10	10	10	10	14	15	15	10	10	10	15
Annual recurrent ed. expend. ($bn.)	7.9	7.7	7.6	7.5	7.4	7.4	7.3	8.5	9.1	10.0	7.7	7.4	7.3	10.5

Other Asia (n = 24)

Primary enrolments (millions)	113.5	141.8	141.8	141.8	141.8	141.8	141.8	141.8	154.0	153.7	153.7	153.7	168.8	
GER	100	100	100	100	100	100	100	100	110	100	100	100	112	
Primary unit costs ($)	134	119	113	108	105	102	102	104	110	118	104	104	108	
Annual recurrent ed. expend. ($bn.)	27.1	30.6	29.4	28.5	28.1	27.5	27.2	27.7	31.4	32.9	30.2	29.1	34.2	

Latin America (n = 22)

Primary enrolments (millions)	72.8	75.9	75.9	75.9	75.9	75.9	75.9	75.9	86.9	80.1	80.1	80.1	94.8	
GER	108	100	100	100	100	100	100	100	116	100	100	100	120	
Primary unit costs ($)	125	126	125	124	124	123	123	125	141	143	126	124	123	
Annual recurrent ed. expend. ($bn.)	18.0	19.4	19.3	19.3	19.2	19.2	19.1	19.3	24.2	20.4	20.1	20.0	28.1	

Other Developing Countries (n = 11)

Primary enrolments (millions)	30.6	33.4	33.4	33.4	33.4	33.4	33.4	33.4	34.2	34.2	34.2	34.2	35.1	
GER	96	100	100	100	100	100	100	100	100	100	100	100	103	
Primary unit costs ($)	392	358	330	307	295	280	280	280	316	347	285	270	306	
Annual recurrent ed. expend. ($bn.)	23.4	22.9	21.6	20.4	20.0	19.3	19.1	19.3	21.9	22.8	19.8	18.9	22.3	

All Developing Countries (n = 98)

Primary enrolments (millions)	522.2	607.1	607.1	607.1	607.1	607.1	607.1	607.1	651.3	658.7	658.7	658.7	714.1	
GER	106	100	100	100	100	100	100	100	108	100	100	100	110	
Primary unit costs ($)	83	79	74	71	69	66	66	69	76	77	67	65	75	
Annual recurrent ed. expend. ($bn.)	85.8	94.9	90.9	87.8	86.6	84.4	83.4	85.7	99.9	101.0	91.9	87.9	110.3	

[a] Calculated by aggregating all country-level simulations within each region shown. In this table all reforms are implemented for countries with GERs <100. For countries with GERs >100 reforms 6–9 only are implemented. GERs are weighted by primary enrolments. Unit costs are weighted by 6–11-year age-groups. All expenditure figures are in constant 1986 US dollars. All reforms are incremental, and for each target year incorporate those shown in earlier columns.

Sources: Calculated from data in Statistical Appendix Tables A.2 and A.3, and from the detailed national simulations of UPE and SFA.

Table 6.1.[4] The information has been derived by adding together the results of the ninety-eight separate national simulations. In the cases summarized in the table, the cost-saving and cost-shifting reforms have not always been implemented. The reasons for this are not at present relevant, and will be explained in a later section of this chapter. Before exploring some of the implications of the table it would be useful to ask whether there is any information presented there which gives some clue as to its general credibility. Is there, for example, any evidence that the enrolments and costs which are derived from the national simulations are realistic?

This question can be partially answered by comparing the information given in the bottom left-hand cells of the table with other evidence for the likely magnitudes of total primary enrolments in 1990 and total public recurrent expenditures on education throughout the developing world. The table indicates that our estimates for total primary enrolments in all developing countries in 1990 are 522 millions, and that pupils throughout these school systems were at that time accounting for some $86 billion of public recurrent expenditures, at 1986 prices. These estimates compare with those given by Unesco, for 1987, of 477 million pupils, and total publicly funded education costs of $110 billion (recurrent plus investment expenditures) (Unesco 1989: Tables 2.2 and 2.12).

However, some (mainly) Eastern European countries included in our simulations, are excluded from Unesco's 'developing country' category. After adjusting for these differences in definition, our estimates imply a 2 per cent rate of growth per year in primary enrolments in developing countries between 1987 and 1990, and that the costs of our simulated school systems account for, on average, about three-quarters of total public expenditures on education in developing countries.[5] This, then, provides useful consistency and accuracy tests for the estimates generated by our models. Aggregated enrolments for all countries are at the levels we would expect. Equally, on the expenditure side, our intention to cost only that part of the system which would be directly affected by

[4] The discussion of costs focuses entirely upon recurrent costs. Capital costs, as Ch. 5 has indicated, are only a small proportion of the total. In most countries they do not represent a major financial obstacle to the expansion of primary schooling. And where they do, self-help and other local construction methods can reduce costs substantially without significant deleterious consequences for school quality.
[5] The countries excluded from the Unesco developing-country category accounted for some 14 m. primary pupils, and some $14 bn. of public expenditure according to our simulations. Subtracting these from our totals leaves an estimated 508 m. pupils, and costs of some $72 bn. Unesco data suggest that public expenditures on education in 1987, expressed in 1986 prices, would have been around $100 bn. Increasing these at 2% per year suggests total expenditures of about $106 bn. in 1990, at 1986 prices. Recurrent expenditure typically accounts for 90% of total educational expenditure. The proper comparison is therefore between $72 bn. implied by our results, and $95 bn. implied by Unesco data. The conclusions given in the text thus follow.

primary expansion results in a plausible relationship between simulated and reported total educational costs.

3.1. Enrolments

Turning now to the more detailed results, it will be useful, first, to consider the pattern of primary enrolments which emerges from the analyses. Here, it is important to notice that not all countries are expected to increase the total number of their primary pupils between 1990 and 2000. (See, for example, the combined enrolments for India and China shown in Table 6.1, which fall by 13 million over the decade.) This is so in the cases of some (but not all) of the countries with GERs greater than 100 in 1990. The simulation of the costs of UPE involves, for all countries, achieving GERs of 100 by the end of the century. Thus, in our analyses, for countries where GERs are presently higher than 100, they fall, whilst UPE is maintained. This will eventually happen in any event, as the numbers of children beyond primary school-age, who missed taking up primary schooling when they were younger, are reduced. By consequence, where population growth is expected to be insufficient to compensate for the school places made available by a declining GER, total primary enrolments would actually fall over the decade. There are twenty-three countries in this category, including five cases where the falling enrolments are mainly caused by smaller school-age populations owing to expected declines in fertility rather than by reductions in the size of the GER.

It follows that, when groups of countries are aggregated together, the simple difference between enrolments in 1990 and expected enrolments with UPE in 2000 would underestimate the total number of new primary-school places required to accommodate all the new pupils. This is because those countries in which enrolments were falling (that is, where there would be a surplus of school places in 2000) would not have been excluded from the calculation. For these purposes, therefore, it is the gross rather than the net number of new school places which is required.

As shown in Table 6.2, the twenty-three countries where enrolments are expected to decline in the event of all GERs moving to 100 by the year 2000 would shed a total of about 29 million pupils at primary level over the decade. More than 22 million of these pupils, however, would be Chinese: the interaction of a very high initial GER (129), a large population but a rather low population growth rate causes China to dominate all other countries in this group.[6] After allowing for all such cases, it can be

---

[6] It should be noted that, even with disaggregation to the national level, some errors of aggregation are not completely avoided, e.g. in China it is urban population growth that has been in sharpest decline. Meanwhile there will continue to be a need for more rural school places in some areas.

TABLE 6.2. *Calculation of total number of new school places required for UPE and SFA in all low- and middle-income countries*

	1990	2000		2005	
		UPE	SFA	UPE	SFA
1. Primary enrolments in all LDCs[a]	522	607	651	659	714
2. Net additional children enrolled 1990–2000[b]		85	129		
1990–2005				137	192
3. Total decreases in enrolments 1990–2000[c]		29	27		
1990–2005				23	20
4. Gross additional places required[d]		114	156	160	212
5. Places required as % of 1990 enrolments		22	30	31	41

[a] As given by aggregation of national simulations, rounded to the nearest million; see Table 6.1.
[b] Calculated by subtraction of 1990 enrolments from those shown for UPE and SFA.
[c] Enrolments decrease in some countries owing either to reductions in GER to 100, and/or negative rates of growth of school-age population.
[d] Sum of data shown in lines 2 and 3.

seen that the move to UPE by the end of the century would require an additional 114 million primary-school places beyond those available in 1990 (amounting to an increase of 22 per cent) rather than the 85 million implied by the simple difference between the enrolments shown for those two years.

The achievement of SFA would, of course, imply a different expansion pattern: it would require improvements to the quality of primary schooling, in most cases, such that sufficient materials were available in classrooms, and that teachers were paid adequately; in addition it would require a more internally efficient school system, with much lower rates of drop-out and repetition than typically exist at present.

We have investigated the implications of achieving such changes in each of the national simulations, some of the results of which are also summarized in Table 6.1. Focusing still upon enrolments, it can be seen that the sets of cost-saving and cost-shifting reforms (reforms 1–5) have no impact upon these, as compared with the UPE levels. The same is true for the improvements in the supply of teaching materials and teachers' salaries (reforms 6 and 7). However, the reduction in the rates of drop-out and repetition generally increase enrolments sharply, although the actual effect in each particular country depends upon the relative magnitudes of these rates at the present time.[7] Thus the SFA enrolment level

[7] Obviously, there are two separate effects here. The reduction in rates of repetition causes enrolments to fall. On the other hand, reducing the rates of drop-out from school causes enrolments to rise. It is the net impact of both of these changes upon enrolments and costs which are shown in the tables.

for all developing countries consequent on achieving reform levels 8 and 9 would amount to some 650 million pupils by the end of the century, or some 7 per cent more than in the case of the achievement of UPE.

For the same reasons as before, the total additional places required for the achievement of SFA are greater than the difference between the net enrolment data shown for 1990 and those shown for SFA in Table 6.1 would suggest. As indicated in Table 6.2, SFA by the year 2000 would require about 156 million additional school places beyond those available in 1990 (an increase of some 30 per cent over the decade). This would be sufficient to achieve net enrolment ratios around the world in the low 90s, which, as was argued in Chapter 2 (Section 2) is probably as high as can be realistically achieved. As Table 6.1 indicates, these net ratios would often be associated with GERs greater than 100 (with a weighted average for all countries of 108). Further reductions in repetition and drop-out rates would thus be possible in the early part of the next century. These would, in turn, reduce GERs, bringing them closer to NERs (and thus achieving further improvements in efficiency). But additional enrolments amongst primary-age children then excluded from school would not be secured, since NERs would already be close to their maximum achievable levels. Faster reductions in drop-out and repetition than those simulated here would be unrealistic within the time proposed. For these reasons, it is justifiable to take these as useful illustrations of the practical achievement of SFA.

In summary, the achievement of UPE during the 1990s would require an estimated 114 million new school places worldwide, representing an increase of around 22 per cent from 1990. On the other hand, SFA, as we have defined it, would require around 156 million additional places, or about 30 per cent more than present levels. By the year 2005, Table 6.2 shows that the required increases would be around 30 and 40 per cent, respectively. Each of these requirements, in fact, seem modest, needing no more than a steady 2 or 3 per cent annual growth in school places, even for SFA to be achieved within ten years. What, then, is all the fuss about? Surely, this target could easily be achieved, in view of the fact that average growth rates of primary enrolments well in excess of these magnitudes were maintained in all developing-country regions over the fifteen years 1960–75?[8]

The answer is simple: the problem only seems easily surmountable because of the way in which the question is posed. The difficulties likely to be faced in achieving UPE and SFA arise not so much from the enrolment challenge in aggregate, but rather from its highly unequal

---

[8] The rates for Africa, Asia, and Latin America are shown in Table 1.1. In fact, only if the average rates of growth of primary enrolments continued at the relatively modest levels witnessed since 1980 would the quantitative aspects of SFA not be achieved by 2000.

TABLE 6.3. *Regional concentration of additional primary enrolments required for SFA, 1990–2005 (millions, with percentages in parentheses)*

	Estimated primary enrolments			Gross additional places required[a]	
	1990	SFA 2000	SFA 2005	1990–2000	1990–2005
All LDCs	522	651	714	156	212
SSA	59	121	144	62	85
(as % of all)	(11)	(19)	(20)	(40)	(40)
Pakistan and Bangladesh	15	46	52	31	37
(as % of all)	(3)	(7)	(7)	(20)	(17)

[a] These data exclude countries where enrolments are expected to fall, and cannot, for the 'all-LDC' case, be derived from the first three columns shown. See Table 6.2.

Source: Calculated from data in Table A.1.

distribution amongst different countries and regions of the world. The scale of the quantitative task is determined by two variables: first by the proportion of the age-group already enrolled, and second by the rate of growth of the school-age population. Thus, those countries with low GERs in 1990 and with high rates of population growth will face the hardest tasks in attempting to achieve SFA over the next ten to fifteen years. Such cases are heavily concentrated amongst the nations of Sub-Saharan Africa, and in Pakistan and Bangladesh. As indicated by Table 6.3, both of these subregions will face a difficult, if not impossible task.

In Sub-Saharan Africa, enrolments would have to double over ten years to reach SFA, requiring an average annual growth of more than 7 per cent. Although, in 1990, SSA accounted for only 11 per cent of total primary enrolments in developing countries, it can be seen from Table 6.3 that fully 40 per cent of all the additional enrolments required to achieve SFA will be in that subcontinent.

Pakistan and Bangladesh face an even more difficult challenge in proportionate terms.[9] There, enrolment would have to triple over the decade, requiring an extraordinarily rapid annual enrolment growth of 12 per cent to the end of the century, or an average rate of 9 per cent over the fifteen years to 2005. These two countries account for only 3 per cent of total enrolments in developing countries in 1990, but for around 20 per cent of all the increases in enrolments needed if SFA is to be achieved.

In other parts of the developing world, the enrolment challenge is more

[9] This statement is true if we compare Pakistan and Bangladesh with the average for SSA as a whole. Nevertheless, in 8 countries of SSA—Burkina Faso, Chad, Ethiopia, Guinea, Liberia, Mali, Niger, and Somalia—the enrolment gap is, in relative terms, even greater than that in Pakistan and Bangladesh. For details, see Table A.1.

evenly distributed. Large absolute increases will be required in India and Brazil, but these could be accommodated by enrolment growth of around 3 per cent per year. Some of the smaller countries outside the regions shown in Table 6.3 also require large proportional increases in primary-school capacity (Nepal, the two Yemens, Lao PDR, Papua New Guinea). But the major task—where both the absolute and relative challenges are very substantial—will be concentrated in the countries of SSA, and in Pakistan and Bangladesh. Here, then, is where both national and international efforts will need to be strongest. We now turn to an examination of the cost and expenditure implications of UPE and SFA, and return to a case-by-case analysis of resources required later in this chapter.

3.2. Recurrent costs and expenditures

3.2.1. The achievement of UPE

Table 6.1 gives details of the changes in the unit recurrent costs of primary schooling, and in the total publicly incurred recurrent expenditures on education brought about by the move to UPE, in each of the developing country regions. As regards unit costs in 1990, it can be seen that there is very large variation between different parts of the world: the weighted average unit costs vary from as little as $11 in India and China to $392 in the 'other' developing-country groups.

Although each of the national simulations assume no change in any of the parameters affecting the costs of education during the move to UPE, it can be seen from the second column of the table that the weighted average primary unit costs at the regional level do change in comparison with those of 1990. This is an inevitable result of enrolments in each country growing at different rates (in turn a consequence of differences in base-year enrolment ratios and in the rates of growth of the 6–11-years age-group). On balance, weighted unit costs at primary level will fall as UPE is approached. This is, first, owing to the increased importance of African enrolments (rising from 11 to 19 per cent of the total), where primary unit costs are amongst the lowest in the world outside India and China, and, secondly, to the relative decline in the proportional importance of enrolments in some high-cost countries included in the 'other developing-countries' group. These latter are mainly Eastern European countries, including Bulgaria, Czechoslovakia, the former GDR, Poland, and Romania, where total primary enrolments are expected to fall over the period, and where recurrent costs, in 1986 prices, exceeded $500 per pupil.

The increased recurrent costs of achieving UPE by the year 2000 would, in aggregate, be relatively modest. The table shows that annual expenditures on education in developing countries as a whole would need to rise from $86 billion in 1990 to about $95 billion by the century's end, and to just over $100 billion five years later. This would represent a real growth of expenditures of only about 1 per cent per year. In fact, as with net enrolment growth, these net expenditure figures include countries where total expenditures would be falling owing to the numbers of pupils declining over the period. However, even after allowing for this, the increased expenditures required would still be small.

As implied by our earlier analysis of enrolments, however, the regional and national variation in the incidence of these additional costs will pose considerable problems. In SSA, for example, annual public expenditures on education would in aggregate need to rise by 70 per cent to 2000 and to double by the year 2005. A regional focus and strategy will thus be vital. This is a theme to which we later return.

3.2.2. The achievement of SFA

The criterion for the achievement of 'schooling for all' that we have adopted in this book is 'the provision of a school system in which all eligible children are enrolled in schools of at least minimally acceptable quality'. The mere achievement of UPE does not satisfy this criterion. This is both because the quality of schooling currently available is often extremely weak, and because the frequent incidence of high levels of repetition and drop-out imply, in the former case, that many school places are occupied by over-age children, and, in the latter case, that many school-age children leave before completing their primary schooling. Thus 'schooling for all' will be more costly than UPE to the extent that the provision of school inputs, such as teaching materials or salaries, needs to be increased, and to the extent that enrolments, as drop-out rates are reduced, have to be higher than would be implied by GERs of 100 in order to allow for however many places continue to be occupied by those who are over-age.

The qualitative improvements to school systems which are required can be at least partly financed in most countries by 'efficiency' reforms to the school system, which either reduce costs, or shift them to other parties. The question arises, however, as to whether, in practice, all countries should be expected to introduce the full set of efficiency reforms, or whether they should be introduced on only a partial basis, as and where necessary.

Should all reforms be implemented?
There is a range of reasons for supposing that the efficiency reforms would, in many countries, be only partially implemented—and that this is not only a realistic, but also an appropriate expectation. First, the politics of policy reform are complex. Although the efficiency measures which

we propose would do least damage to the quality of schooling, and to equitable access to it (in comparison with the other policy choices we have reviewed) it cannot, of course, be argued that double-shifting, increases in average class-size, the introduction of teacher-helpers, and increases in community financing will themselves actually improve the quality of schooling, except in rather special circumstances. If properly managed, we have argued merely that the changes should do little harm, and that if the resources so raised were properly spent elsewhere in the primary system, the end-result for average school quality would be considerably better than a continuation of the status quo. However, because there will be *perceived* educational costs, the reforms may be strongly opposed in some countries, particularly where the efficiency measures hit hardest the well-endowed schools attended by children of the richer, more articulate, and perhaps more powerful groups. In practice, then, this will be an arena for political contest which will ensure a less than comprehensive implementation of the reforms in some countries.

Second, some countries will already have extracted as much as can be gained from the efficiency reforms, and, for technical rather than for political reasons, will be unable to progress much further down that particular path. For example, we have seen in Chapter 3 how Senegal has imaginatively used double-shifting to increase enrolments at lower cost. Although this serves to demonstrate its potential benefits, there will be natural limits on the extent to which this instrument can be further used in that country in order to accelerate progress to SFA. Zimbabwe, too, has used double-shifting to good effect, but little scope for its further extension now remains. Other countries will be in similar circumstances.

Third, in some countries implementation of some or all of the reforms would not be absolutely necessary in order to finance either UPE or SFA. In such cases it would be difficult to sustain the argument that the efficiency reforms were, in any case, always required. Take, for example, the fairly large group of low- and middle-income countries which have already achieved UPE as conventionally defined. Here, further fiscal or education reform should not be necessary to preserve it in future, provided only that resources available from economic and budgetary growth continued to match the growth of the school-age population. In such circumstances the cost-saving and cost-shifting reforms would not be needed in order to maintain GERs of 100 or more.

Furthermore, those countries with GERs already greater than 100 would be able to achieve budgetary savings from the reduced growth of enrolments, relative to both population and public revenues, implied by reducing their GERs to 100 over the decade to 2000. In those countries, therefore, provided per capita incomes (and per capita public revenues) did not fall over the period, the relative budgetary cost of UPE would decline with the GER. Finally, in the countries having initial GER values well in excess of 100, the *absolute* costs of UPE could decline as a consequence of future enrolments actually being lower than those of 1990, notwithstanding the impact of population growth. The strongest example of such a case is China, where, by moving to a GER value of 100 by the year 2000, recurrent expenditures on education would still be about 6 per cent less, in real terms, than those made in 1990. These resources could enable some of the qualitative improvements required for SFA to be financed, which might remove, in China, the need to introduce some or all of the efficiency reforms.

For all of the above reasons, it is necessary to recognize, and incorporate some flexibility into the attempt to simulate the cost impact of achieving SFA around the world. In fact there is no single figure which could identify such costs, since their magnitude depends upon the extent to which the introduction of efficiency reforms, which would reduce the level of publicly incurred unit costs, were necessary, desirable or even feasible in each particular case.

The costs of selective and of full implementation of the reforms
Accordingly, the costs of achieving SFA were simulated not only on the basis of each country implementing all the reforms we have identified, but also for their more selective implementation. In the case of the latter, based upon the considerations outlined above, the cost-saving and cost-shifting policy changes (reforms 1–5) were not implemented in the national simulations for any of the countries with a GER value greater than 100 in 1990. For the forty-two countries so affected, only the quality-enhancing measures (reforms 6–9) were introduced. This allows high- and low-cost estimates for SFA to be shown (together with, of course, any particular combination in between). The high-cost case, where the efficiency reforms have been selectively implemented, is summarized in Table 6.1. The low-cost case, which employs all reforms, is summarized in Table A.4. Tables A.2 and A.3 provide some of the details for each individual country. In order to keep matters straightforward, only the high-cost case will be discussed in any detail in this chapter. However, in our later discussion of financing strategies, both sets of results will be used.

Table 6.1, then, shows the impact that the selective implementation of each of the educational/fiscal reforms would have upon weighted average unit costs and upon recurrent education expenditures for each region of the developing world. It follows from what has been said that the magnitude of this impact will depend not only upon the internal characteristics of the school systems in each country (such as, for example, whether or not average class-sizes at primary and secondary level were, in 1990, less than forty students, and thus upon whether or not reform 2 is implemented), but also upon the proportion of countries, within each region, having GER values in 1990 greater than 100. Because of this, the impact of the cost-saving/shifting reforms appears greatest in Africa, where very few countries had already achieved UPE (in SSA weighted average unit costs are reduced by 37 per cent as a result of reforms 1–5, and in North Africa by 44 per cent), and it appears least in Latin America, where the majority of countries had achieved UPE (and, thus, where weighted average unit costs for the region as a whole are not significantly changed by these reforms).[10] For the same reasons, whilst in most regions the selective implementation of all the reforms, including those which would enhance school quality, leaves primary unit costs somewhat below their 1990 levels, in the cases of Latin America and India/China the reforms leave unit costs somewhat higher than they were before.

The effects of these and other influences upon annual recurrent education expenditures are shown in the last-line entries for each region in Table 6.1. These expenditure figures are a product not only of the primary unit cost and enrolment trends already discussed, but also of enrolment and cost changes in other parts of the simulated education systems. It is not necessary to go into the details of these changes here, since they would add little to the interpretation of the results. A general point of some interest, however, is that the enrolments and associated costs of secondary-school expansion build up more slowly than those at primary level, owing to the six-year lag which exists, on average, between entry to primary and secondary schools for any particular age-cohort. This fact helps to explain why, in SSA for example, primary enrolments would double if UPE were to be reached by 2000, yet total recurrent expenditures on education would increase by only two-thirds above 1990 levels. On the other hand, the impact of the expansion of the more expensive secondary system would be more fully felt in SSA after the year 2000, when annual recurrent educational expenditures would be increasing at over 5 per cent, compared with a 3.6 per cent annual increase in primary enrolments.

The last-line entries in the first and second columns of Table 6.1 show that the additional recurrent expenditure required by a move to UPE by the end of this century throughout the developing world would amount to about \$9 billion per year—an increase of about 10 per cent over 1990 levels. On the other hand if all of the cost-saving/shifting reforms were implemented in countries which had GERs lower than 100 in 1990, UPE

---

[10] The impact of reforms 1–5 on weighted average unit costs in India and China appears, from Table 6.1, to be zero. This, however, is the result of rounding. In China, the cost-saving/shifting reforms are not implemented. India's 1990 unit costs are estimated to be only 25% of the value of China's, and its primary enrolments in the same year were about two-thirds of those in China. Thus, the reduction of India's unit costs following reforms 1–5 does not significantly reduce the weighted average values for the two countries taken together.

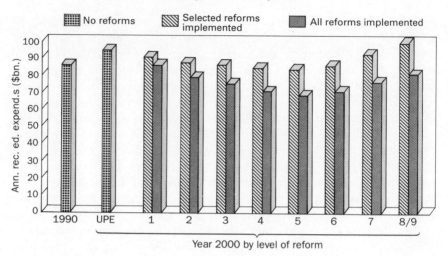

FIG. 6.1 *Costs of reaching UPE and SFA by 2000. All LDCs: alternative patterns of reform*

could then be implemented by the year 2000 with no increase in aggregate expenditures for all countries taken together.[11] But the qualitative improvements which are needed for SFA would again push up costs substantially, to about $100 billion, amounting to an increase of about 16 per cent in comparison with 1990 expenditures.

For purposes of comparison, the aggregate differences in the annual recurrent costs of SFA arising from the selective and from the full implementation of all of the reforms are summarized in Fig. 6.1. In general the full implementation of all reforms by all countries reduces the costs by a further 18 per cent below the 'selective implementation' case. The most striking implication of this is that if all of the reforms were implemented in every country, the total costs of SFA throughout the developing world could be accommodated, in the year 2000, for no more than the expenditures which were actually made, across all countries, in 1990. These figures are instructive. But, as we shall show, they cannot be taken to imply that mere implementation of all policy reforms would solve the financing problem of achieving SFA in every country. Aggregation continues to conceal important differences in the distribution of costs between States. Equally, focusing only upon the beginning and end of a period hides the additional costs which may be being incurred during the

[11] After the implementation of reform 5, we estimate, as shown in Table 6.1, that annual recurrent expenditures would amount to some $83 bn. for all developing countries taken together. This sum is, in fact, slightly lower than the total estimated expenditures for 1990, in the same countries, of some $86 bn.

TABLE 6.4. *Total additional costs of UPE and SFA and likely deficit arising ($bn), 1990–2005: reforms selectively implemented*[a]

	2000									2005		
	UPE No reforms	Cost-saving reforms			Cost-shifting reforms		Quality-enhancing reforms			UPE No reforms	Cost-saving shifting	SFA
		Double-shifting	Increase class-size	Teacher-helpers	Community financing	Freeze higher ed. subsidies	Increase materials	Teacher salaries	SFA Repetition drop-out			
		(1)	(2)	(3)	(4)	(5)	(6)	(7)	(8/9)		(1–5)	(1–9)
Sub-Saharan Africa (n = 35)												
Cumulated additional rec. ed. expend. (net)	19.2	15.1	13.2	11.9	9.4	7.8	9.9	13.4	15.6	46.1	24.0	41.1
Cumulated additional rec. ed. expend. (gross)	19.2	15.1	13.2	11.9	9.4	7.9	10.0	13.4	15.6	46.2	24.0	41.2
Cumulated additional rec. ed. deficits	-8.8	-5.2	-4.0	-3.3	-2.4	-2.0	-2.8	-4.2	-6.1	-21.2	-4.8	-16.9
No. of countries with recurrent deficits	27	22	18	16	14	11	19	24	25	27	15	27
Other Africa (n = 4)												
Cumulated additional rec. ed. expend. (net)	7.0	4.3	2.1	1.4	-0.2	-1.3	-1.1	0.8	0.8	15.9	1.5	5.4
Cumulated additional rec. ed. expend. (gross)	7.0	4.3	2.1	1.4	0.3	0.2	0.2	0.8	0.9	15.9	1.5	5.4
Cumulated additional rec. ed. deficits	-1.7	-0.3	0.0	0.0	0.0	0.0	0.0	-0.1	0.0	-3.7	0.0	0.0
No. of countries with recurrent deficits	3	1	0	0	0	0	0	1	0	3	0	0
India and China (n = 2)												
Cumulated additional rec. ed. expend. (net)	-1.2	-2.0	-2.6	-2.7	-3.2	-3.3	2.9	6.4	11.2	-2.0	-5.4	20.3
Cumulated additional rec. ed. expend. (gross)	0.7	0.0	0.0	0.0	0.0	0.0	2.9	6.4	11.2	1.7	0.0	20.3
Cumulated additional rec. ed. deficits	-0.1	0.0	0.0	0.0	0.0	0.0	-0.7	-2.8	-7.6	-0.2	0.0	-12.3
No. of countries with recurrent deficits	1	0	0	0	0	0	1	2	2	1	0	2
Other Asia (n = 24)												
Cumulated additional rec. ed. expend. (net)	19.4	13.0	8.0	5.8	2.3	0.8	3.3	17.7	24.0	46.9	16.2	56.9
Cumulated additional rec. ed. expend. (gross)	20.2	16.5	14.2	13.3	11.9	11.2	13.1	24.4	30.2	48.4	30.0	65.2
Cumulated additional rec. ed. deficits	-2.9	-1.3	-1.0	-0.8	-0.5	-0.4	-1.8	-7.3	-13.1	-6.2	-1.5	-22.9
No. of countries with recurrent deficits	12	5	4	3	2	2	-7	17	18	12	2	17

TABLE 6.4. (cont'd)

	2000									2005		
	UPE No reforms	Cost-saving reforms			Cost-shifting reforms		Quality-enhancing reforms			UPE No reforms	Cost-saving shifting	SFA
		Double-shifting	Increase class-size	Teacher-helpers	Community financing	Freeze higher ed. subsidies	Increase materials	Teacher salaries	SFA Repetition drop-out			
	(1)	(1)	(2)	(3)	(4)	(5)	(6)	(7)	(8/9)	(1–5)	(1–5)	(1–9)
Latin America (n = 22)												
Cumulated additional rec. ed. expend. (net)	8.0	7.4	7.0	6.8	6.5	6.3	7.1	15.9	34.3	19.0	16.2	80.9
Cumulated additional rec. ed. expend. (gross)	8.2	7.6	7.4	7.3	7.2	7.2	7.8	16.2	34.6	19.3	17.2	81.1
Cumulated additional rec. deficits	-0.3	-0.1	0.0	0.0	0.0	0.0	-0.1	-5.4	-23.5	-0.7	0.0	-56.1
No. of countries with recurrent deficits	7	2	0	0	0	0	2	15	19	7	0	20
Other developing countries (n = 11)												
Cumulated additional rec. ed. expend. (net)	-2.3	-9.8	-16.5	-18.7	-22.6	-23.4	-22.5	-13.6	-8.0	-4.2	-36.0	-8.2
Cumulated additional rec. ed. expend. (gross)	6.4	3.1	0.7	0.1	0.1	0.0	0.1	1.8	4.2	14.2	0.2	10.6
Cumulated additional rec. deficits	-3.0	-0.1	0.0	0.0	0.0	0.0	0.0	-3.3	-5.4	-6.2	0.0	-8.8
No. of countries with recurrent deficits	6	1	1	1	0	0	0	5	5	6	0	5
All developing countries (n = 98)												
Cumulated additional rec. ed. expend. (net)	50.0	28.0	11.3	4.4	-7.8	-13.1	-0.4	40.7	77.9	121.7	16.6	196.5
Cumulated additional rec. ed. expend. (gross)	61.7	46.7	37.6	33.9	28.9	26.6	34.2	63.1	96.7	145.7	72.9	223.8
Cumulated additional rec. deficits	-16.7	-6.9	-5.1	-4.1	-2.9	-2.5	-5.3	-23.1	-55.7	-38.2	-6.2	-116.9
No. of countries with recurrent deficits	56	31	23	20	16	13	29	65	69	56	17	71

[a] In this table the results of implementing all reforms in countries with GER <100 and reforms 6–9 only in countries with GER >100 are shown. All cumulated additional costs have been calculated by summing the projected expenditure differences between the base year and that for each year of the projection period, assuming that expenditures grow at a constant annual rate. All deficits shown in the table are calculated by aggregating all national-level deficits for each individual country, and cumulating them in the way indicated above. Surplus countries are not included in these latter calculations.

Sources: Calculated from data in Statistical Appendix Tables A.2 and A.3, and from the detailed national simulations of UPE and SFA.

intervening years. It is necessary now to strip away some of these covers, in order to see more of the reality beneath.

4. The Cumulated Additional Costs of UPE and SFA

Better estimates of the additional costs generated by UPE and SFA than those given by comparing annual recurrent costs 'before' and 'after' are provided by Table 6.4. Here, the additional costs of the enrolment increases, and of the reforms as selectively implemented, are calculated for each year of the projection period by subtracting from each year's estimated total recurrent costs those which were incurred in 1990. These annual additional costs are then cumulated over the period concerned. Two sets of cumulated additional costs are shown for each developing-country region. The first set is the simple sum of the cumulated costs calculated from each of the national simulations. Since, for some countries, expenditures in the year 2000 (or 2005) are lower than those in 1990, these net figures count any savings made, as a result of the move to UPE or of the introduction of policy reforms, against the additional expenditures incurred by other, less fortunately placed States. In fact, such savings obviously could not be transferred in this way. Thus, of somewhat greater interest, is the second set of cumulated cost figures, which show increased expenditures *gross* of any savings made by States whose simulated expenditures on education decline over the period concerned. What, then do these results show?

Consider, first, the results for all developing countries taken together. It can be seen from the bottom left-hand cell of Table 6.4 that the net additional costs of UPE in 2000, throughout the developing world, would be about $50 billion, but that the gross additional costs (that is, excluding the cost-reductions which would be made possible in some countries by declining enrolments) amount to some $62 billion. The difference between these two estimates suggests that aggregated simulation methods may generally underestimate the gross additional costs of UPE by at least 20 per cent.[12] The size of this error is increased, however, for those estimates showing the cost-impact of the educational/fiscal reforms. As costs progressively fall with the introduction of the reforms, the number of countries able to reduce expenditures below the levels which held in 1990 is increased. Thus, for example, reform level 5 is shown to be associated with net savings of $13 billion for all LDCs (as would also be suggested by Table 6.1, which showed that recurrent costs for all countries would be lower in 2000 than in 1990 after the implementation of

[12] This, of course, provides one of the justifications for performing the cost analyses separately for each individual country.

reform levels 1–5). Yet the second line of the table reports that, in those countries where expenditures do not fall, the cumulated additional costs of UPE would still amount to some $27 billion, even if all cost-saving/ shifting reforms were implemented over the decade. The biases are reduced as expenditures increase again consequent upon the introduction of reforms 6–9, and the difference between the gross and net estimates returns to about 20 per cent with the achievement of SFA.

The table allows the absolute cost-impact of each type of reform to be compared. The impact of double-shift teaching and of increases in class-size are very large: the gross additional recurrent costs of UPE decline, even in the 'selective' case, from $62 billion to $38 billion, after the introduction of reforms 1 and 2. Thus, well over one-third of the cumulated additional gross costs of UPE could be met in these ways. The introduction of teacher-helpers (reform 3) reduces the cumulated gross costs of UPE by 6 per cent—a useful saving, given that its likely negative impact upon the quality of schooling would (if properly managed) be very small. The two sets of cost-shifting reforms further reduce costs by 12 per cent, albeit with potential equity dangers, particularly in the case of increased community support for primary and secondary schooling. Nevertheless, the combined impact of all the cost-saving and cost-shifting reforms, selectively implemented, would be to more than halve the gross additional costs of achieving UPE in those countries where it had not yet been achieved by 1990, and of maintaining it elsewhere.

These reductions in costs are more than outweighed, however, by the likely costs of improvements to the quality of schooling which would be needed in most countries in order to achieve SFA. Each of the reforms shown in the table considerably increases recurrent costs. Even the increased expenditures upon learning resources to the (still modest) figure of $5 per child would cost an additional $7.6 billion at UPE in the year 2000 in comparison with present expenditures. Though large, this may be the single most effective item of expenditure for raising the quality of schooling. These costs would be particularly concentrated in Africa, South Asia, and China, where average recurrent expenditures on learning materials are often much lower than $5 at the present time.[13] Less unexpected are the facts that the increase in teachers' salaries and the sharp reductions in drop-out and repetition would each add about $30 billion to developing-country expenditures. One result of all these changes would be that the achievement of SFA would cost, by the year 2000, rather more than half as much again, in the 'selective' case, as would UPE. Though these costs are substantial, it should be remembered that enrolments would be about 7 per cent higher than in the UPE case, and

---

[13] On the other hand, $5 can buy much more in China and India than in most African countries. China is not actually short of textbooks at primary level, and they are cheap to produce. Typical Indian schools, however, are very poorly resourced.

that the school systems of developing countries would then be considerably more effective and efficient than is the case at the present time.

Four conclusions of importance can, at this stage, be drawn. First, estimates of the additional costs of UPE or SFA that are calculated at a world or regional level are likely to be highly inaccurate, owing to the presence of significant 'biases of aggregation': separate national estimates are required if these errors are to be avoided. Secondly, the aggregated results of our own national estimates suggest that the gross additional recurrent costs of achieving UPE by the year 2000, in all low- and middle-income countries and in the absence of changes being made to education and fiscal policies, would amount to some $60 billion over and above the expenditures made in 1990. Thirdly, although a feasible package of cost-saving and cost-shifting reforms could reduce these additional costs to between $13 billion and $27 billion,[14] they would leave school systems in many countries seriously under-resourced, and many pupils would remain out of school. Finally, in these 162 countries, the gross additional recurrent costs—cumulated over the ten years 1990–2000—of achieving SFA, which would involve remedying some of the qualitative deficiencies mentioned above, would amount to between $50 billion and $100 billion, again depending upon whether the efficiency reforms are fully or selectively implemented. The latter sum is roughly equal to the total amount of recurrent spending on education which occurred in developing countries in 1990.

5. How Can These Costs be Financed?

We now turn to the second set of questions raised at the outset of this chapter. Can developing countries be expected to meet costs of the magnitudes indicated above from their own resources over the next ten to fifteen years? If so, what changes, if any, to existing policies would be required? If not, to what extent can, or should, the international community be expected to help?

5.1. Increased public revenues from economic growth

The first of these questions is important, but difficult to address. In principle, the answer to it would depend, for each individual country, upon the rate of economic growth achieved *ad interim*, upon the proportion of total income which will, or could, be represented by public expenditures, and, within that, upon the proportion of public spending

---

[14] This range depends upon whether reforms are implemented in all countries, or only in those with GERs less than 100, respectively. See Tables 6.4 and A.5.

which will, or could, be devoted to education, particularly to primary schooling. Each of these variables is unknown, the values for which it would be hazardous to attempt to predict in any detail, particularly over periods as long as ten to fifteen years.

Instead, we show, in Table 6.4, the implications of public revenues in each country being such as to allow real educational spending per person to be held constant at their 1990 levels. This, in turn, is consistent with the assumptions that national income per capita, government expenditure as a proportion of GNP, and the relative importance attached to educational spending by each government, each remained constant at 1990 levels. These assumptions are consistent with the World Bank's 'downside' projection of output growth for Sub-Saharan Africa over the 1990s, and its 'more unlikely, but still plausible, "low case" scenario' for other low- and middle-income countries over those years (World Bank 1991*b*: 30). We believe, with the authors of the World Bank study, that these assumptions are realistic for Africa, but probably pessimistic for other developing-country regions. On the other hand, for those countries which are still some way from achieving UPE, and which are a particular focus for the present study—being concentrated, as they are, in SSA and in the poorer parts of Asia and Latin America—more generous assumptions for per capita income growth over the next decade would not, in general, be easy to justify.

The last two lines shown for each regional grouping in Table 6.4 summarize the extent to which UPE, and each of the reforms leading to SFA, would be able to be financed domestically in developing countries, under the above assumptions. Recurrent deficits[15] have been calculated, for each country, by comparing the cumulated additional expenditures required for UPE, and for each of the reforms, with the cumulated resources available, determined as indicated above. In cumulating the deficits, all countries with surpluses have been ignored. The number of countries with recurrent deficits, for each column, are also indicated for each developing-country region shown.

It follows from the methods used, which assume that per capita resources for education will remain constant, that the fifty-six countries[16] with starting values for GER of less than 100 would be unable to finance UPE in the absence of policy reforms. This is because all such countries would have to increase their expenditures upon education at a rate which exceeded that of population growth, in order to raise their GER to 100 by

---

[15] Here, and in what follows, we use the term 'deficit' when the recurrent costs of education at UPE or SFA in 2000 or 2005 are greater than the public resources which are likely to be available for educational spending—using the assumptions for revenue growth and for the fiscal stance adopted, as specified in the text.

[16] These comprise the cases of 55 separate countries together with the composite simulation covering the 65 countries for which data were not separately available.

the end of the century. The first column of Table 6.4 suggests that these countries would face a combined recurrent deficit of about $17 billion by the end of the century if UPE were attained by that date. The table also indicates that the size of these deficits would rather more than double, to about $38 billion, by the year 2005.

It is important to notice that, once again, SSA appears to face the greatest crisis of any region: almost half the countries unable to finance UPE in the absence of policy change are from SSA, and they account for rather more than half the value of the total shortfall of domestic resources worldwide. Moreover, whilst three-quarters of all States in SSA would be unable to finance UPE on the above assumptions, this is true for only one-half of all Asian and Middle Eastern countries, and for only one-third of those in Latin America.

Furthermore, the sheer size of the deficits in the case of SSA indicates the likelihood that these countries will not be able to finance all of the required expansion themselves. The estimated deficit associated with the achievement of UPE by the year 2000, for example, is equivalent to almost 70 per cent *more* than the value of total recurrent spending on education in SSA in 1990. By contrast, the estimated deficit for Asia and the Middle East (excluding China and India) is equal to only 10 per cent of 1990 expenditures, whilst that for Latin America amounts to a mere 2 per cent. Sub-Saharan Africa, then, in moving towards UPE, faces a much heavier financial burden, relative to its capacity to pay, than any other region of the world.

5.2. Policy reform

The contrast between Africa and other world regions sharpens even more—if such is possible—on investigation of the potential role of changes in education and financing policies. It can be seen from Table 6.4 that the implementation of all the five cost-saving/shifting reforms would reduce the likely fiscal deficit facing all developing countries taken together to a mere $2.5 billion by the year 2000 ($6 billion by 2005). However, of the thirteen countries still in deficit after the introduction of reforms 1–5, eleven of them would be from SSA (the others being Pakistan and Bangladesh), and they would account for more than 80 per cent of the estimated total fiscal deficit at that time.

The estimated deficits increase rapidly again with the introduction of the qualitative reforms, and the move to SFA. Their combined value in the year 2000 rises to $56 billion—$117 billion by 2005—and the number of countries so affected, from fifty-six to sixty-nine—seventy-one by 2005. It can be seen from Table 6.4 that these changes are dominated by Asian and Latin American countries, where the costs of SFA are sharply higher than those of UPE. This is mainly because a good number of them had

already achieved UPE by 1990, and thus, in these simulations, benefit
only from the cost-saving consequences of reductions in their GERs
rather than from the impact of the cost-saving/shifting reforms. It is also,
however, strongly influenced by the much larger increases in school
enrolments associated with reforms 8 and 9 in Latin America, and in Asia
than in SSA: as shown by Table 6.1, the sharp reductions in drop-out
and repetition induced by these reforms have the effect of increasing
enrolments by 16 per cent in Latin America and by 9 per cent in Asia
beyong their UPE levels; in SSA, however, the reductions in drop-out
and repetition increase enrolments by only 3 per cent. This is a consequence mainly of rates of repetition being much greater in African
schools than in those of other regions. Drop-out rates are also higher in
SSA, but it is the particularly high repetition rate which, when reduced in
the simulated reforms, acts as a more restraining influence upon incremental enrolments than occurs elsewhere.

These circumstances explain why it is that, whilst the total deficit
associated with SFA in Sub-Saharan Africa is lower than that arising from
achieving UPE, this ranking is reversed in other regions. Nevertheless, it
remains the case that the size of the deficit associated with implementing
SFA, relative to total public spending on education in 1990, would still be
higher in Sub-Saharan Africa than would be the case elsewhere in the
developing world.

5.3. Increased budgetary allocations to education

We have so far talked as though the recurrent and total deficits which
emerge from our analyses were able to be influenced in size only by the
set of educational and financing reforms, the effects of which are demonstrated in the simulations. This, of course, is not so. The deficits shown in
Table 6.4 are premissed upon the assumption that per capita resources
available for education would remain constant in real terms over the
years to 2005. If the available resources were to increase, the size of
the deficits shown would be concomitantly reduced. Now, even if total
budgetary revenues per head of population remained constant over
the period, resources for education could still be increased if governments were to accord education more priority, in state spending, than it
received in the late 1980s. The question thus arises as to whether there is
room for spending to increase in these ways, and, if so, what implications
this might have for the funding of SFA.

Tables 6.5 and 6.6 indicate the extent to which a combination of
policy reform and increased budgetary allocations to education would be
capable of meeting the costs of SFA in each country. The first of these
tables selects, from amongst those which had not achieved UPE by 1990,
all those which are expected to show deficits in the years to 2000 or 2005

were SFA to be achieved by the end of the century. In each of these cases the effects of the full set of cost-saving/shifting and quality-enhancing policy reforms (1–9) are incorporated. In a similar fashion, the second table selects, from amongst those countries where UPE had, by 1990, already been achieved (as proxied by GERs having a value equal to or greater than 100), those expected to incur deficits on reaching SFA without the fiscal assistance of reforms 1–5.

Chapter 2 showed that the proportion of public expenditure allocated to education varies strongly between countries. This is reflected also in Tables 6.5 and 6.6, which indicate a wide range of reported allocations to education, from a minimum of only 4 per cent of total recurrent spending in the case of Pakistan up to as much as 28 per cent in the case of Venezuela. Given that the range is so wide, one approach would be to argue that any additional costs which increased the proportional importance of education in public spending to less than, say, 20 per cent of the total, could and should be financed domestically. This kind of judgement, however, would be naïve. First, it assumes that the different structures of public expenditures between countries are readily adjustable whereas, on the contrary, they change only slowly because they often reflect real and abiding political and economic differences between nations. Small changes may well be possible, but large changes almost certainly would not.

Second, focusing only upon the proportion of budgetary resources going to education ignores the equally important issue of the overall size of state spending in the economy. An example will make the point plain: according to World Bank data (1991*b*: 224), Peru and Tunisia are at similar levels of per capita income, and spend similar proportions of their total budgets upon education. Yet the per capita value of this spending in Tunisia is more than three times that of Peru, because of the much higher proportion of GNP accounted for by Tunisian public spending. Thus, low *proportional* budgetary allocations to education do not, by themselves, imply that the sector is accorded too little priority by a government. More—and more detailed—fiscal information would be needed for such a judgement to be validly based.

For these reasons, it is not particularly helpful to compare critically the proportional allocations of public resources to education shown for different countries in Tables 6.5 and 6.6. Additional information, not provided by these tables, would be needed if such comparisons were to yield sensible results. It is therefore preferable to treat the need to increase public expenditures on education in an incremental rather than an absolute sense. Thus, for most countries, the task of increasing these expenditures, as a proportion of total spending, by one or two percentage points may be a reasonable expectation, whereas hitting a target of *x* per cent of total spending (where *x* may be two or even three times greater

TABLE 6.5. *Public recurrent budgetary implications of financing SFA: deficit countries with GER less than 100 in 1990*[a]

Region	Country	GER 1986	Proportion of recurrent expenditure allocated to education[b]	Cumulated deficit 2000 ($m.) all reforms 1–9 implemented		Cumulated deficit 2005 ($m.) all reforms 1–9 implemented		Budgetary allocation required for fully financed SFA (%)	
				Unchanged budgetary allocation	Budgetary allocation increased by 2%	Unchanged budgetary allocation	Budgetary allocation increased by 2%	2000	2005
SSA	Angola	93	0.13	185		748	346	0.14	0.16
	Benin	64	0.16	47	30	141	104	0.21	0.25
	Burkina Faso	31	0.20	180	149	567	504	0.30	0.38
	Burundi	59	0.16			175		0.15	0.18
	Central African Rep.	66	0.15	151	119	383	327	0.25	0.30
	Chad	43	0.15	323	289	623	568	0.36	0.39
	Ethiopia	36	0.11	1,723	1,507	3,177	2,814	0.26	0.27
	Guinea	29	0.15	83	53	245	206	0.22	0.27
	Liberia	35	0.21	181	164	405	373	0.41	0.46
	Malawi	65	0.12	95	11	518	382	0.15	0.20
	Mali	23	0.10	457	403	1,138	1,045	0.26	0.34
	Mauritania	51	0.15	2		122	32	0.16	0.18
	Mozambique	84	0.16	107	84	266	224	0.23	0.26
	Niger	29	0.16	108	91	303	277	0.31	0.40
	Nigeria	77	0.15	379		2,641	194	0.16	0.18
	Rwanda	65	0.25	176	127	449	361	0.32	0.35
	Senegal	58	0.16	74	20	224	131	0.18	0.20
	Sierra Leone	54	0.14	57	42	156	136	0.21	0.26

Somalia	15	0.16	185	181	468	461	0.77	1.06
Sudan	49	0.16	838	525	1,710	1,181	0.21	0.22
Tanzania	69	0.08			723		0.08	0.09
Uganda	70	0.17	97	57	267	204	0.21	0.24
Zaire	76	0.16	157	29	359	147	0.18	0.19
Subtotal			5,607	3,881	15,812	10,017		
Asia Bangladesh	60	0.11	1,295	1,171	2,772	2,586	0.32	0.41
India	98	0.10	3,325	702	7,601	3,055	0.14	0.16
Myanmar	99	0.13	254	189	561	455	0.21	0.24
Nepal	82	0.13	141	101	313	244	0.20	0.22
Pakistan	44	0.04	1,533	546	4,279	2,612	0.06	0.08
Yemen Arab Rep.	86	0.24	525	348	1,181	891	0.30	0.32
Yemen PDR	66	0.16	32	12	97	70	0.19	0.21
Subtotal			7,105	3,069	16,805	9,913		
LAC Bolivia	87	0.08	109	35	50	293	0.07	0.08
El Salvador	79	0.20	114	32	410	292	0.22	0.26
Guatemala	76	0.16	53	48	420	106	0.19	0.23
Haiti	95	0.23	45		120	36	0.36	0.42
Nicaragua	98	0.12			215		0.13	0.15
Subtotal			321	115	1,216	727		
Other Papua New Guinea	70	0.18	50	1	147	64	0.20	0.22
Total deficits			13,083	7,066	33,980	20,721		

[a] Only those countries with GER <100 and with deficits after implementation of all reforms 1–9 are shown in this table. Twenty countries are expected not to show such deficits, and thus to be able to fully finance SFA domestically without increasing budgetary allocations to education. These countries comprise Côte d'Ivoire, Ghana, Kenya, Zambia, Algeria, Egypt, Morocco, Iraq, Israel, Jordan, Korea, Oman, Thailand, Costa Rica, Trinidad & Tobago, Czechoslovakia, Hungary, Romania, Yugoslavia, and the grouped countries.

[b] These data are typical values from the mid-1980s, based upon UNESCO and World Bank sources.

Sources: Calculated from data in Statistical Appendix and from the detailed national simulations of UPE and SFA.

TABLE 6.6. *Public recurrent budgetary implications of financing SFA: deficit countries with GER greater than 100 in 1990*[a]

		GER 1986	Proportion of recurrent expenditure allocated to education[b]	Cumulated deficit 2000 ($m.)				Cumulated deficit 2005 ($m.)			
				Unchanged budgetary allocation		Budgetary allocation increased by 2%		Unchanged budgetary allocation		Budgetary allocation increased by 2%	
				reforms 6–9	all reforms 1–9	reforms 6–9	all reforms 1–9	reforms 6–9	all reforms 1–9	reforms 6–9	all reforms 1–9
SSA	Cameroon	109	0.14	92				111			
	Lesotho	115	0.17	44		20		82		42	
	Madagascar	121	0.16	287	11	216		711	182	586	57
	Togo	102	0.13	62		13		139		60	
	Subtotal			485	11	249	0	1,042	182	688	57
Asia	China	129	0.16	4,291				4,668			
	Hong Kong	104	0.16	708				944			
	Indonesia	118	0.14	1,292				1,167			
	Iran	110	0.22	1,650				2,376			
	Lao PDR	111	0.07	66	28	52	14	154	76	122	44
	Malaysia	101	0.24	1,065		179		1,544		187	
	Mongolia	102	0.16	35				55			
	Philippines	107	0.17	2,573				4,235			
	Singapore	115	0.25	65							
	Sri Lanka	104	0.13	168				252			
	Syria	111	0.17	518				933		11	
	Turkey	115	0.11	452				485			
	Vietnam	102	0.16	768	154	564		1,507	414	1,174	81
	Subtotal			13,651	182	795	14	18,371	490	1,494	125

Region	Country									
LAC	Argentina	109	0.08	1,325	288		2,839	230	1,292	
	Brazil	103	0.14	17,395	10,805		44,652	8,848	34,535	
	Chile	105	0.17	893	477		1,743		1,131	
	Colombia	114	0.21	696	159		1,176		374	
	Cuba	105	0.16	217			259			
	Dominican Republic	101	0.12	116	72	27	217	65	157	5
	Ecuador	118	0.24	351	137		684		352	
	Honduras	106	0.18	173	56		296		108	
	Jamaica	105	0.13	43			57			
	Mexico	119	0.11	694			837			
	Panama	106	0.18	62			79	30		
	Paraguay	102	0.14	144	83		326		234	
	Peru	122	0.12	261	66		431		119	
	Uruguay	110	0.14	21			16			
	Venezuela	107	0.28	767			1,243			
	Subtotal			23,158	12,143	27	54,854	9,173	38,302	5
Other	Bulgaria	104	0.16	899			1,269			
	Former GDR	105	0.16	2,242	87		4,365		594	
	Greece	104	0.16	275			314			
	Poland	101	0.16	1,897			2,659			
	Subtotal			5,313	87		8,607	0	594	
	Total deficits	220		42,607	13,274	220	82,875	9,845	41,078	187
	TOTAL excluding Brazil[c]	220		25,212	2,469	220	38,223	997	6,543	187

[a] Only those countries with GER >100 and with deficits after implementing reforms 6–9 are shown in this table. Six countries would be expected to have no deficits, and thus to be able to fully finance SFA without introducing cost-saving reforms and without increasing budgetary allocations to education. These are Botswana, Gabon, Mauritius, Zimbabwe, Tunisia, and Portugal.

[b] These data are typical values from the mid-1980s, based upon Unesco and World Bank sources.

[c] Brazil has an unusually large deficit owing to the impact of reducing in reform 9 an exceptionally high drop-out rate at the primary level. This results in primary enrolments increasing by more than 30%, with a concomitant impact upon the current costs.

Sources: Calculated from data in Statistical Appendix and national simulations of UPE and SFA.

than present proportional allocations), for many, clearly would not. Accordingly, the impact of increasing the proportion of public spending allocated to education by 2 percentage points is indicated in Tables 6.5 and 6.6. It will be useful, now, to explore the implications of these results.

5.3.1. *The most educationally disadvantaged countries*

Consider, first, the group of developing countries which had not achieved UPE by the end of the 1980s. There are fifty-six such cases,[17] all of which would be unable to finance UPE by the turn of the century in the absence either of policies to increase real per capita spending on education or to reduce publicly incurred average educational costs. The countries shown in Table 6.5 are those which would still incur deficits in 2000 or 2005, even if the full range of educational/fiscal reforms were introduced, so as to achieve SFA by those dates. There are thirty-six countries in this category. It should be noted, therefore, that implementation of all the reforms would enable full domestic financing not only of UPE, but of SFA, in twenty of the countries which had not yet attained UPE in the 1980s. These twenty countries are listed in the notes to the table. All except three of these are middle-income countries, and in all but four of them GER values greater than 90 had already been attained by the end of the 1980s.

By contrast, the countries where full domestic financing of SFA would still not be possible post-reforms typically have a very different set of characteristics. Most of the thirty-six cases shown in Table 6.5 are low-income countries, and it can be seen that most have starting values for their GERs which are substantially less than 90. Thirty-one of these countries are amongst the world's most educationally disadvantaged States identified in Chapter 2, and they comprise 84 per cent of all countries having GERs less than 90 (see Table 2.1). We can expect, then, a sizeable financing problem to remain for the poorer, more educationally disadvantaged countries, even if they proved willing to introduce policy reforms.

It should be remembered that whether or not the implementation of the full package of reforms would reduce or increase the size of a fiscal deficit (beyond that likely to be associated with achieving UPE in the absence of policy reforms), depends upon the characteristics of each individual case. In circumstances where drop-out rates are currently high, where expenditures upon teaching materials are very low, or where class-

---

[17] This includes the composite simulation (see n. 16, above). Although many of the smaller States in this group will already have achieved UPE, it is nevertheless certain that the total number of countries which had not achieved UPE by the late 1980s was greater than 56.

sizes are large, the SFA reforms would, on balance, tend to increase rather than reduce costs, in comparison with those associated with achieving UPE in an unreformed system. In our simulations, the size of initial UPE deficits are increased in these ways, following the implementation of the SFA reforms, in about one-third (eighteen) of the fifty-six UPE deficit cases—and thus in half of the thirty-six countries shown in Table 6.5. In general, then, we can say that the educational/fiscal reforms simulated here would be able to remove fiscal deficits and secure the move to SFA in countries which are already close to UPE, and particularly where school systems are already reasonably efficient. For those countries with inefficient systems and where only a small proportion of children are presently enrolled, the financial gaps cannot be closed by these means alone.

It can be seen from Table 6.5 that these remaining gaps, after the implementation of reforms 1–9, are quite substantial. They amount to some $13 billion over the period to 2000, and to the much larger sum of $34 billion to 2005 (by which date the impact upon secondary enrolments of having achieved UPE by 2000, in each of the countries shown, is more substantially reflected in the estimates of costs). These deficits are roughly equally shared between African and Asian countries, with particularly large financial gaps appearing for Ethiopia, Mali, Nigeria, and Sudan in Africa, and for Bangladesh, India, and Pakistan in Asia. Outside these two continents, the financial gaps remaining, after implementing all reforms, are relatively small.

The table also demonstrates that if each country were to increase the budgetary allocation shown for 1990 by 2 percentage points, and to keep it constant at that level through to 2005, the total deficits would be reduced by almost one-half, to $7 billion in 2000, and by about one-third, to $21 billion by the year 2005. This change in financing priorities would be sufficient, in combination with the reform package, to finance fully SFA in Burundi, Tanzania, and Bolivia. But in the other countries shown, deficits—albeit smaller than before—would remain.

It must be recognized, however, that it is highly unlikely that all of these low-income countries will be able both to implement the full package of education/fiscal reforms and to reallocate money towards education from other budgetary sources on a permanent basis. Some countries could easily do so, given the necessary commitment. This is particularly so in those cases where large military budgets dwarf allocations to the social sectors. Of those listed in the table, Pakistan is the clearest case of a country which could not expect external support for its education budget in the absence of significant prior shifts in domestic expenditure priorities towards education. But in most of the countries shown such transfers will not be easy. The extent to which they are possible, and the question of whether such shifts could, or should, be linked to levels of external capital or recurrent support, are matters which can be settled only on a case-by-case basis.

5.3.2. Countries which have achieved UPE (but not SFA)

Let us turn now to some consideration of the problems facing the remaining forty-two low- and middle-income countries which had already achieved UPE by the late 1980s. Although there are some important exceptions (China, Indonesia, and the group of countries from SSA), these States are generally better off economically than the first group. Their schools are more widely available to their populations and, again with some exceptions, their school systems are typically more efficient than those in their poorer counterparts. These countries already have the capacity to enrol all the children in the primary school-age group, and there is no reason to suppose that their future financial circumstances would be likely to prevent UPE, in the sense of GERs of at least 100, being maintained.

Yet in many of these countries the quality of the schooling provided remains very low, and many eligible children are prevented from taking up available places by the high levels of repetition and over-age enrolment which remain. Thus, the achievement of SFA—via providing adequate materials support, teacher quality and motivation to secure a good learning environment, and by reducing repetition and drop-out rates to levels which allow schooling opportunities to become genuinely universal—will inevitably involve substantial additional costs in many of these countries over and above those which are presently incurred.

The problem of meeting the additional costs in these countries is similar in nature to that in the first group, where UPE had not, by the late 1980s, yet been attained. There are, however, some differences. First, and most obviously, since the magnitude of the required future expansion of the system is lower for those countries already at UPE, the costs of SFA, relative to resources available, will tend to be less than in the first group. Second, the reduction of GERs towards 100, in a group of countries where values in excess of 115 are not uncommon, provides a source of savings which can help to finance aspects of the move towards SFA. Third, the relevance of some of the cost-saving reforms to countries where UPE has already been attained is less certain than to those where it has not. For example, an increase in the incidence of double-shift teaching, or in the average size of classes, may be entirely defensible if these measures provide the means of financing places for children currently out of school. But if both gross and net enrolments are already high, the question as to whether or not such changes should be used to finance other qualitative reforms—such as improved teaching materials or higher teachers' salaries—has a somewhat more uncertain resolution. In this case, the moral imperative to provide schooling for those currently excluded is removed, and the choice of one set of reforms as compared with the other must depend upon which has greatest impact upon enhanced school-quality. Here, research results in general cannot provide a definitive answer, and the choice would need to depend upon the conditions obtaining in the case of each particular country.

For these reasons, for countries where GERs of 100 or more had already been attained, three sets of questions were posed in our analysis. First, which of these countries would be likely to be able to finance SFA from their own resources, without introducing cost-saving/shifting policies (reforms 1–5), and, for the remaining countries, what pattern of deficits would be likely to emerge? Second, how would the picture change if all reforms (1–9) were to be introduced (as in the case of those countries not having achieved UPE by the late 1980s)? Third, to what extent could the deficits which emerge for some countries, in moving to SFA, be reduced or removed by increasing the priority assigned to education in the public budget, with and without the assistance of reforms 1–5?

The answers to these questions are summarized by the data shown in Table 6.6. Of the forty-two countries which had already achieved UPE, six of them (Botswana, Gabon, Mauritius, Zimbabwe, Tunisia, and Portugal) should be able to finance SFA without introducing any of the cost-saving/shifting policies (reforms 1–5), and without increasing the proportion of the public budget assigned to education. As before, the table shows information on the remaining thirty-six countries which would be likely, according to our analyses, to show a deficit in 2000 or 2005 if SFA were to be achieved without the assistance of reforms 1–5.

It can be seen from the table that the cumulated deficits for this group of countries, in moving to SFA, are likely to be large, in the absence of the cost-saving/shifting reforms. The combined deficit for the whole group is estimated at some $43 billion over the decade to the year 2000, and at some $83 billion by 2005. Clearly, some mix of cost-saving/shifting measures and/or increased expenditures, would be necessary even in most of the countries where UPE has already been reached if SFA were to be attained over the decade. Accordingly, the impact on these deficits of implementing the full package of policy reforms in these countries, i.e., including reforms 1–5, is also shown in the table. It is clear that this would be sufficient to accommodate most of the deficits. Only four of the countries would still have a deficit in the year 2000, and the number would be seven by 2005. A large deficit would remain for Brazil in the latter year, caused by the impact of reducing in reform 9 an exceptionally high drop-out rate at primary level, which causes enrolments to increase by more than 30 per cent with a concomitant impact upon recurrent costs. Elsewhere, however the implementation of the full package of policy reforms would reduce the deficits to insignificant proportions for the year

2000, and they would remain less than $1 billion, excluding Brazil, in 2005.

On the other hand, many of these countries may prefer to finance SFA by allocating increased priority to education within the public budget rather than by introducing some or all of the cost-saving/shifting reforms. Many of the large deficits shown in the table could be removed by devoting only a small additional proportion of public expenditure to the education sector. Those for sixteen of the countries shown (including those for China, Indonesia, Iran, and Mexico) could be removed by devoting an additional 1 per cent of public spending to education. Furthermore, the table shows that a 2 per cent shift in favour of education would remove the deficits in more than half (nineteen) of these countries, even in the absence of reforms 1–5.

By using some mix of policy reforms together with small increases in the proportion of the budget allocated to education, the costs of moving to SFA could, therefore, be easily met by virtually every country shown in Table 6.6. Even in the case of Brazil, the combination of all of the cost-saving/shifting reforms and a 2 per cent budgetary shift would be capable of fully financing the costs of SFA. Our calculations suggest that some small deficits might remain in the cases of Madagascar, Lao PDR, Vietnam, and Dominican Republic, but the table shows that the combined value of those remaining deficits would amount to less than $200 million over the whole period to 2005. Thus, the financial challenge of achieving SFA in the group of countries where UPE has already been attained is considerably less onerous than that in the first group of countries, shown in Table 6.5. By consequence, the levels of external support which would be needed to achieve SFA targets are also small. Their importance would be determined more by questions of strategy than by the magnitude of the financial transfers which were strictly required.

5.4. Increased financial aid to education

The question as to how much aid will be needed to achieve SFA in low- and middle-income countries has no single, reliable answer. As we have gone to some lengths to show, the aid requirements would depend upon what developing countries actually do themselves in order to increase expenditures on education, and to reform both their systems of schooling and the methods whereby they are financed. Nevertheless, some informed judgements can now be made, based upon the conditional financial outcomes that we have simulated for each country.

Table 6.7 provides a broad summary of the financing problem as it has emerged from the analysis of this chapter. It indicates the total additional recurrent costs of achieving SFA over the years to 2005, for all low- and

TABLE 6.7. *Summary of additional recurrent costs of achieving SFA and financing requirements, 1990–2005 ($US bn., 1986 prices)*

	SSA		All LDCs	
Additional costs 1990–2005[a]				
UPE by 2000	46		146	
Cost-saving/shifting reforms[b]		−24		−110
Quality-enhancing reforms[b]		+17		+104
SFA by 2000[b]	39		140	
Total deficits[c]	−16		−44	
Countries below UPE 1990		−16		−34
Countries at UPE 1990		0		−10
Deficits if ed. budget increased 2%[d]	−10		−21	
Countries below UPE 1990		−10		−21
Countries at UPE 1990		0		0
Additional aid 1990–2005	15		30	
Countries below UPE 1990		14		20–25
Countries at UPE 1990		1		5–10
Additional annual aid 1990–2005				
1986 prices	1		2	
1990 prices	1.25		2.5	

[a] These are the cumulated additional recurrent costs, as compared with those of 1990, for each year of the period, as given by Tables 6.4 and A.5.
[b] All reforms are here implemented in all countries, as summarized by Table A.5.
[c] These are expenditures on education which remain unfinanced after expected budgetary growth and implementation of all reforms. See Tables 6.5 and 6.6.
[d] See Tables 6.5 and 6.6.

middle-income countries, and for those in Sub-Saharan Africa separately. It demonstrates once again that, if all countries were to introduce all the policy reforms which we have simulated, the costs of achieving SFA worldwide would be slightly less than those associated with an unreformed UPE. In other words, the higher quality and better coverage of schooling required to achieve SFA, as compared with UPE, can be financed by the package of efficiency reforms. The quantity–quality trade-off could in this way be avoided, as expansion proceeds.

Most of these costs can be met by normal budgetary growth in developing countries. However, we have shown that, unless per capita incomes grow faster than is currently expected, deficits (in the sense of unfinanced expenditures on education) for many countries would emerge. This would be particularly so for the countries identified in Table 6.5. Those are currently amongst the most educationally disadvantaged in the world, and are likely to need a significant amount of additional financial aid over at least a fifteen-year period if SFA is to be reached. If all the thirty-six countries shown were prepared and able to implement the full package of educational/fiscal reforms during the move to SFA, a minimum of around $21 billion and a maximum of around $34 billion would be likely to be needed in external support over the fifteen years 1990–2005. This range of estimates corresponds to whether or not an additional two per cent of total budgetary resources were diverted annually to education in all or none of these countries, respectively. These sums translate into flows of about $1.4–2.2 billion per year in aid for these purposes throughout the period which would need to be allocated to different countries in roughly similar proportions to the incidence of the deficits shown in the table.

It is, however, unlikely that total aid requirements could, in practice, turn out to be close to the lower limit of this range. First, not all countries will be in a position to increase real spending on education to the extent which this would imply. Many of the African countries shown in Table 6.5, for example, are already in receipt of adjustment loans which have been premissed upon real per capita public spending falling quite sharply over the 1990s. Whilst this does not imply that education spending would also have to fall, the achievement of real increases for any particular sector is obviously much more difficult than it would be if the wider policy environment were less contractionary. Equally a diversion of funds towards education from other sectors, such as defence, would be easier to achieve if such expenditures were not already set to decline for reasons of broad macroeconomic strategy.

Secondly, there are good reasons to suppose that other countries, apart from those mentioned in Table 6.5 would need support from external aid if SFA is to be achieved. Obvious candidates would include some of the African countries mentioned in the notes to the table, which are still some way from achieving UPE, but where the burden of adjustment has led to some exhaustion with the process of policy reform. Thus, Ivory Coast, Ghana, Kenya, and Zambia, could each achieve SFA with a tolerable, and affordable, amount of policy change. But in order to initiate further reforms each of these States would almost certainly need the mixture of 'carrot and stick' provided by an aid relationship.

Similar points can be made of some of the countries shown in Table 6.6. In general, as we have seen, these States are generally better off than those in the first group in both educational and economic terms. Here, SFA could be afforded, either by introducing the cost-saving/shifting reforms, by increasing budgetary allocations, or by a mixture of both. Assuming that such reforms were implemented, little if any external support would be needed to achieve SFA. But in order to secure their implementation, aid transfers on a regular basis would, in some cases, probably turn out to be required. The countries from SSA—Cameroon,

Lesotho, Madagascar, and Togo—would be in this category. Equally, the case for the strategic use of aid to support educational policy reforms in Indonesia, Philippines, Sri Lanka, Vietnam, Brazil, and some of the other Latin American countries shown in Table 6.6 is strong.

As suggested by Table 6.7, therefore, it is difficult to see how the additional aid bill for achieving SFA could in practice be less than about $30 billion over the fifteen years 1990–2005. This translates into a flow of, on average, about $2 billion per year in 1986 prices, or about $2.5 billion in 1990 prices. It can be seen from the table that most of this external finance would be needed for countries where UPE had not been achieved by 1990, and that about half of it would be required for the countries of Sub-Saharan Africa. In view of the considerations discussed above, it would seem sensible to expect resources of that order to be required.

Even so, it is important to recognize the fairly wide range of other conditions which would need to be met if such resources were in fact to secure SFA goals. This raises questions about the use and effectiveness of aid, its appropriate modalities in support of primary schooling, and of the technical and political obstacles to securing policy reform in the South, with or without the involvement of aid agencies. There are then, other reasons to fear that SFA may still not be achieved within ten to fifteen years. How soundly based are such fears? Is the heart of the problem the availability of resources, or are there other constraints of equal, or perhaps of greater importance? These questions provide the agenda for the final chapter.

7

Aid to Education and Policy Reform

1. Introduction

A bargain needs to be struck between the countries of the North and those of the South if all of the world's children are to be accommodated in primary schools of reasonable quality over the next ten to fifteen years. In its absence, it seems certain that SFA will remain an elusive goal. The main parties to the bargain will now be familiar, as will be the dimensions of the challenge which they face. We have shown that most countries in the low- and middle-income groups will be unable to finance SFA without significant policy change. Further, it seems that in at least thirty of those countries even the introduction of a rather demanding set of policy reforms, plus significantly increased allocations of public expenditure to the education sector, would still fail to raise the resources required. In this final chapter, we ask whether aid transfers sufficient to fill these gaps are likely to be feasible in the light of the recent history of international aid to education. Although the answer to this question is in the affirmative, we show that the types of aid which are given, the criteria by which aid is allocated, and the purposes for which it is used, will each have to change markedly from past practice if it is to be effective in supporting SFA. Finally, we return to some questions raised earlier in this book, which suggest that other categories of policy change—in addition to those we have simulated—will be necessary in some countries if SFA is to be secured. The fuller details of the North–South bargain, to which we allude, are thereby explored.

2. The Aid Record

An examination of long-term trends in aid to education in developing countries reveals some disturbing facts. The aggregate picture is summarized in Table 7.1. It shows that education was accorded far less priority by aid agencies during the 1980s than had been the case in earlier years. The proportion of aid allocated to education fell from 17 per cent in the early 1970s to scarcely more than 10 per cent of the total from 1985 onwards. The final two columns of Table 7.1 show the values of total and

TABLE 7.1. *Official development assistance from OECD countries: education and total flows, 1970–1989*

	current prices ($USbn.)		(2) as % of (1)	constant 1986 prices ($USbn.)[a]	
	Total aid (1)	Aid to education (2)	(3)	Total aid (4)	Aid to education (5)
1970	7.0	1.1	16.0	22.1	3.5
1975	13.9	2.4	17.3	26.0	4.5
1980	27.3	3.4	12.5	32.5	4.1
1985	29.4	3.2	10.9	34.9	3.8
1986	36.7	4.0	10.9	36.7	4.0
1987	41.6	4.4	10.6	37.0	3.9
1988	48.1	5.3	11.0	39.9	4.4
1989	46.7	5.0	10.7	38.9	4.2

[a] Constant price series calculated by applying World Bank GDP deflator (World Bank 1991*a*: 240) to data shown in columns (1) and (2).

Sources: Coombs (1985: 295); OECD (1990); World Bank (1991*b*: Table 19).

educational aid in constant 1986 prices. It can be seen that aid to education in 1975 amounted to about $4.5 billion. By 1985 it had fallen to $3.8 billion and it climbed back to more than $4 billion again only as recently as 1988/9. Thus, even though the real value of development assistance, taken as a whole, almost doubled between 1970 and 1989, that of aid to education actually fell by about 15 per cent over the decade 1975–85. Subsequently, it increased slightly, but its 1975 value had still not been regained by 1989.

Our estimates of the amount of aid required to secure SFA need to be set against this background of a sharp decline in the value and relative importance of educational aid after 1975. As argued earlier, transfers of an additional $2 billion per year, in 1986 prices, would seem to be needed from 1990 onwards, over a fifteen-year period. The last column of Table 7.1 indicates that such increases would raise total aid for education by about 50 per cent beyond its 1986–9 values. This is a large proportional increase, which might seem, at first sight, unlikely to be achieved. Such a sharp expansion in the level of aid to a single sector would require a major and widespread change in the relative priority accorded to it by the international community. How likely is this?

The first point is that the magnitudes involved are not large in comparison with the increased aid flows to other sectors which occurred after 1975, but which were noticeably absent in the case of education. In particular, it should be noted that if aid to education had increased *pari passu* with that to other sectors after 1975, fully $6.7 billion would have been provided as aid to education by 1989. This compares with the $4.2 billion which was actually allocated in that year (Table 7.1). The difference between these two figures is rather more than the extra $2 billion which we now estimate to be required. Thus, the provision of the additional aid needed to secure SFA in the developing world would do no more than reassert the relative importance of education in total aid flows which held in the early 1970s. In one sense, then, such an adjustment could be seen more as the correction of a historical anomaly than as a major new departure which existing spending priorities would be unable to accommodate.

Secondly, there is ample evidence that the aid community could muster the monies required relatively easily, at least as regards the aggregate additional sums involved. For example, at the World Conference on Education for All, held in Jomtien, Thailand, in March 1990, the then President of the World Bank, Barber Conable, promised that the Bank would double its education lending over the following three years to an annual figure of more than $1.5 billion. Later in the same year, at the World Summit for Children, convened by Unicef, Conable further promised that lending for primary education would increase substantially in the future, to become the largest single element in the Bank's education programme.

Table 7.2, which summarizes aspects of the Bank's recent record, indicates that these pledges are being honoured. The table shows that

TABLE 7.2. *World Bank education lending, 1963–1991*

Fiscal year[a]	Education lending ($m. current)		Proportion of total allocated to primary schooling (%)
	Total	IDA	
1963–9	34.8	n/a	0.0
1970–4	163.0	n/a	4.5
1975–80	353.6	n/a	14.2
1981–5	692.2	200.0	22.4
1986–9	776.8	324.0	27.8
1989	963.7	449.0	31.0
1990	1,486.6	957.0	24.0
1991	2,251.1	737.0	36.0

[a] Where more than one year is shown, data in table are annual averages.

Sources: World Bank (1990: 54; 1991*c*: Table A.18; 1991*d*: Annexe Table 2).

education lending by the Bank increased by almost $1.3 billion (current prices) between 1989 and 1991, thereby comfortably exceeding Conable's predictions made at Jomtien. At the same time, lending for primary schooling, which had accounted for negligible proportions of the programme prior to the mid-1970s, increased to over one-third of education lending by 1991, and was expected to reach nearly half of the total during 1992 (World Bank 1991*c*: 54).

These increases in total education lending by the Bank are the equivalent of about $1 billion in 1986 prices, and thus amount to about half of the total additional external finance which we estimate to be required on an annual basis to support SFA. It should be noted, however, that most loans from the World Bank are only slightly more concessional than commercial loans. IDA funds, the terms of which are highly concessional, represent only about one-quarter of total financial flows from the Bank. As shown in Table 7.2, a somewhat higher proportion of educational lending (amounting to some 46 per cent over the years 1989–91) has been on IDA terms, and both the absolute and proportional importance of IDA support to education have increased significantly since the mid-1980s. Nevertheless, in spite of this recent progress, the greater part of the new Bank lending to education has remained on close to commercial terms. Thus, many of these recent loans will not have been particularly relevant—because of the high costs associated with them—to many of the most educationally disadvantaged countries which remain far from achieving SFA.

If these countries are to be supported in ways promised by the World Bank, it would be necessary for the structure of educational lending to change more sharply in favour of IDA financing. Thirty-two of the thirty-six countries shown in Table 6.4, which—on the basis of the criteria set out in Chapter 6—should be assigned the first priority in new aid allocations, are in fact eligible for IDA funds on per capita income grounds.[1] Furthermore, some of the other countries, which are not generally eligible, could still qualify for IDA support in the social sectors, as has happened in the case of Zimbabwe. Thus, at least in principle, a shift of funding allocations by the Bank towards the countries most in need could result in a significant part of the increased funds allocated for education being transferred on 'aid' rather than loan terms over the 1990s.

The difficulty with this proposed strategy, however, is that the education sector would then take a very large share of total IDA funds available. For example, in 1991, about 20 per cent of IDA resources were allocated to education. Yet, in view of the flows of aid we expect to be needed over the 1990s, adequate IDA support for SFA would have required at least a further $500 million of the total $2.2 billion lent by the

---

[1] The exceptions are El Salvador, Guatemala, Nicaragua, and Papua New Guinea.

Bank to education in that year.[2] That would raise the IDA allocation needed for education to about one-third of all IDA resources available at the present time. It is an open question as to whether such an increase could be engineered within the current ceilings for IDA. There are many other competing needs from environmental, health, population, and infrastructure programmes. Nevertheless, the choice is clear. If the recently increased World Bank support to education is fully to promote the achievement of SFA, about one-third of the present IDA budget would need to be utilized. Alternatively it would be necessary to increase the overall size of the IDA budget, on the understanding that these resources would support increased priority for schooling for all.

In summary, the magnitude of lending to education by the World Bank has increased sharply since 1989, in ways promised by its President in 1990. However, it is clear that further structural changes will be needed in the composition of this lending towards a greater utilization of IDA finance if SFA is to be facilitated. If these changes were achieved, and provided that Bank programmes were sustained in real terms at 1991 levels, other donors (mainly the OECD bilateral programmes) would need to increase their aid to education by around 25 per cent, in real terms, beyond the levels achieved in the late 1980s in order to provide the additional $2 billion (in 1986 prices) of annual aid transfers which we expect to be required. The commitments made by many of the northern governments and aid organizations, both at Jomtien and at the meetings which followed, suggest that—at least in aggregate—the necessary additional financial resources to support SFA throughout the world can be found.

3. Danger Signals (1): Aid Effectiveness and Donor Policies

Raising sufficient additional aid monies to support SFA is by no means a foregone conclusion, but it is perhaps within reach. Its achievement, however, would be the beginning rather than the end of the task in hand. If schooling for all is to be attained, the additional aid monies raised will have to be carefully managed, they will have to be directed towards those countries most in need of external support, and they will have to be applied in the context of clear policy reforms implemented—in ways discussed in earlier chapters—in recipient States. If the aid costs of SFA are to be kept within the bounds we have estimated, an unusually tight approach to aid management will need to be applied. In its absence the

---

[2] For reasons given later in this chapter, it is not implied that support for SFA would require that all these loans would need to be allocated directly to primary schooling. Support to the education sector as a whole, within the context of an agreed policy framework for primary schooling, can in some circumstances be equally promotive of SFA goals.

TABLE 7.3. *World Bank education project approvals, 1991:*
recipient-country characteristics

Region	No. of countries			Total value of projects approved ($USm.)	Distribution of column 5 (%)
	with project approvals	with GER <100	with expected SFA deficits		
(1)	(2)	(3)	(4)	(5)	(6)
SSA	7	6	5	265.9	11.8
N. Africa	3	2	0	222.0	9.9
Asia/Pacific	7	3	3	918.5	40.8
L. America	5	2	3	595.3	26.4
E. Europe	2	1	0	250.0	11.1
TOTAL	24	14	11	2,251.7	100.0

Notes: Columns (3) and (4) refer to characteristics of countries included in column (2) only. Column (4) shows the number of countries, amongst those in column (2), which are expected to show deficits on implementing SFA, after introducing the full set of policy reforms 1–9.

Sources: Calculated from World Bank (1990: Table 7.2) and our national simulations of SFA.

costs of SFA would turn out to be much higher, and, in turn, its attainment would again be postponed. There are some critical dangers here which will need to be addressed by both donors and recipients of aid for SFA. These will be discussed in turn.

3.1. Focus upon the educationally disadvantaged countries

First, and most obvious, is the point that the aid funds must be directed towards the right countries if SFA is to be achieved. As we have seen, the countries which will need most financial help are those which have the lowest primary GERs at the present time. Yet they will not receive particular attention from the aid community unless deliberate measures to redirect and restructure aid programmes towards them are taken.

We have already hinted that the geographical allocations made in 1991 by the World Bank seem not to be obviously compatible with the aims of SFA. In order to illustrate the real difficulties involved here, Table 7.3 summarizes the composition of the additional $2.25 billion approved for education in that year.

It should be recognized, of course, the programmes cannot be instantaneously, or even quickly, switched to reflect new priorities. The history of involvement with particular countries, and indeed the set of ongoing project commitments approved in earlier years, constrain budgets to a modest pace of change. Thus, the projects summarized in Table 7.3 represent only the most recent characteristics of the Bank's lending programme; they account for only perhaps 25–30 per cent of the value of all loans outstanding in the education sector, and a somewhat larger proportion of the number of countries that are recipients of that support.

Notwithstanding these cautions, the table reveals a surprisingly different set of priorities from those which would be necessary if the Bank were to help secure a move to SFA over the next decade. The $2.2 billion is to be allocated to education projects in some twenty-four countries of the developing world. Of these, only seven are from SSA, and they are due to receive scarcely 12 per cent of the total value of project funds approved. By contrast, our analysis has shown that support to SSA would need to be much more prominent. Two-thirds of the aid-dependent countries (shown in Table 6.4) are from SSA, and they are likely to require approximately half of the total aid supplied. Morover, even outside of SSA, only a minority of the countries to which education loans were approved by the Bank in 1991 were high-priority cases from the perspective of SFA. For example, we have shown that the countries of North Africa, and of Eastern Europe, would be capable of financing SFA from domestic resources, given state willingness to introduce educational and financial reforms. It seems difficult to justify the fact that each of these regions, each having around one-fifth of the population of SSA in fewer countries, with much stronger economies and educational systems, received in 1991 broadly similar financial allocations for education as the whole of the SSA region combined.

All of this implies that the recently increased allocations of finance for education by the World Bank do not give immediate cause for complacency. This would remain true even if they were subsequently matched by similar pledges from other agencies. Increased financial allocations of these magnitudes are needed. But the disposition selected for these funds, and the terms on which they are allocated amongst different countries, will be critical if they are to facilitate the move to SFA worldwide.

3.2. Ensure that aid genuinely supports SFA

A second major danger, even if funds of the right magnitude reach the countries in need, is that they will be used for the wrong purposes. Large amounts of aid to provide tertiary education facilities, or staff to teach in them, will not necessarily help to get more children into primary school. Such a result is possible where the project would have been implemented even in the absence of the donor, and thus, where domestic funds were released by aid for use in the primary system. But this kind of substitution depends strongly on the policy environment, and often upon the policy conditionality attached to the use of the funds involved. Where such safeguards were absent, it would be foolish to suppose that the funds concerned would be able to serve any particular set of indirect purposes, whether in the education sector or elsewhere. Thus, the choice facing the agencies appears to be either to support the primary-school system directly, or to provide more finance for education generally, on condition that agreed actions in the primary sector were taken by the recipient government itself.[3]

Historically, the amount of direct aid to primary schooling has been tiny. Even during 1981–6, by which time the World Bank's interest in primary schooling had started to rise (see Table 7.2), such support from all sources amounted to an average of only $180 million per year, equivalent to about 5 per cent of total aid to education in developing countries over those years. As with education aid in general, the real value of this support to the primary sector declined at that time.[4] This neglect, as explained in Chapter 1, primarily reflected the agencies' reluctance to accept the idea that expenditure upon primary schooling constituted effective investment. Although there was mounting evidence that helping to build up sound and broadly based primary-school systems would be more socially profitable than many of the roads, bridges, dams, and airports which had been the more usual targets for aid finance, its implications were slow to affect the practice of aid policy.

3.3. Shift the emphasis away from capital aid

Apart from these concerns, however, there was also a range of more practical reasons which led agencies to favour the secondary and higher levels of education as more suitable objects for their attention than primary schooling. The main factor here is that it is administratively easier to support projects which require substantial capital facilities, and which are geographically centralized. The higher levels of the education system satisfy these conditions more fully than the primary system, where the wide dispersion of schools, each needing only minimal capital facilities, makes for relatively large administrative demands per dollar of aid spent. In addition, it seemed less likely that donor comparative advantage lay strongly in the primary sector. Most of the teaching materials could be locally produced, often using national languages, and

---

[3] To say that there is a choice may often be too strong: even where primary schooling is supported directly, safeguards are still required to ensure that the aid monies genuinely provide additional support, and that domestic financing for primary schooling will not be concomitantly reduced.

[4] Estimates of annual flows of aid to primary schooling can be found in Lockheed and Verspoor (1990: Table 8.1).

the teaching staff at primary level were not usually candidates for foreign training. At the higher levels of education, where circumstances to the contrary often held, donors felt that they could be of much more use.

Not surprisingly, when agencies did change their views as regards the importance of supporting primary schooling, they began their involvement by doing the things which they knew best how to do. Table 7.4 shows the type of aid given to the primary sector during the early 1980s. Three points of importance emerge. First, the financing of hardware (buildings, furniture, and equipment) accounted for almost 30 per cent of total aid to primary schooling over 1981–6, and for almost 40 per cent of that received by the poorest countries. Second, expenditure on books and teaching materials has been extremely modest, accounting for less than 5 per cent of aid to primary schooling overall. Third, although general recurrent support has been provided in some places, this was mainly confined to the richer countries, whilst the low-income group received insignificant amounts of such support. We shall argue that the implicit priorities revealed by each of these figures are wrong.

The provision of project-based capital aid is not generally appropriate for primary schooling. This is not only because of the problems of administrative cost mentioned above. More significant from an economic perspective is that, unless procurement and disbursement procedures are unusually flexible, such assistance runs the risk of over-design of school buildings, producing higher-cost schools than are either necessary or desirable. In countries where a good proportion of primary schools are built simply, using materials which are available in the immediate locality of the schools, and perhaps using a proportion of voluntary labour, the introduction of standardized school designs, at greater construction cost, brings uncertain benefits. One effect has often been to raise the unit capital costs of primary education. Where only a minority of schools were funded by aid this would lead to an increase in the funding gap which the aid was attempting to alleviate. Thus, only where some strategic objective needs to be attained, such as the correction of regional inequalities, the provision of school storerooms or toilet facilities, or the provision of staff housing as means of retaining or attracting staff to disadvantaged areas, should capital assistance to the primary sector be maintained.[5]

[5] A useful example of this is provided by the Swedish International Development Authority's support to primary schooling in Zimbabwe. Between 1985 and 1990, in a project to upgrade primary schools in disadvantaged areas, classrooms and staff houses were provided for more than 600 schools serving poor rural communities. In 1984, the building of primary schools in Zimbabwe had become the responsibility of local communities, on a self-help basis. In the more disadvantaged areas, however, households were so poor that local authorities were unable to collect the funds necessary to purchase building materials. Thus, classes were still commonly held out-of-doors. The SIDA project provided funds for materials and transport to overcome this constraint. Labour continued to be provided by the community, and local materials were also supplied wherever possible. Careful management

TABLE 7.4. *Different types of aid to primary education, 1981–1986 (%)*

Types of aid	All countries	Low-income countries	Lower-middle-income countries	Upper-middle-income countries
Books and instructional materials	4.8	7.5	3.9	0.8
Furniture and equipment	6.3	16.2	2.6	1.0
Technical assistance	14.0	17.6	13.1	0.9
Food/scholarships	15.3	20.7	14.3	0.7
Buildings	23.4	22.1	25.8	3.3
Budgetary assistance	29.9	5.7	34.8	90.3
Other	6.3	10.2	5.6	3.0
TOTAL	100.0	100.0	100.0	100.0

Source: IREDU (1989), cited in World Bank (1991c: Table A.17).

As Table 7.4 indicates, there has been great reluctance amongst donors to become involved with the details of materials supply. This reflected the commonly held view amongst agency staff that direct support to pupils and teachers would surely be less efficient than concentrating upon funding teacher-education, curriculum-development centres, educational planning, and other central units, which could help to enhance the effectiveness of the entire system. It is now clear that these initiatives, whilst still needed, are insufficient. We have documented in this book the ways in which rural and urban schools throughout the southern continents, but particularly those in Africa, are often short of the most rudimentary items, including exercise books, chalk, pencils, rulers, maps, and so on. But the most pressing need is for more textbooks. As reported in Chapter 1, a large number of research studies have now confirmed the commonsense assumption that the availability and the quality of primary textbooks have a strong influence upon the amount and nature of what pupils learn. They also seem to be a factor in reducing rates of drop-out from schools. Whilst most governments aspire to providing each schoolchild with an adequate set of texts free of charge, very few have succeeded in doing so. In most cases texts, where they are available, have to be bought by pupils, thereby significantly adding to the direct private

of costs prevented over-design; structures were easily replicated; location planning allowed the scheme to become an instrument for reducing some of the sharp inequalities which have existed in Zimbabwe between the facilities available in rural and urban primary schools. Further details can be found in Colclough *et al.* (1990: 112–15).

costs of schooling, and increasing the probability of drop-out or non-attendance, particularly amongst pupils from poorer families. Some governments, either through shortages of foreign exchange or deficiencies in printing and distributing capacities, fail to make textbooks consistently and universally available, thereby preventing even richer families from obtaining them. Similar problems often affect the availability of writing and drawing materials.

For all of the above reasons, funding the provision of more and better teaching materials, and of textbooks in particular, will be a critically important ingredient in the strategies to achieve SFA in most countries. Our simulations show that the additional costs involved in making available such materials up to a level of $5 per child would amount to about $8 billion by the year 2000, with UPE being attained by that date.[6] There are, then, important opportunities here for the selective use of aid funds, in ways which could have a substantial pay-off for the quality of learning in developing countries. In most cases this would involve the provision of financial and technical support to local production and distribution systems. Where these remained inadequate, textbooks could be produced abroad, notwithstanding the cost increases that this would inevitably bring (see below). Here, the design of textbooks would be undertaken by curriculum-development units in recipient countries, but printing and publishing could be done initially by firms on contract to donor agencies, pending transfer to publishing houses in developing countries themselves. A number of potential models for this type of activity exist.[7]

We estimate that the cumulated additional recurrent costs of achieving SFA in all developing countries will be about five times greater than the additional capital costs. We have shown in this book that the major financing problems will be recurrent in nature, and it follows that the greatest benefits from aid policy to the primary sector would be derived by increasing the amount of recurrent support. This goes well beyond the provision of teaching materials (which are usually treated as recurrent rather than capital items) to include budgetary support for teachers' salaries and other associated costs.

3.4. Northern purchasing often involves a waste of aid

The case for supporting recurrent costs is strengthened by a further danger which aid for SFA will need to avoid. Our estimates for the total costs of reaching SFA are based, ultimately, upon the unit costs of

[6] This can be seen by comparing the difference between the gross additional recurrent education expenditures for reforms 5 and 6, for all developing countries, shown in Table 6.3.

[7] See Colclough *et al.* (1985: 302–3).

schooling in each of the low- and middle-income countries separately, and upon changes in these costs which would be consequent upon implementing a range of policy reforms in each country. They therefore indicate the resources needed to reach SFA, expressed in terms of developing-country price and cost levels around 1986. By contrast, the values of aid flows summarized by earlier tables in this chapter are expressed in terms of OECD prices and costs. Thus, to the extent that aid for primary schooling supplied by the North, valued in northern price terms, exceeded its value in southern price terms, so the aid requirements, as conventionally valued, would be increased beyond the $2 billion per year which we have shown to be required. This point is of very considerable practical importance. It encompasses, but goes well beyond the risk of capital aid inadvertently pushing up school construction costs, mentioned earlier. There, the point was that such aid was inappropriate if it increased the unit costs of both aided and non-aided schools. Here, it is that such aid may be inappropriate where the cost of the inputs supplied (equipment, materials, training, expertise) are higher than the cost of their local equivalents, even if their provision had no impact on the cost of the non-aided sector.

In fact, of course, most conventional project aid would not pass this test. The cost of school equipment made in Birmingham is far greater than it would be if it were made in India. The cost of a trainer sent from USA to work in Zambia is more than twenty times greater than that of hiring a Zambian to do the job, were someone available and suitably qualified to do it. In cases where substitutes cannot be found in the recipient country, such high cost differentials do not invalidate the benefits of the aid. Provided the items are really needed, their opportunity costs are the same as their northern costs. But, if they are not really needed, or if local substitutes are available, their supply will involve a waste of resources. In such circumstances, the aid requirements for SFA would be increased, beyond the additional annual sum of $2 billion, by the difference between the local and international values of the goods supplied, and financing recurrent costs would provide much better value per dollar of aid spent.

3.5. Aid for SFA must support local and recurrent costs

There are three main considerations which have typically led aid agencies to resist funding recurrent costs. The first of these is that the benefits of such finance are less visible to northern political constituencies than funds spent on capital projects. An additional school built with the help of aid funds seems, at first sight, to provide a more lasting and appropriate benefit than would be the case if the aid were used to employ twenty additional schoolteachers. The obvious reply is that if the real constraint is recurrent rather than capital finance, the project approach will lead, at the margin, to schools without teachers, and thus to a waste of aid. The second consideration is that the provision of recurrent finance may lead to a loss of donor control over the ultimate disposition of the funds. If, for example, a recipient government chose to award large salary increases to public employees during the period covered by recurrent support, the real benefits of the financial transfer would be changed in ways which the aid agency had little chance to influence. The third point is that recurrent subventions may risk a requirement for continued donor support well beyond the comfortable medium-term time-horizon contemplated by most projects supported by capital aid. For example, it is almost always assumed that once a school is built, the responsibility for meeting the costs of its running and maintenance will pass to the recipient government. Agencies argue that a distinction between the short-term responsibilities of the donor and the longer-term ones of the recipient cannot be so conveniently delineated in the case of the use of aid funds for recurrent purposes. Thus, there is a worry that the initial willingness to provide recurrent support would impose constraints upon the future use of aid funds in ways which would be resisted by northern parliaments as well as by aid officials.

There are, in fact, agreed procedures established by the OECD, which partly address these concerns. Guidelines on the financing of maintenance and recurrent expenditures have been issued by the Development Assistance Committee (OECD 1979, 1982), which recognize the increasing need for such forms of aid support in the light of the budgetary problems faced by a growing number of countries. These guidelines explicitly incorporate the assumption that aid recipients will eventually take over responsibility for these expenditures, and arrangements for phasing out recurrent support are incorporated in typical agreements for its provision.

Although this is no doubt sensible, a more comprehensive means of tackling the three problems of increasing the visibility of the benefits of recurrent support, of retaining control over its disposition, and of avoiding the acquisition of commitments which stretch indefinitely into the future is available. This is provided by the possibility of increasing the number and nature of policy conditions upon which the aid transfer is given. We have shown in this book that significant policy change will be necessary in a large number of countries if SFA is to be achieved. It follows that the judicious use of policy conditions attached to flows of budgetary aid could not merely improve the efficiency of the education sector, but, by directing attention towards the most critical areas for reform, could become an important instrument, internationally, by which SFA was secured.

3.6. From policy dialogue to conditionality

It has always been accepted that donor agencies can reasonably expect to discuss with recipient governments the design of projects upon which their money is to be spent. For those agencies providing large-scale development funding, such as the World Bank and some of the major bilaterals, it has long been customary for such discussions also to encompass the broader policy framework, at sectoral or national levels, which may influence project performance. Although many developing-country governments have not been entirely happy with this custom, it was seen as necessary to secure large amounts of external funding, and most donors involved indicated that they merely sought a dialogue, where opinions about desirable changes in policy would be offered, but not binding upon the recipient to enact.

The deterioration in the economic circumstances of many developing countries since the late 1970s—the onset of recession, high levels of debt, and widespread economic decline—have changed the nature of this dialogue. Increasingly, general balance of payments support, rather than project aid, became vital as means of overcoming shortages of foreign exchange. Since the general macroeconomic environment was viewed as critical to the sound use of such funds, a much stronger element of policy conditionality was often attached to their transfer, and the frequency with which such policy conditions have been used has increased enormously in recent years. These policy conditions are still negotiated with recipient governments, rather than imposed, but the room for flexibility on the part of donors is judged by them to be far smaller than was the case with the dialogues of earlier years. Moreover, the World Bank takes the lead more often, on behalf of the rest of the aid community. This ensures a monopolistic bargaining framework which is more difficult for developing countries to gainsay.

There are parallels here between the macroeconomic debate and the nature of the dialogue which is now needed between aid agencies and recipients in order to secure SFA. The move away from project aid to general sectoral support, and the shift which will be required from capital to recurrent budgetary assistance each imply that policy conditionality, more specific and more binding than that used in earlier negotiations over aid to education, will probably be necessary.

Although, as indicated earlier, such conditionality is in any case likely to be demanded by the northern constituencies, who would now be supplying aid to education on rather more 'risky' terms, as they would see it, than in the past, it could nevertheless serve a critical role in securing the move to UPE and SFA. Some countries would need such pressure in order to secure the real intent (as opposed to merely the promise) to implement UPE/SFA. Many others would need it if policy reforms of the kind we have examined in this book are to be considered, let alone implemented.

It would, however, be necessary to avoid the trap of making universal prescriptions for policy change. The great weakness of many of the policy reforms urged on countries by the World Bank and the Fund, is the extent to which they have been 'recipes' for liberalization which take little account of the relevant structural features of, and differences between, the countries in which they have been applied. We have attempted, in the policy simulations undertaken in the present study, to introduce a modest amount of flexibility based upon what is known about countries' circumstances. As we have indicated, by no means all of these policies are suitable for all countries. Nevertheless, much more country-specific analysis than has been possible in these pages would be needed in order to determine the particular set of policy reforms which were economically, politically, and educationally desirable for countries engaging in an aid discussion. This analysis would best be initiated by the recipient countries themselves, either as research studies or as planning documents. Their critical ingredients would be an analysis of the major cost and resource characteristics of their school systems, and a specification of the actions proposed, or options which the State confronts, in order to secure UPE and SFA.

In summary, it should now be clear that raising additional aid for education of about $2 billion per year is only one of many preconditions which must be satisfied if northern countries are to help the South to achieve SFA. It will be necessary for these funds to be channelled to the countries which are likely to be most aid-dependent (in practice, those with primary GERs less than 90), and the type of aid provided will need to be different from that which has typified the process in the past. In particular there will need to be a major shift away from capital towards recurrent support. If these conditions were not met the costs of achieving SFA, in aid terms, would be considerably more than those which we currently expect. Dialogue with recipient States about the set of policies intended to be pursued would be a necessary part of the aid process, whether the primary sector or aid to education more generally was the chosen target.

4. Danger Signals (2): Limits to the Impact of Policy Reform

We have suggested a similarity between the macroeconomic policy dialogue amongst donor and recipient countries, and that which is now needed to help reshape educational policy. In one important sense, the debate about education should prove to be considerably easier than that about the management of the economy as a whole. This is because the set of policy reforms which we have identified as being helpful, from the perspective of securing better-quality schooling for all the children of school-age, should prove to be less politically contentious than those usually associated with economic stabilization and adjustment. Indeed, to the extent that the reforms, and the expansion to SFA which they facilitate, responded to popular demands for more and better schooling, they could, in principle, add greatly to the popularity of the governments concerned.

Nevertheless, the political constraints will in some cases be considerable. Where prospects exist for increasing class-size, and for introducing double-shift teaching, these will often tend to be located in schools in the more densely populated urban centres. Their burden will thus fall more heavily upon some communities than others. Similarly, measures to shift part of the costs of education at tertiary level on to private households can be expected to be strongly opposed by some of the groups most affected. It is obvious that some of the most important reasons whereby the distribution of access to education resources remain highly skewed in particular contexts and, in turn, why particular reform initiatives appear to succeed or to fail, are to be found in the realm of political economy rather than in that of educational enquiry. For these reasons not all governments will be willing to introduce all, or even some, of the reforms, notwithstanding their efficiency and equity benefits. Conditional offers of aid could, in such circumstances, perform a strategically important role in facilitating policy changes which were perceived to be difficult and which States would otherwise resist.

The full set of policy reforms will be less comprehensively implemented than is posited in our analysis, not only for the politico-economic reasons alluded to above, but also because not all of them will be technically relevant, or possible to implement, in some countries. No data are available from international sources on the present incidence of double-shift sessions in each country, nor on the present extent of community financing, nor the current funding arrangements in higher education. Our simulations examined the cost implications of marginal changes in these variables via their proportional impact upon the unit costs of schooling—an approach which allowed independence from their current values. Nevertheless, in some countries (though probably a minority) we must accept that it will not prove possible to move much further in some of these directions than has already occurred. This need not be important in countries which face choices in the means by which they approach SFA, i.e. most of those with GERs presently greater than 100, where not all reforms need be implemented. But it is likely to have some impact on those countries which we have called aid-dependent, where choices between different reforms cannot easily be made and where substantial deficits, post-reform, in financing SFA, would be likely to remain.

A third source of difficulty may arise from the responses of teachers and administrators to the reform process. Teachers would often be responsible for larger classes than before, or working double-shifts. They would have to adapt to the curriculum changes needed to reduce pupil failure and drop-out, to enhance their use of textbooks and other teaching materials, to develop skills in managing teacher-assistants, and to increase their co-operation with colleagues to secure efficiency gains. Equally, administrators will need to adopt more flexible and rapid planning approaches, and be willing to devolve more financial and administrative authority to the local level, particularly in those countries which are presently far from SFA.

Our case-studies, and the examples drawn from the wider literature in Chapters 3 and 4, have demonstrated that these problems, though real, can be overcome. Nevertheless, in seeking such changes in well over half of all LDCs—which will require at least some of these reforms in order to finance SFA, with or without increased budgetary provision and enhanced levels of aid—substantial and rapid administrative change will be needed if SFA is to be achieved by the early years of next century. Equally, the primary-teaching service, staffed as it often is by people who themselves have had little formal education and training, will be put to the test.

In this context, some of the reforms will make the task easier. The qualitative improvements to the school environment, financed by the efficiency reforms, are likely to be very popular with teachers. Better teaching materials, and lower drop-outs from school will enhance teacher satisfaction; lower rates of repetition would help to reduce class-size, particularly in the final year of primary schooling; shift and multigrade teaching bring opportunities for higher teacher earnings; and the salary increases incorporated in the reforms would boost flagging morale. Equally, the additional responsibilities and productivity now required of teachers would usually be critical, in political terms, to securing the pay increases envisaged. Notwithstanding these positive factors, however, it is likely that the scale of changes required by the reforms will be the source of delay in some countries, where the year 2005 would become a more realistic target for the achievement of SFA than the century's end.

A fourth type of restraint upon the efficacy of the reforms which we have investigated concerns the quality of the economic environment within which they are implemented. The central condition here would be that economic growth over the ten to fifteen years after 1990 should proceed at least as fast as that of population. To the extent that growth turned out to be slower than that, i.e. that per capita incomes were not maintained in real terms, so the per capita value of resources available to governments to finance education would, with no change in the fiscal stance, fall. The result of these circumstances would, again, be higher deficits than those shown in Chapter 6. As indicated earlier, it is considered that these assumptions about economic growth are, on balance, conservative, and that the revenue position is more likely to be better than that estimated, rather than worse, taking all countries together.[8] Nevertheless, the economic growth assumptions may still prove too optimistic in some countries where the recent growth record has been bad, and where its causes have not yet been removed. For example, those African countries which remain in deep recession, often close to collapse (Sudan, Ethiopia, Mozambique, and Mali amongst others), would be likely to experience even higher deficits than those shown in Chapter 6, in the absence of a rapid end to war, drought, famine, and steep economic decline.

For all of these reasons—political, technical, professional, and economic—there are some limits to what can in practice be expected from the policy reform process, which will almost certainly mean that the costs of reaching SFA in the developing world as a whole will in fact be greater than those we have estimated, and that the speed of its delivery will, in some countries, be delayed. Furthermore, it is likely that the range of constraints that conspire to produce this result are clustered more strongly in the poorer countries which are presently furthest from UPE, most heavily indebted, or where growth prospects remain particularly dismal. In such cases there will be little alternative to the provision of greater financial assistance than that envisaged in Chapter 6 if SFA is to be reached. None the less, important to that process would remain evidence of real attempts to raise more internal resources for education using the efficiency reforms we have identified (or others where they particularly suit national circumstances) together with the production of agreed plans for the move to UPE and SFA within a reasonable period of time. In the absence of such undertakings by the recipient government concerned it is doubtful that enhanced levels of assistance, for these purposes, would be either justifiable or forthcoming.

5. Danger Signals (3): Problems on the Demand Side

As Chapter 2 made clear, there is, of course, a quite separate set of circumstances which may lead to the objectives both of aid and of policy reforms not being achieved. This is where there are factors inhibiting the demand for primary education, irrespective of the relative supply of school places. Here, there are three categories of explanation which have special importance: cases where the direct costs of schooling are strong

---

[8] As for the individual national estimates of revenues and deficits, these are considerably less reliable than the cost estimates for each country, depending as they do upon additional layers of assumptions for their derivation.

enough to serve as a disincentive to parents sending their children to school; cases where the opportunity costs of school attendance act in such a way; cases where the customary or cultural attitudes of families place a lower value on the schooling of children of a particular sex, age-group, caste, or other attribute. These circumstances may, of course, all be present together, in which case their effects would interact. In this penultimate section of the chapter, we shall investigate some possible state responses to these circumstances, beginning, however, with one which is commonly believed to be important but which is shown often not to be so.

5.1. Compulsory schooling

It seems fairly obvious that a government which genuinely intended to provide sufficient school places for all, and that these should be fully utilized, would introduce legislation to make school attendance compulsory for the relevant age-group. Such legislation is widespread around the world, typically stipulating both the minimum duration of school attendance in years, and the ages during which it should occur. Table 7.5 shows that 85 per cent of developing countries have enacted laws which make schooling compulsory, and that on average they require attendance for about eight years. Both the incidence of legislation and the length of attendance required are less in Africa and Asia than in Latin America. The industrialized countries, on the other hand, all have regulations making schooling compulsory, the average duration being slightly more than nine years. The question arises, therefore, as to whether there is any relationship between the non-enactment of legislation and the incidence

TABLE 7.5. *The incidence of compulsory schooling legislation around the world*

	No. of countries	No. of countries with compulsory schooling	(2) as % of (1)	Average duration of compulsory schooling (years)
	(1)	(2)	(3)	(4)
Africa	55	44	80.0	7.4
Latin America	44	42	95.4	8.3
Asia	36	29	80.6	7.0
Subtotals				
Developing countries	135	115	85.2	7.6
Developed countries	34	34	100.0	9.4

Source: Calculated from Unesco (1989: Table 3.1).

of low enrolment ratios caused by low demand for schooling. If so, the act of legislating could be expected to be a useful response.

This apparently straightforward question is in fact too complicated to answer accurately, given the available evidence. Observed enrolment ratios are the result of the interaction of supply and demand, and as regards the determinants of supply, the state provision of school places may in any case not be independent of the demand for them. What can be said is that a puzzlingly large number of countries with low GERs have laws making primary-school attendance compulsory. For example there are seventeen countries with primary GERs of less than seventy having such legislation. Sixteen of these are in SSA, and they include five cases where primary enrolments in the late 1980s were equal to less than one-third of the eligible age-group.[9]

In Africa, there is actually some evidence of an inverse relationship between the incidence of compulsory schooling legislation and the value of the GER: for the group of eleven African countries not having such legislation the mean GER for 1986 was 85, whereas for the continent as a whole it was sharply lower, with a value of 74 for the same year.[10]

We should note that in most cases the legislation exempts children from attending if there is no suitable school within reasonable distance of their homes. The question whether or not such regulations ensure attendance where schools exist thus remains open. However, the cases of Ghana, Liberia, Mozambique, Nigeria, Somalia, Tanzania, and Zaïre are instructive in this context. In those countries, all of which have compulsory schooling legislation, the GER fell by between 10 and 50 per cent over the years 1980–6, partly as a result of economic hardships which caused families to withdraw children from school. Here, then, the laws were not sufficient to sustain enrolment in the face of falling demand.[11]

Thus, across developing countries, the existence of compulsory schooling regulations often seems to have had little impact upon the proportion of children actually enrolled. Historically, these laws were introduced in most countries in response to international convention and pressure. Often they date back to the years following the Unesco conferences of the 1960s which, as indicated in Chapter 1, adopted targets for universal compulsory primary enrolment in each region of the developing world.

[9] The list of countries is as follows: Bangladesh, Benin, Burkina Faso, Burundi, Central African Republic, Chad, Ivory Coast, Ethiopia, Guinea, Liberia, Malawi, Mali, Niger, Rwanda, Senegal, Somalia, and Tanzania.

[10] These are calculated from the GER data shown in Table A.1. Those African countries without compulsory schooling legislation are Botswana, Western Cameroon, Gambia, Kenya, Mauritania, Mauritius, Sierra Leone, Sudan, Swaziland, Tunisia, and Uganda.

[11] There were, of course, supply-side pressures where public expenditures on primary schooling were falling along with other budgetary items, and where the provision of school facilities was not keeping pace with population growth. But in a number of these countries many children were withdrawn from school because their parents needed their labour.

Sometimes, as in India, Taiwan, North Vietnam, and South Korea, the legislation was on the statute books much earlier, although in India it has never actually been enforced.[12] It is now clear that these regulations were often introduced too early to be of much help: where large numbers of school children do not attend school because sufficient places are not available, it is difficult for the law to insist that attendance should be compulsory for those who do not seek it. The evidence from the industrialized countries suggests that compulsory schooling regulations do promote continued high levels of enrolment once school places for all children are genuinely available. They would thus become important for countries to adopt and enforce as net enrolment ratios move up towards 90. But where the coverage of school systems remains partial, such regulations are probably of little help.

5.2. Mitigating the costs

One of the causes of the concentration of low enrolment ratios amongst the poorest countries is that state expenditures upon schooling cannot completely remove the costs to poor households of their children's attendance. Even if fees are not charged, there are usually the costs of some books to meet, and often there are school uniforms to buy. Moreover, the opportunity costs of school attendance are, in practice, a negative function of household income. It is the poor who depend upon the income from child labour. For the middle classes, by contrast, household incomes often benefit directly from the child-minding role which full-time schooling provides, and indirectly by allowing more of the time of other members of the household to be spent on income-earning tasks. As pointed out in Chapter 2, in order to move gross enrolment ratios up towards 100, it is not only necessary, at given unit cost levels, that public expenditures on education should rise, but it is a requirement that this should also happen within the budgets of private households. By consequence, the poorer are the households concerned, and the higher the direct and indirect costs which they would need to meet, the more likely is it that public measures to increase primary provision would fail to elicit the required enrolment response.

Crucial, therefore, to the success of state policies for UPE and SFA, particularly where (as is usually the case) it is the children of the poorest families who remain out of school, will be the introduction of measures to mitigate the costs of school attendance. Methods of community financing at primary level would need to be confined to the wealthier communities and schools (with the possible exception, as indicated earlier, of contributions to capital costs via own construction), and all direct costs of

[12] See Weiner (1991: 101–8).

attendance, such as fees or charges for books, materials, and other consumables, would need to be reduced and, where possible, removed. In a number of African countries a strong positive enrolment response to the abolition of school fees has already been demonstrated,[13] even in circumstances where such charges were the equivalent of only a few dollars per year. Thus, price and income elasticities of demand for primary schooling are sometimes high. This will need to be both recognized and utilized by strategies for UPE and SFA.

Even so, policies which substantially reduce the direct costs of school attendance may yet prove insufficient to overcome problems of low demand for primary schooling where the opportunity costs of sending a child to school are judged, by its parents, to be high. Unhappily, this happens in a wide variety of countries and circumstances. As household incomes have fallen in Africa in recent years, the widespread withdrawal of children from school indicated not just an increasing inability by parents to meet the direct costs of schooling, but also an increased dependence by them upon the incomes, however meagre, which their children could earn. More serious, because more long-standing, is the issue of the institutionalization of child labour which has been tolerated in a significant number of States, particularly those of South Asia and North Africa. In India, as Myron Weiner observes:

Indians of virtually all political persuasions oppose the notion that education should be imposed. The major objection is that poverty forces children to drop out of school to find employment to augment the income of their families. It is an argument widely subscribed to by all political groups. . . . In the debate over the government's new policy toward child-labour laws, critics were distressed that the government accepted child labour as a 'harsh reality', but virtually no one urged the government to remove children from employment in cottage industries and agriculture by forcing them to go to school, irrespective of their parents' wishes. (Weiner 1991: 186)

These circumstances obtain in India owing to the set of interests served by the system of child labour. Poor parents seek the income it provides. Employers, and ultimately consumers, profit from the much lower wages commanded by children in comparison with adult labour. The middle classes find it convenient not to disrupt a system which prevents large numbers of those from poorer backgrounds from entering their own ranks. The conspiracy of silence to which this array of interests leads will not be overcome merely by further reductions in the direct costs of schooling. What is required is a change in attitudes within the State, leading to firmer action against child labour and in support of more universal attendance at school.

---

[13] This was particularly so during the 1970s in Malawi and Botswana.

5.3. The critical importance of focusing upon female enrolments

Earlier in this book we reviewed evidence which shows (Chapter 1) that providing girls with primary (and secondary) education is critical to economic progress, and that it probably provides an even greater set of social and economic benefits than that which is provided by the schooling of boys. We have also shown (Chapter 2) that one of the three most important characteristics associated with countries having low primary GERs is that the schooling of girls is not treated so importantly as that of boys. It is, then, a profound irony that the benefits of primary schooling are especially high for girls, yet that underenrolments are strongly concentrated amongst them: we estimate that almost two-thirds of primary school-age children who are out of school are girls. Correction of this imbalance—which itself would do much to secure SFA—is one of the most important challenges facing educational policy in developing countries in the 1990s.

The extent to which this would happen *pari passu* with the expansion of school places depends upon the reasons for the existence of female underenrolment in each particular country. In cases where low female enrolments reflect merely a preference to educate boys in the face of a restricted number of school places, one would expect the male/female enrolment ratio to be responsive to the expansion of school facilities. Such cases, however, will probably be the minority. More usually, a strong imbalance in the sex ratio of enrolments will be indicative of the presence of systematic biases which depress the demand for the schooling of girls relative to that for boys. These biases can usefully be grouped into three different categories, as indicated below.

First, the opportunity costs of sending girls to school are often high, and, at primary level, higher than those for boys. There is a considerable amount of evidence that, whether in school or not, girls of primary school-age spend significantly more time on household chores than do boys.[14] For older children, the time spent working appears to become more equal between the sexes, but the girls tend to spend more time in household activities than in the labour force, whereas the reverse is the case for boys.[15] Girls' labour time is typically spent looking after younger children, cleaning, cooking, collecting fuel and water, and other household tasks. This liberates the time of other family members, and particularly of mothers, for work outside the household. For young children the opportunity costs of school attendance are more strongly those associated with work in the household rather than in the labour force.

[14] See Davison and Kanyuka (1990) for Malawi; Sijogyo *et al.* (1980) for Burkina Faso; World Bank (1991e) for India.
[15] See Evenson *et al.* (1980) for Philippines, and Pitt and Rozenzweig (1989) for Bangladesh.

Thus, owing to the specialization of tasks between the sexes, which appears in many societies to start early, the *de facto* opportunity costs of sending girls to primary school tend to be higher than those for boys.

Second, the perceived economic returns to parents of sending their daughters to school tend to be lower than those for their sons. As noted in Chapter 1, there is little systematic evidence to show that private returns to education for girls are, in general, lower than those for boys. Nevertheless, in some countries, as in India, discrimination in the labour market does sharply reduce women's earnings in comparison with those of similarly educated men (Sambamoorthi 1984; Tilak 1987). But even where this is not so, the differences between male and female participation rates in the market economy mean that, on average, expected returns to schooling will be lower—from the perspective of parents—for girls than is the case for boys.

Third, strong customary or traditional attitudes often assign greater constraints, or restrictions, upon the education of girls in comparison with that of boys. Girls have special needs for physical protection which may not be acknowledged by the disposition of school facilities. Some national cultures require the privacy or seclusion of girls, and place special value on the protection of their reputations. In some societies convention requires that girls be taught by women rather than men, yet the public school system may not reflect this requirement. In such cases, these and other customary attitudes lead to female education being assigned lower value than that of males, in turn reflecting the roles which society expects women to fulfil. For example, the strong association, reported in Chapter 2, between the proportion of Muslims in the population and female underenrolment, after allowing for income differences between countries, indicates the importance of such 'demand-side' constraints upon the achievement of SFA. In these cases, then it is the set of attitudes at the level of the household—which may or may not reflect, or be supported by the prevailing ideology of the State—which would need to be changed if moves towards SFA were to succeed.

In order to tackle these problems, measures to reduce the direct costs of schooling would obviously be influential in increasing the level of female enrolments. Scholarships, or fee-waivers are needed for girls first, in societies where fees are charged. Elsewhere, subsidies for school uniforms, meals, and free transport to school need to be focused particularly upon increasing the incentives for girls to attend. But broader measures will also be required.[16]

Actions by the State to attempt to reduce the resistance towards

---

[16] Hardly any systematic information is available on the relative costs and effects of policy alternatives to improve the incentives to educate girls. However, a useful review of what is known can be found in Herz *et al.* (1991).

educating girls could be extremely important, including publicizing, in simple, accessible terms, the impressively wide range of benefits of female education (accruing both to society and to individual households) which are now known to exist. Nevertheless, attitudes will often change only slowly. It will be necessary in some societies to facilitate girls' schooling in ways which recognize this. Single-sex schools, the recruitment of more female teachers, and more flexible timetabling to reduce conflict with household responsibilities each provide some means of increasing the incentives to enrol girls. The BRAC programme in Bangladesh, discussed earlier, appears to owe much of its success in enrolling girls to some of these characteristics.

The most important ingredient for successful policy design will be careful analysis of the factors which constrain enrolments in each case. Circumstances differ widely from country to country, and there is no single package of demand-side policies which are relevant in all circumstances. Usually there are a number of factors which act together to influence enrolment outcomes. It must be expected therefore, that a range of different policies will be needed, affecting both demand and supply, in order effectively and rapidly to enhance the enrolment of both girls and boys.

6. Conclusion

This book has attempted to identify the changed policies which would be required if all the children of primary-school age in developing countries were to be accommodated in schools of at least minimally acceptable quality by the turn of the century. The approach adopted has been, first, to ask why large numbers of children still remain out of school. Such an understanding is necessary if effective policy solutions are to be found. Second, on the basis of detailed country case-studies, and the results of more general research in developing countries, we have asked how, and to what extent, educational and other policy reforms could facilitate a more rapid transition to schooling for all. Promising sets of policy reforms were derived from this experience. Third, the cost and enrolment impact of introducing these reforms were investigated for all low- and middle-income countries separately, using a simulation approach. The results show that the policy agenda is extremely demanding, requiring a major collaborative venture by countries of both the North and the South.

Most low- and middle-income countries could reach SFA, as we have defined it, by using a mix of education and fiscal policy reforms, together with some modest increase in the budgetary priority accorded to education over the coming years. Not all of the reforms we have identified will prove possible in all countries, for a variety of reasons. But the analysis provides a framework within which the potential for, and impact of, policy change can be assessed in each particular case.

There is, however, a significant minority of developing countries which will be unable, from their own resources, to reach SFA over the next ten to fifteen years, even with sharp changes in policy. These are generally amongst the poorer countries, half of them from Sub-Saharan Africa, where primary gross enrolment ratios are currently very low. Here, the costs of bridging the enrolment gap, and of keeping up with population growth will prove too demanding to be financed entirely from domestic resources, on most scenarios for the extent of feasible policy change.

In order to secure SFA in these countries a substantial amount of additional financial aid will be needed from the North. But the politics of policy reform imply that additional aid will also be needed in other countries, both to secure greater willingness to implement the reform process, and indeed to encourage a central place being given to the achievement of SFA in the praxis of education policy.

The list of reforms which turn out to be both practical and politically manageable will differ from place to place. They will also differ from the particular combinations illustrated for each country in this book. Nationally prepared programmes for the achievement of SFA are therefore needed as a condition of the aid bargain. There is, then, an important diagnostic task facing each country. Each national programme for SFA would need to set out the resources necessary to universalize primary schooling over the decade, and to examine the impact upon these resource requirements of the policy reforms we have identified, and of others which may seem appropriate in particular national circumstances. Funding strategies would need to be explored, over a somewhat longer time-span than ten years, to allow for the fiscal impact of primary expansion on secondary enrolments to be absorbed. Equally important, the reasons for underenrolment of children would need to be carefully examined in each case. Is the problem of universalizing enrolments merely one of supplying sufficient school facilities, or are people voluntarily choosing not to send their children to school? As we have seen, in many cases the presence of low demand for schooling will be at least part of the answer. Convincing strategies would therefore need to be proposed for tackling problems of demand, as well as those of supply, as part of national programmes for SFA. Thus, in the large number of countries where the proportion of girls enrolled in primary school is significantly less than the proportion of boys,[17] a national strategy for SFA would

[17] Table A.1 shows that there are 26 countries in which the value of the female primary enrolment ratio is less than 80% of that for males. As with so many of the other characteristics associated with educational deprivation which have been documented in this book, the list consists almost entirely of countries from Sub-Saharan Africa and South Asia. The countries comprise: Benin, Burkina Faso, Burundi, Central African Republic, Chad,

need both to encompass financial provision for school expansion under various policy reforms, and to identify specific initiatives which would be taken in order to raise the level of female enrolments. Equally, in other countries, more general measures to combat voluntary underenrolment will be required.

This book has shown that the total additional costs of achieving UPE over the years 1990–2000 in developing countries would amount to rather more than $60 billion (in 1986 prices), and that the additional costs would have grown to more than $140 billion by the year 2005, assuming, *inter alia*, that unit costs and average transition rates to secondary schooling remained unchanged. About 160 million new school places would be required for UPE over the fifteen years 1990–2005, whereas SFA, which includes qualitative improvements to school systems, and lower rates of drop-out and repetition, would require about 212 million additional places over the same period. Accordingly, the costs of SFA are considerably higher than those of UPE, but they could be kept down to UPE cost levels in most countries if the set of efficiency reforms which we have identified were to be introduced. These efficiency savings, therefore, would be capable of financing the improvements to both the quality and capacity of school systems which typically separate UPE from SFA. Normal budgetary growth, together with some shift of spending priorities towards education—most notably away from defence—would then meet a large part of the additional costs of UPE/SFA.

It is not possible to predict exactly the amount of aid that would be needed to support those countries unable to achieve SFA from their own budgetary resources. Obviously, it would depend upon the amount of policy reform which each country were able and prepared to introduce. If all countries implemented all the reforms we have identified, and increased by 2 percentage points the proportion of the recurrent budget which they presently allocate to education, about $20 billion (in 1986 prices) would then be needed in aid over the period 1990–2005. However not all reforms will prove practically possible, and some governments, particularly some of the most needy African ones, would be unable to increase education spending during years when real per capita public expenditures remain set to decline further. Equally there would be a need for additional aid to countries other than the thirty-six most disadvantaged, in order to encourage them to adopt SFA targets, and to implement the reforms which could allow them to be financed.

All in all, we estimate that a figure of around $30 billion (in 1986 prices) will be required in aid to education over the years 1990–2005, in

Ivory Coast, Ethiopia, Ghana, Guinea, Malawi, Mali, Mauritania, Mozambique, Niger, Nigeria, Senegal, Somalia, Sudan, Togo, Morocco, Bangladesh, India, Nepal, Pakistan, Yemen Arab Republic, and Yemen PDR (see Table A.1).

order to achieve SFA. This would be in addition to existing levels of support to education in developing countries, and would represent an increase of such aid flows by about 50 per cent. This support would need to be predominantly recurrent in nature, and should take a number of different forms, including relief for debt-service in those highly indebted countries which demonstrate a clear commitment to SFA. International financial pledges for education rose substantially during 1990/1, to meet, in value terms, about half of the additional finance required on an annual basis. But some restructuring of these flows would be required, directing more towards the countries in greatest need, and more centrally espousing the objectives of SFA. In particular, about half of this external support would be needed for the countries of Sub-Saharan Africa, where it would enhance the value of present aid flows to education by around two-thirds.

These are large magnitudes. However, it should be remembered that over the years 1975 to 1989 aid to education fell from 17 per cent to scarcely more than 10 per cent of total concessional flows. This would therefore represent only a modest correction to a sustained downward, and highly undesirable, trend of support to human resources in the developing world. Equally, although it would secure a school place for each eligible child, it would provide school quality barely beyond a basic level for many countries, particularly those in Sub-Saharan Africa.

The years since 1989 have been characterized by bold and imaginative steps in world affairs. This has been a time of great hope and optimism for peace in the North, and for the financial savings and human freedoms which that would bring. Meanwhile in the South, one set of great human freedoms—that delivered by access to schooling—is at present denied to about 130 million children of primary school-age. Furthermore, schooling of adequate quality is denied to very many more. We have shown that a combination of reforms to educational policy in developing countries, some modest switching of expenditures by them towards primary schooling, and additional transfers of around $2 billion per year (or about $2.5 billion in 1990 prices) from northern countries are needed to provide schooling of minimally acceptable quality for all of the world's children. There are many difficulties which lie along the path. Delays are likely owing to an array of political, technical, bureaucratic, and economic factors which have been discussed in earlier pages. But this is a challenge which can and should be met, and it provides one of the finest targets for human development over these closing years of the twentieth century.

Technical Appendix

The Simulation Model

We have utilized a computerized model to project the enrolments and costs of education systems over a fifteen-year period.[1] In its basic form this is an enrolment-transition model which provides data on flows of students through each part of the school system. These are linked to unit cost data to generate estimates of the costs of the system at different times. The cost estimates can be compared, within the model, with projections of resources available, based upon assumptions for budgetary growth and for the future priority assigned to educational spending in the budgetary process.

This Technical Appendix describes the component parts of the model, the central assumptions which have been built into its configuration, and the ways in which the cost-saving, cost-shifting, and quality-enhancing reforms referred to in the text have been applied.

The Component Parts

The first component of the model is an enrolment-transition spreadsheet which projects enrolments by grade for primary, secondary, and technical and vocational schools, and for teacher training. The model allows the duration of each of these levels of schooling to be separately specified. The length of the primary- and secondary-school systems used in each of the ninety-seven national simulations reported in Chapter 6 are as given by national data. These vary between extreme values of three and nine years, with the most common cycle lengths being six years in each case. In the case of the composite simulation covering sixty-five countries (but only 2 per cent of the population of LDCs) for which national data were not available (see below), and in the example based on SSA data discussed in Chapter 5, primary and secondary cycle lengths of six years each are used. There is much greater variation in the duration of post-secondary training, not only between, but also within, particular countries. Accordingly all simulations assume that technical and vocational schooling, and teacher training, each last for three years, and run in parallel with the final three years of secondary schooling. Higher education is treated as exogenous to the model, and is the subject of separate assumptions, to be outlined later.

The starting-point for the projections is the enrolment pattern for all grades and levels of the school system in the base year, 1990. This is determined by a set of

---

[1] The original software for the model was developed by Unesco (see Unesco 1990), and was enhanced by ourselves for the purpose of this research.

parameters, the values for which are separately specified for each of the national simulations. These are:

1. The population of 6-year-olds.
2. The population of 6–11-year-olds.
3. The number of entrants to primary grade 1 as a proportion of 6-year-olds.
4. The repetition rates (RR) for all grades.
5. The promotion rate (PR) for all grades.
6. The drop-out rate (DOR) which is defined by the relationship:
   DOR = 1 − (RR + PR).
7. The promotion rate from primary to secondary school.
8. The number of students per class (SC).
9. The number of teachers per class (TC).
10. The student/teacher ratio (STR) defined as: STR = SC/TC.
11. The annual rate of teacher attrition.

On the basis of these inputs, enrolments for each grade can be projected forward and requirements for additional teachers and classrooms can be computed.

The second component of the model consists of a spreadsheet where the unit costs for each type of enrolment can be entered. These comprise:

- The salaries of all categories of staff at school level, including teachers and non-teaching staff.
- School-operating expenses including the cost of learning material, scholar-ships, and boarding subsidies.
- The salaries and operating expenses associated with inspection, and with regional and national administration.

In addition it is necessary to specify a number of other parameters. These comprise:

- The proportion of private enrolments and the public subsidy associated with these.
- The extent of double-shifting.
- The capital cost per classroom.
- The planned growth in salary costs which results from salary awards, over successive five-year periods.

The two spreadsheets are dynamically linked using macros[2] so that data from both the enrolment-transition and unit cost spreadsheets can be integrated to arrive at estimates of the total publicly incurred costs of each cycle of the education system. It should be stressed that these costs, in our simulations, are those which are incurred by the State. It would be straightforward to use the model also to compute the costs, for each level of the system, incurred by private households. However, this is not at present possible for more than one or two countries, owing to the dearth of reliable data on the private costs of schooling. In its simplest mathematical form recurrent and capital costs are calculated using the simple linear equations below:[3]

---

[2] The most recent version of the model uses Quattro Pro software; it utilizes its macro-facilities to integrate data from several different spreadsheets.

[3] The meaning of the terms is as follows: E = enrolments; U = unit cost; SC = number of pupils per class; H = higher-education costs; r = recurrent; i = investment; p = primary;

Total Recurrent Cost (T_r)

$$T_r = (E_{pn} \times U_{prn}) + (E_{sn} \times U_{srn}) + (E_{vn} \times U_{vrn}) + (E_{tn} \times U_{trn}) + (H_{rn}).$$

Total Investment Cost (T_i)

$$T_i = ((E_{p(n+1)} - E_{pn})/SC \times U_{pc}) + ((E_{s(n+1)} - E_{sn})/SC \times U_{sc})$$
$$+ ((E_{v(n+1)} - E_{vn})/SC \times U_{vc}) + ((E_{t(n+1)} - E_{tn})/SC \times U_{tc}) + (H_{in}).$$

All the terms necessary to arrive at cost estimates are therefore determined by the two spreadsheets except for those relating to higher-education costs. Higher education is treated as exogenous to the model. Accordingly, assumptions concerning public expenditures on higher education are made separately, based on available data, and entered directly to complete the computation of the total costs of the system.

The third component of the model is concerned with projecting resources rather than costs. Resources available from the public budget in the base year (1990) are assumed equal to costs. The distribution of these costs determines the initial proportions of the recurrent budget allocated to primary, secondary, and higher levels of education. The proportion allocated to capital expenditure in the base year is determined by the total cost of the number of new classrooms needed, as generated by the enrolment-transition spreadsheet. Assumptions concerning the expected growth of resources available to the public sector, and to education within it, are separately specified. Thus, comparisons between projected costs and projected resources available, can be made.

Assumptions

In principle, if data are available to provide reliable estimates for all of the above variables and parameters, it is a simple matter to produce estimates of the future costs of expanded school systems. Unfortunately, however, for a minority of these items tolerably accurate data are not available on a comparable international basis, and for a rather larger number of items, there are at least some countries where there are data gaps. In each of these cases, therefore, assumptions have to be made. Those which affect all simulations are as follows:

1. The number of students per class (SC) and the number of teachers per class (TC) are statistics which are often not available. However, the student/teacher ratio (STR) is widely calculated. We therefore derive SC from the identity:

   SC = STR × TC

assuming that TC = 1.00 in primary, 1.4 in secondary, and 1.5 in teacher training.

2. Initially, private enrolments at primary level and in teacher training are assumed to be zero, and to account for 5 per cent of secondary, technical, and

---

s = secondary; v = vocational and technical; t = teacher training; n = year for which costs are calculated; c = cost of a classroom.

vocational enrolments. Five per cent of the unit cost of private places is assumed to be a charge on the public budget.

3. It is assumed that there is no double-shifting at any level of schooling in the base year.

4. Unit costs for teacher training are assumed to be 50 per cent greater than those for general secondary schools.

5. The capital costs of classrooms have been assumed to be $US3,500 for primary, $US6,500 for secondary, $US8,000 for teacher training, and $US7,000 for technical and vocational schools.

6. Technical and vocational education are treated together in the modelling such that only one enrolment pattern is generated and unit costs are estimated on the basis of an average for both.

In cases where data necessary to calculate any of the parameters for the modelling exercise were missing, a standard procedure was used in order to estimate them. The method was to insert the mean value for the parameter concerned as calculated, from our data-base, for other developing countries, or for regional subgroupings of them. This procedure was used where data for any of the following parameters were absent: average class-size at primary level, repetition and promotion rates, length of school system at primary and general secondary levels, pupil/teacher ratios at secondary, technical, teacher-training, and vocational levels, the proportion of vocational and teacher-training pupils relative to those enrolled in general secondary schools, public recurrent expenditure as a proportion of total public expenditure, recurrent expenditure on education as a proportion of total education expenditure, and the constituent parts of recurrent expenditures on education broken down by salary, materials, and 'other' heads.

In each of the above cases, the value used to replace the missing parameter was an arithmetic mean calculated from groups of countries where the value was known. In the cases of expenditure proportions 'all LDC' means were used. For others, a non-African or African mean was assigned, depending upon the continental location of the country concerned.

In some cases, primary or secondary unit costs were also not known. Here, an approach to their estimation using arithmetic or population-weighted means would have been inappropriate. Instead, the values were estimated on the basis of a simple regression equation, linking primary and secondary unit costs to per capita income (in 1986) for those developing countries where data on unit costs were known. The estimating equations, with t values in parentheses, were as follows:

Predicted primary unit cost = $-23.63 + 0.15$ (GNP/capita) (1)
t-statistics: (-1.4) (18.4)
Adjusted R^2: 0.83
F-value: 339.7 (significant at 1% level).

Predicted secondary unit cost = $-26.26 + 0.33$ (GNP/capita) (2)
t-statistics: (-0.34) (10.78)
Adjusted R^2: 0.75
F-value: 116.1 (significant at 1% level).

The high correlations between publicly financed unit costs and per capita incomes indicate that the latter can be expected to be fairly efficient in predicting the former.

The final category of countries with 'data-gaps' concerns those for which there were simply insufficient data to undertake separate national simulations. This group, which comprises sixty-five countries, includes all those for which a primary GER value was not available, together with some others where the paucity of data was so extreme that reliable national estimates were not possible, even though the GER was known.

Most of the countries in this group had populations of less than 1 million persons in 1986. However, ten larger countries are also included. They comprise Afghanistan, Albania, Bhutan, Congo, Kampuchea, Lebanon, Namibia, Puerto Rico, South Africa, and Taiwan. These ten countries had a combined population of 88 million in the mid-1980s. The remaining fifty-five countries, on the other hand, which include most of the small island States of the Pacific and the Caribbean, had a combined population of about 12 million at that time.

All of these countries were grouped together in a single simulation. The group was assigned a GER equal to the arithmetic mean for all countries in the database (89.5), and a similar approach was adopted for estimating the size of the school-age population (14.6 per cent of the total), and its rate of growth over the period to 2005 (1.4 per cent per annum). Estimated values for all other parameters were obtained by following the standard procedure for dealing with missing data, described above.

The above sets of assumptions provide estimates, in the absence of reported values, for some of the parameters needed for the national simulations. There is, however, a further set of assumptions made, which concern the methods used rather than the data available. These can best be understood by considering the first step in the simulation exercise, that of building up primary enrolments such as to achieve UPE—defined as a GER of 100—by the end of the century. This is achieved by gradually (and, in some cases where initial GERs are low, sharply) increasing the proportion of 6-year-olds enrolled in the first grade of primary school, over the intervening years. By these means the GER rises to 100 by the year 2000 and stabilizes at that level through 2005. During this process, each of the parameters mentioned in earlier paragraphs is held constant. Thus, the simulation provides estimates of the costs of reaching UPE, assuming that there are no changes in any of the underlying conditions which determine the costs of schooling in each particular country. In the language of economics, it is a 'partial-equilibrium' approach, which abstracts from the impact which the projected changes may have upon other sectors, which in turn may change the cost and demand conditions within the education sector itself.

Second, all national data, upon which the projections are based, are for 1986, the most recent year for which the required information was available from international published sources. In view of the lag which always attends the publication of international statistics, two alternative methods for dealing with it present themselves. One could simply project forward for a ten- or fifteen-year period using 1986 as the base year. Alternatively, the parameters for 1986 could be applied to the estimated school population in a more recent year, thereby producing cost estimates, expressed in 1986 prices, of achieving UPE and SFA from, say 1990. The latter method was adopted. Analytically, it is the same as the former approach, with the first four years of the projection period omitted.

Third, the estimated populations, in 1990, of 6–11-year-olds, and of 6-year-olds, are derived for all countries from World Bank sources. The same sources are used to provide population estimates for these groups over the period 1990–2005. Primary enrolments in 1990 are derived by applying the GER reported for 1986 to the 1990 6–11-age-group, which latter is, in turn, adjusted for the actual length of primary schooling in each individual country. Enrolments throughout the whole school system are then determined by the interaction between the estimated primary school-age population, the GER, and the parameters for cycle-length, and for repetition and promotion rates mentioned earlier in this Appendix. This approach thus assumes that these enrolment parameters, including rates of population growth, have been stable for some time in the past, and that the GER has not changed significantly over the years 1986–90.

Fourth, the promotion rate from primary to secondary school is set at 40 per cent, equal to the weighted mean value for all developing countries in the mid-1980s. This therefore assumes that the move to UPE will not result in increased relative provision at secondary level. For higher education, a more conservative assumption—that public expenditures would here increase at the same rate as the school-age population—was employed.

Finally, the assumptions made for changes in public resources available for education are that these will increase, in real terms, at the same rate as the population of the country concerned. With no change in fiscal stance, and no change in the priority assigned to educational expenditures, this is consistent with an assumption that real per capita incomes in each country would not fall over the projection period. Comments on the plausibility of these assumptions are given in Chapter 6.

The Introduction of Policy Reforms

The particular benefit of the modelling approach described above is that it can be used to explore the effects of changing any or all of the cost parameters in ways which simulate educational or fiscal reforms. In general, changes to parameters are translated by the model into smooth growth (or decline) in their values over the projection period. Thus, for example, the effects of reducing repetition, or of increasing teachers' salaries, can be examined by selecting both their initial values and those expected after five years; the model then implements changes incrementally for each year of the period, and for subsequent periods, as required.

It will be remembered that the first set of simulation results obtained for each country concerns the cost and enrolment implications of achieving UPE by the year 2000. This is the product of increasing GERs to 100 by that date without changing any of the other parameters. A separate set of results is produced for both the years 2000 and 2005, both of which maintain the same target date for the achievement of UPE. Subsequently, the impact of changing the cost parameters can be investigated. Nine sets of reforms are introduced, the effects of which cumulate successively. The policy changes implied by each of these reforms, together with the ways in which particular parameter values are altered in order to simulate them, are summarized below:

Cost-Saving Reforms

Reform 1: Introduce double-shifting at primary and secondary levels.

Implementation: Reduce teacher/pupil ratio by 15 per cent over ten years at primary and secondary level.

Reform 1 has an effect on both recurrent and capital costs and implies an increase in teacher productivity. If double-shifting is already practised, this reform assumes that some further increase is possible to the extent of a reduction of 15 per cent in unit costs.

Reform 2: Increase class-size.

Implementation: Increase average class-size, at primary and secondary levels, by five pupils in all countries where the current value is forty or less, over a ten-year period. Increase average class-size by five pupils in teacher-training and vocational schools in all countries where the current value is thirty or less, over a ten-year period.

Reform 2 allows class-sizes to increase to maxima of forty-five in primary and secondary schools, and thirty-five in teacher-training and vocational schools. Countries with average class-sizes larger than this are unaffected by the reform. It assumes that measures are taken to reduce the dispersion of class-size from the mean. These would have no effect on costs, but would have equity benefits and should improve quality in those schools with the highest student/teacher ratios.

Reform 3: Reduce primary unit costs by the increased use of self-study, teaching assistants, and community helpers.

Implementation: Reduce primary teachers' unit costs by 10 per cent over a ten-year peroid.

Reform 3 implies the substitution of some trained-teacher-time by untrained/ volunteer teachers and community assistants. Cost reductions of 10 per cent could be achieved if one period per day were occupied by self-study, peer-group learning, or unpaid/nominally rewarded community helpers.

Cost-Shifting Reforms

Reform 4a: Increase community contributions to financing schooling.

Implementation: Decrease unit recurrent costs for primary and secondary schools by 10 per cent over a ten-year period.

Reform 4a assumes that any of a number of mechanisms will be used to shift some costs from the State to the community. These include an increase in private-school enrolments and/or the introduction of school fees in ways that do not discourage enrolment by children from relatively poor families. If 10 per cent of students were enrolled in private schools at primary and secondary level this could, depending upon the level of state subsidy of private education, be sufficient to capture these savings. Alternatively, other forms of cost recovery would need to be introduced at levels sufficient to finance 10 per cent of recurrent costs, focused, of course, mainly upon richer communities and families. There are well-known equity risks with both of these options.

Reform 4b: Decrease the capital costs of classroom construction at primary level, in part by passing costs to local communities.

Implementation: Reduce the cost of primary classrooms to the State by 50 per cent over five years.

There are ways of reducing construction costs, via better design and planning, in many countries. In many others, greater devolution of the responsibility for constructing classrooms to local communities could achieve significant savings at little equity cost.

Reform 5: Freeze higher-education subsidies at current levels.

Implementation: Keep the public sector recurrent and capital expenditures on higher education constant at 1990 levels.

Reform 5 fixes public subsidies to higher education at current levels. This does not prevent enrolments from growing. It implies that any such growth will have to be financed through mechanisms other than the public budget. This reform decreases the share of the education budget taken by higher education.

Quality-Enhancing Reforms

Reform 6: Increase learning resources per child.

Implementation: Increase learning resources per child to $US5 over five years at all levels for all cases where these are less than $US5 in 1990.

The intention here is to ensure that there is a minimally adequate supply of textbooks and writing material, and to preserve the non-salary recurrent budget from extinction in some countries.

Reform 7: Increase teachers' salaries.

Implementation: Increase teachers' salaries by 15 per cent in real terms over a ten-year period.

Reform 7 could take the form of general salary increases. But in many countries it would be better to integrate some salary restructuring, to provide more incentives for good performance and to those teachers working in educationally disadvantaged areas.

Reform 8: Reduce repetition rates by introducing automatic promotion.

Implementation: Reduce repetition rates to 25 per cent of existing values at all levels over ten years, whilst keeping drop-out unchanged and allowing promotion rates to increase concomitantly.

Reform 8 implies the introduction of automatic promotion in two stages, so that repetition drops to half its initial level over the first five years and halves again over the next five years. Faster rates of reduction may be desirable but are probably unrealistic. As repetition falls, internal efficiency increases, thereby reducing both the GER and recurrent costs.

Reform 9: Reduce drop-out rates.

Implementation: Reduce drop-out to 50 per cent of existing values at all levels over ten years and allow promotion rates to increase concomitantly.

Faster reduction in rates of drop-out than are contemplated here are probably not feasible given their dependence on a range of factors, of which improved school quality is but one. This reform has the effect of increasing GERs, and, with all quality-enhancing reforms in place, provides our proxy for the achievement of SFA. Thus, SFA does not have a single definition in terms of enrolment targets, since the level of GER reached, by reform 9, depends on starting conditions. However, the process through which final GERs are identified remains constant, and in this sense our operational definition is the same for all countries.

Procedures for Estimating the Additional Costs of UPE and SFA

There are two different ways in which the simulation model can be used to generate estimates of the costs of achieving SFA around the world. The first is to use estimates for the parameters of the model which are mean values derived from data for all the countries concerned. This involves calculation of weighted or arithmetic means for all the cost-related variables, both those covering enrolments and expenditures. This done, the introduction of the total populations of school-age children, of six-year-olds, and of their respective rates of growth, for the countries concerned, together with their combined (population-weighted) GER, allows the model to project the costs of achieving UPE and SFA for any group of States.

A second approach to estimation is to perform separate simulations for each individual country, using national enrolment, population, and cost data in each case. These results can then be added together, to provide the costs of UPE and SFA in different groups of countries or regions, and, indeed, for the world as a whole.

It is obvious that the second method will provide more accurate estimates of the costs of school expansion than the first. This is because, in practice, weighting each of the parameters used in the model by school-age population—whilst adequate for calculating the costs of school systems in the base year—is not adequate for estimating future costs in circumstances where each of the national systems are changing, over time, at substantially different rates. Thus, for example, weighted-mean world costs of primary schooling in 1990 are substantially influenced by India and China, which both have very large school-age populations, and very low publicly funded unit costs of schooling. Yet, since these countries have low rates of population growth by world standards, and are already beyond (China), or close to achieving (India), UPE, the cost influence of other countries, facing higher unit costs, with higher rates of growth of population, and starting from a position which is much farther from UPE, may be underestimated by an approach which assumes that base-year weighted mean cost values will remain unchanged at world level during the shift towards UPE.[4]

For these, and other reasons, the first method has not been used, except, in Chapter 5, to illustrate the range of conclusions which the simulation model will support, and (as explained earlier in this Appendix) for the purpose of aggregating a group of countries where there is insufficient national-level data to support separate simulations.

On the basis of the results of the second method, each of the national simulations were added together to produce estimates of regional and LDC total costs of

---

[4] In fact, it is interesting to note that, notwithstanding the influence of India and China, unit costs at primary level are expected to fall with the approach of UPE, owing to the much greater importance of relatively low-cost African enrolments in the total, and to the relative decline in importance of some very high-cost States in Eastern Europe and elsewhere (see Ch. 6).

reaching UPE and SFA, using various combinations of the nine reforms, as explained in Chapter 6. Deficits and surpluses on the education budget (using assumptions indicated earlier in this Appendix) were calculated both for UPE and each level of reform leading to SFA. Aggregation of these deficits allows estimates for external resource requirements at the regional level to be compiled. This analysis is not possible where more aggregated methods are used, since they falsely presuppose that surpluses in one country are, both in principle and practice, available to finance deficits arising elsewhere. Our analysis shows that aggregation would underestimate additional costs of UPE and SFA by about 20 per cent over the fifteen-year period.

Finally, the national simulations are used to calculate the cumulated additional costs of UPE and SFA over a ten- and fifteen-year period, for comparison with resources available. Since additional costs (in comparison with those in the base year) are highly sensitive to the phasing of the introduction of individual reforms, it is assumed that the difference between final-year and base-year costs build up in equal annual increments over the ten- and fifteen-year periods for which results are separately shown. The same assumption is used for revenue growth, allowing calculation and comparison of cumulated deficits and surpluses for different countries and regions, both with and without policy reforms. These analyses are the basis for the identification of the likely aid-dependent countries in the move to SFA, and for the estimates of aid requirements which are discussed in Chapter 6.

A Note on Data Sources

The data upon which our analyses and simulations are based comprise information on more than ninety variables for ninety-seven countries. It is, therefore, impractical to cite sources for each of these separately. However, with very few exceptions, the information in our national data-bases was built up from published international statistical sources. Of these, the most frequently used have been the Unesco Statistical Yearbook (Unesco 1989), and the World Development Indicators, published by the World Bank (World Bank 1989*a*, 1991*b*). Data from the UNDP Human Development Reports (UNDP 1990, 1991), from World Military and Social Expenditures (Sivard 1990), and from Lockheed and Verspoor (1990) were also frequently used. In addition, data on the population of 6-year-olds in 1989 are from Bulatao *et al.* (1990), and those on the Muslim population are mainly from Weekes (1978), but also from Europa (1990) and *Statesman's Yearbook* (1990).

In the course of building up these data, many inaccuracies in and inconsistencies between the original sources became plain. These shortcomings are well known, and will not be expanded upon here. Nevertheless, the results which they support, via our simulations, and the inferences which we have drawn from them, do pass important tests of common sense and consistency, which give us faith that the exercise has been worthwhile.

The Statistical Appendix which follows reproduces a small part of the results from our national simulations, which are felt to be of some general interest. However, the interpretations which are given in Chapter 6, and the assumptions which underlie them should be remembered when focusing upon the results for individual countries. In particular, the financial data shown in Tables A.2 and A.3 are mainly useful to show the impact of successive policy reforms on educational costs and financing in each country. It is the relative change in these expenditures which is more important than their absolute amounts.

Statistical Appendix

TABLE A.1. *Primary enrolments and enrolment ratios in developing countries, 1986–1990, and the enrolment implications of UPE and SFA*[a]

	Gross enrolment ratios (1986)			Net enrolment ratio (1986)	Estimated primary enrolments (000s) 1990[b]	Primary enrolments implied by UPE and SFA (000s)			
	Males	Females	Total			UPE 2000	SFA 2000	UPE 2005	SFA 2005[c]
SSA									
Angola			93		996	1,412	1,853	1,621	2,169
Benin	87	43	64	51	502	1,095	1,231	1,325	1,496
Botswana	109	115	112	95	269	323	313	372	360
Burkina Faso	39	23	31	26	448	2,039	2,003	2,543	2,407
Burundi	68	50	59	46	529	1,301	1,203	1,615	1,448
Cameroon	118	100	109		1,995	2,633	2,410	3,129	2,850
Cent. African Rep.	82	50	66	51	302	628	854	742	1,058
Chad	62	24	43	38	378	1,191	1,624	1,409	2,008
Ethiopia	44	28	36	27	3,071	11,353	13,081	13,232	15,465
Gabon	124	121	123		175	216	204	262	249
Ghana	81	63	72		1,708	3,218	3,021	3,817	3,507
Guinea	41	17	29	22	335	1,464	1,422	1,796	1,628
Ivory Coast	82	58	70		1,443	2,852	2,644	3,471	3,121
Kenya	100	94	97	71	5,636	8,437	8,429	10,217	10,228
Lesotho	102	127	115		367	437	450	504	525
Liberia			35		131	615	655	775	810
Madagascar	125	118	121		1,931	2,229	2,611	2,620	3,138

Malawi	73	57	65	48	1,152	2,429	2,787	2,969	3,498
Mali	29	17	23	19	350	2,043	2,307	2,538	2,784
Mauritania	63	39	51		165	449	412	548	484
Mauritius	107	107	107	92	135	119	107	115	103
Mozambique	94	74	84	49	1,384	2,237	2,464	2,609	2,887
Niger	38	20	29	27	345	1,695	1,677	2,108	2,024
Nigeria	103	81	77		14,779	27,075	27,000	32,550	32,217
Rwanda	66	64	65	62	1,117	2,643	2,902	3,387	3,783
Senegal	69	47	58	49	687	1,591	1,496	1,898	1,732
Sierra Leone			54		413	1,017	1,130	1,248	1,402
Somalia	20	10	15	11	207	1,943	2,299	2,480	2,966
Sudan	58	41	49		2,000	5,431	5,520	6,459	6,441
Tanzania	69	69	69	52	3,775	8,099	7,874	10,204	9,696
Togo	126	78	102	73	570	796	764	948	904
Uganda	77	63	70	53	2,510	4,914	4,863	5,906	5,764
Zaïre	84	68	76		4,515	7,985	8,099	9,367	9,434
Zambia	102	92	97		1,586	2,306	2,250	2,743	2,656
Zimbabwe	140	132	136	100	2,623	2,694	2,663	3,121	3,129
TOTAL					58,527	116,910	120,623	140,650	144,373
North Africa									
Algeria	105	85	95		3,924	5,287	5,175	5,987	5,846
Egypt	97	79	88		6,750	9,168	9,340	10,061	10,253
Morocco	90	58	74		2,385	3,929	3,820	4,358	4,216
Tunisia	127	107	117	94	1,373	1,349	1,199	1,425	1,269
TOTAL					14,432	19,733	19,534	21,831	21,585

TABLE A.1. (cont'd)

	Gross enrolment ratios (1986)			Net enrolment ratio (1986)	Estimated primary enrolments (000s) 1990[b]	Primary enrolments implied by UPE and SFA[c] (000s)			
	Males	Females	Total			UPE 2000	SFA 2000	UPE 2005	SFA 2005
Asia									
Bangladesh	70	50	60	53	9,238	17,520	23,896	18,701	26,352
China	138	120	129	95	140,489	117,932	120,632	122,597	125,821
Hong Kong	105	103	104		552	575	566	598	588
India	115	81	98		91,752	101,396	115,395	105,672	123,697
Indonesia	120	115	118		30,771	27,684	27,128	28,403	27,781
Iran	120	100	110	91	7,804	9,722	9,556	11,376	11,162
Iraq	107	91	99	87	3,227	4,688	4,444	5,625	5,313
Israel	93	97	95		695	732	822	735	849
Jordan	98	99	99	88	672	844	802	941	887
Korea, Rep.	97	99	98	96	4,876	4,829	4,580	4,759	4,473
Lao PDR	78	100	111		572	659	968	746	1,140
Malaysia	101	101	101		2,316	2,558	2,442	2,702	2,560
Mongolia	101	103	102	95	167	197	187	217	204
Myanmar			99		4,915	5,539	7,040	5,851	7,629
Nepal	104	47	82		2,001	3,216	4,073	3,694	4,795
Oman	102	86	94	80	209	288	273	328	308
Pakistan	56	32	44		6,422	19,615	21,674	22,788	25,400
Philippines	108	106	107	94	9,615	9,927	10,365	10,431	10,963
Singapore	118	113	115	100	284	259	248	265	252
Sri Lanka	106	102	104	100	2,303	2,446	2,384	2,569	2,498
Syria	117	105	111	100	2,313	2,720	2,824	3,103	3,241
Thailand	96	96	96		7,245	7,776	8,102	7,899	8,276

Turkey	119	111	115	83	7,205	7,343	7,208	7,945	7,777
Vietnam	105	99	102	88	8,643	10,329	11,342	11,403	12,648
Yemen, Arab Rep.	134	38	86		1,169	1,706	2,406	1,913	2,834
Yemen, PDR	96	35	66		333	616	705	699	826
TOTAL					345,790	361,117	390,060	381,959	418,277
Latin America									
Argentina	109	109	109		4,829	4,656	5,243	4,739	5,492
Bolivia	92	82	87	79	1,302	1,824	2,047	2,037	2,348
Brazil	108	99	103	83	27,386	29,663	37,236	31,257	41,493
Chile	106	104	105		2,038	1,961	2,337	1,964	2,439
Colombia	113	115	114	73	3,977	3,703	3,789	3,808	3,905
Costa Rica	99	97	98	85	382	435	427	459	449
Cuba	109	101	105	95	1,114	1,138	1,083	1,177	1,113
Dominican Rep.	99	103	101	73	1,041	1,185	1,378	1,269	1,508
Ecuador	119	117	118		1,896	1,939	2,152	2,127	2,399
El Salvador	77	81	79		1,063	1,457	1,709	1,542	1,876
Guatemala	82	70	76		849	1,336	1,602	1,462	1,798
Haiti	101	89	95	55	884	1,059	1,499	1,130	1,682
Honduras	104	108	106	91	899	1,096	1,226	1,244	1,413
Jamaica	104	106	105	98	346	336	329	340	331
Mexico	120	118	119	100	15,853	14,861	15,050	15,639	15,877
Nicaragua	93	103	98	75	593	745	989	826	1,144
Panama	108	104	106	89	343	324	314	323	311
Paraguay	105	99	102	87	639	794	871	894	993
Peru	125	120	122	97	3,895	3,633	3,873	3,853	4,162
Trinidad & Tobago	97	99	98	86	180	203	205	213	216
Uruguay	111	109	110	92	357	328	315	328	314
Venezuela	107	107	107	89	2,978	3,230	3,258	3,475	3,511
TOTAL					72,844	75,905	86,929	80,108	94,775

TABLE A.1. (cont'd)

Other	Gross enrolment ratios (1986)			Net enrolment ratio (1986)	Estimated primary enrolments (000s) 1990[b]	Primary enrolments implied by UPE and SFA[c] (000s)			
	Males	Females	Total			UPE 2000	SFA 2000	UPE 2005	SFA 2005
Bulgaria	105	103	104		1,073	952	958	911	919
Czechoslovakia	98	98	98		1,965	1,724	1,724	1,602	1,604
German Dem. Rep.	106	104	105	91	860	819	944	817	968
Greece	104	104	104	99	872	805	763	789	741
Hungary	98	98	98	96	1,158	918	909	810	802
Papua New Guinea	76	64	70	70	410	700	725	769	798
Poland	101	101	101	99	4,944	4,656	4,598	4,536	4,478
Portugal	127	121	124	100	1,209	918	826	879	786
Romania	98	97	97		2,900	2,760	3,100	2,648	3,061
Yugoslavia	97	95	96	79	1,388	1,334	1,322	1,281	1,269
Omitted Countries			90		13,848	17,799	18,290	19,139	19,674
TOTAL					30,627	33,385	34,160	34,181	35,101
GRAND TOTAL					522,219	607,050	651,307	658,729	714,110

[a] Blanks indicate that data are not available. Items may not add to totals owing to rounding.

[b] These enrolment estimates have been derived by applying the 1986 GER to the estimated 1990 school-age population, adjusted for the length of schooling in each country. They thus indicate what enrolments in 1990 would have been, had the proportion of children attending school remained unchanged since 1986. See Ch. 6 for comment.

[c] These are estimated by national simulations. UPE is defined as achieving a GER of 100, calculated on the basis of projections of the school-age population. SFA applies efficiency reforms to the UPE position, causing enrolments to change as a result of lower rates of repetition and drop-out.

TABLE A.2. *Simulated costs and financing of UPE and SFA in 2000 and 2005, all policy reforms implemented, all developing countries separately (in $m. at constant 1986 prices)*

	1990	2000 UPE No reform	Cost-saving reforms — Double-shifting (1)	Increase class-size (2)	Teacher-helpers (3)	Cost-shifting reforms — Community financing (4)	Freeze higher ed. subsidies (5)	Quality-enhancing reforms — Increase materials (6)	Teacher salaries (7)	SFA Repetition & drop-out (8/9)	2005 UPE No reform	Cost-saving (1–3)	Cost-shifting (1–5)	SFA (1–9)
Sub-Saharan Africa														
Angola (GER 93)														
Total recurrent education expenditure	216	300	269	243	232	215	201	201	220	318	346	268	226	420
Budgetary allocation required for balance	13%	13%	12%	11%	10%	10%	9%	9%	10%	14%	14%	10%	9%	16%
Cumulated additional recurrent expenditure		463	295	151	88	–6	–82	–80	23	563	1,043	413	78	1,634
Cumulated recurrent surplus/deficit		–86	83	226	290	384	459	457	355	–185	–156	473	809	–748
Benin (GER 64)														
Total recurrent education expenditure	17	31	28	26	25	23	22	27	29	33	40	33	28	46
Budgetary allocation required for balance	16%	20%	18%	17%	16%	15%	14%	17%	18%	21%	22%	18%	15%	25%
Cumulated additional recurrent expenditure		77	59	49	43	32	25	51	62	85	183	121	82	232
Cumulated recurrent surplus/deficit		–39	–21	–11	–5	6	13	–12	–24	–47	–92	–30	9	–141
Burundi (GER 59)														
Total recurrent education expenditure	96	165	150	141	137	130	121	127	137	132	244	203	177	189
Budgetary allocation required for balance	16%	18%	17%	16%	15%	15%	14%	14%	15%	15%	23%	19%	16%	18%
Cumulated additional recurrent expenditure		380	297	247	230	188	139	171	226	200	1,191	858	648	749
Cumulated recurrent surplus/deficit		–142	–60	–9	8	50	98	67	12	38	–617	–285	–75	–175
Burkina Faso (GER 31)														
Total recurrent education expenditure	45	111	100	97	93	86	81	89	97	96	176	148	126	146
Budgetary allocation required for balance	20%	35%	31%	31%	29%	27%	25%	28%	30%	30%	47%	39%	33%	38%
Cumulated additional recurrent expenditure		365	304	291	269	229	198	246	289	281	1,052	825	652	808
Cumulated recurrent surplus/deficit		–264	–203	–190	–168	–128	–97	–146	–188	–180	–811	–585	–412	–567
Cameroon (GER 109)														
Total recurrent education expenditure	428	587	531	522	502	469	431	434	474	464	691	591	490	535
Budgetary allocation required for balance	14%	13%	12%	12%	11%	10%	10%	10%	11%	10%	13%	11%	9%	10%
Cumulated additional recurrent expenditure		875	567	520	410	225	19	37	255	199	2,103	1,310	500	857
Cumulated recurrent surplus/deficit		155	464	510	621	805	1,011	994	775	831	375	1,169	1,979	1,621

Table A.2. (cont'd)

	1990	2000 UPE No reform	Cost-saving reforms Double-shifting (1)	Increase class-size (2)	Teacher-helpers (3)	Cost-shifting reforms Community financing (4)	Freeze higher ed. subsidies (5)	Quality-enhancing reforms Increase materials (6)	Teacher salaries (7)	SFA Repetition & drop-out (8/9)	2005 UPE No reform	Cost-saving (1–3)	Cost-shifting (1–5)	SFA (1–9)
Central African Republic (GER 66)														
Total recurrent education expenditure	33	63	56	56	52	48	45	47	53	73	75	62	52	101
Budgetary allocation required for balance	15%	22%	19%	19%	18%	16%	15%	16%	18%	25%	22%	18%	15%	30%
Cumulated additional recurrent expenditure		164	124	124	103	81	67	79	107	218	333	228	156	543
Cumulated recurrent surplus/deficit		–97	–57	–57	–36	–13	0	–12	–40	–151	–174	–69	3	–383
Chad (GER 43)														
Total recurrent education expenditure	33	92	81	81	75	69	66	69	77	103	109	89	78	130
Budgetary allocation required for balance	15%	32%	28%	28%	26%	24%	23%	24%	27%	36%	32%	26%	23%	39%
Cumulated additional recurrent expenditure		324	264	264	233	197	184	201	243	388	606	449	357	776
Cumulated recurrent surplus/deficit		–259	–199	–199	–168	–132	–119	–136	–178	–323	–453	–296	–204	–623
Ethiopia (GER 36)														
Total recurrent education expenditure	166	522	460	460	427	390	379	420	464	533	619	508	445	651
Budgetary allocation required for balance	11%	25%	22%	22%	21%	19%	18%	20%	22%	26%	26%	21%	19%	27%
Cumulated additional recurrent expenditure		1,960	1,618	1,618	1,441	1,235	1,175	1,401	1,644	2,024	3,628	2,738	2,239	3,886
Cumulated recurrent surplus/deficit		–1,659	–1,317	–1,316	–1,140	–934	–874	–1,099	–1,343	–1,723	–2,919	–2,029	–1,530	–3,177
Ghana (GER 72)														
Total recurrent education expenditure	283	443	397	353	344	315	303	313	340	336	580	452	393	438
Budgetary allocation required for balance	27%	31%	28%	24%	24%	22%	21%	22%	24%	23%	34%	27%	23%	26%
Cumulated additional recurrent expenditure		879	630	386	338	178	111	166	315	291	2,377	1,351	881	1,238
Cumulated recurrent surplus/deficit		–323	–74	170	218	378	445	390	240	265	–1,062	–36	434	77
Guinea (GER 29)														
Total recurrent education expenditure	28	61	54	49	47	44	41	47	52	51	87	67	57	71
Budgetary allocation required for balance	15%	27%	24%	21%	20%	19%	18%	21%	22%	22%	34%	26%	22%	27%
Cumulated additional recurrent expenditure		181	144	117	105	88	70	105	129	125	474	309	228	342
Cumulated recurrent surplus/deficit		–140	–102	–76	–63	–46	–29	–64	–88	–83	–378	–212	–132	–245

Ivory Coast														
Total recurrent education expenditure	390	675	603	553	527	488	463	463	508	468	854	667	575	572
Budgetary allocation required for balance	18%	22%	20%	18%	17%	16%	15%	15%	17%	15%	24%	19%	16%	16%
Cumulated additional recurrent expenditure		1,572	1,175	900	757	542	401	401	652	432	3,711	2,218	1,483	1,458
Cumulated recurrent surplus/deficit		−750	−353	−78	65	280	421	421	170	390	−1,755	−262	473	498
Kenya (GER 97)														
Total recurrent education expenditure	380	564	507	465	443	411	376	406	441	443	683	537	441	530
Budgetary allocation required for balance	22%	22%	20%	18%	18%	16%	15%	16%	17%	18%	22%	18%	14%	17%
Cumulated additional recurrent expenditure		1,008	694	467	345	166	−24	138	334	342	2,423	1,253	481	1,195
Cumulated recurrent surplus/deficit		−62	252	479	601	780	969	808	612	604	−141	1,029	1,801	1,087
Lesotho (GER 115)														
Total recurrent education expenditure	26	34	30	28	27	25	23	26	28	31	38	31	25	36
Budgetary allocation required for balance	17%	16%	14%	13%	13%	12%	11%	12%	13%	15%	16%	12%	10%	15%
Cumulated additional recurrent expenditure		43	20	10	5	−6	−16	−4	11	24	94	34	−8	75
Cumulated recurrent surplus/deficit		11	33	44	49	60	70	58	43	30	33	94	135	53
Liberia (GER 35)														
Total recurrent education expenditure	23	85	75	67	63	57	55	56	62	67	115	85	74	92
Budgetary allocation required for balance	21%	52%	46%	41%	38%	35%	34%	34%	38%	41%	58%	43%	37%	46%
Cumulated additional recurrent expenditure		342	286	241	218	188	176	180	214	241	732	494	407	549
Cumulated recurrent surplus/deficit		−282	−227	−182	−158	−129	−117	−121	−155	−181	−588	−350	−264	−405
Madagascar (GER 121)														
Total recurrent education expenditure	76	91	77	69	65	58	58	69	78	108	104	74	66	148
Budgetary allocation required for balance	16%	13%	11%	10%	9%	9%	9%	10%	11%	16%	13%	9%	8%	18%
Cumulated additional recurrent expenditure		83	7	−37	−62	−97	−97	−36	12	177	228	−18	−76	577
Cumulated recurrent surplus/deficit		82	158	202	228	263	263	202	153	−11	167	413	471	−182
Malawi (GER 65)														
Total recurrent education expenditure	64	104	95	93	90	83	78	88	94	106	141	121	104	168
Budgetary allocation required for balance	12%	14%	13%	13%	12%	11%	11%	12%	13%	15%	17%	14%	12%	20%
Cumulated additional recurrent expenditure		217	169	156	138	101	73	73	164	226	610	455	313	830
Cumulated recurrent surplus/deficit		−86	−38	−25	−7	30	58	1	−33	−95	−298	−144	−2	−518
Mali (GER 23)														
Total recurrent education expenditure	38	151	131	116	107	98	95	102	115	134	207	148	130	202
Budgetary allocation required for balance	10%	30%	26%	23%	21%	19%	19%	20%	22%	26%	35%	25%	22%	34%
Cumulated additional recurrent expenditure		623	511	430	382	331	314	354	424	530	1,351	880	736	1,309
Cumulated recurrent surplus/deficit		−551	−439	−358	−309	−259	−242	−282	−351	−457	−1,180	−709	−565	−1,138
Mauritania (GER 51)														
Total recurrent education expenditure	54	99	90	86	84	77	72	73	79	75	145	121	103	103
Budgetary allocation required for balance	15%	21%	19%	18%	17%	16%	15%	15%	17%	16%	26%	21%	18%	18%
Cumulated additional recurrent expenditure		249	198	179	165	130	100	107	142	115	726	541	392	392
Cumulated recurrent surplus/deficit		−135	−85	−66	−51	−17	14	6	−28	−2	−457	−271	−122	−122

TABLE A.2. (cont'd)

	1990	2000									2005			
		UPE No reform	Cost-saving reforms			Cost-shifting reforms		Quality-enhancing reforms			UPE No reform	Cost-saving	Cost-shifting	SFA
			Double-shifting	Increase class-size	Teacher-helpers	Community financing	Freeze higher ed. subsidies	Increase materials	Teacher salaries	SFA Repetition & drop-out				
			1	2	3	4	5	6	7	8/9	1–3	1–5	1–9
Mozambique (GER 84)														
Total recurrent education expenditure	31	45	41	41	40	37	34	45	49	61	55	48	40	82
Budgetary allocation required for balance	16%	17%	15%	15%	15%	14%	13%	17%	18%	23%	18%	15%	13%	26%
Cumulated additional recurrent expenditure		82	58	57	50	33	21	82	99	167	193	137	79	408
Cumulated recurrent surplus/deficit		−22	2	3	10	27	39	−22	−39	−107	−51	5	63	−266
Niger (GER 29)														
Total recurrent education expenditure	14	42	37	34	32	30	29	36	39	40	66	52	46	62
Budgetary allocation required for balance	16%	33%	29%	27%	25%	23%	22%	28%	30%	31%	43%	34%	30%	40%
Cumulated additional recurrent expenditure		152	127	110	101	87	81	121	137	141	416	303	254	381
Cumulated recurrent surplus/deficit		−120	−95	−78	−69	−55	−48	−89	−105	−108	−338	−225	−176	−303
Nigeria (GER 77)														
Total recurrent education expenditure	974	1,497	1,361	1,359	1,338	1,240	1,160	1,273	1,373	1,443	1,974	1,764	1,501	1,963
Budgetary allocation required for balance	15%	16%	15%	15%	15%	14%	13%	14%	15%	16%	18%	16%	14%	18%
Cumulated additional recurrent expenditure		2,873	2,129	2,117	1,999	1,462	1,022	1,642	2,192	2,580	8,001	6,321	4,212	7,906
Cumulated recurrent surplus/deficit		−672	72	84	202	739	1,179	558	9	−379	−2,736	−1,056	1,052	−2,641
Rwanda (GER 65)														
Total recurrent education expenditure	73	153	137	135	127	118	110	119	131	144	201	167	141	195
Budgetary allocation required for balance	25%	34%	30%	30%	28%	26%	24%	26%	29%	32%	36%	30%	25%	35%
Cumulated additional recurrent expenditure		443	351	343	298	247	204	253	318	391	1,027	750	546	977
Cumulated recurrent surplus/deficit		−227	−135	−127	−83	−32	12	−37	−103	−176	−499	−221	−18	−449
Senegal (GER 58)														
Total recurrent education expenditure	62	113	101	101	97	89	85	90	99	96	148	127	110	124
Budgetary allocation required for balance	16%	21%	19%	19%	18%	17%	16%	17%	18%	18%	24%	21%	18%	20%
Cumulated additional recurrent expenditure		282	218	218	194	150	127	158	204	191	692	527	386	499
Cumulated recurrent surplus/deficit		−166	−101	−101	−77	−34	−10	−41	−87	−74	−417	−252	−111	−224

Sierra Leone (GER 54)														
Total recurrent education expenditure	16	32	28	26	24	22	21	25	28	31	41	31	27	44
Budgetary allocation required for balance	14%	22%	19%	17%	16%	15%	14%	17%	19%	21%	24%	18%	16%	26%
Cumulated additional recurrent expenditure		88	69	55	47	37	31	53	65	86	200	124	91	224
Cumulated recurrent surplus/deficit		-60	-40	-26	-18	-8	-2	-24	-36	-57	-133	-56	-23	-156
Somalia (GER 15)														
Total recurrent education expenditure	6	39	34	29	27	25	24	32	35	42	57	40	35	69
Budgetary allocation required for balance	16%	72%	63%	53%	50%	45%	44%	58%	64%	77%	87%	61%	54%	106%
Cumulated additional recurrent expenditure		183	157	127	116	103	100	143	158	198	404	269	233	501
Cumulated recurrent surplus/deficit		-170	-143	-114	-103	-89	-86	-129	-145	-185	-372	-237	-201	-468
Sudan (GER 49)														
Total recurrent education expenditure	341	793	703	641	601	552	529	535	592	607	974	740	641	738
Budgetary allocation required for balance	16%	27%	24%	22%	21%	19%	18%	18%	20%	21%	29%	22%	19%	22%
Cumulated additional recurrent expenditure		2,486	1,988	1,645	1,430	1,156	1,032	1,067	1,378	1,460	5,059	3,186	2,397	3,173
Cumulated recurrent surplus/deficit		-1,865	-1,367	-1,024	-809	-534	-410	-445	-756	-838	-3,597	-1,723	-934	-1,710
Tanzania (GER 69)														
Total recurrent education expenditure	277	467	424	385	378	352	336	343	370	396	665	537	472	588
Budgetary allocation required for balance	8%	9%	8%	8%	7%	7%	7%	7%	7%	8%	11%	9%	8%	9%
Cumulated additional recurrent expenditure		1,048	810	599	559	418	326	367	517	657	3,108	2,086	1,560	2,495
Cumulated recurrent surplus/deficit		-318	-79	131	171	313	405	364	214	73	-1,336	-314	212	-723
Togo (GER 102)														
Total recurrent education expenditure	40	57	52	51	49	46	41	44	48	50	68	58	47	61
Budgetary allocation required for balance	13%	13%	12%	11%	11%	10%	9%	10%	11%	11%	13%	11%	9%	12%
Cumulated additional recurrent expenditure		91	65	56	49	32	6	23	41	56	219	145	54	165
Cumulated recurrent surplus/deficit		2	29	37	45	62	88	71	53	38	7	80	171	60
Uganda (GER 70)														
Total recurrent education expenditure	45	70	64	58	57	52	49	73	77	79	94	76	64	105
Budgetary allocation required for balance	17%	19%	17%	16%	15%	14%	13%	20%	21%	21%	22%	17%	15%	24%
Cumulated additional recurrent expenditure		140	103	72	65	41	23	152	175	189	392	246	155	484
Cumulated recurrent surplus/deficit		-48	-12	19	27	50	69	-60	-83	-97	-175	-28	62	-267
Zaire (GER 76)														
Total recurrent education expenditure	139	226	202	186	177	164	154	190	205	215	272	212	181	261
Budgetary allocation required for balance	16%	19%	17%	15%	15%	14%	13%	16%	17%	18%	20%	15%	13%	19%
Cumulated additional recurrent expenditure		480	349	260	207	136	84	279	362	420	1,063	587	339	979
Cumulated recurrent surplus/deficit		-217	-86	3	55	126	179	-16	-99	-157	-442	33	282	-359
Zambia (GER 97)														
Total recurrent education expenditure	132	190	171	168	160	149	138	145	159	158	226	191	159	184
Budgetary allocation required for balance	18%	18%	16%	16%	15%	14%	13%	14%	15%	15%	18%	15%	13%	15%
Cumulated additional recurrent expenditure		319	214	199	154	92	32	75	149	145	757	470	221	414
Cumulated recurrent surplus/deficit		-21	84	99	144	206	265	223	149	152	-45	242	491	298

TABLE A.2. (cont'd)

	1990	2000 UPE No reform	Cost-saving reforms Double-shifting	Increase class-size	Teacher-helpers	Cost-shifting reforms Community financing	Freeze higher ed. subsidies	Quality-enhancing reforms Increase materials	Teacher salaries	SFA Repetition & drop-out	2005 UPE No reform	Cost-saving	Cost-shifting	SFA
			1	2	3	4	5	6	7	8/9		1–3	1–5	1–9
North Africa														
Algeria (GER 95)														
Total recurrent education expenditure	2,152	2,829	2,563	2,347	2,282	2,112	1,992	1,992	2,157	2,145	3,243	2,617	2,228	2,410
Budgetary allocation required for balance	16%	17%	15%	14%	13%	12%	12%	12%	13%	13%	17%	14%	12%	13%
Cumulated additional recurrent expenditure		3,724	2,258	1,072	716	-219	-882	-882	28	-39	8,729	3,716	607	2,061
Cumulated recurrent surplus/deficit		-409	1,058	2,244	2,600	3,535	4,198	4,198	3,287	3,354	-1,010	4,003	7,112	5,658
Egypt (GER 88)														
Total recurrent education expenditure	1,171	1,513	1,362	1,242	1,193	1,109	1,064	1,080	1,174	1,236	1,694	1,335	1,170	1,408
Budgetary allocation required for balance	13%	14%	13%	12%	11%	10%	10%	10%	11%	12%	15%	11%	10%	12%
Cumulated additional recurrent expenditure		1,878	1,051	388	117	-341	-592	-501	12	358	4,178	1,312	-10	1,895
Cumulated recurrent surplus/deficit		-623	204	867	1,138	1,596	1,847	1,756	1,243	897	-1,310	1,556	2,877	973
Morocco (GER 74)														
Total recurrent education expenditure	473	696	625	564	541	500	479	486	529	527	807	628	547	610
Budgetary allocation required for balance	14%	17%	15%	14%	13%	12%	12%	12%	13%	13%	18%	14%	12%	13%
Cumulated additional recurrent expenditure		1,227	838	500	377	151	37	71	308	299	2,672	1,245	598	1,097
Cumulated recurrent surplus/deficit		-657	-269	69	192	418	532	498	261	270	-1,364	63	709	211
Asia														
Bangladesh (GER 60)														
Total recurrent education expenditure	106	182	170	169	163	148	147	231	240	356	204	184	165	475
Budgetary allocation required for balance	11%	17%	15%	15%	15%	14%	13%	21%	22%	32%	17%	16%	14%	41%
Cumulated additional recurrent expenditure		416	350	348	315	233	225	690	737	1,375	787	628	474	2,954
Cumulated recurrent surplus/deficit		-336	-270	-268	-235	-152	-144	-610	-656	-1,295	-605	-446	-292	-2,772
China (GER 129)														
Total recurrent education expenditure	6,433	6,087	5,549	5,034	4,928	4,589	4,483	5,045	5,370	5,737	5,966	4,837	4,347	5,752
Budgetary allocation required for balance	16%	14%	12%	11%	11%	10%	10%	11%	12%	13%	13%	10%	9%	12%
Cumulated additional recurrent expenditure		-1,907	-4,862	-7,696	-8,278	-10,143	-10,729	-7,636	-5,849	-3,833	-3,744	-12,775	-16,694	-5,448
Cumulated recurrent surplus/deficit		4,842	7,797	10,631	11,212	13,077	13,664	10,570	8,784	6,768	10,278	19,310	23,228	11,982

Hong Kong (GER 104)														
Total recurrent education expenditure	1,338	1,420	1,277	1,160	1,122	1,054	1,024	1,025	1,114	1,126	1,467	1,159	1,043	1,151
Budgetary allocation required for balance	16%	15%	14%	12%	12%	11%	11%	11%	12%	12%	15%	12%	11%	12%
Cumulated additional recurrent expenditure		452	−334	−981	−1,191	−1,566	−1,728	−1,724	−1,235	−1,166	1,033	−1,435	−2,358	−1,499
Cumulated recurrent surplus/deficit		158	945	1,591	1,802	2,176	2,339	2,334	1,846	1,776	326	2,794	3,717	2,858
India (GER 98)														
Total recurrent education expenditure	1,513	1,648	1,487	1,390	1,362	1,281	1,257	1,771	1,878	2,243	1,728	1,428	1,306	2,655
Budgetary allocation required for balance	10%	10%	9%	8%	8%	8%	8%	11%	11%	14%	10%	8%	8%	16%
Cumulated additional recurrent expenditure		741	−142	−678	−831	−1,276	−1,410	1,420	2,009	4,015	1,722	−680	−1,659	9,138
Cumulated recurrent surplus/deficit		−51	833	1,368	1,521	1,967	2,100	−730	−1,318	−3,325	−186	2,217	3,196	−7,601
Indonesia (GER 118)														
Total recurrent education expenditure	3,487	3,403	3,119	2,867	2,786	2,620	2,561	2,646	2,819	2,940	3,395	2,783	2,529	2,931
Budgetary allocation required for balance	14%	13%	12%	11%	11%	10%	10%	10%	11%	12%	13%	11%	10%	11%
Cumulated additional recurrent expenditure		−461	−2,025	−3,412	−3,855	−4,768	−5,095	−4,626	−3,672	−3,010	−733	−5,634	−7,664	−4,445
Cumulated recurrent surplus/deficit		1,644	3,208	4,594	5,038	5,950	6,277	5,808	4,855	4,192	3,352	8,252	10,283	7,064
Iran (GER 110)														
Total recurrent education expenditure	3,595	4,660	4,225	3,865	3,749	3,489	3,223	3,223	3,492	3,599	5,360	4,313	3,580	4,051
Budgetary allocation required for balance	22%	21%	19%	17%	17%	15%	14%	14%	15%	16%	20%	16%	14%	15%
Cumulated additional recurrent expenditure		5,855	3,461	1,486	848	−586	−2,050	−2,050	−568	21	14,120	5,739	−124	3,647
Cumulated recurrent surplus/deficit		1,466	3,860	5,836	6,474	7,907	9,371	9,371	7,889	7,300	3,252	11,633	17,496	13,725
Iraq (GER 99)														
Total recurrent education expenditure	2,051	2,966	2,662	2,389	2,292	2,137	1,943	1,954	2,139	2,085	3,564	2,754	2,248	2,429
Budgetary allocation required for balance	16%	16%	14%	13%	12%	11%	10%	10%	11%	11%	16%	12%	10%	11%
Cumulated additional recurrent expenditure		5,034	3,358	1,862	1,326	473	−591	−534	482	186	12,105	5,626	1,575	3,025
Cumulated recurrent surplus/deficit		−92	1,583	3,080	3,616	4,468	5,532	5,475	4,459	4,756	−217	6,262	10,313	8,863
Israel (GER 95)														
Total recurrent education expenditure	792	815	748	660	639	600	600	600	638	706	824	647	607	764
Budgetary allocation required for balance	7%	8%	7%	6%	6%	6%	6%	6%	6%	7%	8%	6%	6%	7%
Cumulated additional recurrent expenditure		128	−244	−723	−839	−1,056	−1,056	−1,056	−848	−473	257	−1,163	−1,483	−220
Cumulated recurrent surplus/deficit		−128	244	723	839	1,056	1,056	1,056	848	473	−257	1,163	1,483	220
Jordan (GER 99)														
Total recurrent education expenditure	282	353	316	285	275	255	242	242	264	263	395	307	264	286
Budgetary allocation required for balance	4%	4%	4%	3%	3%	3%	3%	3%	3%	3%	4%	3%	3%	3%
Cumulated additional recurrent expenditure		389	186	14	−43	−148	−224	−224	−99	−107	897	195	−151	27
Cumulated recurrent surplus/deficit		−12	192	363	421	526	601	601	476	484	−25	677	1,023	845
Korea (GER 98)														
Total recurrent education expenditure	3,197	3,150	2,788	2,594	2,457	2,258	2,258	2,261	2,498	2,446	3,112	2,429	2,231	2,397
Budgetary allocation required for balance	31%	31%	27%	26%	24%	22%	22%	22%	25%	24%	31%	24%	22%	24%
Cumulated additional recurrent expenditure		−258	−2,251	−3,317	−4,068	−5,166	−5,166	−5,146	−3,847	−4,133	−678	−6,147	−7,725	−6,397
Cumulated recurrent surplus/deficit		−262	1,731	2,797	3,547	4,645	4,645	4,625	3,326	3,612	−449	5,020	6,598	5,270

TABLE A.2. (cont'd)

	1990	2000										2005			
		UPE No reform	Cost-saving reforms			Cost-shifting reforms		Quality-enhancing reforms				UPE No reform	Cost-saving	Cost-shifting	SFA
			Double-shifting	Increase class size	Teacher-helpers	Community financing	Freeze higher ed. subsidies	Increase materials	Teacher salaries	SFA Repetition & drop-out					
			1	2	3	4	5	6	7	8/9			1–3	1–5	1–9
Laos PDR (GER 111)															
Total recurrent education expenditure	9	11	10	9	8	8	7	10	11	17		12	9	8	22
Budgetary allocation required for balance	7%	7%	6%	5%	5%	5%	5%	6%	7%	11%		7%	5%	4%	13%
Cumulated additional recurrent expenditure		9	3	-2	-4	-7	-10	5	9	42		24	2	-10	108
Cumulated recurrent surplus/deficit		5	10	16	18	21	24	8	5	-28		8	30	42	-76
Malaysia (GER 101)															
Total recurrent education expenditure	1,729	1,917	1,707	1,518	1,458	1,348	1,315	1,315	1,442	1,448		2,021	1,536	1,370	1,506
Budgetary allocation required for balance	24%	24%	21%	19%	18%	17%	16%	16%	18%	18%		24%	18%	16%	18%
Cumulated additional recurrent expenditure		1,034	-120	-1,158	-1,493	-2,098	-2,279	-2,279	-1,579	-1,544		2,335	-1,541	-2,873	-1,780
Cumulated recurrent surplus/deficit		65	1,220	2,258	2,592	3,197	3,378	3,378	2,678	2,643		132	4,007	5,340	4,247
Mongolia (GER 102)															
Total recurrent education expenditure	56	67	61	56	54	51	48	49	52	53		73	60	52	57
Budgetary allocation required for balance	16%	15%	14%	13%	13%	12%	11%	11%	12%	12%		15%	12%	11%	12%
Cumulated additional recurrent expenditure		59	25	-2	-8	-29	-42	-41	-20	-15		137	29	-33	11
Cumulated recurrent surplus/deficit		5	38	65	72	93	106	104	83	78		9	117	179	135
Myanmar (GER 99)															
Total recurrent education expenditure	71	80	72	69	67	62	60	86	92	126		84	71	63	154
Budgetary allocation required for balance	13%	13%	12%	11%	11%	10%	10%	14%	15%	21%		13%	11%	10%	24%
Cumulated additional recurrent expenditure		48	6	-11	-23	-51	-60	84	112	299		107	-2	-66	663
Cumulated recurrent surplus/deficit		-3	39	56	68	96	105	-39	-67	-254		-5	104	167	-561
Nepal (GER 82)															
Total recurrent education expenditure	40	61	54	50	47	44	41	56	60	78		71	55	47	99
Budgetary allocation required for balance	13%	15%	14%	13%	12%	11%	11%	14%	15%	20%		16%	12%	10%	22%
Cumulated additional recurrent expenditure		115	80	55	41	23	9	89	111	211		247	123	59	476
Cumulated recurrent surplus/deficit		-45	-10	14	28	47	61	-19	-41	-141		-84	40	104	-313

	1	2	3	4	5	6	7	8	9	10	11	12	13	14
Oman (GER 94)														
Total recurrent education expenditure	435	585	523	463	444	409	392	392	428	426	674	512	444	482
Budgetary allocation required for balance	12%	12%	11%	10%	9%	8%	8%	8%	9%	9%	12%	9%	8%	9%
Cumulated additional recurrent expenditure		823	483	152	51	−144	−239	−239	−37	−50	1,913	618	69	372
Cumulated recurrent surplus/deficit		−123	217	548	650	845	940	940	738	751	−278	1,016	1,566	1,263
Pakistan (GER 44)														
Total recurrent education expenditure	266	590	529	483	467	428	409	495	533	637	820	650	563	950
Budgetary allocation required for balance	4%	6%	5%	5%	5%	4%	4%	5%	5%	6%	7%	6%	5%	8%
Cumulated additional recurrent expenditure		1,781	1,446	1,193	1,105	886	786	1,256	1,466	2,037	4,426	3,071	2,376	5,468
Cumulated recurrent surplus/deficit		−1,277	−942	−689	−601	−383	−282	−752	−962	−1,533	−3,237	−1,882	−1,187	−4,279
Philippines (GER 107)														
Total recurrent education expenditure	4,866	5,111	4,593	4,195	3,979	3,705	3,603	3,603	3,922	4,071	5,354	4,168	3,724	4,255
Budgetary allocation required for balance	17%	17%	15%	14%	13%	12%	12%	12%	13%	13%	17%	13%	12%	13%
Cumulated additional recurrent expenditure		1,347	−1,499	−3,692	−4,880	−6,385	−6,945	−6,945	−5,191	−4,370	3,907	−5,584	−9,132	−4,891
Cumulated recurrent surplus/deficit		1,453	4,299	6,491	7,680	9,185	9,745	9,745	7,991	7,170	2,360	11,850	15,398	11,158
Singapore (GER 115)														
Total recurrent education expenditure	831	816	749	689	669	632	618	618	659	664	818	672	614	659
Budgetary allocation required for balance	25%	24%	22%	20%	19%	18%	18%	18%	19%	19%	23%	19%	17%	19%
Cumulated additional recurrent expenditure		−85	−451	−783	−891	−1,095	−1,170	−1,170	−948	−919	−103	−1,277	−1,735	−1,380
Cumulated recurrent surplus/deficit		319	685	1,017	1,125	1,329	1,403	1,403	1,182	1,153	620	1,793	2,252	1,896
Sri Lanka (GER 104)														
Total recurrent education expenditure	197	213	193	177	171	161	157	166	178	183	222	179	161	190
Budgetary allocation required for balance	13%	13%	12%	11%	10%	10%	9%	10%	11%	11%	13%	10%	9%	11%
Cumulated additional recurrent expenditure		89	−21	−112	−141	−200	−222	−171	−103	−80	200	−148	−288	−61
Cumulated recurrent surplus/deficit		24	135	225	255	313	336	285	216	193	54	402	541	315
Syria (GER 111)														
Total recurrent education expenditure	657	791	694	602	571	517	516	523	581	621	885	637	576	715
Budgetary allocation required for balance	17%	16%	14%	12%	11%	10%	10%	10%	12%	12%	16%	11%	10%	13%
Cumulated additional recurrent expenditure		737	202	−302	−474	−771	−773	−738	−417	−201	1,820	−159	−647	463
Cumulated recurrent surplus/deficit		366	901	1,406	1,577	1,874	1,876	1,841	1,521	1,304	762	2,741	3,229	2,119
Thailand (GER 96)														
Total recurrent education expenditure	1,584	1,682	1,493	1,291	1,229	1,132	1,126	1,132	1,241	1,322	1,717	1,255	1,147	1,384
Budgetary allocation required for balance	21%	22%	19%	17%	16%	14%	14%	14%	16%	17%	22%	16%	14%	17%
Cumulated additional recurrent expenditure		536	−503	−1,611	−1,955	−2,489	−2,522	−2,491	−1,886	−1,440	1,062	−2,635	−3,502	−1,607
Cumulated recurrent surplus/deficit		−271	768	1,876	2,220	2,754	2,787	2,756	2,151	1,705	−480	3,217	4,084	2,189
Turkey (GER 115)														
Total recurrent education expenditure	895	944	812	712	675	614	614	658	741	749	995	710	645	790
Budgetary allocation required for balance	11%	10%	8%	7%	7%	6%	6%	7%	8%	8%	9%	7%	6%	7%
Cumulated additional recurrent expenditure		268	−456	−1,006	−1,211	−1,546	−1,548	−1,304	−849	−804	799	−1,479	−1,999	−837
Cumulated recurrent surplus/deficit		579	1,303	1,853	2,058	2,393	2,395	2,151	1,696	1,651	1,126	3,405	3,924	2,762

TABLE A.2. (cont'd)

	1990	2000 UPE No reform	Cost-saving reforms			Cost-shifting reforms		Quality-enhancing reforms			2005 UPE No reform	Cost-saving	Cost-shifting	SFA
			Double-shifting	Increase class-size	Teacher-helpers	Community financing	Freeze higher ed. subsidies	Increase materials	Teacher salaries	SFA Repetition & drop-out				
			1	2	3	4	5	6	7	8/9		1–3	1–5	1–9
Vietnam (GER 102)														
Total recurrent education expenditure	247	297	270	248	241	227	216	267	284	329	327	265	232	383
Budgetary allocation required for balance	16%	15%	14%	13%	12%	12%	11%	14%	15%	17%	15%	12%	11%	18%
Cumulated additional recurrent expenditure		279	127	8	-29	-110	-169	110	207	451	642	150	-116	1,096
Cumulated recurrent surplus/deficit		18	170	289	325	407	466	187	90	-154	40	532	798	-414
Yemen Arab Republic (GER 86)														
Total recurrent education expenditure	304	431	385	384	360	333	317	317	350	478	484	405	349	576
Budgetary allocation required for balance	24%	27%	24%	24%	23%	21%	20%	20%	22%	30%	27%	23%	20%	32%
Cumulated additional recurrent expenditure		694	441	436	307	155	69	69	249	953	1,436	803	356	2,171
Cumulated recurrent surplus/deficit		-267	-13	-9	121	273	358	358	178	-525	-446	187	633	-1,181
Yemen PDR (GER 66)														
Total recurrent education expenditure	25	40	36	32	30	28	27	29	32	36	48	36	31	46
Budgetary allocation required for balance	16%	21%	18%	16%	16%	14%	14%	15%	16%	19%	22%	17%	15%	21%
Cumulated additional recurrent expenditure		85	61	40	31	18	12	23	37	62	182	90	53	166
Cumulated recurrent surplus/deficit		-55	-31	-10	-1	12	18	7	-7	-32	-114	-21	15	-97
Latin America														
Argentina (GER 109)														
Total recurrent education expenditure	715	742	679	574	570	552	544	563	598	710	729	562	533	800
Budgetary allocation required for balance	8%	8%	7%	6%	6%	6%	6%	6%	6%	7%	7%	6%	5%	8%
Cumulated additional recurrent expenditure		145	-203	-776	-798	-901	-941	-838	-647	-30	108	-1,225	-1,457	674
Cumulated recurrent surplus/deficit		56	404	977	999	1,102	1,143	1,039	848	231	337	1,669	1,902	-230
Bolivia (GER 87)														
Total recurrent education expenditure	119	158	142	128	122	114	109	114	124	139	180	139	121	167
Budgetary allocation required for balance	8%	8%	7%	7%	6%	6%	6%	6%	7%	7%	9%	7%	6%	8%
Cumulated additional recurrent expenditure		213	126	46	16	-30	-58	-29	24	106	484	157	15	380
Cumulated recurrent surplus/deficit		-70	18	98	128	173	202	172	119	38	-153	173	315	-50

Brazil (GER 103)

Total recurrent education expenditure	7,516	8,230	7,409	6,619	6,325	5,944	5,770	5,770	6,262	7,957	8,660	6,656	5,987	9,963
Budgetary allocation required for balance	14%	14%	13%	11%	11%	10%	10%	10%	11%	14%	14%	11%	10%	16%
Cumulated additional recurrent expenditure		3,923	−588	−4,933	−6,552	−8,649	−9,605	−9,605	−6,897	2,422	9,147	−6,882	−12,234	19,571
Cumulated recurrent surplus/deficit		856	5,367	9,712	11,331	13,429	14,384	14,384	11,677	2,357	1,576	17,606	22,957	−8,848

Chile (GER 105)

Total recurrent education expenditure	633	619	557	508	484	450	449	449	487	569	618	483	448	609
Budgetary allocation required for balance	17%	17%	15%	14%	13%	12%	12%	12%	13%	15%	16%	13%	12%	16%
Cumulated additional recurrent expenditure		−80	−421	−688	−822	−1,007	−1,014	−1,014	−803	−356	−125	−1,202	−1,486	−196
Cumulated recurrent surplus/deficit		115	456	723	857	1,042	1,049	1,049	838	391	202	1,279	1,562	272

Colombia (GER 114)

Total recurrent education expenditure	967	957	869	797	776	726	714	720	775	853	958	776	709	885
Budgetary allocation required for balance	21%	20%	18%	17%	16%	15%	15%	15%	16%	18%	19%	16%	14%	18%
Cumulated additional recurrent expenditure		−55	−539	−933	−1,052	−1,322	−1,388	−1,356	−1,054	−627	−73	−1,523	−2,061	−653
Cumulated recurrent surplus/deficit		383	866	1,261	1,380	1,650	1,716	1,684	1,381	955	799	2,249	2,787	1,379

Costa Rica (GER 98)

Total recurrent education expenditure	171	193	179	168	163	155	147	148	157	159	204	172	152	166
Budgetary allocation required for balance	18%	18%	17%	16%	15%	14%	14%	14%	15%	15%	18%	15%	13%	15%
Cumulated additional recurrent expenditure		119	40	−22	−48	−90	−134	−131	−82	−68	264	7	−157	−46
Cumulated recurrent surplus/deficit		−10	69	131	157	199	243	240	191	177	−19	238	402	290

Cuba (GER 105)

Total recurrent education expenditure	528	550	496	418	405	379	372	372	401	405	564	415	378	411
Budgetary allocation required for balance	16%	15%	14%	11%	11%	10%	10%	10%	11%	11%	15%	11%	10%	11%
Cumulated additional recurrent expenditure		121	−174	−604	−679	−820	−859	−859	−700	−676	286	−908	−1,205	−940
Cumulated recurrent surplus/deficit		88	384	814	889	1,029	1,069	1,069	910	886	180	1,374	1,671	1,406

Dominican Republic (GER 101)

Total recurrent education expenditure	41	47	41	41	39	36	35	41	44	52	50	42	37	58
Budgetary allocation required for balance	12%	11%	10%	10%	10%	9%	9%	10%	11%	13%	11%	10%	8%	13%
Cumulated additional recurrent expenditure		32	4	3	−10	−25	−33	−1	19	61	73	8	−33	141
Cumulated recurrent surplus/deficit		2	30	30	43	58	66	35	15	−27	3	67	109	−65

Ecuador (GER 118)

Total recurrent education expenditure	372	410	372	338	328	308	293	296	320	363	435	348	303	402
Budgetary allocation required for balance	24%	22%	20%	18%	18%	17%	16%	16%	17%	20%	22%	17%	15%	20%
Cumulated additional recurrent expenditure		206	−3	−187	−245	−354	−439	−420	−291	−53	501	−194	−556	237
Cumulated recurrent surplus/deficit		218	427	611	670	778	863	844	715	477	471	1,165	1,527	735

El Salvador (GER 79)

Total recurrent education expenditure	129	158	142	137	132	124	122	126	137	159	174	144	132	196
Budgetary allocation required for balance	20%	22%	20%	19%	18%	17%	17%	18%	19%	22%	23%	19%	18%	26%
Cumulated additional recurrent expenditure		161	74	48	15	−28	−40	−18	43	167	360	124	29	541
Cumulated recurrent surplus/deficit		−102	−15	11	43	87	99	76	16	−109	−229	7	102	−410

TABLE A.2. (cont'd)

	1990	2000 UPE No reform	Cost-saving reforms Double-shifting (1)	Increase class-size (2)	Teacher-helpers (3)	Cost-shifting Community financing (4)	Freeze higher ed. subsidies (5)	Quality-enhancing Increase materials (6)	Teacher salaries (7)	SFA Repetition & drop-out (8/9)	2005 UPE No reform	Cost-shifting (1-3)	Cost-saving (1-5)	SFA (1-9)
Guatemala (GER 76)														
Total recurrent education expenditure	98	137	124	113	109	102	98	102	111	138	159	127	112	180
Budgetary allocation required for balance	16%	19%	17%	16%	15%	14%	14%	14%	15%	19%	20%	16%	14%	23%
Cumulated additional recurrent expenditure		218	143	86	63	22	1	23	71	219	493	231	115	660
Cumulated recurrent surplus/deficit		-114	-38	19	42	83	104	82	34	-114	-253	9	125	-420
Haiti (GER 95)														
Total recurrent education expenditure	15	18	16	14	13	12	12	17	18	27	19	14	13	33
Budgetary allocation required for balance	23%	24%	21%	19%	18%	16%	16%	23%	24%	36%	24%	18%	16%	42%
Cumulated additional recurrent expenditure		15	4	-4	-9	-15	-16	11	18	65	32	-5	-17	146
Cumulated recurrent surplus/deficit		-4	7	15	20	26	27	0	-7	-53	-7	30	43	-120
Honduras (GER 106)														
Total recurrent education expenditure	146	181	164	151	145	135	127	128	140	154	205	163	139	172
Budgetary allocation required for balance	18%	18%	16%	15%	14%	13%	12%	12%	13%	15%	17%	14%	12%	15%
Cumulated additional recurrent expenditure		196	97	29	-7	-59	-106	-97	-35	45	471	138	-57	209
Cumulated recurrent surplus/deficit		39	137	205	242	294	341	332	269	193	77	410	605	336
Jamaica (GER 105)														
Total recurrent education expenditure	82	82	74	69	67	63	62	64	69	69	82	67	62	69
Budgetary allocation required for balance	13%	13%	12%	11%	10%	10%	10%	10%	11%	11%	13%	10%	10%	11%
Cumulated additional recurrent expenditure		-3	-44	-72	-86	-109	-12	-102	-76	-72	-4	-124	-163	-106
Cumulated recurrent surplus/deficit		12	53	82	95	119	121	111	85	81	24	144	184	126
Mexico (GER 119)														
Total recurrent education expenditure	2,998	3,105	2,910	2,754	2,695	2,581	2,426	2,465	2,586	2,677	3,221	2,804	2,448	2,733
Budgetary allocation required for balance	11%	10%	10%	9%	9%	9%	8%	8%	9%	9%	10%	9%	8%	9%
Cumulated additional recurrent expenditure		585	-486	-1,344	-1,667	-2,298	-3,149	-2,931	-2,266	-1,766	1,781	-1,556	-4,406	-2,121
Cumulated recurrent surplus/deficit		1,321	2,392	3,250	3,573	4,204	5,056	4,837	4,173	3,673	2,497	5,834	8,683	6,399

Nicaragua (GER 98)														
Total recurrent education expenditure	97	121	109	101	96	89	84	88	95	128	135	106	91	160
Budgetary allocation required for balance	12%	12%	11%	10%	10%	9%	9%	9%	10%	13%	12%	10%	8%	15%
Cumulated additional recurrent expenditure		133	66	20	-8	-44	-72	-52	-11	168	301	73	-49	500
Cumulated recurrent surplus/deficit		-9	57	104	132	168	195	176	134	-45	-17	212	334	-215
Panama (GER 106)														
Total recurrent education expenditure	196	189	172	155	149	140	140	140	151	152	188	148	139	151
Budgetary allocation required for balance	18%	17%	16%	14%	14%	13%	13%	13%	14%	14%	17%	13%	13%	14%
Cumulated additional recurrent expenditure		-37	-131	-224	-255	-305	-305	-305	-249	-240	-66	-381	-452	-357
Cumulated recurrent surplus/deficit		37	131	224	255	305	305	305	249	240	66	381	452	357
Paraguay (GER 102)														
Total recurrent education expenditure	60	75	68	62	61	57	54	57	61	73	84	69	59	89
Budgetary allocation required for balance	14%	13%	12%	11%	11%	10%	10%	10%	11%	13%	13%	11%	9%	14%
Cumulated additional recurrent expenditure		85	48	15	9	-15	-32	-16	7	74	194	71	-8	235
Cumulated recurrent surplus/deficit		3	40	73	79	103	120	104	81	14	10	134	212	-30
Peru (GER 122)														
Total recurrent education expenditure	192	190	167	149	142	131	129	149	163	185	194	144	131	199
Budgetary allocation required for balance	12%	11%	10%	8%	8%	7%	7%	8%	9%	11%	10%	8%	7%	11%
Cumulated additional recurrent expenditure		-9	-138	-239	-276	-338	-345	-238	-157	-37	13	-382	-491	57
Cumulated recurrent surplus/deficit		155	284	385	422	484	491	384	303	183	316	711	819	271
Trinidad and Tobago (GER 98)														
Total recurrent education expenditure	225	252	222	192	182	165	165	165	184	187	266	193	174	200
Budgetary allocation required for balance	16%	16%	14%	12%	11%	10%	10%	10%	11%	12%	16%	11%	10%	12%
Cumulated additional recurrent expenditure		150	-19	-181	-235	-328	-332	-329	-228	-209	331	-260	-412	-204
Cumulated recurrent surplus/deficit		-21	149	310	365	458	462	458	357	338	-41	550	701	494
Uruguay (GER 110)														
Total recurrent education expenditure	119	113	103	93	90	84	84	84	90	91	112	89	83	90
Budgetary allocation required for balance	14%	13%	12%	11%	10%	10%	10%	10%	10%	10%	13%	10%	9%	10%
Cumulated additional recurrent expenditure		-29	-85	-141	-159	-189	-191	-191	-158	-154	-51	-239	-285	-232
Cumulated recurrent surplus/deficit		36	92	148	166	196	198	198	164	161	65	253	299	247
Venezuela (GER 107)														
Total recurrent education expenditure	2,575	2,918	2,762	2,623	2,567	2,488	2,247	2,258	2,352	2,384	3,132	2,757	2,297	2,456
Budgetary allocation required for balance	28%	27%	26%	24%	24%	23%	21%	21%	22%	22%	27%	24%	20%	21%
Cumulated additional recurrent expenditure		1,884	1,029	265	-42	-479	-1,805	-1,744	-1,228	-1,050	4,452	1,457	-2,227	-953
Cumulated recurrent surplus/deficit		390	1,245	2,009	2,316	2,752	4,078	4,018	3,502	3,324	703	3,698	7,382	6,108
Other LDCs														
Bulgaria (GER 104)														
Total recurrent education expenditure	1,519	1,373	1,241	1,086	1,049	991	1,015	1,015	1,092	1,138	1,305	998	977	1,107
Budgetary allocation required for balance	16%	15%	14%	12%	12%	11%	11%	11%	12%	13%	15%	12%	11%	13%
Cumulated additional recurrent expenditure		-805	-1,531	-2,381	-2,585	-2,903	-2,774	-2,774	-2,353	-2,095	-1,711	-4,172	-4,337	-3,297
Cumulated recurrent surplus/deficit		160	886	1,736	1,940	2,259	2,130	2,130	1,708	1,450	331	2,792	2,957	1,917

TABLE A.2. (cont'd)

	1990	2000									2005			
		UPE No reform	Cost-saving reforms			Cost-shifting reforms		Quality-enhancing reforms			UPE No reform	Cost-saving	Cost-shifting	SFA
			Double-shifting	Increase class-size	Teacher-helpers	Community financing	Freeze higher ed. subsidies	Increase materials	Teacher salaries	SFA Repetition & drop-out				
			1	2	3	4	5	6	7	8/9		1–3	1–5	1–9
Czechoslovakia (GER 98)														
Total recurrent education expenditure	5,246	4,551	4,188	3,749	3,657	3,472	3,472	3,631	3,843	3,867	4,245	3,411	3,237	3,705
Budgetary allocation required for balance	9%	9%	8%	8%	7%	7%	7%	7%	8%	8%	9%	7%	7%	8%
Cumulated additional recurrent expenditure		−3,823	−5,823	−8,238	−8,739	−9,761	−9,761	−8,882	−7,720	−7,585	−8,011	−14,685	−16,072	−12,330
Cumulated recurrent surplus/deficit		−224	1,776	4,190	4,692	5,713	5,713	4,835	3,673	3,538	−502	6,172	7,559	3,817
German Democratic Republic (GER 105)														
Total recurrent education expenditure	1,790	1,735	1,564	1,331	1,275	1,191	1,191	1,191	1,285	1,466	1,721	1,265	1,182	1,556
Budgetary allocation required for balance	16%	15%	14%	12%	11%	10%	10%	10%	11%	13%	15%	11%	10%	13%
Cumulated additional recurrent expenditure		−301	−1,245	−2,524	−2,831	−3,292	−3,292	−3,292	−2,777	−1,783	−549	−4,198	−4,862	−1,875
Cumulated recurrent surplus/deficit		301	1,245	2,524	2,831	3,292	3,292	3,292	2,777	1,783	549	4,198	4,862	1,875
Greece (GER 104)														
Total recurrent education expenditure	781	733	664	595	574	536	542	542	584	586	714	559	531	571
Budgetary allocation required for balance	16%	15%	14%	12%	12%	11%	11%	11%	12%	12%	15%	12%	11%	12%
Cumulated additional recurrent expenditure		−262	−645	−1,023	−1,138	−1,348	−1,312	−1,312	−1,085	−1,074	−539	−1,779	−1,998	−1,682
Cumulated recurrent surplus/deficit		94	476	855	970	1,180	1,144	1,144	916	905	174	1,415	1,634	1,318
Hungary (GER 98)														
Total recurrent education expenditure	135	106	96	82	79	74	74	76	82	83	94	70	66	75
Budgetary allocation required for balance	2%	2%	2%	1%	1%	1%	1%	1%	1%	1%	2%	1%	1%	1%
Cumulated additional recurrent expenditure		−160	−218	−294	−310	−338	−338	−327	−294	−289	−330	−523	−559	−484
Cumulated recurrent surplus/deficit		−6	51	127	143	171	171	160	127	121	−13	180	216	144
Papua New Guinea (GER 70)														
Total recurrent education expenditure	67	101	90	88	84	78	75	77	84	89	117	98	86	106
Budgetary allocation required for balance	18%	23%	20%	20%	19%	17%	17%	17%	19%	20%	24%	20%	18%	22%
Cumulated additional recurrent expenditure		185	128	117	94	58	44	52	91	122	402	247	153	312
Cumulated recurrent surplus/deficit		−113	−56	−45	−22	14	28	20	−19	−50	−237	−82	12	−147

Poland (GER 101)														
Total recurrent education expenditure	3,862	3,650	3,286	2,817	2,699	2,523	2,561	2,561	2,762	2,776	3,552	2,627	2,512	2,725
Budgetary allocation required for balance	16%	15%	14%	12%	11%	11%	11%	11%	12%	12%	15%	11%	11%	12%
Cumulated additional recurrent expenditure		-1,167	-3,165	-5,748	-6,394	-7,362	-7,154	-7,154	-6,047	-5,970	-2,479	-9,878	-10,800	-9,097
Cumulated recurrent surplus/deficit		128	2,126	4,709	5,355	6,323	6,116	6,116	5,009	4,932	242	7,640	8,562	6,859
Romania (GER 96)														
Total recurrent education expenditure	2,870	2,688	2,420	2,194	2,104	1,996	1,996	1,996	2,164	2,408	2,591	2,029	1,924	2,494
Budgetary allocation required for balance	2%	2%	2%	2%	2%	2%	2%	2%	2%	2%	2%	2%	2%	2%
Cumulated additional recurrent expenditure		-1,002	-2,476	-3,723	-4,213	-4,810	-4,810	-4,810	-3,886	-2,541	-2,236	-6,734	-7,572	-3,009
Cumulated recurrent surplus/deficit		-363	1,111	2,358	2,848	3,445	3,445	3,445	2,522	1,177	-676	3,822	4,659	97
Yugoslavia (GER 96)														
Total recurrent education expenditure	1,210	1,146	1,041	940	917	859	859	859	923	959	1,108	887	830	935
Budgetary allocation required for balance	16%	16%	14%	13%	13%	12%	12%	12%	13%	13%	16%	13%	12%	14%
Cumulated additional recurrent expenditure		-351	-929	-1,481	-1,609	-1,931	-1,931	-1,931	-1,578	-1,380	-813	-2,583	-3,035	-2,194
Cumulated recurrent surplus/deficit		-162	416	967	1,095	1,417	1,417	1,417	1,064	867	-285	1,484	1,936	1,096
Grouped omitted countries (GER 90)														
Total recurrent education expenditure	4,957	6,091	5,491	5,059	4,865	4,516	4,367	4,367	4,745	5,138	6,678	5,335	4,718	5,795
Budgetary allocation required for balance	16%	17%	15%	14%	13%	12%	12%	12%	13%	14%	17%	14%	12%	15%
Cumulated additional recurrent expenditure		6,236	2,934	558	-505	-2,427	-3,246	-3,246	-1,166	994	13,767	3,021	-1,910	6,706
Cumulated recurrent surplus/deficit		-2,138	1,164	3,540	4,603	6,525	7,344	7,344	5,264	3,104	-4,499	6,247	11,178	2,562

Notes: All countries are included with the exception of six countries with GER >100 which would be able to finance SFA without reforms 1–5 being implemented.

Total Recurrent Expenditure on Education: these data are all as derived from national simulations of UPE and SFA.

Budgetary Allocation Required: data for 1990 are estimates based upon reported data from UNESCO and World Bank sources for the mid-1980s. Estimates for 2000 and 2005 and for each level of reform are the proportions which would be required to finance all the expenditures shown in the first line entry, for each country, as calculated in national simulations.

Cumulated Additional Recurrent Expenditure on Education: calculated in national simulations, as described in technical appendix.

Cumulated Surplus/Deficit: calculated by comparing cumulated additional expenditures and revenues, assuming per capita public revenues available to finance education remain constant over 1990–2005. See technical appendix.

TABLE A.3. *Simulated costs and financing of UPE and SFA in 2000 and 2005, all countries with GERs greater than 100 separately, policy reforms 6–9 only (in $m at constant 1986 prices)*

	1990	2000									2005			
		UPE No reform	Cost saving			Cost shifting		Quality enhancing		SFA	UPE No reform	Cost saving	Cost shifting	SFA
			1	2	3	4	5	6	7	8/9		1–3	1–5	1–9
Sub-Saharan Africa														
Botswana (GER 112)														
Total recurrent education expenditure	105	135	135	135	135	135	135	135	144	141	149	149	149	156
Budgetary allocation required for balance	20%	19%	19%	19%	19%	19%	19%	19%	21%	20%	19%	19%	19%	19%
Cumulated additional recurrent expenditure		161	161	161	161	161	161	161	211	197	350	350	350	407
Cumulated recurrent surplus/deficit		38	38	38	38	38	38	38	-12	2	119	119	119	63
Cameroon (GER 109)														
Total recurrent education expenditure	428	587	587	587	587	587	587	590	645	632	691	691	691	751
Budgetary allocation required for balance	14%	13%	13%	13%	13%	13%	13%	13%	14%	14%	13%	13%	13%	14%
Cumulated additional recurrent expenditure		875	875	875	875	875	875	894	1,195	1,123	2,103	2,103	2,103	2,589
Cumulated recurrent surplus/deficit		155	155	155	155	155	155	136	-165	-92	375	375	375	-111
Gabon (GER 123)														
Total recurrent education expenditure	143	195	195	195	195	195	195	195	213	210	231	231	231	255
Budgetary allocation required for balance	13%	12%	12%	12%	12%	12%	12%	12%	13%	13%	11%	11%	11%	12%
Cumulated additional recurrent expenditure		285	285	285	285	285	285	285	384	368	704	704	704	892
Cumulated recurrent surplus/deficit		128	128	128	128	128	128	128	29	45	306	306	306	117
Lesotho (GER 115)														
Total recurrent education expenditure	26	34	34	34	34	34	34	36	40	44	38	38	38	53
Budgetary allocation required for balance	17%	16%	16%	16%	16%	16%	16%	17%	19%	21%	16%	16%	16%	21%
Cumulated additional recurrent expenditure		43	43	43	43	43	43	56	78	97	94	94	94	210
Cumulated recurrent surplus/deficit		11	11	11	11	11	11	-2	-24	-44	33	33	33	-82
Madagascar (GER 121)														
Total recurrent education expenditure	76	91	91	91	91	91	91	103	117	158	104	104	104	214
Budgetary allocation required for balance	16%	13%	13%	13%	13%	13%	13%	15%	17%	23%	13%	13%	13%	27%
Cumulated additional recurrent expenditure		83	83	83	83	83	83	151	225	453	228	228	228	1,106
Cumulated recurrent surplus/deficit		82	82	82	82	82	82	.15	-59	-287	167	167	167	-711

Mauritius (GER 107)

Total recurrent education expenditure	40	36	36	36	36	36	36	36	40	34	34	34	34	31
Budgetary allocation required for balance	15%	14%	14%	14%	14%	14%	14%	14%	16%	13%	14%	14%	14%	13%
Cumulated additional recurrent expenditure		−20	−20	−20	−20	−20	−20	−20	1	−32	−44	−44	−44	−69
Cumulated recurrent surplus/deficit		7	7	7	7	7	7	7	−14	19	16	16	16	41

Togo (GER 102)

Total recurrent education expenditure	40	57	57	57	57	57	57	60	65	69	68	68	68	86
Budgetary allocation required for balance	13%	13%	13%	13%	13%	13%	13%	14%	15%	16%	13%	13%	13%	16%
Cumulated additional recurrent expenditure		91	91	91	91	91	91	110	136	156	219	219	219	364
Cumulated recurrent surplus/deficit		2	2	2	2	2	2	−16	−42	−62	7	7	7	−139

Zimbabwe (GER 136)

Total recurrent education expenditure	338	386	386	386	386	386	386	386	426	438	426	426	426	489
Budgetary allocation required for balance	25%	20%	20%	20%	20%	20%	20%	20%	22%	23%	19%	19%	19%	22%
Cumulated additional recurrent expenditure		263	263	263	263	263	263	263	482	550	700	700	700	1,207
Cumulated recurrent surplus/deficit		476	476	476	476	476	476	476	257	189	1,063	1,063	1,063	556

North Africa

Tunisia (GER 117)

Total recurrent education expenditure	444	473	473	473	473	473	473	476	525	483	487	487	487	490
Budgetary allocation required for balance	15%	14%	14%	14%	14%	14%	14%	14%	15%	14%	13%	13%	13%	13%
Cumulated additional recurrent expenditure		160	160	160	160	160	160	177	445	213	343	343	343	366
Cumulated recurrent surplus/deficit		204	204	204	204	204	204	187	−81	151	481	481	481	458

Asia

China (GER 129)

Total recurrent education expenditure	6,433	6,087	6,087	6,087	6,087	6,087	6,087	6,710	7,235	7,747	5,965	5,965	5,965	7,834
Budgetary allocation required for balance	16%	14%	14%	14%	14%	14%	14%	15%	16%	17%	13%	13%	13%	17%
Cumulated additional recurrent expenditure		−1,907	−1,907	−1,907	−1,907	−1,907	−1,907	1,520	4,410	7,225	−3,744	−3,744	−3,744	11,202
Cumulated recurrent surplus/deficit		4,842	4,842	4,842	4,842	4,842	4,842	1,415	−1,475	−4,291	10,278	10,278	10,278	−4,668

Hong Kong (GER 104)

Total recurrent education expenditure	1,338	1,420	1,420	1,420	1,420	1,420	1,420	1,421	1,561	1,578	1,467	1,467	1,467	1,632
Budgetary allocation required for balance	16%	15%	15%	15%	15%	15%	15%	15%	17%	17%	15%	15%	15%	17%
Cumulated additional recurrent expenditure		452	452	452	452	452	452	457	1,227	1,318	1,033	1,033	1,033	2,353
Cumulated recurrent surplus/deficit		158	158	158	158	158	158	153	−616	−708	326	326	326	−994

Indonesia (GER 118)

Total recurrent education expenditure	3,487	3,403	3,403	3,403	3,403	3,403	3,403	3,497	3,776	3,937	3,395	3,395	3,395	3,960
Budgetary allocation required for balance	14%	13%	13%	13%	13%	13%	13%	14%	15%	15%	13%	13%	13%	15%
Cumulated additional recurrent expenditure		−462	−462	−462	−462	−462	−462	57	1,587	2,475	−734	−734	−734	3,786
Cumulated recurrent surplus/deficit		1,644	1,644	1,644	1,644	1,644	1,644	1,125	−405	−1,292	3,353	3,353	3,353	−1,167

TABLE A.3. (cont'd)

	1990	2000 UPE No reform	2000 Cost saving 1	2000 Cost saving 2	2000 Cost saving 3	2000 Cost shifting 4	2000 Cost shifting 5	2000 Quality enhancing 6	2000 Quality enhancing 7	2000 SFA 8/9	2005 UPE No reform	2005 Cost saving 1-3	2005 Cost shifting 1-5	2005 SFA 1-9
Iran (GER 110)														
Total recurrent education expenditure	3,595	4,660	4,660	4,660	4,660	4,660	4,660	4,660	5,086	5,226	5,360	5,360	5,360	6,064
Budgetary allocation required for balance	22%	21%	21%	21%	21%	21%	21%	21%	22%	23%	20%	20%	20%	23%
Cumulated additional recurrent expenditure		5,855	5,855	5,855	5,855	5,855	5,855	5,855	8,196	8,971	14,120	14,120	14,120	19,748
Cumulated recurrent surplus/deficit		1,466	1,466	1,466	1,466	1,466	1,466	-875	-1,650	3,252	3,252	3,252	3,252	-2,376
Laos PDR (GER 111)														
Total recurrent education expenditure	9	11	11	11	11	11	11	14	15	23	12	12	12	32
Budgetary allocation required for balance	7%	7%	7%	7%	7%	7%	7%	9%	9%	15%	7%	7%	7%	18%
Cumulated additional recurrent expenditure		9	9	9	9	9	9	27	32	80	24	24	24	186
Cumulated recurrent surplus/deficit		5	5	5	5	5	5	-13	-18	-66	8	8	8	-154
Malaysia (GER 101)														
Total recurrent education expenditure	1,729	1,917	1,917	1,917	1,917	1,917	1,917	1,917	2,122	2,122	2,021	2,021	2,021	2,230
Budgetary allocation required for balance	24%	24%	24%	24%	24%	24%	24%	24%	26%	26%	24%	24%	24%	26%
Cumulated additional recurrent expenditure		1,035	1,035	1,035	1,035	1,035	1,035	1,035	2,164	2,165	2,336	2,336	2,336	4,011
Cumulated recurrent surplus/deficit		65	65	65	65	65	65	65	-1,065	-1,065	130	130	130	-1,544
Mongolia (GER 102)														
Total recurrent education expenditure	56	67	67	67	67	67	67	67	73	74	73	73	73	81
Budgetary allocation required for balance	16%	15%	15%	15%	15%	15%	15%	15%	17%	17%	15%	15%	15%	17%
Cumulated additional recurrent expenditure		59	59	59	59	59	59	61	93	99	137	137	137	201
Cumulated recurrent surplus/deficit		5	5	5	5	5	5	3	-30	-35	9	9	9	-55
Philippines (GER 107)														
Total recurrent education expenditure	4,866	5,111	5,111	5,111	5,111	5,111	5,111	5,111	5,617	5,843	5,354	5,354	5,354	6,179
Budgetary allocation required for balance	17%	17%	17%	17%	17%	17%	17%	17%	18%	19%	17%	17%	17%	19%
Cumulated additional recurrent expenditure		1,347	1,347	1,347	1,347	1,347	1,347	1,347	4,131	5,373	3,907	3,907	3,907	10,502
Cumulated recurrent surplus/deficit		1,453	1,453	1,453	1,453	1,453	1,453	1,453	-1,331	-2,573	2,360	2,360	2,360	-4,235
Singapore (GER 115)														
Total recurrent education expenditure	831	816	816	816	816	816	816	816	881	885	818	818	818	886
Budgetary allocation required for balance	25%	24%	24%	24%	24%	24%	24%	24%	25%	26%	23%	23%	23%	25%
Cumulated additional recurrent expenditure		-85	-85	-85	-85	-85	-85	-85	273	298	-104	-104	-104	439
Cumulated recurrent surplus/deficit		319	319	319	319	319	319	319	-39	-65	620	620	620	77

Sri Lanka (GER 104)														
Total recurrent education expenditure	197	213	213	213	213	213	213	224	243	248	222	222	222	260
Budgetary allocation required for balance	13%	13%	13%	13%	13%	13%	13%	14%	15%	15%	13%	13%	13%	15%
Cumulated additional recurrent expenditure		89	89	89	89	89	145	253	281	200	200	200	506	
Cumulated recurrent surplus/deficit		24	24	24	24	24	-32	-139	-168	54	54	54	-252	
Syria (GER 111)														
Total recurrent education expenditure	657	791	791	791	791	791	791	798	893	952	885	885	885	1,096
Budgetary allocation required for balance	17%	16%	16%	16%	16%	16%	16%	16%	18%	19%	16%	16%	16%	19%
Cumulated additional recurrent expenditure		737	737	737	737	737	776	1,299	1,621	1,821	1,821	1,821	3,515	
Cumulated recurrent surplus/deficit		366	366	366	366	366	327	-196	-518	761	761	761	-933	
Turkey (GER 115)														
Total recurrent education expenditure	895	944	944	944	944	944	944	993	1,121	1,131	995	995	995	1,196
Budgetary allocation required for balance	11%	10%	10%	10%	10%	10%	10%	10%	11%	11%	9%	9%	9%	11%
Cumulated additional recurrent expenditure		267	267	267	267	267	536	1,244	1,299	799	799	799	2,410	
Cumulated recurrent surplus/deficit		579	579	579	579	579	311	-397	-452	1,126	1,126	1,126	-485	
Vietnam (GER 102)														
Total recurrent education expenditure	247	297	297	297	297	297	297	353	380	440	327	327	327	520
Budgetary allocation required for balance	16%	15%	15%	15%	15%	15%	15%	18%	20%	23%	15%	15%	15%	24%
Cumulated additional recurrent expenditure		279	279	279	279	279	587	736	1,065	642	642	642	2,190	
Cumulated recurrent surplus/deficit		18	18	18	18	18	-290	-439	-768	40	40	40	-1,507	
Latin America														
Argentina (GER 109)														
Total recurrent education expenditure	715	742	742	742	742	742	742	763	825	993	729	729	729	1,126
Budgetary allocation required for balance	8%	8%	8%	8%	8%	8%	8%	8%	8%	10%	7%	7%	7%	11%
Cumulated additional recurrent expenditure		145	145	145	145	145	260	601	1,526	108	108	108	3,284	
Cumulated recurrent surplus/deficit		56	56	56	56	56	-59	-399	-1,325	337	337	337	-2,839	
Brazil (GER 103)														
Total recurrent education expenditure	7,517	8,230	8,230	8,230	8,230	8,230	8,230	8,230	9,032	11,549	8,660	8,660	8,660	14,439
Budgetary allocation required for balance	14%	14%	14%	14%	14%	14%	14%	14%	15%	20%	14%	14%	14%	23%
Cumulated additional recurrent expenditure		3,923	3,923	3,923	3,923	3,923	3,923	8,336	22,174	9,146	9,146	9,146	55,375	
Cumulated recurrent surplus/deficit		857	857	857	857	857	857	-3,556	-17,395	1,578	1,578	1,578	-44,652	
Chile (GER 105)														
Total recurrent education expenditure	633	619	619	619	619	619	619	619	680	802	618	618	618	861
Budgetary allocation required for balance	17%	17%	17%	17%	17%	17%	17%	17%	18%	21%	16%	16%	16%	23%
Cumulated additional recurrent expenditure		-80	-80	-80	-80	-80	-80	254	928	-125	-125	-125	1,819	
Cumulated recurrent surplus/deficit		115	115	115	115	115	115	-219	-893	202	202	202	-1,743	

TABLE A.3. (cont'd)

	1990	2000 UPE No reform	Cost saving 1	2	3	Cost shifting 4	5	Quality enhancing 6	7	SFA 8/9	2005 UPE No reform	Cost saving 1-3	Cost shifting 1-5	SFA 1-9
Colombia (GER 114)														
Total recurrent education expenditure	967	957	957	957	957	957	957	963	1,049	1,153	958	958	958	1,205
Budgetary allocation required for balance	21%	20%	20%	20%	20%	20%	20%	20%	22%	24%	19%	19%	19%	24%
Cumulated additional recurrent expenditure		-55	-55	-55	-55	-55	-55	-20	453	1,023	-73	-73	-73	1,902
Cumulated recurrent surplus/deficit		383	383	383	383	383	383	348	-125	-696	799	799	799	-1,176
Cuba (GER 105)														
Total recurrent education expenditure	528	550	550	550	550	550	550	550	603	606	564	564	564	619
Budgetary allocation required for balance	16%	15%	15%	15%	15%	15%	15%	15%	17%	17%	15%	15%	15%	16%
Cumulated additional recurrent expenditure		122	122	122	122	122	122	122	410	427	286	286	286	725
Cumulated recurrent surplus/deficit		88	88	88	86	88	88	88	-201	-217	180	180	180	-259
Dominican Republic (GER 101)														
Total recurrent education expenditure	41	47	47	47	47	47	47	53	58	68	50	50	50	77
Budgetary allocation required for balance	12%	11%	11%	11%	11%	11%	11%	13%	14%	17%	11%	11%	11%	18%
Cumulated additional recurrent expenditure		32	32	32	32	32	32	66	94	149	73	73	73	293
Cumulated recurrent surplus/deficit		2	2	2	2	2	2	-33	-60	-116	3	3	3	-217
Ecuador (GER 118)														
Total recurrent education expenditure	372	410	410	410	410	410	410	414	451	513	435	435	435	579
Budgetary allocation required for balance	24%	22%	22%	22%	22%	22%	22%	22%	24%	28%	22%	22%	22%	29%
Cumulated additional recurrent expenditure		206	206	206	206	206	206	227	431	775	501	501	501	1,656
Cumulated recurrent surplus/deficit		218	218	218	218	218	218	197	-7	-351	471	471	471	-684
Honduras (GER 106)														
Total recurrent education expenditure	146	181	181	181	181	181	181	183	201	220	205	205	205	251
Budgetary allocation required for balance	18%	18%	18%	18%	18%	18%	18%	18%	19%	21%	17%	17%	17%	21%
Cumulated additional recurrent expenditure		196	196	196	196	196	196	206	302	408	471	471	471	844
Cumulated recurrent surplus/deficit		39	39	39	39	39	39	29	-67	-173	77	77	77	-296
Jamaica (GER 105)														
Total recurrent education expenditure	82	82	82	82	82	82	82	84	91	92	82	82	82	92
Budgetary allocation required for balance	13%	13%	13%	13%	13%	13%	13%	13%	14%	14%	13%	13%	13%	14%
Cumulated additional recurrent expenditure		-3	-3	-3	-3	-3	-3	8	48	52	-4	-4	-4	78
Cumulated recurrent surplus/deficit		12	12	12	12	12	12	1	-39	-43	24	24	24	-57

Mexico (GER 119)

Total recurrent education expenditure	2,998	3,105	3,105	3,105	3,105	3,105	3,105	3,149	3,339	3,471	3,221	3,221	3,221	3,638
Budgetary allocation required for balance	11%	10%	10%	10%	10%	10%	10%	11%	11%	12%	10%	10%	10%	12%
Cumulated additional recurrent expenditure		585	585	585	585	585	585	827	1,875	2,600	1,780	1,780	1,780	5,114
Cumulated recurrent surplus/deficit		1,322	1,322	1,322	1,322	1,322	1,322	1,080	32	-694	2,498	2,498	2,498	-837

Panama (GER 106)

Total recurrent education expenditure	196	189	189	189	189	189	189	189	206	207	188	188	188	206
Budgetary allocation required for balance	18%	17%	17%	17%	17%	17%	17%	17%	19%	19%	17%	17%	17%	19%
Cumulated additional recurrent expenditure		-37	-37	-37	-37	-37	-37	-37	55	62	-66	-66	-66	79
Cumulated recurrent surplus/deficit		37	37	37	37	37	37	37	-55	-62	66	66	66	-79

Paraguay (GER 102)

Total recurrent education expenditure	60	75	75	75	75	75	75	79	85	102	84	84	84	126
Budgetary allocation required for balance	14%	13%	13%	13%	13%	13%	13%	14%	15%	18%	13%	13%	13%	20%
Cumulated additional recurrent expenditure		85	85	85	85	85	85	103	139	232	194	194	194	530
Cumulated recurrent surplus/deficit		3	3	3	3	3	3	-15	-51	-144	10	10	10	-326

Peru (GER 122)

Total recurrent education expenditure	192	190	190	190	190	190	190	212	235	266	194	194	194	287
Budgetary allocation required for balance	12%	11%	11%	11%	11%	11%	11%	12%	13%	15%	10%	10%	10%	15%
Cumulated additional recurrent expenditure		-9	-9	-9	-9	-9	-9	108	234	407	13	13	13	759
Cumulated recurrent surplus/deficit		155	155	155	155	155	155	37	-89	-261	316	316	316	-431

Uruguay (GER 110)

Total recurrent education expenditure	119	113	113	113	113	113	113	113	123	124	112	112	112	122
Budgetary allocation required for balance	14%	13%	13%	13%	13%	13%	13%	13%	14%	14%	13%	13%	13%	14%
Cumulated additional recurrent expenditure		-29	-29	-29	-29	-29	-29	-29	26	28	-51	-51	-51	30
Cumulated recurrent surplus/deficit		36	36	36	36	36	36	36	-19	-21	65	65	65	-16

Venezuela (GER 107)

Total recurrent education expenditure	2,575	2,918	2,918	2,918	2,918	2,918	2,918	2,930	3,082	3,128	3,132	3,132	3,132	3,375
Budgetary allocation required for balance	28%	27%	27%	27%	27%	27%	27%	27%	29%	29%	27%	27%	27%	29%
Cumulated additional recurrent expenditure		1,884	1,884	1,884	1,884	1,884	1,884	1,951	2,788	3,040	4,452	4,452	4,452	6,398
Cumulated recurrent surplus/deficit		390	390	390	390	390	390	323	-514	-767	703	703	703	-1,243

Other LDCs

Bulgaria (GER 104)

Total recurrent education expenditure	1,519	1,373	1,373	1,373	1,373	1,373	1,373	1,373	1,502	1,565	1,305	1,305	1,305	1,505
Budgetary allocation required for balance	16%	15%	15%	15%	15%	15%	15%	15%	17%	17%	15%	15%	15%	17%
Cumulated additional recurrent expenditure		-805	-805	-805	-805	-805	-805	-805	-95	-254	-1,711	-1,711	-1,711	-110
Cumulated recurrent surplus/deficit		160	160	160	160	160	160	160	-550	-899	331	331	331	-1,269

TABLE A.3. (cont'd)

	1990	2000									2005			
		UPE No reform	Cost saving 1	2	3	Cost shifting 4	5	Quality enhancing 6	7	SFA 8/9	UPE No reform	Cost saving 1–3	Cost shifting 1–5	SFA 1–9
German Democratic Republic (GER 105)														
Total recurrent education expenditure	1,790	1,735	1,735	1,735	1,735	1,735	1,735	1,735	1,903	2,198	1,721	1,721	1,721	2,336
Budgetary allocation required for balance	16%	15%	15%	15%	15%	15%	15%	15%	17%	19%	15%	15%	15%	20%
Cumulated additional recurrent expenditure		−301	−301	−301	−301	−301	−301	−301	624	2,242	−549	−549	−549	4,365
Cumulated recurrent surplus/deficit		301	301	301	301	301	301	301	−624	−2,242	549	549	549	−4,365
Greece (GER 104)														
Total recurrent education expenditure	781	733	733	733	733	733	733	733	801	800	714	714	714	775
Budgetary allocation required for balance	16%	15%	15%	15%	15%	15%	15%	15%	17%	17%	15%	15%	15%	16%
Cumulated additional recurrent expenditure		−262	−262	−262	−262	−262	−262	−262	112	107	−539	−539	−539	−51
Cumulated recurrent surplus/deficit		93	93	93	93	93	93	93	−281	−275	174	174	174	−314
Poland (GER 101)														
Total recurrent education expenditure	3,862	3,650	3,650	3,650	3,650	3,650	3,650	3,650	4,005	4,018	3,552	3,552	3,552	3,914
Budgetary allocation required for balance	16%	15%	15%	15%	15%	15%	15%	15%	17%	17%	15%	15%	15%	17%
Cumulated additional recurrent expenditure		−1,165	−1,165	−1,165	−1,165	−1,165	−1,165	−1,165	789	859	−2,476	−2,476	−2,476	421
Cumulated recurrent surplus/deficit	127	127	127	127	127	127	127	127	−1,828	−1,897	239	239	239	−2,659
Portugal (GER 124)														
Total recurrent education expenditure	928	772	772	772	772	772	772	772	846	778	714	714	714	706
Budgetary allocation required for balance	16%	14%	14%	14%	14%	14%	14%	14%	15%	14%	13%	13%	13%	13%
Cumulated additional recurrent expenditure		−859	−859	−859	−859	−859	−859	−859	−452	−829	−1,715	−1,715	−1,715	−1,779
Cumulated recurrent surplus/deficit		561	561	561	561	561	561	561	154	531	1,074	1,074	1,074	1,138

Notes: All financial data in this table are in $ millions at constant 1986 prices.

Total Recurrent Expenditure on Education: these data are all as derived from national simulations of UPE and SFA.

Budgetary Allocation Required: data for 1990 are estimates based upon reported data from UNESCO and World Bank sources for the mid-1980s. Estimates for 2000 and 2005 and for each level of reform are the proportions which would be required to finance all the expenditures shown in the first line entry, for each country, as calculated in national simulations.

Cumulated Additional Recurrent Expenditure on Education: calculated in national simulations, as described in technical appendix.

Cumulated Surplus/Deficit: calculated by comparing cumulated additional expenditures and revenues, assuming per capita public revenues available to finance education remain constant over 1990–2005. See technical appendix.

TABLE A.4. *The impact of UPE and SFA on annual costs and enrolments by major region, all reforms implemented*[a]

	1990	2000 UPE No reforms	Cost-saving reforms			Cost-shifting reforms		Quality-enhancing reforms			2005 UPE No reforms	Cost-saving	Cost-shifting	SFA
			Double-shifting	Increase class size	Teacher-helpers	Community financing	Freeze higher ed. subsidies	Increase materials	Teacher salaries	SFA Repetition & drop-out				
			1	2	3	4	5	6	7	8/9		1–3	1–5	1–9
Sub-Saharan Africa (n = 35)														
Primary enrolments (millions)	58.5	116.9	116.9	116.9	116.9	116.9	116.9	116.9	116.9	120.6	140.7	140.7	140.7	144.4
GER	69	100	100	100	100	100	100	100	100	104	102	102	102	106
Primary unit costs ($US)	41	40	35	33	30	28	28	31	34	35	39	30	28	34
Annual recurrent ed. expend. ($USbn.)	5.2	8.7	7.8	7.5	7.2	6.7	6.4	6.8	7.4	7.8	10.9	9.1	7.9	10.0
Other Africa (n = 4)														
Primary enrolments (millions)	14.4	19.7	19.7	19.7	19.7	19.7	19.7	19.7	19.7	19.5	21.8	21.8	21.8	21.6
GER	89	100	100	100	100	100	100	100	100	99	100	100	100	99
Primary unit costs ($US)	129	127	112	99	92	84	84	86	96	95	128	93	85	96
Annual recurrent ed. expend. ($USbn.)	4.2	5.5	5.0	4.6	4.5	4.2	4.0	4.0	4.4	4.4	6.2	5.1	4.4	4.9
India and China (n = 2)														
Primary enrolments (millions)	232.2	219.3	219.3	219.3	219.3	219.3	219.3	219.3	219.3	236.0	228.3	228.3	228.3	249.5
GER	117	100	100	100	100	100	100	100	100	108	100	100	100	110
Primary unit costs ($US)	11	10	9	8	7	6	6	11	12	11	10	7	6	11
Annual recurrent ed. expend. ($USbn.)	7.9	7.7	7.0	6.4	6.3	5.9	5.7	6.8	7.2	8.0	7.7	6.3	5.7	8.4
Other Asia (n = 24)														
Primary enrolments (millions)	113.5	141.8	141.8	141.8	141.8	141.8	141.8	141.8	141.8	154.0	153.7	153.7	153.7	168.8
GER	100	100	100	100	100	100	100	100	100	110	100	100	100	112
Primary unit costs ($US)	134	119	103	90	83	75	75	77	87	81	118	82	74	80
Annual recurrent ed. expend. ($USbn.)	27.1	30.6	27.5	25.0	24.0	22.3	21.5	21.9	23.8	24.8	32.9	25.8	22.7	26.8

TABLE A.4. (cont'd)ᵃ

	1990	2000 UPE No reforms	Cost-saving reforms: Double-shifting (1)	Increase class-size (2)	Teacher-helpers (3)	Cost-shifting reforms: Community financing (4)	Freeze higher ed. subsidies (5)	Quality-enhancing reforms: Increase materials (6)	Teacher salaries (7)	SFA Repetition & drop-out (8/9)	2005 UPE No reforms	Cost-saving (1–3)	Cost-shifting (1–5)	SFA (1–9)
Latin America (N = 22)														
Primary enrolments (millions)	72.8	75.9	75.9	75.9	75.9	75.9	75.9	75.9	75.9	86.9	80.1	80.1	80.1	94.8
GER	108	100	100	100	100	100	100	100	100	116	100	100	100	120
Primary unit costs ($)	125	126	110	95	88	79	79	81	91	92	126	88	79	92
Annual recurrent ed. expend. ($bn.)	18.0	19.4	17.8	16.2	15.7	14.8	14.2	14.3	15.3	17.6	20.4	16.4	14.5	20.2
Other developing countries (N = 11)														
Primary enrolments (millions)	30.6	33.4	33.4	33.4	33.4	33.4	33.4	33.4	33.4	34.2	34.2	34.2	34.2	35.1
GER	96	100	100	100	100	100	100	100	100	103	100	100	100	103
Primary unit costs ($)	392	358	313	268	249	226	226	226	253	254	347	241	219	247
Annual recurrent ed. expend. ($bn.)	23.4	22.9	20.9	18.7	18.1	17.0	16.9	17.1	18.4	19.3	22.8	18.0	16.8	19.8
All developing countries (N = 98)														
Primary enrolments (millions)	522.2	607.0	607.0	607.0	607.0	607.0	607.0	607.0	607.0	651.3	658.7	658.7	658.7	714.1
GER	106	100	100	100	100	100	100	100	100	108	100	100	100	110
Primary unit costs ($)	83	79	69	60	55	50	50	53	60	58	77	54	49	57
Annual recurrent ed. expend. ($bn.)	85.8	94.9	86.0	78.4	75.7	70.9	68.7	70.9	76.5	81.8	101.0	80.6	72.0	90.0

ᵃ Calculated by aggregating all country-level simulations within each region shown. In this table all reforms are implemented for all countries with the exception of 6 countries with GER > 100 which would be able to finance SFA without reforms 1–5. These countries are included in this table but only reforms 6–9 are implemented. GERs are weighted by 6–11-year age-groups. Unit costs are weighted by primary enrolments. All expenditure figures are in constant 1986 dollars. All reforms are incremental, and for each target year incorporate those shown in earlier columns.

TABLE A.5. *Total additional costs of UPE and SFA and likely deficit arising ($bn.), 1990–2005, all reforms implemented*

	2000									2005		
	UPE No reforms	Cost-saving reforms			Cost-shifting reforms		Quality-enhancing reforms			UPE No reforms	Cost-saving shifting	SFA
		Double-shifting	Increase class-size	Teacher-helpers	Community financing	Freeze higher ed. subsidies	Increase materials	Teacher salaries	SFA Repetition & drop-out			
		1	2	3	4	5	6	7	8/9		1–5	1–9
Sub-Saharan Africa (n = 35)												
Cumulated additional rec. ed. expend. (net)	19.2	14.7	12.7	11.2	8.5	6.6	8.7	12.1	14.2	46.1	21.8	38.5
Cumulated additional rec. ed. expend. (gross)	19.2	14.7	12.7	11.2	8.6	6.8	8.9	12.1	14.3	46.2	21.9	38.6
Cumulated additional rec. deficits	−8.8	−5.2	−4.0	−3.3	−2.4	−2.0	−2.7	−3.9	−5.6	−21.2	−4.8	−16.0
No. of countries with recurrent deficits	27	22	18	16	14	11	17	20	22	27	15	24
Other Africa (n = 4)												
Cumulated additional rec. ed. expend. (net)	7.0	4.3	2.1	1.4	−0.2	−1.3	−1.1	0.8	0.8	15.9	1.5	5.4
Cumulated additional rec. ed. expend. (gross)	7.0	4.3	2.1	1.4	0.3	0.2	0.2	0.8	0.9	15.9	1.5	5.4
Cumulated additional rec. deficits	−1.7	−0.3	0.0	0.0	0.0	0.0	0.0	−0.1	0.0	−3.7	0.0	0.0
No. of countries with recurrent deficits	3	1	0	0	0	0	0	1	0	3	0	0
India and China (n = 2)												
Cumulated additional rec. ed. expend. (net)	−1.2	−5.0	−8.4	−9.1	−11.4	−12.1	−6.2	−3.8	0.2	−2.0	−18.4	3.7
Cumulated additional rec. ed. expend. (gross)	0.7	0.0	0.0	0.0	0.0	0.0	1.4	2.0	4.0	1.7	0.0	9.1
Cumulated additional rec. deficits	−0.1	0.0	0.0	0.0	0.0	0.0	−0.7	−1.3	−3.3	−0.2	0.0	−7.6
No. of countries with recurrent deficits	1	0	0	0	0	0	1	1	1	1	0	1
Other Asia (n = 24)												
Cumulated additional rec. ed. expend. (net)	18.2	−2.7	−19.9	−26.2	−37.8	−42.9	−34.6	−21.7	−12.5	19.4	−30.8	−12.7
Cumulated additional rec. ed. expend. (gross)	20.2	10.2	5.6	4.0	1.8	1.1	2.3	3.4	5.6	48.4	4.8	20.6
Cumulated additional rec. deficits	−2.9	−1.3	−1.0	−0.8	−0.5	−0.4	−1.4	−1.7	−4.0	−6.2	−1.5	−9.7
No. of countries with recurrent deficits	12	5	4	3	2	2	5	5	8	12	2	8

Table A.5. (cont'd)

	2000									2005		
	UPE No reforms	Cost-saving reforms			Cost-shifting reforms		Quality-enhancing reforms			UPE No reforms	Cost-saving shifting	SFA
		Double-shifting	Increase class-size	Teacher-helpers	Community financing	Freeze higher ed. subsidies	Increase materials	Teacher salaries	SFA Repetition & drop-out			
		1	2	3	4	5	6	7	8/9		1–5	1–9
Latin America (n = 22)												
Cumulated additional rec. ed. expend. (net)	8.0	−1.2	−9.8	−12.8	−17.4	−21.0	−20.2	−14.7	−2.0	19.0	−27.6	17.5
Cumulated additional rec. ed. expend. (gross)	8.2	5.9	5.0	4.7	4.7	4.8	4.8	9.3	23.5	19.3	7.8	59.1
Cumulated additional rec. deficits	−0.3	−0.1	0.0	0.0	0.0	0.0	0.0	−0.0	−0.3	−0.7	0.0	−10.4
No. of countries with recurrent deficits	7	2	0	0	0	0	0	2	7	7	0	10
Other developing countries (n = 11)												
Cumulated additional rec. ed. expend. (net)	−2.3	−13.8	−25.6	−29.1	−35.0	−35.4	−34.5	−27.3	−22.4	−4.2	−52.7	−28.7
Cumulated additional rec. ed. expend. (gross)	6.4	3.1	0.7	0.1	0.1	0.0	0.1	0.1	1.1	14.2	0.2	7.0
Cumulated additional rec. deficits	−3.0	−0.1	−0.0	−0.0	0.0	0.0	0.0	−0.0	−0.1	−6.2	0.0	−0.1
No. of countries with recurrent deficits	6	1	1	1	0	0	0	1	1	6	0	1
All developing countries (n = 98)												
Cumulated additional rec. ed. expend. (net)	50.0	1.3	−40.5	−55.6	−82.0	−94.0	−81.8	−50.8	−21.9	121.7	−110.3	33.9
Cumulated additional rec. ed. expend. (gross)	61.7	38.2	26.1	21.4	15.5	13.0	17.8	27.8	49.4	145.7	36.2	139.9
Cumulated additional rec. deficits	−16.7	−6.9	−5.1	−4.1	−2.9	−2.5	−4.9	−7.1	−13.3	−38.2	−6.2	−43.8
No. of countries with recurrent deficits	56	31	23	20	16	13	23	30	39	56	17	44

Note: In this table all reforms are implemented for all countries with the exception of 6 countries with GER >100 which would be able to finance SFA without reforms 1–5. These countries are included in this table but only reforms 6–9 are implemented. GERs are weighted by 6–11-year age-groups. All expenditure data are in billions of constant 1986 dollars. All cumulated additional costs have been calculated by summing the projected expenditure differences between the base year and that for each year of the projection period, assuming that expenditures grow at a constant annual rate. All deficits shown in the table are calculated by aggregating all national-level deficits for each individual country, and cumulating them in the way indicated above. Surplus countries are not included in these latter calculations.

Sources: Calculated from data in Statistical Appendix and from the detailed national simulations of UPE and SFA.

Bibliography

Anandalakshmy, S., Sriniwas, S., and Jain, D. (1991), 'Shiksha Karmi Project, Assessment of Children's Achievement' (Institute of Development Studies, Jaipur, India).

Ariyadasa, M., Wijeraten, S., and Genaratne, D. 1986, *Some Indicators and Projections Relevant to First and Second Level General Education: Sri Lanka*. Ministry of Education, Cultural Affairs and Information, Columbo

Armitage, J., Batista, J., Harbison, R. W., Holsinger, D. B., and Helio, R. (1986), 'School Quality and Achievement in Rural Brazil', EDT Paper 25 (World Bank, Washington, DC).

Aubret, P. (1989), *Rapport d'Evaluation des Classes à Double Flux* (SODETEG, Paris).

Baker, V. (1986), 'Going to School in Black Thicket Jungle', *Colombo Research Report* 6 (Institute of Cultural and Social Studies, Leiden University, The Netherlands).

Beebout, H. S. (1972), 'The Production Surface for Academic Achievement: An Economic Study of Malaysian Secondary Schools', Ph.D. Dissertation, University of Wisconsin-Madison.

Berstecher, D., and Carr-Hill, R. (1990), *Primary Education and Economic Recession in the Developing World since 1980* (Unesco, Paris).

Blaug, M. (1979), 'The Case for Universal Primary Education', in Smith (1979).

Bloom, B. S. (1964), *Stability and Change in Human Characteristics* (John Wiley, New York).

Bray, M. (1988), 'Policy Implications and Conclusions', in Bray with Lillis (1988).

—— (1989), *Multiple-Shift Schooling: Design and Operation for Cost-Effectiveness* (Commonwealth Secretariat, London).

—— with Lillis, K. (1988) (eds.), *Community Financing of Education: Issues and Policy Implications in Less Developed Countries* (Pergamon, Oxford).

BRIDGES (1988), 'Impact of Management Reforms on Cluster Innovation, Principals' Effectiveness, Teacher Behaviour, and School Community Relations' (National Institute of Education, Sri Lanka, and Graduate School of Education, Harvard University).

Bulatao, R. A., *et al.* (1990), *World Population Projections: Short and Long-Term Estimates* (Johns Hopkins University Press for the World Bank, Baltimore).

Caillods, F., and Gottelman-Duret, G. (1992), 'Formation Scientifique dans l'Enseignement Secondaire Générale; Organisation et État', International Institute for Educational Planning (Unesco, Paris).

Carr Hill, R., and Lintott, J. (1984), 'Comparative Analysis of Statistical Data on Adult Education for 84 Countries' (Office of Statistics, Unesco, Paris).

Carron, G., and Chau, T. N. (1980) (eds.), *Regional Disparities in Educational Development: A Controversial Issue* (Unesco-IIEP, Paris).

Castillo, Z., and Rojas, C. (1988), *Evaluación del Programa Escuela Nueva en Colombia* (Instituto SER de Investigación, Bogotá).

Chiswick, C. U. (1976), 'On Estimating Earnings Functions for LDCs', *Journal of Development Studies*, 4: 67–78.

Chunga, B. (1991), 'Evaluating Educational Innovations; A Study of the Zambian Upper Primary Schools' Practical Subjects Innovation', Unpublished D.Phil thesis, University of Sussex, Brighton.

Cochrane, S. (1979), *Fertility and Education. What Do We Really Know?* (Johns Hopkins University Press, Baltimore).

—— (1988), 'The Effects of Education, Health and Social Security on Fertility in Developing Countries', Working Paper WPS 93 (Population and Human Resources Dept., World Bank, Washington, DC).

—— O'Hara, D., and Leslie, J. (1980), 'The Effects of Education on Health', Staff Working Paper 399 (World Bank, Washington, DC).

Colbert, V., and Arboleda, J. (1990), 'Universalisation of Primary Education in Colombia: The New School Programme', *Notes, Comments*, 191 (Unesco, Paris).

Colclough, C. (1976), 'Basic Education: Samson or Delilah?', *Convergence*, 9/2: 48–63.

—— (1982), 'The Impact of Primary Schooling on Economic Development: A Review of the Evidence', *World Development*, 10/3: 167–86.

—— (1990), 'Raising Additional Resources for Education in Developing Countries: Are Graduate Payroll Taxes Preferable to Student Loans?' *International Journal of Educational Development*, 10/2–3: 169–80.

—— (1991), 'Who Should Learn to Pay? An Assessment of Neo-liberal Approaches to Education Policy', in Colclough and Manor (1991: 197–213).

—— Lewin, K., and Oxenham, J. (1985), 'Donor Agency Support for Primary Education: Strategies Reconsidered', *International Journal of Educational Development*, 5/4: 295–306.

—— Löfstedt, J. I., Manduvi-Moyo, J., Maravanyika, O., and Ngwata, W. (1990), 'Education in Zimbabwe: Issues of Quantity and Quality', *Education Division Documents*, 50 (Swedish International Development Authority, Stockholm).

—— and Manor, J. (1991) (eds.), *States or Markets? Neo-liberalism and the Development Policy Debate* (Clarendon Press, Oxford).

Coleman, J., Campbell, E., Hobson, C., MacPartland, J., Mood, A., Weinfall, F., and York, R. (1966), *Equality of Educational Opportunity* (Government Printing Office, Washington, DC).

Commonwealth Secretariat (1980), *Universal Primary Education in Commonwealth Africa: Report of a Commonwealth Regional Seminar, Lesotho* (London).

Coombs, P. H. (1985), *The World Crisis in Education: The View from the Eighties* (Oxford University Press, New York).

Cope, J., Denning, C., and Ribeiro, L. (1989), *Content Analysis of Reading and Mathematics Textbooks in Fifteen Developing Countries* (Book Development Council, London).

Cornia, G. A. (1984), 'A Summary and Interpretation of the Evidence', in Jolly and Cornia (1984).

Cummings, C. E. (1988), 'Curriculum Costs: Vocational Subjects', in Lauglo and Lillis (1988).

—— Davies, M., Lillis, K., and Nyagah, B. (1985), 'Practical Subjects in Kenyan Academic Secondary Schools', *Education Division Documents*, 22 (Swedish International Development Authority, Stockholm).

Cummings, W. K. (1986), 'Low Cost Primary Education: Implementing an Innovation in Six Nations' (International Development Research Centre, Ottawa).

Davison, J., and Kanyuka, M. (1990), 'An Ethnographic Study of Factors that affect the Education of Girls in Southern Malawi' (USAID, Lilongwe, mimeo).

De Bosch, J., Kemper, J., and Hugh, M. (1985), 'Les Installations Scolaires en Afrique Francophone' (Unesco, Dakar).

Dore, R. (1976), *The Diploma Disease* (Unwin Education, London).

Easterlin, R. A. (1975), 'An Economic Framework for Fertility Analysis', *Studies in Family Planning*, 6 (Mar.): 54–63.

Eicher, J. C. (1984), 'Educational Costing and Financing in Developing Countries—with special reference to Sub-Saharan Africa', Staff Working Paper, 655 (World Bank, Washington, DC).

Europa (1990), *Africa South of the Sahara 1990* (Europa Publications, London).

Evenson, R., Popkin, B., and Quizon, E. (1980), 'Nutrition, Work and Demographic Behaviour in Rural Philippine Households', in H. Binswanger, *et al.* (eds), *Rural Households in Asia* (Singapore University Press, Singapore).

FAO (1985), *Women in Developing Agriculture* (Food and Agriculture Organization, Rome).

Farrell, J. P., and Schiefelbein, E. (1974), 'Expanding the Scope of Educational Planning: The Experience of Chile', *Interchange*, 5/2: 18–30.

Foster, P. (1965), 'The Vocational School Fallacy in Development Planning', repr. in C. A. Anderson and M. J. Bowman (1965), *Education and Economic Development* (Aldine Publishing Co., Chicago).

Fredriksen, B. (1981), 'Progress Towards Regional Targets for Universal Primary Education: A Statistical Review', *International Journal of Educational Development*, 1/1: 2–15.

—— (1983), 'The Arithmetic of Achieving Universal Primary Education', *International Review of Education*, 29/2: 141–66.

Fuller, B. (1985), 'Raising School Quality in Developing Countries; What Investments Boost Learning?', Education and Training Series, Discussion Paper EDT7 (World Bank, Washington, DC).

—— (1986), 'Is Primary School Quality Eroding in the Third World?', *Comparative Education Review*, 30/4: 491–507.

—— (1987), 'What School Factors Raise Achievement in the Third World?', *Review of Educational Research*, 57/3: 255–92.

Govt. of Ghana (1975), *Report of the National Consultative Committee on Education Finance* (Accra).

Govt. of India (1977), 'Interim Report from Working Group on Universalisation of Elementary Education' (Ministry of Education, New Delhi).

—— (1985), Planning for the Universalisation of Elementary Education and its Implications.

Govt. of Sri Lanka (1984), *Report on Consumer Finances and the Socio-Economic Survey* (Colombo).

—— (1988), *School Census* (Ministry of Education, Cultural Affairs and Information, Colombo).

Govt. of Zambia (1989), 'A Report on the Performance of School Production Units during 1986/87', Self-Help Action Plan for Education (SHAPE) (Ministry of General Education, Youth and Sport, Zambia).

Govt. of Zimbabwe (1979–89), 'Annual Report of the Secretary for Education' (Ministry of Education, Harare).

—— (1984–9), Financial Statements (Harare).

—— (1987), *Statistical Yearbook 1987* (Central Statistical Office, Harare).

—— (1989), *Quarterly Digest of Statistics* (Central Statistical Office, Harare).

—— (1990), *Estimates of Expenditure, 1990* (Ministry of Finance, Harare).

Green, R. H. (1991), 'Neo-liberalism and the Political Economy of War: Sub-Saharan Africa as a Case-Study of a Vacuum', in Colclough and Manor (1991: 238–59).

Gustaffson, I. (1988), 'Work as Education—Perspectives on the Role of Work in Current Educational Reform in Zimbabwe', in Lauglo and Lillis (1988).

Haffenden, I. (1991), 'The National Youth Service in the Seychelles', in Lewin and Stuart (1991).

Hallak, J. (1990), 'Investing in the Future: Setting Priorities for Education in the Developing World' (International Institute for Educational Planning, Unesco, Paris).

Hartley, M., and Swanson, E. (1984), 'Achievement and Wastage: An Analysis of the Retention of Basic Skills in Primary Education' (Development Research Dept., World Bank, Washington, DC, mimeo).

Hawes, H. (1988), *Child-to-Child: A New Path to Learning* (Unesco Institute of Education, Hamburg).

Herz, B., Subbarao, K., Habib, M., and Raney, L. (1991), 'Letting Girls Learn: Promising Approaches in Primary and Secondary Education', Discussion Paper, 133 (World Bank, Washington, DC).

Heyneman, S. (1978), 'Textbooks and Achievement: What We Know', Staff Working Paper 298 (World Bank, Washington, DC).

—— Farrell, J., and Sepulveda-Stuardo, M. (1981), 'Textbooks and Achievement in Developing Countries: What we Know', *Journal of Curriculum Studies*, 13/3: 227–46.

—— and Jamison, D. (1980), 'Student Learning in Uganda: Textbook Availability and Other Factors', *Comparative Education Review*, 24/2: 206–20.

—— —— and Montenegro, X. (1984), 'Textbooks in the Philippines: Evaluation of the Pedagogical Impact of a Nationwide Investment', *Educational Evaluation and Policy Analysis*, 6/2: 139–50.

—— and Loxley, W. A. (1983), 'The Effect of Primary School Quality on Academic Achievement across Twenty-nine High- and Low-Income Countries', *American Journal of Sociology*, 88/6: 1162–94.

Hill, M. A., and King, E. M. (1991), 'Women's Education in the Third World: An Overview', in King and Hill (1991: 1–42).

Hinchliffe, K. (1983), 'Cost Structures of Secondary Schooling in Tanzania and Colombia', DiSCus Project Paper (Education Division, World Bank, Washington, DC).

—— (1987), 'Education and the Labour Market', in Psacharopoulos (1987*b*: 141–5).

Horn, R., and Arriagada, A. (1986), 'The Educational Attainment of the World's Population: Three Decades of Progress', Education and Training Department Discussion Paper EDT, 37 (World Bank, Washington, DC).

Husen, T., Saha, L., and Noonan, R. (1978), 'Teacher Training and Student Achievement in Less Developed Countries', Staff Working Paper, 310 (World Bank, Washington, DC).

ILO (1981), *The Paper Qualification Syndrome and the Unemployment of School Leavers*, Jobs and Skills Programme for Africa (Addis Ababa).

IMF (1991), *International Financial Statistics* (International Monetary Fund, Washington, DC).

IREDU (1989), 'External Aid for Primary Education in Developing Countries' (Institut de Recherche Sur l'Économie de l'Éducation, University of Bourgogne, Dijon).

Jamison, D. T., Searle, B., Golda, K., and Heyneman, S. (1981), 'Improving Elementary Mathematics Education in Nicaragua: An Experimental Study of the Impact of Textbooks and Radio on Achievement', *Journal of Educational Psychology*, 73: 556–67.

Jencks, C., Smith, M., Acland, H., Bane, M., Cohen, D., Gintis, H., Heyns, B., and Michelson, S. (1972), *Inequality: A Reassessment of the Effects of Family and Schooling in America* (Basic Books, New York).

Jimenez, E., Lockheed, M., and Watanawaka, N. (1988), 'The Relative Efficiency of Private and Public Schools: the Case of Thailand', *World Bank Economic Review*, 2/2: 139–64.

Jolly, R., and Cornia, G. A. (1984) (eds.), *The Impact of World Recession on Children*, a study prepared for Unicef (Pergamon, Oxford).

King, E., and Hill, M. A. (1991) (eds.), 'Women's Education in Developing Countries: Barriers, Benefits and Policy', PHREE Background Paper, 91/40 (World Bank, Washington, DC).

Knight, J. B., and Sabot, R.H. (1990), *Education, Production and Inequality: The East African Natural Experiment* (Oxford University Press for the World Bank, Oxford).

Komba, D., and Temu, E. (1987), 'State of the Art Review of Education for Self Reliance Implementation' (Ministry of Education, Tanzania and Foundation of Education with Production, Botswana).

Komenan, A. (1987), 'World Education Indicators', Education and Training Department Discussion Paper EDT, 88 (World Bank, Washington, DC).

Kyereme, S., and Thorbecke, E. (1991), 'Factors Affecting Food Poverty in Ghana', *Journal of Development Studies*, 28/1: 39–52.

Lauglo, J., and Lillis, K. (1988) (eds.), *Vocationalising Education: An International Perspective* (Pergamon, Oxford).

Lee, K. H. (1988), 'Universal Primary Education: An African Dilemma', *World Development*, 16/12: 1481–91.

Leslie, J., and Cochrane, S. (1979), 'Parental Education and Child Health:

Malnutition and Morbidity' (World Bank, Washington, DC, mimeo).

Levin, H., and Lockheed, M. (1991) (eds.), 'Effective Schools in Developing Countries', Education and Employment Division Background Paper Series No. PHREE 91/38 (World Bank, Washington, DC).

Lewin, K. M. (1987), *Education in Austerity: Options for Planners*, Fundamentals of Educational Planning 36 (International Institute of Educational Planning, Unesco, Paris).

—— (1991), 'Science Education in Developing Countries; Issues and Perspectives for Planners' (International Institute for Educational Planning, Unesco, Paris).

—— with Berstecher, D. (1989), 'The Costs of Recovery; Are User Fees the Answer?' *IDS Bulletin*, 20/1.

—— and Jones, R. (1985), 'Learning about Science and Technology Outside School: A Report to the Commonwealth Secretariat Education Programme', mimeo (Commonwealth Secretariat, London).

—— and Little, A. W. (1984), 'Examination Reform and Educational Change in Sri Lanka; Modernisation or Dependent Underdevelopment', in Watson (1984).

—— with Stuart, J. (1991) (eds.), *Educational Innovation in Developing Countries: Case Studies of Changemakers* (Macmillan).

—— Wang, Y. J., Wang, L., Qu, H. C., Wu, Z. K., Qian, J., and Li, J. Y. (1991), *China Basic Education Project*, Interim Reports on Tongxian and Ansai Case Studies. (Beijing Normal University/Unicef, Beijing, mimeo).

—— and Xu, H. (1989), 'Rethinking Revolution; Reflections on China's 1985 Educational Reforms', *Comparative Education*, 25/1.

Lillis, K., and Ayot, H. (1988), 'Community Financing of Education in Kenya', in Bray with Lillis (1988).

Little, A., Cyril, H. M., and Samuel, E. (1991), 'Towards Effective Schools in Disadvantaged Areas: The Case of Two Pairs of Schools in the Badulla Integrated Rural Development Programme 1984–1987', mimeo (BIRDP Education Project Office, Bandarawela, Sri Lanka).

—— and Sivasithambaram, R. (1991), 'Improving Educational Effectiveness in a Plantation School: The Case of the Goonekelle School in Sri Lanka', in Levin and Lockheed (1991).

Lockheed, M. E., Jamison, D., and Lau, L. (1980), 'Farmer Education and Farm Efficiency: A Survey', *Economic Development and Cultural Change*, 29 (Oct.): 37–76.

—— and Verspoor, A. M., with Bloch, D., Englebert, P., Fuller, B., King, E., Middleton, J., Paqueo, V., Rodd, A., Romain, R., and Welmond, M. (1990), *Improving Primary Education in Developing Countries: A Review of Policy Options*, Draft document prepared for the World Conference on Education for All, Jomtien, Thailand (World Bank, Washington, DC).

Lofstedt, J.-I. (1990), 'Human Resources in Chinese Development; Needs and Supply of Competencies', *Research Report*, 80 (International Institute for Educational Planning, Unesco, Paris).

—— Jayaweera, S., and Little, A. (1985), 'Human Resources Development in Sri Lanka: An Analysis of Education and Training', *Education Division Documents* 24 (Swedish International Development Agency, Stockholm).

Lovell, C. H., Fatema, K. (1989), 'Assignment Children: The BRAC Non-

Formal Primary Education Programme in Bangladesh' (Unicef, New York).

McPartland, J. M., and Karweit, N. (1979), 'Research on Educational Effects', in Walberg (1979).

Madaus, G. F., (1979), *Schooling Effectiveness: A Reassessment of the Evidence* (McGraw-Hill, New York).

Meyer, J., Ramirez, F., and Soysal, Y. (1989), 'World Expansion of Mass Education, 1870–1980', paper presented at the annual meeting of the American Educational Research Association, San Francisco.

Mingat A., and Tan, J. P. (1985), 'Subsidisation of Higher Education versus Expansion of Primary Enrolments: What Can a Shift of Resources Achieve in Sub-Saharan Africa?' *International Journal of Educational Development*, 5/4: 259–68.

Mondon, P., and Thelot, C. (1989), 'Le Succès de l'École au Sénégal', report to the Ministry of Education (Dakar, Senegal).

OECD (1979), *Guidelines on Local and Recurrent Cost Financing* (Development Assistance Committee, OECD, Paris).

—— (1982), *Guidelines on Aid for Maintenance* (OECD, Paris).

—— (1990), *Development Co-Operation Review* (OECD, Paris).

O'Hara, D. (1979), 'Multivariate Analysis of Mortality', mimeo (World Bank, Washington, DC).

Orivel, F., and Sergent, F. (1988) 'Foreign Aid to Education in Sub-Saharan Africa: How Useful Is It?' *Prospects*, 18/4: 460–9.

Oxenham, J. C. P. (1984) (ed.), *Education versus Qualification* (Unwin Education, London).

Pitt, M., and Rosenzweig, M. (1989), 'Estimating the Intrafamily Incidence of Illness: Child Health and Gender Inequality in the Allocation of Time in Indonesia', mimeo (Yale University, New Haven, Conn.).

Perraton, H. (1986) (ed.), Distance Education: An Economic and Educational Assessment of Its Potential in Africa, report EDT43 (World Bank, Washington, DC).

Postlethwaite, T. N., and Wiley, D. E. (1991), *Science Achievement in Twenty-Three Countries* (Pergamon, Oxford).

Psacharopoulos, G. (1973), *Returns to Education: An International Comparison* (Elsevier, Amsterdam and New York).

—— (1985*a*), 'Curriculum Diversification, Cognitive Achievement and Economic Performance: Evidence from Tanzania and Colombia', in Lauglo and Lillis (1988).

—— (1985*b*), 'Returns to Education: A Further International Update and Implications', *Journal of Human Resources*, 20/4: 583–604.

—— (1987*a*), 'Public versus Private Schools in Developing Countries: Evidence from Colombia and Tanzania', *International Journal of Educational Development*, 7/1: 59–67.

—— (1987*b*) (ed.), *Economics of Education, Research and Studies* (Pergamon, Oxford).

Pudasaini, S. P. (1983), 'The Effects of Education in Agriculture: Evidence from Nepal', *American Journal of Agricultural Economics*, 65/3: 509–15.

Republic of China (1989), *The Development and Reform of Basic Education in China*, World Conference on Education for All—Meeting Basic Learning

Needs, Jomtien, Thailand (Country Documents, People's Republic of China).

Rodriguez, J. (1982), *El Logro en Matemática y Lenguaje en la Educàción Primaria Columbiana* (Instituto SER de Investigaciones, Bogotá).

Romain, R. (1985), 'Lending in Primary Education: Bank Perfomance Review 1962–1985', Discussion Paper EDT, 20 (World Bank, Washington, DC).

Rosenzweig, M., and Schultz, T. P. (1982), 'Market Opportunities, Genetic Endowments and the Intrafamily Distribution of Resources: Child Survival in Rural India', *American Economic Review*, 72/4: 803–15.

Sajogjo, P. *et al.* (1980), 'Different Perspectives: West Java Project on Rural Household Economics and the Role of Women', in FAO (1985).

Sambamoorthi, V. (1984), 'Labour Market Discrimination against Women in India', Working Paper 58, Women in Development Series (Michigan State University, East Lansing, Mich.).

Samoff, J. (1990), 'The Politics of Privatisation in Tanzania', *International Journal of Education and Development*, 10/1: 1–15.

Schultz, T. P. (1991), 'Returns to Women's Education', in King and Hill (1991: 43–78).

Schultz, T. W. (1975), 'The Value of the Ability to Deal with Disequilibrium', *Journal of Economic Literature*, 13: 872–6.

SIHRD (1991), *Basic Education and National Development: Forty Years of Chinese Experience* Shanghai Institute of Human Resource Development (People's Education Press, Beijing, China).

Simmons, J. (ed.) (1980), *The Education Dilemma: Policy Issues for Developing Countries in the 1980s* (Pergamon, Oxford).

—— and Alexander L. (1980), 'Factors which Promote School Achievement in Developing Countries: A Review of the Research', in Simmons (1980: 77–95).

Sinclair, M. E., with Lillis, K. (1980), *School and Community in the Third World* (Croom Helm, London).

Sivard, R. L. (1990), *World Military and Social Expenditures 1990–91*, 15th edn. (World Priorities Inc., Washington, DC).

Smith, R. L. (1979), 'Universal Primary Education: Report of a Workshop', (Institute of Education, University of London).

Smyth, J. A. (1988), 'Costs and Financing Obstacles to Universal Primary Education in Africa', Educational Financing Occasional Paper 6 (Unesco, Paris).

Solmon, L. C. (1987), 'The Range of Educational Benefits', in Psacharopoulos (1987*b*: 83–93).

Statesman's Yearbook (1990–1) (Macmillan Press, London).

Stewart, F. (1991), 'Education and Adjustment: the Experience of the 1980s and Lessons for the 1990s', mimeo (Commonwealth Secretariat, London).

Swartland, J., and Taylor, D. (1988), 'Community Financing of Schools in Botswana', in Bray with Lillis (1988).

Thobani, M. (1984), 'Charging User Fees for Social Services: Education in Malawi', *Comparative Education Review*, 28/3: 402–23.

Thorndike, R. (1973), *Reading Comprehension in Fifteen Countries* (Halsted Press, New York).

Tibi, C. (1986), 'Report on the Costs of Technical and Vocational Institutions in

Thailand', mimeo (International Institute for Educational Planning, Unesco, Paris).

—— (1990), 'What Policies for Teachers?', Working Paper (Unesco, Paris).

Tilak, J. B. G. (1983), 'The Political Economy of Investment in Education in South Asia', *International Journal of Educational Development*, 4/2: 155–66.

—— (1987), *The Economics of Inequality in Education* (Sage Publications, New Delhi).

—— (1991), 'Family and Government Investments in Education', *International Journal of Educational Development*, 11/2: 91–106.

Toye, J. (1991), 'Ghana: Socio-Economic Review', mimeo (Institute of Development Studies, Sussex).

UN (1987), 'Fertility Behaviour in the Context of Development', *Population Studies*, 100 (United Nations, New York).

UNDP (1990), *Human Development Report* (United Nations Development Programme, Oxford University Press).

—— (1991), *Human Development Report* (United Nations Development Programme, Oxford University Press).

Unesco (1956), Report of meeting on 'Free and Compulsory Education in Latin America and the Caribbean' held in Lima (Unesco, Paris).

—— (1960), *Conference of Ministers of Education in Asia, Final Report*, Karachi (Unesco Paris; updated Tokyo, 1962).

—— (1961*a*), *Outline of a Plan for African Educational Development*, Addis Ababa (Unesco, Paris).

—— (1961*b*), *Conference of African States on the Development of Education in Africa*, Final Report, Addis Ababa (Unesco, Paris).

—— (1962), *Conference on Education and Economic and Social Development*, Santiago, Chile, 1962 (Unesco, Paris).

—— (1966), *Conference of Ministers of Education and Ministers responsible for Economic Planning in the Arab States*, Tripoli, Libya, 9–14 Apr. 1966 (Unesco, Paris).

—— (1977*a*), 'Regional Seminar on Alternative Approaches to School Education at Primary Level, Final Report', Manila December 1976 (Unesco, Paris).

—— (1977*b*), *Statistical Yearbook 1977* (Unesco, Paris).

—— (1984), 'The Drop-out Problem in Primary Education: Some Case Studies', Bangkok (Unesco, Paris).

—— (1985), 'Universal Primary Education in Asia and the Pacific: Regional Overview', Bangkok (Unesco, Paris).

—— (1989), *Statistical Yearbook 1989* (Unesco, Paris).

—— (1990), 'Presentation Model for Educational Development' (Unesco, Paris).

Unicef (1990), *The State of the World's Children 1990* (Unicef, Oxford).

Vulliamy, G. (1983), 'Core Subject—Core Project Integration: Practice and Possibilities', *Papua New Guinea Journal of Education* 19: 41–62.

Walberg, H. J. (1979) (ed.), *Educational Environments and Effects: Evaluation Policy and Productivity* (McCutchan, Berkeley, Calif.).

Watson, K. (1984) (ed.), *Dependence and Interdependence in Education, International Perspectives* (Croom Helm, London).

Weekes, R. V. (1978) (ed.), *Muslim Peoples—A World Ethnography Survey*

(Greenwood Press, Westport, Conn.).

Weiner, M. (1991). *The Child and the State in India* (Princeton University Press, Princeton, NJ.)

Welch, F. (1970), 'Education in Production', *Journal of Political Economy*, 78/1: 35–59.

Whalley, J., and Ziderman, A. (1989), 'Payroll Taxes for Financing Training in Developing Countries', PPR Working Paper 141 (World Bank, Washington, DC).

Williams, P. R. C. (1975), 'Education in Developing Countries: The View from Mount Olympus', *Prospects*, 5/4: 457–78 (Unesco, Paris).

—— (1979), 'Universal Primary Education and the Future', in Smith (1979: 92–3).

—— (1983), 'The Last Ten Per Cent', *International Review of Education*, 29/2: 159–63.

Wolff, L. (1983), 'Controlling the Costs of Primary and Secondary Education in Eastern Africa: A Review of Data and Policy Options', mimeo (World Bank, Washington, DC).

Woodhall, M. (1983), 'Student Loans as a Means of Financing Higher Education: Lessons from International Experience', Staff Working Paper 500 (World Bank, Washington, DC).

World Bank (1974), Education Sector Working Paper (World Bank, Washington, DC).

—— (1980), Education Sector Policy Paper (World Bank, Washington, DC).

—— (1982), 'Staff Appraisal Report Colombia: Sub-Sector Project for Rural Basic Education' (World Bank, Washington, DC).

—— (1983), 'Senegal: Sub-Sector Memorandum for Primary Education', (World Bank, Washington, DC).

—— (1984a), 'China Issues and Prospects in Education', *Annexe C1 of Long-Term Development Issues and Options*, World Bank Country Study (World Bank, Washington, DC).

—— (1984b), *World Development Report* (Oxford University Press, New York).

—— (1986a), *Financing Education in Developing Countries: An Exploration of Policy Options* (World Bank, Washington, DC).

—— (1986b), *World Development Report* (Oxford University Press, New York).

—— (1987), *Zimbabwe: A Strategy for Sustained Growth*, Report 6981-21M, 2 vols. (World Bank, Washington, DC).

—— (1988a), *Education in Sub-Saharan Africa: Policies for Adjustment, Revitalisation and Expansion* (World Bank, Washington, DC).

—— (1988b), *World Development Report 1988* (Oxford University Press, New York).

—— (1988c), 'Senegal Primary Education Development Project', Back-to-office and supervision reports, mimeo (World Bank, Washington, DC).

—— (1989a), *World Development Report 1989* (Oxford University Press, New York).

—— (1989b), 'Ghana Basic Education for Self-Employment and Rural Development: A Sub-Sector Study' (World Bank, Washington, DC).

—— (1989c), 'Staff Appraisal Report, China: Textbook Development Project' (World Bank, Washington, DC).

—— (1989*d*), 'Staff Appraisal Report: Sri Lanka, General Education Project', Report 7918-CE (World Bank, Washington, DC).

—— (1990), *Annual Report 1991* (World Bank, Washington, DC).

—— (1991*a*), *Vocational and Technical Education and Training*, Policy Paper (World Bank, Washington, DC).

—— (1991*b*), *World Development Report* (Oxford University Press, New York).

—— (1991*c*), *Primary Education*, Policy Paper (World Bank, Washington, DC).

—— (1991*d*), *Annual Operational Review: Fiscal 1991, Education and Training*, PHREE Background Paper, 91/44R (World Bank, Washington, DC).

—— (1991*e*), *Gender and Poverty in India* (World Bank, Washington, DC).

Index

Index